THE DEATH AND LIFE OF GREAT AMERICAN CITIES

THE DEATH AND LIFE OF GREAT AMERICAN CITIES

JANE JACOBS

50TH ANNIVERSARY EDITION

WITH A NEW INTRODUCTION BY
JASON EPSTEIN
AND A FOREWORD BY THE AUTHOR

MODERN LIBRARY
NEW YORK

2011 Modern Library Edition

Introduction copyright © 2011 by Jason Epstein
Biographical note copyright © 1993 by Random House, Inc.
Copyright © 1961, 1989, 1993 by Jane Jacobs

Published in the United States by Modern Library, an
imprint of The Random House Publishing Group,
a division of Random House, Inc., New York.

MODERN LIBRARY and the TORCHBEARER Design
are registered trademarks of Random House, Inc.

Portions of this work were originally published in
*Architectural Forum, Columbia University Forum,
Harper's Magazine,* and *The Reporter.*

LIBRARY OF CONGRESS CATALOGING-IN-PUBLICATION
Jacobs, Jane, 1916–2006
The death and life of great American cities/Jane Jacobs;
with a new foreword by the author.—Modern Library ed.
p.   cm.
Includes index.
ISBN 978-0-679-64433-0
1. City planning—United States.   2. Urban renewal—United
States.   3. Urban policy—United States.   I. Title.
HT167.J33   1993
307.76'0973—dc20   92-32407

Printed in the United States of America on acid-free paper

www.modernlibrary.com

8   9

JANE JACOBS

Jane Jacobs was born on May 4, 1916, in Scranton, Pennsylvania. Her father was a physician and her mother taught school and worked as a nurse. After high school and a year spent as a reporter on the *Scranton Tribune,* Jacobs went to New York, where she found a succession of jobs as a stenographer and wrote freelance articles about the city's many working districts, which fascinated her. In 1952, after a number of writing and editing jobs ranging in subject matter from metallurgy to a geography of the United States for foreign readers, she became an associate editor of *Architectural Forum.* She was becoming increasingly skeptical of conventional planning beliefs as she noticed that the city rebuilding projects she was assigned to write about seemed neither safe, interesting, alive, nor good economics for cities once the projects were built and in operation. She gave a speech to that effect at Harvard in 1956, and this led to an article in *Fortune* magazine entitled "Downtown Is for People," which in turn led to *The Death and Life of Great American Cities.* The book was published in 1961 and produced permanent changes in the debate over urban renewal and the future of cities.

In opposition to the kind of large-scale, bulldozing government intervention in city planning associated with Robert Moses and with federal slum-clearing projects,

Jacobs proposed a renewal from the ground up, emphasizing mixed use rather than exclusively residential or
commercial districts, and drawing on the human vitality
of existing neighborhoods: "Vital cities have marvelous
innate abilities for understanding, communicating, contriving, and inventing what is required to combat their
difficulties. . . . Lively, diverse, intense cities contain the
seeds of their own regeneration, with energy enough to
carry over for problems and needs outside themselves."
Although Jacobs's lack of experience as either architect or
city planner drew criticism, *The Death and Life of Great
American Cities* was quickly recognized as one of the most
original and powerfully argued books of its day. It was
variously praised as "the most refreshing, provocative,
stimulating, and exciting study of this greatest of our
problems of living which I have seen" (Harrison Salisbury) and "a magnificent study of what gives life and
spirit to the city" (William H. Whyte).

Jacobs married an architect, who she said taught her
enough to become an architectural writer. They had two
sons and a daughter. In 1968 they moved to Toronto,
where Jacobs often assumed an activist role in matters relating to development and was an adviser on the reform
of the city's planning and housing policies. She was a
leader in the successful campaign to block construction of
a major expressway on the grounds that it would do more
harm than good, and helped prevent the demolition of an
entire downtown neighborhood. Her writings include
The Economy of Cities (1969); *The Question of Separatism*

(1980), a consideration of the issue of sovereignty for Quebec; *Cities and the Wealth of Nations* (1984), a major study of the importance of cities and their regions in the global economy; and *Systems of Survival* (1993).

She died April 25, 2006.

INTRODUCTION

Jason Epstein

I first heard of Jane Jacobs in 1956 when a friend suggested that I read her article "Downtown Is for People" in *Fortune* in which she laid out the case against Le Corbusier's Radiant City ideology which had infected much postwar city planning including that of New York City's master builder, Robert Moses. I was immediately sympathetic to Jane's argument that cities are complex organisms that create their own logic but are in danger of being smothered by the arrogant fantasies of modernist planners with their sinuous interchanges, sterile towers, and depopulated vistas. I had lived for a while in Greenwich Village not far from Jane and shared her devotion to that eccentric section of New York City with its streets and alleys of nineteenth-century town houses, its mixed commercial, residential, and industrial uses, and its cultural vitality, qualities distilled from the vigorous city itself whose diverse economy of light industry, garment and shoe manufacturing, food processing, publishing, metalwork, electronics, graphics, and so on made New York with its conurbation the largest manufacturing employer in the United States at that time. Unlike Detroit or Pittsburgh, New York was not defined by a dominant industry. New York was a cornucopia of possibility and improvisation, an incubator of vital neighborhoods and local citizenship.

There were problems: segregation, slums, crime, redlining, a calcified school system, corruption great and small, but the city and its enlightened citizens, one felt, were strong enough to overcome these miseries. Moses' high-rise slum clearance, however, was not a solution but a brutal intensification of the problems, as Jane Jacobs argued in "Downtown Is for People" and at greater length in her masterpiece, *The Death and Life of Great American Cities*.

I had been working for Doubleday at the time and offered Jane a contract for a book based on her *Fortune* article which I had reprinted in a collection of essays called *The Exploding Metropolis*. Two years later I moved to Random House. Jane moved with me and in January 1961 delivered the manuscript of *Death and Life* which I read without interruption or emendation. There was little to edit. I would eventually publish all but the last of the several books that followed, many composed on her old Remington for which she must have laid in a supply of ribbons before typewriters became obsolete.

Editors and their authors seldom form deep friendships for the same reason that psychiatrists and their patients keep their distance: the relationship requires candor which mixes poorly with intimacy. Perhaps because her manuscripts needed little editing and were usually delivered on time Jane and I were an exception to this rule. We were kindred spirits. She did not use a literary agent. We negotiated directly, book by book and formed a lifelong intellectual and professional friendship that survived her move to Toronto during the Vietnam War. Together we explored eastern Canada, from the great provincial parks to the mining towns along the permafrost above the tree line and still farther north to Moose Factory at the bottom of James Bay, a once flourishing entrepôt of the Hudson's

Bay Company, where we were surprised to find amid the ramshackle Cree dwellings two Chinese restaurants offering Mets Canadien et Chinois, a relic of the Chinese laborers who built the railroad in the 1920s that terminates there—an example, as Jane pointed out, of how one kind of work leads to another.

We seldom discussed our personal lives. I knew that Jane's father had been a family physician and her mother a nurse and that she was fond of her brother John, a federal judge, that she had been born and raised in Scranton, Pennsylvania, and had come to New York in 1943 hoping to become a journalist. I was not surprised to learn later from a biographer that she had been a defiant high school student with a sense of humor, a sharp eye for cant, and a problem for her uninspiring teachers: a contrarian even then. She was rewarded for her candor with poor grades and planned to skip college. She took instead courses in the Extension program at Columbia, where she could take only the courses she wanted and write a book, *Constitutional Chaff*, which was published by the Columbia University Press, an impressive debut for a self-educated, nonmatriculated, and uncredentialed scholar at the age of twenty-five. The book was a study of the rejected proposals for the United States Constitution. Jane who was her own best critic refused to show me a copy and chose not to discuss this first effort.

Like all of Jane's work *Death and Life* is about how human beings by their own devices instinctively create vital communities and how these communities and their economies are subject to corruption or obliteration by ambitious individuals in positions of power, whether well-meaning, vicious, or foolish. *Death and Life* and especially her subsequent books are thus about the dynamics of civilization, how vital economies and their societies are formed, elaborated, and sustained, and the forces that thwart and ruin them. This, rather more than her critique of city planning, I believe, accounts for the continued interest in her work. Her sympathies are with the slow accretion of custom and skills, of social norms and ingenious solutions to practical problems. She was fascinated by how new kinds of work evolve, in vital societies, from older forms, a process often stifled by its own success: for example, how Detroit's early Great Lakes traders learned to build their own boats, then to make paint varnishes and brass fittings, and eventually master steam-engine technology and metallurgic skills, which led to engines for cars, so that the combination of Detroit's skills made it the logical center of automobile manufacturing, whose dominance by the twentieth century created an industrial monoculture which led to Detroit's collapse and an irrational, environmentally pernicious national transportation system.

To use a much abused term, Jane was a conservative, indeed a radical conservative, mistrustful of abstraction, suspicious of large ideas and concentrations of political and economic power: a "genius of common sense," as far from an ideologue as it is possible to be.* Toward the end of her life Jane was fascinated by urban traffic tangles as evidence of bureaucratic idiocy resulting in perverse, even deadly, outcomes: the man-made difficulty of get-

*Genius of Common Sense: Jane Jacobs and the Story of The Death and Life of Great American Cities by Glenna Lang and Marjory Wunsch.

ting safely where one wanted to go when one wanted to go there. Jane herself used a bicycle. She thought of these tangles as fractal versions of Soviet five-year plans. But she preferred to expose such faults in her own country than indulge in anti-Soviet bombast. I never asked Jane if she admired Edmund Burke but I believe that Burke, were he alive, would admire her. Predictably Jane's book was praised by the libertarian right and denounced by the social engineers of the left. Jane took little note of either group.

Jane thought of herself primarily as a writer and was happiest and most productive at her Remington. Events however made her an activist, a role in which she excelled but which she resented as a distraction from her writing. Her adversary was Robert Moses, who had amassed what amounted to dictatorial power over the physical development of New York City and its environs by appointing himself, with the help of complacent politicians, to the chairmanship of various public authorities. From the 1930s to the '60s these high positions provided him the money and the power to reshape the area according to his vision in which the automobile and its infrastructure were the necessary engines of modernity. Ruthlessly he uprooted long settled neighborhoods to build his expressways; erected high-rise slum clearance projects, which almost overnight became deracinated vertical slums; built bridges and parkways that shaped the city's northern and eastern suburbs, creating traffic tangles that made access to and from the city at rush hour a nightmare to which suffering commuters, breathing carbon monoxide, are inured as if this planning disaster were a natural phenomenon and not a human error. Moses' tools were raw political power, vast financial resources, and an exhausted, Radiant City ideology. By the 1950s his power to damage New York City appeared limitless.

His fatal error was to make Jane his enemy by proposing to extend Fifth Avenue through Washington Square Park, at the center of Greenwich Village, as far south as Broome Street in what is now SoHo, where it would join a projected multilane, elevated crosstown expressway linking New Jersey via the Holland Tunnel to the Manhattan and Williamsburg bridges to Brooklyn. Since the proposed Broome Street Expressway qualified as an interstate highway it was eligible for 90 percent federal funding though Canal Street, the existing link between the Manhattan Bridge and the Holland Tunnel, was and is to this day adequate. Nevertheless, Moses knew that with his federal bonanza he could count on the complicity of politicians, developers, construction unions and their minions who had supported his previous depredations. The uprooted residents of these impoverished neighborhoods believed they were powerless. The residents of Greenwich Village suffered no such delusion.

Washington Square Park, two blocks wide by three blocks long is an urban masterpiece with a long history and many cultural associations from Henry James to Bob Dylan, a place where children and dogs safely play and city dwellers catch their breath, a place, as one writer said, "to enjoy grass and trees in a city that could feel very paved and gray." The Fifth Avenue extension would destroy the treasured park and devastate the thriving Village streets to the south as it bulldozed a two-mile swath to Broome Street and the projected expressway. Furious Village residents distributed circulars and posters, held meetings, and appealed to City Hall as Moses went ahead with his plans. Jane wrote to the mayor that she and her husband had restored their old house on Hudson Street, which she said had been a slum, and wondered why the city would now destroy the park where she took her children to play. "It is very discouraging," she wrote, "to do our best to make the city more habitable and then to learn that the city itself is thinking up ways to make it uninhabitable." The mayor didn't answer and Jane joined the protesters who appealed for support to their local politicians. Since their careers were in the hands of the Village voters and not in those of the City Hall politicians and upstate power brokers on whom Moses depended, the local politicians joined the struggle. So did the two Village newspapers until the fight for the park became a citywide issue. Moses, facing for the first time an articulate and politically sophisticated community, capitulated but retained the major, and undisclosed, part of his plan—the federally funded Broome Street Expressway. He also retaliated by declaring the West Village area where Jane and her family lived a slum eligible for clearance, "the cheerful hurly-burly" of whose street life Jane celebrated in *Death and Life* as the very essence of cityness. Her house at 555 Hudson was right in the cross hairs. This time Jane conceived an ingenious guerrilla strategy and once again the villagers upended Moses who was unprepared for opponents who could not be bullied. Jane returned to her Remington unaware of the great battle that lay ahead.

The successful struggle by the threatened communities with Jane's help to defeat the monstrous Broome Street Expressway would last nine years, send Moses into retirement, and convince Jane that if she wanted to be a

writer she had better pack her Remington and leave New
York. She settled in Toronto where her husband, a distinguished hospital architect, joined a local firm and then
their two sons joined them to escape the Vietnam War, the
crowning absurdity of a political establishment as dan-
gerously out of touch with reality as Moses. Later Jane
said that "I just wasn't cut out to be the citizen of an empire."

The Broome Street Expressway would cut Manhattan
in two just below the waist and with its ramps hollow out
the entire nine-block area between Houston and Canal
from river to river. The utter insanity of this scheme was
breathtaking. Because Jane was now well known for her
previous encounters with Moses, the Broome Street
neighbors asked her to help. For six years until victory
was assured and only the mopping up was left to do Jane
devoted herself to this last great battle, sensing that if
Moses lost again the City would be rid of him.

With the expressway's defeat the area, with its handsome old cast-iron facades, came spontaneously to life as
artists moved illegally into the vast lofts that had been
abandoned by their industrial occupants who had fled the
area believing that the expressway would come and they
would be evicted. With the artists there soon came the galleries, and with the galleries came the restaurants and
trendy shops. Today the area known as SoHo is perhaps
the most vibrant of New York's many vibrant neighborhoods. The artists have left, priced out of their lofts, but
the cultural echo remains. SoHo is New York's Left Bank.

I now live in the handsome old beaux arts police
headquarters building on the corner of Broome and Cen-
tre streets, once scheduled by Moses for demolition and

now a Landmark. It is widely assumed that it was to this building that Jane was taken to be booked when she broke up a meeting of the New York State Transportation Authority scheduled without adequate notice to approve an essential stage of the expressway project. In fact she was taken to the nearby Seventh Precinct Station, but the impact was the same. Jane's arrest made headlines. The issue was no longer the expressway but the struggle between the widely praised author of *The Death and Life of Great American Cities* and the tyrannical Robert Moses, now seen as killer of cities, a battle that Moses and the politicians could not win.

With advance word from a friendly insider Jane had packed the meeting with local citizens. As the Transportation Authority was about to approve the motion to proceed she rose to demand her First Amendment right to assemble on the stage which she then mounted followed by her neighborhood entourage, who exercised their right to free expression by destroying the stenotypist's tape in the hope that without a record the hearing could not be said to have occurred. With a scrap of tape still in her hand Jane was led away by the police who apologized for what they had to do amid the cheers of her followers. Two days later she was charged with three felonies which were eventually reduced to lesser charges and a fine, but by this time the absurdity of the expressway was obvious and the political price to City Hall was more than the mayor and his fellow politicians wanted to pay. Today a scrawny tree planted on Broome Street before the church that served as protest headquarters commemorates the victory.

Jane had hoped to preserve the neighborhood for its

working-class inhabitants, some of whom still manage to live here in their rent-controlled tenement apartments, but lofts in the handsome old cast-iron buildings where the artists once squatted are now beyond the reach of all but the very rich. That wildly expensive gentrification should have been the fate not only of SoHo but of Jane's West Village has led some critics to question Jane's determination to rescue these old neighborhoods from urban renewal. The question is tendentious. Had Jane not intervened, the crooked streets and human scale of the West Village with its active street life and diverse economy would have been replaced by cookie-cutter condos that blight much of the outer boroughs, while what is now SoHo would be a wasteland in the shadow of an elevated highway.

When I think of Jane and what she taught me I think of her exuberance, her chuckle that seemed to engage her whole body, her vast curiosity, her kindness, the clarity of her vision, and of the irrepressible schoolgirl whose uncomprehending teachers instilled in her at an early age the joy and necessity of thinking for oneself. That her great book has survived for half a century seems to me not so much remarkable as inevitable.

When Robert Moses received a copy of *Death and Life* from the publisher he replied, "Dear Bennett [Cerf]: I am returning the book that you sent me. Aside from the fact that it is intemperate it is also libelous. . . .

Sell this junk to someone else.

Cordially, Robert Moses."

—*September, 2011*

JASON EPSTEIN launched the trade paperback format in the United States in 1952 as a young editor at Doubleday. In 1963 he was a founder of *The New York Review* and in 1979 co-founder with the late Edmund Wilson of the Library of America. In 2007 he co-founded On Demand Books. Among his many awards are the National Book Award Medal for Distinguished Contribution to American Letters, the Lifetime Achievement Award of the National Book Critics Circle, and the Curtis Benjamin Award given by the American Association of Publishers for enriching the world of books.

Foreword to the Modern Library Edition

Jane Jacobs

When I began work on this book in 1958, I expected merely to describe the civilizing and enjoyable services that good city street life casually provides—and to deplore planning fads and architectural fashions that were expunging these necessities and charms instead of helping to strengthen them. Some of Part One of this book: that's all I intended.

But learning and thinking about city streets and the trickiness of city parks launched me into an unexpected treasure hunt. I quickly found that the valuables in plain sight—streets and parks—were intimately mingled with clues and keys to other peculiarities of cities. Thus one discovery led to another, then another. . . . Some of the findings from the hunt fill the rest of this book. Others, as they turned up, have gone into four further books. Obviously, this book exerted an influence on me, and lured me into my subsequent life's work. But has it been influential otherwise? My own appraisal is yes and no.

Some people prefer doing their workaday errands on foot, or feel they would like to if they lived in a place where they could. Other people prefer hopping into the car to do errands, or would like to if they had a car. In the old days, before automobiles, some people liked ordering up carriages or sedan chairs and many wished they could. But as we know from novels, biographies, and legends, some people whose social positions required them to ride—except for rural rambles—

wistfully peered out at passing street scenes and longed to participate in their camaraderie, bustle, and promises of surprise and adventure.

In a kind of shorthand, we can speak of foot people and car people. This book was instantly understood by foot people, both actual and wishful. They recognized that what it said jibed with their own enjoyment, concerns, and experiences, which is hardly surprising, since much of the book's information came from observing and listening to foot people. They were collaborators in the research. Then, reciprocally, the book collaborated with foot people by giving legitimacy to what they already knew for themselves. Experts of the time did not respect what foot people knew and valued. They were deemed old-fashioned and selfish—troublesome sand in the wheels of progress. It is not easy for uncredentialed people to stand up to the credentialed, even when the so-called expertise is grounded in ignorance and folly. This book turned out to be helpful ammunition against such experts. But it is less accurate to call this effect "influence" than to see it as corroboration and collaboration. Conversely, the book neither collaborated with car people nor had an influence on them. It still does not, as far as I can see.

The case of students of city planning and architecture is similarly mixed, but with special oddities. At the time of the book's publication, no matter whether the students were foot or car people by experience and temperament, they were being rigorously trained as anticity and antistreet designers and planners: trained as if they were fanatic car people and so was everybody else. Their teachers had been trained or indoctrinated that way too. So in effect, the whole establishment concerned with the physical form of cities (including bankers, developers, and politicians who had assimilated the planning and architectural visions and theories) acted as gatekeepers protecting forms and visions inimical to city life. However, among architectural students especially, and to some extent among planning students, there were foot people. To them, the book made sense. Their teachers (though not all) tended to consider it trash or "bitter, coffee-house rambling" as one planner put it. Yet the book, curiously enough, found its way onto required or optional reading lists—sometimes, I suspect, to arm students with awareness of the benighted ideas they would be up against as practitioners. Indeed, one university teacher told me just that. But for foot people among students, the book was subversive. Of course their subversion was by no means all my doing. Other authors and researchers—notably William H. Whyte—were also exposing the unworkability and joylessness of anticity visions. In London, editors and writers of *The Architectural Review* were already up to the same thing in the mid-1950s.

Nowadays, many architects, and some among the younger generation of planners, have excellent ideas—beautiful, ingenious ideas—for strengthening city life. They also have the skills to carry out their plans. These people are a far cry from the ruthless, heedless city manipulators I have castigated.

But here we come to something sad. Although the numbers of arrogant old gatekeepers have dwindled with time, the gates themselves are another matter. Anticity planning remains amazingly sturdy in American cities. It is still embodied in thousands of regulations, bylaws, and codes, also in bureaucratic timidities owing to accepted practices, and in unexamined public attitudes hardened by time. Thus, one may be sure that there have been enormous and dedicated efforts in the face of these obstacles wherever one sees stretches of old city buildings that have been usefully recycled for new and different purposes; wherever sidewalks have been widened and vehicular roadways narrowed precisely where they should be—on streets in which pedestrian traffic is bustling and plentiful; wherever downtowns are not deserted after their offices close; wherever new, fine-grained mixtures of street uses have been fostered successfully; wherever new buildings have been sensitively inserted among old ones to knit up holes and tatters in a city neighborhood so that the mending is all but invisible. Some foreign cities have become pretty good at these feats. But to try to accomplish such sensible things in America is a daunting ordeal at best, and often enough heartbreaking.

In Chapter Twenty of this book I proposed that the ground levels of self-isolating projects within cities could be radically erased and reconstituted with two objects in view: linking the projects into the normal city by fitting them out with plentiful, new, connecting streets; and converting the projects themselves into urban places at the same time, by adding diverse new facilities along those added streets. The catch here, of course, is that new commercial facilities would need to work out economically, as a measure of their genuine and not fake usefulness.

It is disappointing that this sort of radical replanning has not been tried—as far as I know—in the more than thirty years since this book was published. To be sure, with every decade that passes, the task of carrying out the proposal would seem to be more difficult. That is because anticity projects, especially massive public housing projects, tend to cause their city surroundings to deteriorate, so that as time passes, less and less healthy adjoining city is available to tie into.

Even so, good opportunities still exist for converting city projects into city. Easy ones ought to be tried first on the premise that this is a learning challenge, and it is good policy for all learning to start with easy cases and work up to more difficult ones. The time is coming when we will sorely need to apply this learning to suburban sprawls since it is unlikely we can continue extending them without limit. The costs in energy waste, infrastructure waste, and land waste are too high. Yet if already existing sprawls are intensified, in favor of thriftier use of resources, we need to have learned how to make the intensifications and linkages attractive, enjoyable, safe, and sustainable—for foot people as well as car people.

Occasionally this book has been credited with having helped halt urban-renewal and slum-clearance programs. I would be delighted to take credit if this were true. It isn't. Urban renewal and slum clearance succumbed to their own failures and fiascos, after continuing with their extravagant outrages for many years after this book was published. Even now they pop up when wishful thinking and forgetfulness set in, abetted by sufficient cataclysmic money lent to developers and sufficient political hubris and public subsidies. A recent example, for instance, is the grandiose but bankrupt Canary Wharf project set in isolation in what were London's dilapidated docklands and the demolished, modest Isle of Dogs community, beloved by its inhabitants.

To return to the treasure hunt that began with the streets and one thing leading to another and another: at some point along the trail I realized I was engaged in studying the ecology of cities. Offhand, this sounds like taking note that raccoons nourish themselves from city backyard gardens and garbage bags (in my own city they do, sometimes even downtown), that hawks can possibly reduce pigeon populations among skyscrapers, and so on. But by city ecology I mean something different from, yet similar to, natural ecology as students of wilderness address the subject. A natural ecosystem is defined as "composed of physical-chemical-biological processes active within a space-time unit of any magnitude." A city ecosystem is composed of physical-economic-ethical processes active at a given time within a city and its close dependencies. I've made up this definition, by analogy.

The two sorts of ecosystems—one created by nature, the other by human beings—have fundamental principles in common. For instance, both types of ecosystems—assuming they are not barren—require much diversity to sustain themselves. In both cases, the diversity develops organically over time, and the varied components are interdependent in complex ways. The more niches for diversity of life and livelihoods in either kind of ecosystem, the greater its carrying capacity for life. In both types of ecosystems, many small and obscure components—easily overlooked by superficial observation—

can be vital to the whole, far out of proportion to their own tininess of scale or aggregate quantities. In natural ecosystems, gene pools are fundamental treasures. In city ecosystems, kinds of work are fundamental treasures; furthermore, forms of work not only reproduce themselves in newly created proliferating organizations, they also hybridize, and even mutate into unprecedented kinds of work. And because of their complex interdependencies of components, both kinds of ecosystems are vulnerable and fragile, easily disrupted or destroyed.

If not fatally disrupted, however, they are tough and resilient. And when their processes are working well, ecosystems appear stable. But in a profound sense, the stability is an illusion. As a Greek philosopher, Heraclitus, observed long ago, everything in the natural world is in flux. When we suppose we see static situations, we actually see processes of beginning and processes of ending occurring simultaneously. Nothing is static. It is the same with cities. Thus, to investigate either natural or city ecosystems demands the same kind of thinking. It does not do to focus on "things" and expect them to explain much in themselves. Processes are always of the essence; things have significances as participants in processes, for better or worse.

This way of seeing is fairly young and new, which is perhaps why the hunt for knowledge to understand either natural or city ecology seems so inexhaustible. Little is known; so much yet to know.

We human beings are the only city-building creatures in the world. The hives of social insects are fundamentally different in how they develop, what they do, and their potentialities. Cities are in a sense natural ecosystems too—for us. They are not disposable. Whenever and wherever societies have flourished and prospered rather than stagnated and decayed, creative and workable cities have been at the core of the phenomenon; they have pulled their weight and more. It is the same still. Decaying cities, declining economies, and mounting social troubles travel together. The combination is not coincidental.

It is urgent that human beings understand as much as we can about city ecology—starting at any point in city processes. The humble, vital services performed by grace of good city streets and neighborhoods are probably as good a starting point as any. So I find it heartening that The Modern Library is issuing this beautiful new edition for a new generation of readers who, I hope, will become interested in city ecology, respect its marvels, discover more.

Toronto, Canada
October 1992

To NEW YORK CITY
where I came to seek my fortune
and found it by finding
Bob, Jimmy, Ned and Mary
for whom this book is written too

Acknowledgments

So many scores of persons helped me with this book, wittingly and unwittingly, that I shall never fully be able to acknowledge the appreciation I owe and feel. In particular I am grateful for information, aid or criticism given by the following persons: Saul Alinsky, Norris C. Andrews, Edmund Bacon, June Blythe, John Decker Butzner, Jr., Henry Churchill, Grady Clay, William C. Crow, Vernon De Mars, Monsignor John J. Egan, Charles Farnsley, Carl Feiss, Robert B. Filley, Mrs. Rosario Folino, Chadbourne Gilpatric, Victor Gruen, Frank Havey, Goldie Hoffman, Frank Hotchkiss, Leticia Kent, William H. Kirk, Mr. and Mrs. George Kostritsky, Jay Landesman, The Rev. Wilbur C. Leach, Glennie M. Lenear, Melvin F. Levine, Edward Logue, Ellen Lurie, Elizabeth Manson, Roger Montgomery, Richard Nelson, Joseph Passonneau, Ellen Perry, Rose Porter, Ansel Robison, James W. Rouse, Samuel A. Spiegel, Stanley B. Tankel, Jack Volkman, Robert C. Weinberg, Erik Wensberg, Henry Whitney, William H. Whyte, Jr., William Wilcox, Mildred Zucker, Beda Zwicker. None of these people is, of course, responsible for what I have written; indeed, some disagree heartily with my point of view but have helped me generously nevertheless.

I am grateful also to the Rockefeller Foundation for the financial support which made my research and writing possible, to the New School for Social Research for its hospitality, and to Douglas Haskell, the Editor of *Archi-tectural Forum*, for his encouragement and forbearance. Most of all I am grateful to my husband, Robert H. Jacobs, Jr.; by this time I do not know which ideas in this book are mine and which are his.

CONTENTS

ILLUSTRATIONS

The scenes that illustrate this book are all about us. For illustrations, please look closely at real cities. While you are looking, you might as well also listen, linger and think about what you see.

THE DEATH AND LIFE OF GREAT AMERICAN CITIES

"Until lately the best thing that I was able to
think of in favor of civilization, apart from
blind acceptance of the order of the universe,
was that it made possible the artist, the poet,
the philosopher, and the man of science. But I
think that is not the greatest thing. Now I
believe that the greatest thing is a matter that
comes directly home to us all. When it is
said that we are too much occupied with the means
of living to live, I answer that the chief worth
of civilization is just that it makes the means
of living more complex; that it calls for great
and combined intellectual efforts, instead of
simple, uncoordinated ones, in order that the
crowd may be fed and clothed and housed and moved
from place to place. Because more complex and
intense intellectual efforts mean a fuller and
richer life. They mean more life. Life is an
end in itself, and the only question as to
whether it is worth living is whether you have
enough of it.
"I will add but a word. We are all very near
despair. The sheathing that floats us over its
waves is compounded of hope, faith in the
unexplainable worth and sure issue of effort,
and the deep, sub-conscious content which comes
from the exercise of our powers."

OLIVER WENDELL HOLMES, JR.

1

INTRODUCTION

This book is an attack on current city planning and rebuilding. It is also, and mostly, an attempt to introduce new principles of city planning and rebuilding, different and even opposite from those now taught in everything from schools of architecture and planning to the Sunday supplements and women's magazines. My attack is not based on quibbles about rebuilding methods or hairsplitting about fashions in design. It is an attack, rather, on the principles and aims that have shaped modern, orthodox city planning and rebuilding.

In setting forth different principles, I shall mainly be writing about common, ordinary things: for instance, what kinds of city streets are safe and what kinds are not; why some city parks are marvelous and others are vice traps and death traps; why some slums stay slums and other slums regenerate themselves even against financial and official opposition; what makes downtowns shift their centers; what, if anything, is a city neighborhood, and what jobs, if any, neighborhoods in great cities do. In short, I shall be writing about how cities work in real life, because this is the only way to learn what principles of planning and what practices in rebuilding can promote social and economic vitality in cities, and what practices and principles will deaden these attributes.

There is a wistful myth that if only we had enough money to spend—the figure is usually put at a hundred billion dollars—we could wipe out all our slums in ten years, reverse decay in the great, dull, gray belts that were yesterday's and day-before-yesterday's suburbs, anchor the wandering middle class and its wandering tax money, and perhaps even solve the traffic problem.

But look what we have built with the first several billions: Low-income projects that become worse centers of delinquency, vandalism and general social hopelessness than the slums they were supposed to replace. Middle-income housing projects which are truly marvels of dullness and regimentation, sealed against any buoyancy or vitality of city life. Luxury housing projects that mitigate their inanity, or try to, with a vapid vulgarity. Cultural centers that are unable to support a good bookstore. Civic centers that are avoided by everyone but bums, who have fewer choices of loitering place than others. Commercial centers that are lackluster imitations of standardized suburban chain-store shopping. Promenades that go from no place to nowhere and have no promenaders. Expressways that eviscerate great cities. This is not the rebuilding of cities. This is the sacking of cities.

Under the surface, these accomplishments prove even poorer than their poor pretenses. They seldom aid the city areas around them, as in theory they are supposed to. These amputated areas typically develop galloping gangrene. To house people in this planned fashion, price tags are fastened on the population, and each sorted-out chunk of price-tagged populace lives in growing suspicion and tension against the surrounding city. When two or more such hostile islands are juxtaposed the result is called "a balanced neighborhood." Monopolistic shopping centers and monumental cultural centers cloak, under the public relations hoohaw, the subtraction of commerce, and of culture too, from the intimate and casual life of cities.

That such wonders may be accomplished, people who get marked with the planners' hex signs are pushed about, expropriated, and uprooted much as if they were the subjects of a conquering power. Thousands upon thousands of small businesses are destroyed, and their proprietors ruined, with hardly a gesture at compensation. Whole communities are torn apart and sown to the winds, with a reaping of cynicism, resentment and despair that must be heard and seen to be believed. A group of clergymen in Chicago, appalled at the fruits of planned city rebuilding there, asked,

> Could Job have been thinking of Chicago when he wrote:
>
>> Here are men that alter their neighbor's landmark . . . shoulder the poor aside, conspire to oppress the friendless.
>>
>> Reap they the field that is none of theirs, strip they the vineyard wrongfully seized from its owner . . .
>>
>> A cry goes up from the city streets, where wounded men lie groaning . . .

If so, he was also thinking of New York, Philadelphia, Boston, Washington, St. Louis, San Francisco and a number of other places. The economic rationale of current city rebuilding is a hoax. The economics of city rebuilding do not rest soundly on reasoned investment of public tax subsidies, as urban renewal theory proclaims, but also on vast, involuntary subsidies wrung out of helpless site victims. And the increased tax returns from such sites, accruing to the cities as a result of this "investment," are a mirage, a pitiful gesture against the ever increasing sums of public money needed to combat disintegration and instability that flow from the cruelly shaken-up city. The means to planned city rebuilding are as deplorable as the ends.

Meantime, all the art and science of city planning are helpless to stem decay—and the spiritlessness that precedes decay—in ever more massive swatches of cities. Nor can this decay be laid, reassuringly, to lack of opportunity to apply the arts of planning. It seems to matter little whether they are applied or not. Consider the Morningside Heights area in New York City. According to planning theory it should not be in trouble at all, for it enjoys a great abundance of parkland, campus, playground and other open spaces. It has plenty of grass. It occupies high and pleasant ground with magnificent river views. It is a famous educational center with splendid institutions—Columbia University, Union Theological Seminary, the Juilliard School of Music, and half a dozen others of eminent respectability. It is the beneficiary of good hospitals and churches. It has no industries. Its streets are zoned in the main against "incompatible uses" intruding into the preserves for solidly constructed, roomy, middle- and upper-class apartments. Yet by the early 1950's Morningside Heights was becoming a slum so swiftly, the surly kind of slum in which people fear to walk the streets, that the situation posed a crisis for the

institutions. They and the planning arms of the city government got together, applied more planning theory,
wiped out the most run-down part of the area and built in
its stead a middle-income cooperative project complete
with shopping center, and a public housing project, all
interspersed with air, light, sunshine and landscaping.
This was hailed as a great demonstration in city saving.

After that, Morningside Heights went downhill even
faster.

Nor is this an unfair or irrelevant example. In city
after city, precisely the wrong areas, in the light of planning theory, are decaying. Less noticed, but equally significant, in city after city the wrong areas, in the light of
planning theory, are refusing to decay.

Cities are an immense laboratory of trial and error,
failure and success, in city building and city design. This
is the laboratory in which city planning should have been
learning and forming and testing its theories. Instead the
practitioners and teachers of this discipline (if such it can
be called) have ignored the study of success and failure
in real life, have been incurious about the reasons for
unexpected success, and are guided instead by principles
derived from the behavior and appearance of towns, suburbs, tuberculosis sanatoria, fairs, and imaginary dream
cities—from anything but cities themselves.

If it appears that the rebuilt portions of cities and the
endless new developments spreading beyond the cities
are reducing city and countryside alike to a monotonous,
unnourishing gruel, this is not strange. It all comes, first-,
second-, third- or fourth-hand, out of the same intellectual
dish of mush, a mush in which the qualities, necessities,
advantages and behavior of great cities have been utterly

confused with the qualities, necessities, advantages and behavior of other and more inert types of settlements.

There is nothing economically or socially inevitable about either the decay of old cities or the fresh-minted decadence of the new unurban urbanization. On the contrary, no other aspect of our economy and society has been more purposefully manipulated for a full quarter of a century to achieve precisely what we are getting. Extraordinary governmental financial incentives have been required to achieve this degree of monotony, sterility and vulgarity. Decades of preaching, writing and exhorting by experts have gone into convincing us and our legislators that mush like this must be good for us, as long as it comes bedded with grass.

Automobiles are often conveniently tagged as the villains responsible for the ills of cities and the disappointments and futilities of city planning. But the destructive effects of automobiles are much less a cause than a symptom of our incompetence at city building. Of course planners, including the highwaymen with fabulous sums of money and enormous powers at their disposal, are at a loss to make automobiles and cities compatible with one another. They do not know what to do with automobiles in cities because they do not know how to plan for workable and vital cities anyhow—with or without automobiles.

The simple needs of automobiles are more easily understood and satisfied than the complex needs of cities, and a growing number of planners and designers have come to believe that if they can only solve the problems of traffic, they will thereby have solved the major problem of cities. Cities have much more intricate economic and social concerns the automobile traffic. How can you know what to try with traffic until you know how the city itself works, and what else it needs to do with its streets? You can't.

It may be that we have become so feckless as a people that we no longer care how things do work, but only what kind of quick, easy outer impression they give. If so, there is little hope for our cities or probably for much else in our society. But I do not think this is so.

Specifically, in the case of planning for cities, it is clear that a large number of good and earnest people do care deeply about building and renewing. Despite some corruption, and considerable greed for the other man's vineyard, the intentions going into the messes we make are, on the whole, exemplary. Planners, architects of city design, and those they have led along with them in their beliefs are not consciously disdainful of the importance of knowing how things work. On the contrary, they have gone to great pains to learn what the saints and sages of modern orthodox planning have said about how cities *ought* to work and what *ought* to be good for people and businesses in them. They take this with such devotion that when contradictory reality intrudes, threatening to shatter their dearly won learning, they must shrug reality aside.

Consider, for example, the orthodox planning reaction to a district called the North End in Boston.* This is an old, low-rent area merging into the heavy industry of the

* Please remember the North End. I shall refer to it frequently in this book.

waterfront, and it is officially considered Boston's worst slum and civic shame. It embodies attributes which all enlightened people know are evil because so many wise men have said they are evil. Not only is the North End bumped right up against industry, but worse still it has all kinds of working places and commerce mingled in the greatest complexity with its residences. It has the highest concentration of dwelling units, on the land that is used for dwelling units, of any part of Boston, and indeed one of the highest concentrations to be found in any American city. It has little parkland. Children play in the streets. Instead of super-blocks, or even decently large blocks, it has very small blocks; in planning parlance it is "badly cut up with wasteful streets." Its buildings are old. Everything conceivable is presumably wrong with the North End. In orthodox planning terms, it is a three-dimensional text-book of "megalopolis" in the last stages of depravity. The North End is thus a recurring assignment for M.I.T. and Harvard planning and architectural students, who now and again pursue, under the guidance of their teachers, the paper exercise of converting it into super-blocks and park promenades, wiping away its nonconforming uses, trans-forming it to an ideal of order and gentility so simple it could be engraved on the head of a pin.

Twenty years ago, when I first happened to see the North End, its buildings—town houses of different kinds and sizes converted to flats, and four- or five-story tene-ments built to house the flood of immigrants first from Ireland, then from Eastern Europe and finally from Sicily—were badly overcrowded, and the general effect was of a district taking a terrible physical beating and cer-tainly desperately poor.

When I saw the North End again in 1959, I was amazed at the change. Dozens and dozens of buildings had been rehabilitated. Instead of mattresses against the windows there were Venetian blinds and glimpses of fresh paint. Many of the small, converted houses now had only one or two families in them instead of the old crowded three or four. Some of the families in the tenements (as I learned later, visiting inside) had uncrowded themselves by throwing two older apartments together, and had equipped these with bathrooms, new kitchens and the like. I looked down a narrow alley, thinking to find at least here the old, squalid North End, but no: more neatly repointed brickwork, new blinds, and a burst of music as a door opened. Indeed, this was the only city district I had ever seen—or have seen to this day—in which the sides of buildings around parking lots had not been left raw and amputated, but repaired and painted as neatly as if they were intended to be seen. Mingled all among the buildings for living were an incredible number of splendid food stores, as well as such enterprises as upholstery making, metal working, carpentry, food processing. The streets were alive with children playing, people shopping, people strolling, people talking. Had it not been a cold January day, there would surely have been people sitting.

The general street atmosphere of buoyancy, friendliness and good health was so infectious that I began asking directions of people just for the fun of getting in on some talk. I had seen a lot of Boston in the past couple of days, most of it sorely distressing, and this struck me, with relief, as the healthiest place in the city. But I could not imagine where the money had come from for the rehabilitation, because it is almost impossible today to get any appreciable mortgage money in districts of American cities that are not either high-rent, or else imitations of suburbs. To find out, I went into a bar and restaurant (where an animated conversation about fishing was in progress) and called a Boston planner I know.

"Why in the world are you down in the North End?" he said. "Money? Why, no money or work has gone into the North End. Nothing's going on down there. Eventually, yes, but not yet. That's a slum!"

"It doesn't seem like a slum to me," I said.

"Why, that's the worst slum in the city. It has two hundred and seventy-five dwelling units to the net acre! I hate to admit we have anything like that in Boston, but it's a fact."

"Do you have any other figures on it?" I asked.

"Yes, funny thing. It has among the lowest delinquency, disease and infant mortality rates in the city. It also has the lowest ratio of rent to income in the city. Boy, are those people getting bargains. Let's see . . . the child population is just about average for the city, on the nose. The death rate is low, 8.8 per thousand, against the average city rate of 11.2. The TB death rate is very low, less than 1 per ten thousand, can't understand it, it's lower even than Brookline's. In the old days the North End used to be the city's worst spot for tuberculosis, but all that has changed. Well, they must be strong people. Of course it's a terrible slum."

"You should have more slums like this," I said. "Don't tell me there are plans to wipe this out. You ought to be down here learning as much as you can from it."

"I know how you feel," he said. "I often go down

there myself just to walk around the streets and feel that wonderful, cheerful street life. Say, what you ought to do, you ought to come back and go down in the summer if you think it's fun now. You'd be crazy about it in summer. But of course we have to rebuild it eventually. We've got to get those people off the streets."

Here was a curious thing. My friend's instincts told him the North End was a good place, and his social statistics confirmed it. But everything he had learned as a physical planner about what is good for people and good for city neighborhoods, everything that made him an expert, told him the North End had to be a bad place.

The leading Boston savings banker, "a man 'way up there in the power structure," to whom my friend referred me for my inquiry about the money, confirmed what I learned, in the meantime, from people in the North End. The money had not come through the grace of the great American banking system, which now knows enough about planning to know a slum as well as the planners do. "No sense in lending money into the North End," the banker said. "It's a slum! It's still getting some immigrants! Furthermore, back in the Depression it had a very large number of foreclosures; bad record." (I had heard about this too, in the meantime, and how families had worked and pooled their resources to buy back some of those foreclosed buildings.)

The largest mortgage loans that had been fed into this district of some 15,000 people in the quarter-century since the Great Depression were for $3,000, the banker told me, "and very, very few of those." There had been some others for $1,000 and for $2,000. The rehabilitation work had been almost entirely financed by business and housing earnings within the district, plowed back in, and by skilled work bartered among residents and relatives of residents.

By this time I knew that this inability to borrow for improvement was a galling worry to North Enders, and that furthermore some North Enders were worried because it seemed impossible to get new building in the area except at the price of seeing themselves and their community wiped out in the fashion of the students' dreams of a city Eden, a fate which they knew was not academic because it had already smashed completely a socially similar—although physically more spacious— nearby district called the West End. They were worried because they were aware also that patch and fix with nothing else could not do forever. "Any chance of loans for new construction in the North End?" I asked the banker.

"No, absolutely not!" he said, sounding impatient at my denseness. "That's a slum!"

Bankers, like planners, have theories about cities on which they act. They have gotten their theories from the same intellectual sources as the planners. Bankers and government administrative officials who guarantee mortgages do not invent planning theories nor, surpris- ingly, even economic doctrine about cities. They are enlightened nowadays, and they pick up their ideas from idealists, a generation late. Since theoretical city planning has embraced no major new ideas for considerably more than a generation, theoretical planners, financers and bureaucrats are all just about even today.

And to put it bluntly, they are all in the same stage of

elaborately learned superstition as medical science was early in the last century, when physicians put their faith in bloodletting, to draw out the evil humors which were believed to cause disease. With bloodletting, it took years of learning to know precisely which veins, by what rituals, were to be opened for what symptoms. A superstructure of technical complication was erected in such deadpan detail that the literature still sounds almost plausible. However, because people, even when they are thoroughly enmeshed in descriptions of reality which are at variance with reality, are still seldom devoid of the powers of observation and independent thought, the science of bloodletting, over most of its long sway, appears usually to have been tempered with a certain amount of common sense. Or it was tempered until it reached its highest peaks of technique in, of all places, the young United States. Bloodletting went wild here. It had an enormously influential proponent in Dr. Benjamin Rush, still revered as the greatest statesman-physician of our revolutionary and federal periods, and a genius of medical administration. Dr. Rush Got Things Done. Among the things he got done, some of them good and useful, were to develop, practice, teach and spread the custom of bloodletting in cases where prudence or mercy had heretofore restrained its use. He and his students drained the blood of very young children, of consumptives, of the greatly aged, of almost anyone unfortunate enough to be sick in his realms of influence. His extreme practices aroused the alarm and horror of European bloodletting physicians. And yet as late as 1851, a committee appointed by the State Legislature of New York solemnly defended the thoroughgoing use of bloodletting. It scathingly ridiculed and censured a physician, William Turner, who had the temerity to write a pamphlet criticizing Dr. Rush's doctrines and calling "the practice of taking blood in diseases contrary to common sense, to general experience, to enlightened reason and to the manifest laws of the divine Providence." Sick people needed fortifying, not draining, said Dr. Turner, and he was squelched.

Medical analogies, applied to social organisms, are apt to be farfetched, and there is no point in mistaking mammalian chemistry for what occurs in a city. But analogies as to what goes on in the brains of earnest and learned men, dealing with complex phonemena they do not understand at all and trying to make do with a pseudoscience, do have point. As in the pseudoscience of bloodletting, just so in the pseudoscience of city rebuilding and planning, years of learning and a plethora of subtle and complicated dogma have arisen on a foundation of nonsense. The tools of technique have steadily been perfected. Naturally, in time, forceful and able men, admired administrators, having swallowed the initial fallacies and having been provisioned with tools and with public confidence, go on logically to the greatest destructive excesses, which prudence or mercy might previously have forbade. Bloodletting could heal only by accident or insofar as it broke the rules, until the time when it was abandoned in favor of the hard, complex business of assembling, using and testing, bit by bit, true descriptions of reality drawn not from how it ought to be, but from how it is. The pseudoscience of city planning and its companion, the art of city design, have not yet broken with the specious comfort of wishes, familiar superstitions, oversimplifications, and symbols, and have not yet embarked upon the adventure of probing the real world.

So in this book we shall start, if only in a small way, adventuring in the real world, ourselves. The way to get at what goes on in the seemingly mysterious and perverse behavior of cities is, I think, to look closely, and with as little previous expectation as is possible, at the most ordinary scenes and events, and attempt to see what they mean and whether any threads of principle emerge among them. This is whit I try to do in the first part of this book.

One principle emerges so ubiquitously, and in so many and such complex different forms, that I turn my attention to its nature in the second part of this book, a part which becomes the heart of my argument. This ubiquitous principle is the need of cities for a most intricate and close-grained diversity of uses that give each other constant mutual support, both economically and socially. The components of this diversity can differ enormously, but they must supplement each other in certain concrete ways.

I think that unsuccessful city areas are areas which lack this kind of intricate mutual support, and that the science of city planning and the art of city design, in real life for real cities, must become the science and art of catalyzing and nourishing these close-grained working relationships. I think, from the evidence I can find, that there are four primary conditions required for generating useful great city diversity, and that by deliberately inducing these four conditions, planning can induce city vitality (something that the plans of planners alone, and the designs of designers alone, can never achieve). While Part I is principally about the social behavior of people in cities, and is necessary for understanding what follows, Part II is principally about the economic behavior of cities and is the most important part of this book.

Cities are fantastically dynamic places, and this is strikingly true of their successful parts, which offer a fertile ground for the plans of thousands of people. In the third part of this book, I examine some aspects of decay and regeneration, in the light of how cities are used, and how they and their people behave, in real life.

The last part of the book suggests changes in housing, traffic, design, planning and administrative practices, and discusses, finally, the *kind* of problem which cities pose— a problem in handling organized complexity.

The look of things and the way they work are inextricably bound together, and in no place more so than cities. But people who are interested only in how a city "ought" to look and uninterested in how it works will be disappointed by this book. It is futile to plan a city's appearance, or speculate on how to endow it with a pleasing appearance of order, without knowing what sort of innate, functioning order it has. To seek for the look of things as a primary purpose or as the main drama is apt to make nothing but trouble.

In New York's East Harlem there is a housing project with a conspicuous rectangular lawn which became an object of hatred to the project tenants. A social worker frequently at the project was astonished by how often the subject of the lawn came up, usually gratuitously as far as she could see, and how much the tenants despised it and urged that it be done away with. When she asked why, the usual answer was, "What good is it?" or "Who wants it?" Finally one day a tenant more articulate than the others made this pronouncement: "Nobody cared what we wanted when they built this place. They threw our houses down and pushed us here and pushed our friends somewhere else. We don't have a place around here to get a cup of coffee or a newspaper even, or borrow fifty cents. Nobody cared what we need. But the big men come and look at that grass and say, 'Isn't it wonderful! Now the poor have everything!' "

This tenant was saying what moralists have said for thousands of years: Handsome is as handsome does. All that glitters is not gold.

She was saying more: There is a quality even meaner than outright ugliness or disorder, and this meaner quality is the dishonest mask of pretended order, achieved by ignoring or suppressing the real order that is struggling to exist and to be served.

In trying to explain the underlying order of cities, I use a preponderance of examples from New York because that is where I live. But most of the basic ideas in this book come from things I first noticed or was told in other cities. For example, my first inkling about the powerful effects of certain kinds of functional mixtures in the city came from Pittsburgh, my first speculations about street safety from Philadelphia and Baltimore, my first notions about the meanderings of downtown from Boston, my first clues to the unmaking of slums from Chicago. Most of the material for these musings was at my own front door, but perhaps it is easiest to see things first where you don't take them for granted. The basic idea, to try to begin understanding the intricate social and economic order under the seeming disorder of cities, was not my idea at all, but that of William Kirk, head worker of Union Settlement in East Harlem, New York, who, by showing me East Harlem, showed me a way of seeing other neighborhoods, and downtowns too. In every case, I have tried to test out what I saw or heard in one city or neighborhood against others, to find how relevant each city's or each place's lessons might be outside its own special case.

I have concentrated on great cities, and on their inner areas, because this is the problem that has been most consistently evaded in planning theory. I think this may also have somewhat wider usefulness as time passes, because many of the parts of today's cities in the worst, and apparently most baffling, trouble were suburbs or dignified, quiet residential areas not too long ago; eventually many of today's brand-new suburbs or semisuburbs are going to be engulfed in cities and will succeed or fail in that condition depending on whether they can adapt to functioning successfully as city districts. Also, to be frank, I like dense cities best and care about them most.

But I hope no reader will try to transfer my observations into guides as to what goes on in towns, or little cities, or in suburbs which still are suburban. Towns, suburbs and even little cities are totally different organisms from great cities. We are in enough trouble already from trying to understand big cities in terms of the behavior, and the imagined behavior, of towns. To try to understand towns in terms of big cities will only compound confusion.

I hope any reader of this book will constantly and skeptically test what I say against his own knowledge of cities and their behavior. If I have been inaccurate in observations or mistaken in inferences and conclusions, I hope these faults will be quickly corrected. The point is, we need desperately to learn and to apply as much knowledge that is true and useful about cities as fast as possible.

I have been making unkind remarks about orthodox city planning theory, and shall make more as occasion arises to do so. By now, these orthodox ideas are part of our folklore. They harm us because we take them for granted. To show how we got them, and how little they are to the point, I shall give a quick outline here of the most influential ideas that have contributed to the verities of orthodox modern city planning and city architectural design.*

The most important thread of influence starts, more or less, with Ebenezer Howard, an English court reporter for whom planning was an avocation. Howard looked at the living conditions of the poor in late-nineteenth-century London, and justifiably did not like what he smelled or saw or heard. He not only hated the wrongs and mistakes of the city, he hated the city and thought it an outright evil and an affront to nature that so many people should get themselves into an agglomeration. His prescription for saving the people was to do the city in.

---

*Readers who would like a fuller account, and a sympathetic account which mine is not, should go to the sources, which are very interesting, especially: *Garden Cities of Tomorrow*, by Ebenezer Howard; *The Culture of Cities*, by Lewis Mumford; *Cities in Evolution*, by Sir Patrick Geddes; *Modern Housing*, by Catherine Bauer; *Toward New Towns for America*, by Clarence Stein; *Nothing Gained by Overcrowding*, by Sir Raymond Unwin; and *The City of Tomorrow and Its Planning*, by Le Corbusier. The best short survey I know of is the group of excerpts under the title "Assumptions and Goals of City Planning," contained in *Land Use Planning, A Casebook on the Use, Misuse and Re-use of Urban Land*, by Charles M. Haar.

The program he proposed, in 1898, was to halt the growth of London and also repopulate the countryside, where villages were declining, by building a new kind of town—the Garden City, where the city poor might again live close to nature. So they might earn their livings, industry was to be set up in the Garden City, for while Howard was not planning cities, he was not planning dormitory suburbs either. His aim was the creation of self-sufficient small towns, really very nice towns if you were docile and had no plans of your own and did not mind spending your life among others with no plans of their own. As in all Utopias, the right to have plans of any significance belonged only to the planners in charge. The Garden City was to be encircled with a belt of agriculture. Industry was to be in its planned preserves; schools, housing and greens in planned living preserves; and in the center were to be commercial, club and cultural places, held in common. The town and green belt, in their totality, were to be permanently controlled by the public authority under which the town was developed, to prevent speculation or supposedly irrational changes in land use and also to do away with temptations to increase its density—in brief, to prevent it from ever becoming a city. The maximum population was to be held to thirty thousand people.

Nathan Glazer has summed up the vision well in *Architectural Forum*: "The image was the English country town—with the manor house and its park replaced by a community center, and with some factories hidden behind a screen of trees, to supply work."

The closest American equivalent would probably be the model company town, with profit-sharing, and with the Parent-Teacher Associations in charge of the routine, custodial political life. For Howard was envisioning not simply a new physical environment and social life, but a paternalistic political and economic society.

Nevertheless, as Glazer has pointed out, the Garden City was "conceived as an alternative to the city, and as a solution to city problems; this was, and is still, the foundation of its immense power as a planning idea." Howard managed to get two garden cities built, Letchworth and Welwyn, and of course England and Sweden have, since the Second World War, built a number of satellite towns based on Garden City principles. In the United States, the suburb of Radburn, N.J., and the depression-built, government-sponsored Green Belt towns (actually suburbs) were all incomplete modifications on the idea. But Howard's influence in the literal, or reasonably literal, acceptance of his program was as nothing compared to his influence on conceptions underlying all American city planning today. City planners and designers with no interest in the Garden City, as such, are still thoroughly governed intellectually by its underlying principles.

Howard set spinning powerful and city-destroying ideas: He conceived that the way to deal with the city's functions was to sort and sift out of the whole certain simple uses, and to arrange each of these in relative self-containment. He focused on the provision of wholesome housing as the central problem, to which everything else was subsidiary; furthermore he defined wholesome housing in terms only of suburban physical qualities and small-town social qualities. He conceived of commerce in terms of routine, standardized supply of goods, and as serving a self-limited market. He conceived of good planning as a

series of static acts; in each case the plan must anticipate all
that is needed and be protected, after it is built, against any
but the most minor subsequent changes. He conceived of
planning also as essentially paternalistic, if not authoritarian. He was uninterested in the aspects of the city which
could not be abstracted to serve his Utopia. In particular,
he simply wrote off the intricate, many-faceted, cultural
life of the metropolis. He was uninterested in such problems as the way great cities police themselves, or exchange
ideas, or operate politically, or invent new economic
arrangements, and he was oblivious to devising ways to
strengthen these functions because, after all, he was not
designing for this kind of life in any case.

Both in his preoccupations and in his omissions,
Howard made sense in his own terms but none in terms
of city planning. Yet virtually all modern city planning
has been adapted from, and embroidered on, this silly
substance.

Howard's influence on American city planning con-
verged on the city from two directions: from town and
regional planners on the one hand, and from architects on
the other. Along the avenue of planning, Sir Patrick Geddes, a Scots biologist and philosopher, saw the Garden
City idea not as a fortuitous way to absorb population
growth otherwise destined for a great city, but as the
starting point of a much grander and more encompass-
ing pattern. He thought of the planning of cities in terms
of the planning of whole regions. Under regional planning, garden cities would be rationally distributed
throughout large territories, dovetailing into natural
resources, balanced against agriculture and woodland,
forming one far-flung logical whole.

Howard's and Geddes' ideas were enthusiastically adopted in America during the 1920's, and developed further by a group of extraordinarily effective and dedicated people—among them Lewis Mumford, Clarence Stein, the late Henry Wright, and Catherine Bauer. While they thought of themselves as regional planners, Catherine Bauer has more recently called this group the "Decentrists," and this name is more apt, for the primary result of regional planning, as they saw it, would be to decentralize great cities, thin them out, and disperse their enterprises and populations into smaller, separated cities or, better yet, towns. At the time, it appeared that the American population was both aging and leveling off in numbers, and the problem appeared to be not one of accommodating a rapidly growing population, but simply of redistributing a static population.

As with Howard himself, this group's influence was less in getting literal acceptance of its program—that got nowhere—than in influencing city planning and legislation affecting housing and housing finance. Model housing schemes by Stein and Wright, built mainly in suburban settings or at the fringes of cities, together with the writings and the diagrams, sketches and photographs presented by Mumford and Bauer, demonstrated and popularized ideas such as these, which are now taken for granted in orthodox planning: The street is bad as an environment for humans; houses should be turned away from it and faced inward, toward sheltered greens. Frequent streets are wasteful, of advantage only to real estate speculators who measure value by the front foot. The basic unit of city design is not the street, but the block and more particularly the super-block. Commerce should be

segregated from residences and greens. A neighborhood's demand for goods should be calculated "scientifically," and this much and no more commercial space
allocated. The presence of many other people is, at best,
a necessary evil, and good city planning must aim for at
least an illusion of isolation and suburbany privacy. The
Decentrists also pounded in Howard's premises that the
planned community must be islanded off as a self-contained unit, that it must resist future change, and that
every significant detail must be controlled by the planners
from the start and then stuck to. In short, good planning
was project planning.

To reinforce and dramatize the necessity for the new
order of things, the Decentrists hammered away at the
bad old city. They were incurious about successes in great
cities. They were interested only in failures. All was failure. A book like Mumford's *The Culture of Cities* was
largely a morbid and biased catalog of ills. The great city
was Megalopolis, Tyrannopolis, Nekropolis, a monstrosity, a tyranny, a living death. It must go. New York's midtown was "solidified chaos" (Mumford). The shape and
appearance of cities was nothing but "a chaotic accident . . . the summation of the haphazard, antagonistic
whims of many self-centered, ill-advised individuals"
(Stein). The centers of cities amounted to "a foreground of
noise, dirt, beggars, souvenirs and shrill competitive
advertising" (Bauer).

How could anything so bad be worth the attempt to
understand it? The Decentrists' analyses, the architectural
and housing designs which were companions and off-
shoots of these analyses, the national housing and home
financing legislation so directly influenced by the new

vision—none of these had anything to do with understanding cities, or fostering successful large cities, nor
were they intended to. They were reasons and means for
jettisoning cities, and the Decentrists were frank about
this.

But in the schools of planning and architecture, and in
Congress, state legislatures and city halls too, the Decentrists' ideas were gradually accepted as basic guides for
dealing constructively with big cities themselves. This is
the most amazing event in the whole sorry tale: that
finally people who sincerely wanted to strengthen great
cities should adopt recipes frankly devised for undermining their economies and killing them.

The man with the most dramatic idea of how to get all
this anti-city planning right into the citadels of iniquity
themselves was the European architect Le Corbusier. He
devised in the 1920's a dream city which he called the
Radiant City, composed not of the low buildings beloved
of the Decentrists, but instead mainly of skyscrapers
within a park. "Suppose we are entering the city by way
of the Great Park," Le Corbusier wrote. "Our fast car
takes the special elevated motor track between the majes-
tic skyscrapers: as we approach nearer, there is seen the
repetition against the sky of the twenty-four skyscrapers;
to our left and right on the outskirts of each particular
area are the municipal and administrative buildings; and
enclosing the space are the museums and university
buildings. The whole city is a Park." In Le Corbusier's
vertical city the common run of mankind was to be
housed at 1,200 inhabitants to the acre, a fantastically high
city density indeed, but because of building up so high, 95
percent of the ground could remain open. The skyscrap-

ers would occupy only 5 percent of the ground. The high-income people would be in lower, luxury housing around courts, with 85 percent of their ground left open. Here and there would be restaurants and theaters.

Le Corbusier was planning not only a physical environment. He was planning for a social Utopia too. Le Corbusier's Utopia was a condition of what he called maximum individual liberty, by which he seems to have meant not liberty to do anything much, but liberty from ordinary responsibility. In his Radiant City nobody, presumably, was going to have to be his brother's keeper any more. Nobody was going to have to struggle with plans of his own. Nobody was going to be tied down.

The Decentrists and other loyal advocates of the Garden City were aghast at Le Corbusier's city of towers in the park, and still are. Their reaction to it was, and remains, much like that of progressive nursery school teachers confronting an utterly institutional orphanage. And yet, ironically, the Radiant City comes directly out of the Garden City. Le Corbusier accepted the Garden City's fundamental image, superficially at least, and worked to make it practical for high densities. He described his creation as the Garden City made attainable. "The garden city is a will-o'-the-wisp," he wrote. "Nature melts under the invasion of roads and houses and the promised seclusion becomes a crowded settlement . . . The solution will be found in the 'vertical garden city.' "

In another sense too, in its relatively easy public reception, Le Corbusier's Radiant City depended upon the Garden City. The Garden City planners and their ever increasing following among housing reformers, students and architects were indefatigably popularizing the ideas of the super-block, the project neighborhood, the unchangeable plan, and grass, grass, grass; what is more they were successfully establishing such attributes as the hallmarks of humane, socially responsible, functional, high-minded planning. Le Corbusier really did not have to justify his vision in either humane or city-functional terms. If the great object of city planning was that Christopher Robin might go hoppety-hoppety on the grass, what was wrong with Le Corbusier? The Decentrists' cries of institutionalization, mechanization, depersonalization seemed to others foolishly sectarian.

Le Corbusier's dream city has had an immense impact on our cities. It was hailed deliriously by architects, and has gradually been embodied in scores of projects, ranging from low-income public housing to office building projects. Aside from making at least the superficial Garden City principles superficially practicable in dense city, Le Corbusier's dream contained other marvels. He attempted to make planning for the automobile an integral part of his scheme, and this was, in the 1920's and early 1930's, a new, exciting idea. He included great arterial roads for express one-way traffic. He cut the number of streets because "cross-roads are an enemy to traffic." He proposed underground streets for heavy vehicles and deliveries, and of course like the Garden City planners he kept the pedestrians off the streets and in the parks. His city was like a wonderful mechanical toy. Furthermore, his conception, as an architectural work, had a dazzling clarity, simplicity and harmony. It was so orderly, so visible, so easy to understand. It said everything in a flash, like a good advertisement. This vision and its bold symbolism have been all but irresistible to planners, housers, designers, and to developers, lenders and mayors too. It exerts a great pull on "progressive" zoners, who write rules calculated to encourage nonproject builders to reflect, if only a little, the dream. No matter how vulgarized or clumsy the design, how dreary and useless the open space, how dull the close-up view, an imitation of Le Corbusier shouts "Look what I made!" Like a great, visible ego it tells of someone's achievement. But as to how the city works, it tells, like the Garden City, nothing but lies.

Although the Decentrists, with their devotion to the ideal of a cozy town life, have never made peace with the Le Corbusier vision, most of their disciples have. Virtually all sophisticated city designers today combine the two conceptions in various permutations. The rebuilding technique variously known as "selective removal" or "spot renewal" or "renewal planning" or "planned conservation"—meaning that total clearance of a run-down area is avoided—is largely the trick of seeing how many old buildings can be left standing and the area still converted into a passable version of Radiant Garden City. Zoners, highway planners, legislators, land-use planners, and parks and playground planners—none of whom live in an ideological vacuum—constantly use, as fixed points of reference, these two powerful visions and the more sophisticated merged vision. They may wander from the visions, they may compromise, they may vulgarize, but these are the points of departure.

We shall look briefly at one other, less important, line of ancestry in orthodox planning. This one begins more or less with the great Columbian Exposition in Chicago in 1893, just about the same time that Howard was formulating his Garden City ideas. The Chicago fair snubbed the exciting modern architecture which had begun to emerge in Chicago and instead dramatized a retrogressive imitation Renaissance style. One heavy, grandiose monument after another was arrayed in the exposition park, like frosted pastries on a tray, in a sort of squat, decorated forecast of Le Corbusier's later repetitive ranks of towers in a park. This orgiastic assemblage of the rich and monumental captured the imagination of both planners and public. It gave impetus to a movement called the City Beautiful, and indeed the planning of the exposition was dominated by the man who became the leading City Beautiful planner, Daniel Burnham of Chicago.

The aim of the City Beautiful was the City Monumental. Great schemes were drawn up for systems of baroque boulevards, which mainly came to nothing. What did come out of the movement was the Center Monumental, modeled on the fair. City after city built its civic center or its cultural center. These buildings were arranged along a boulevard as at Benjamin Franklin Parkway in Philadelphia, or along a mall like the Government Center in Cleveland, or were bordered by park, like the Civic Center at St. Louis, or were interspersed with park, like the Civic Center at San Francisco. However they were arranged, the important point was that the monuments had been sorted out from the rest of the city, and assembled into the grandest effect thought possible, the whole being treated as a complete unit, in a separate and well-defined way.

People were proud of them, but the centers were not a success. For one thing, invariably the ordinary city around them ran down instead of being uplifted, and they always acquired an incongruous rim of ratty tattoo parlors and second-hand-clothing stores, or else just nondescript, dispirited decay. For another, people stayed away from them to a remarkable degree. Somehow, when the fair became part of the city, it did not work like the fair.

The architecture of the City Beautiful centers went out of style. But the idea behind the centers was not questioned, and it has never had more force than it does today. The idea of sorting out certain cultural or public functions and decontaminating their relationship with the workaday city dovetailed nicely with the Garden City teachings. The conceptions have harmoniously merged, much as the Garden City and the Radiant City merged, into a sort of Radiant Garden City Beautiful, such as the immense Lincoln Square project for New York, in which a monumental City Beautiful cultural center is one among a series of adjoining Radiant City and Radiant Garden City housing, shopping and campus centers.

And by analogy, the principles of sorting out—and of bringing order by repression of all plans but the planners'—have been easily extended to all manner of city functions, until today a land-use master plan for a big city is largely a matter of proposed placement, often in relation to transportation, of many series of decontaminated sortings.

From beginning to end, from Howard and Burnham to the latest amendment on urban-renewal law, the entire concoction is irrelevant to the workings of cities. Unstudied, unrespected, cities have served as sacrificial victims.

PART ONE

THE PECULIAR
NATURE OF CITIES

2

THE USES OF SIDEWALKS: SAFETY

Streets in cities serve many purposes besides carrying vehicles, and city sidewalks—the pedestrian parts of the streets—serve many purposes besides carrying pedestrians. These uses are bound up with circulation but are not identical with it and in their own right they are at least as basic as circulation to the proper workings of cities.

A city sidewalk by itself is nothing. It is an abstraction. It means something only in conjunction with the buildings and other uses that border it, or border other sidewalks very near it. The same might be said of streets, in the sense that they serve other purposes besides carrying wheeled traffic in their middles. Streets and their sidewalks, the main public places of a city, are its most vital organs. Think of a city and what comes to mind? Its streets. If a city's streets look interesting, the city looks interesting; if they look dull, the city looks dull.

More than that, and here we get down to the first problem, if a city's streets are safe from barbarism and fear, the city is thereby tolerably safe from barbarism and fear. When people say that a city, or a part of it, is dangerous or is a jungle what they mean primarily is that they do not feel safe on the sidewalks.

But sidewalks and those who use them are not passive beneficiaries of safety or helpless victims of danger. Sidewalks, their bordering uses, and their users, are active participants in the drama of civilization versus barbarism in cities. To keep the city safe is a fundamental task of a city's streets and its sidewalks.

This task is totally unlike any service that sidewalks and streets in little towns or true suburbs are called upon to do. Great cities are not like towns, only larger. They are not like suburbs, only denser. They differ from towns and suburbs in basic ways, and one of these is that cities are, by definition, full of strangers. To any one person, strangers are far more common in big cities than acquaintances. More common not just in places of public assembly, but more common at a man's own doorstep. Even residents who live near each other are strangers, and must be, because of the sheer number of people in small geographical compass.

The bedrock attribute of a successful city district is that a person must feel personally safe and secure on the street among all these strangers. He must not feel automatically menaced by them. A city district that fails in this respect also does badly in other ways and lays up for itself, and for its city at large, mountain on mountain of trouble.

Today barbarism has taken over many city streets, or people fear it has, which comes to much the same thing in the end. "I live in a lovely, quiet residential area," says a friend of mine who is hunting another place to live. "The only disturbing sound at night is the occasional scream of someone being mugged." It does not take many incidents of violence on a city street, or in a city district, to make people fear the streets. And as they fear them, they use them less, which makes the streets still more unsafe.

To be sure, there are people with hobgoblins in their heads, and such people will never feel safe no matter

THE USES OF SIDEWALKS: SAFETY

what the objective circumstances are. But this is a different matter from the fear that besets normally prudent, tolerant and cheerful people who show nothing more than
common sense in refusing to venture after dark—or in a
few places, by day—into streets where they may well be
assaulted, unseen or unrescued until too late.

The barbarism and the real, not imagined, insecurity
that gives rise to such fears cannot be tagged a problem
of the slums. The problem is most serious, in fact, in gen-
teel-looking "quiet residential areas" like that my friend
was leaving.

It cannot be tagged as a problem of older parts of
cities. The problem reaches its most baffling dimensions
in some examples of rebuilt parts of cities, including supposedly the best examples of rebuilding, such as middle-
income projects. The police precinct captain of a
nationally admired project of this kind (admired by planners and lenders) has recently admonished residents not
only about hanging around outdoors after dark but has
urged them never to answer their doors without knowing
the caller. Life here has much in common with life for the
three little pigs or the seven little kids of the nursery
thrillers. The problem of sidewalk and doorstep insecurity is as serious in cities which have made conscientious
efforts at rebuilding as it is in those cities that have
lagged. Nor is it illuminating to tag minority groups, or
the poor, or the outcast with responsibility for city danger. There are immense variations in the degree of civilization and safety found among such groups and among
the city areas where they live. Some of the safest sidewalks in New York City, for example, at any time of day
or night, are those along which poor people or minority

groups live. And some of the most dangerous are in streets occupied by the same kinds of people. All this can also be said of other cities.

Deep and complicated social ills must lie behind delinquency and crime, in suburbs and towns as well as in great cities. This book will not go into speculation on the deeper reasons. It is sufficient, at this point, to say that if we are to maintain a city society that can diagnose and keep abreast of deeper social problems, the starting point must be, in any case, to strengthen whatever workable forces for maintaining safety and civilization do exist—in the cities we do have. To build city districts that are custom made for easy crime is idiotic. Yet that is what we do.

The first thing to understand is that the public peace—the sidewalk and street peace—of cities is not kept primarily by the police, necessary as police are. It is kept primarily by an intricate, almost unconscious, network of voluntary controls and standards among the people themselves, and enforced by the people themselves. In some city areas—older public housing projects and streets with very high population turnover are often conspicuous examples—the keeping of public sidewalk law and order is left almost entirely to the police and special guards. Such places are jungles. No amount of police can enforce civilization where the normal, casual enforcement of it has broken down.

The second thing to understand is that the problem of insecurity cannot be solved by spreading people out more thinly, trading the characteristics of cities for the characteristics of suburbs. If this could solve danger on the city streets, then Los Angeles should be a safe city because superficially Los Angeles is almost all suburban. It has virtually no districts compact enough to qualify as dense city areas. Yet Los Angeles cannot, any more than any other great city, evade the truth that, being a city, it *is* composed of strangers not all of whom are nice. Los Angeles' crime figures are flabbergasting. Among the seventeen standard metropolitan areas with populations over a million, Los Angeles stands so pre-eminent in crime that it is in a category by itself. And this is markedly true of crimes associated with personal attack, the crimes that make people fear the streets.

Los Angeles, for example, has a forcible rape rate (1958 figures) of 31.9 per 100,000 population, more than twice as high as either of the next two cities, which happen to be St. Louis and Philadelphia; three times as high as the rate of 10.1 for Chicago, and more than four times as high as the rate of 7.4 for New York.

In aggravated assault, Los Angeles has a rate of 185, compared with 149.5 for Baltimore and 139.2 for St. Louis (the two next highest), and with 90.9 for New York and 79 for Chicago.

The overall Los Angeles rate for major crimes is 2,507.6 per 100,000 people, far ahead of St. Louis and Houston, which come next with 1,634.5 and 1,541.1, and of New York and Chicago, which have rates of 1,145.3 and 943.5.

The reasons for Los Angeles' high crime rates are undoubtedly complex, and at least in part obscure. But of this we can be sure: thinning out a city does not insure safety from crime and fear of crime. This is one of the conclusions that can be drawn within individual cities too, where pseudosuburbs or superannuated suburbs are ideally suited to rape, muggings, beatings, holdups and the like.

Here we come up against an all-important question about any city street: How much easy opportunity does it offer to crime? It may be that there is some absolute amount of crime in a given city, which will find an outlet somehow (I do not believe this). Whether this is so or not, different kinds of city streets garner radically different shares of barbarism and fear of barbarism.

Some city streets afford no opportunity to street barbarism. The streets of the North End of Boston are outstanding examples. They are probably as safe as any place on earth in this respect. Although most of the North End's residents are Italian or of Italian descent, the district's streets are also heavily and constantly used by people of every race and background. Some of the strangers from outside work in or close to the district; some come to shop and stroll; many, including members of minority groups who have inherited dangerous districts previously abandoned by others, make a point of cashing their paychecks in North End stores and immediately making their big weekly purchases in streets where they know they will not be parted from their money between the getting and the spending.

Frank Havey, director of the North End Union, the local settlement house, says, "I have been here in the North End twenty-eight years, and in all that time I have never heard of a single case of rape, mugging, molestation of a child or other street crime of that sort in the district. And if there had been any, I would have heard of it even if it did not reach the papers." Half a dozen times or so in the past three decades, says Havey, would-be molesters have made an attempt at luring a child or, late at night, attacking a woman. In every such case the try was thwarted by passers-by, by kibitzers from windows, or shopkeepers.

Meantime, in the Elm Hill Avenue section of Roxbury, a part of inner Boston that is suburban in superficial character, street assaults and the ever present possibility of more street assaults with no kibitzers to protect the victims, induce prudent people to stay off the sidewalks at night. Not surprisingly, for this and other reasons that are related (dispiritedness and dullness), most of Roxbury has run down. It has become a place to leave.

I do not wish to single out Roxbury or its once fine Elm Hill Avenue section especially as a vulnerable area; its disabilities, and especially its Great Blight of Dullness, are all too common in other cities too. But differences like these in public safety within the same city are worth noting. The Elm Hill Avenue section's basic troubles are not owing to a criminal or a discriminated against or a poverty-stricken population. Its troubles stem from the fact that it is physically quite unable to function safely and with related vitality as a city district.

Even within supposedly similar parts of supposedly similar places, drastic differences in public safety exist. An incident at Washington Houses, a public housing project in New York, illustrates this point. A tenants' group at this project, struggling to establish itself, held some outdoor ceremonies in mid-December 1958, and put up three Christmas trees. The chief tree, so cumbersome it was a problem to transport, erect, and trim, went into the project's inner "street," a landscaped central mall and promenade. The other two trees, each less than six feet tall and easy to carry, went on two small fringe plots at the outer corners of the project where it abuts a busy avenue and lively cross streets of the old city. The first night, the large tree and all its trimmings were stolen. The two smaller trees remained intact, lights, ornaments and all, until they were taken down at New Year's. "The place where the tree was stolen, which is *theoretically* the most safe and sheltered place in the project, is the same place that is unsafe for people too, especially children," says a social worker who had been helping the tenants' group. "People are no safer in that mall than the Christmas tree. On the other hand, the place where the other trees were safe, where the project is just one corner out of four, happens to be safe for people."

This is something everyone already knows: A well-used city street is apt to be a safe street. A deserted city street is apt to be unsafe. But how does this work, really? And what makes a city street well used or shunned? Why is the sidewalk mall in Washington Houses, which is supposed to be an attraction, shunned? Why are the sidewalks of the old city just to its west not shunned? What about streets that are busy part of the time and then empty abruptly?

A city street equipped to handle strangers, and to make a safety asset, in itself, out of the presence of strangers, as the streets of successful city neighborhoods always do, must have three main qualities:

First, there must be a clear demarcation between what is public space and what is private space. Public and private spaces cannot ooze into each other as they do typically in suburban settings or in projects.

Second, there must be eyes upon the street, eyes belonging to those we might call the natural proprietors of the street. The buildings on a street equipped to handle strangers and to insure the safety of both residents and strangers, must be oriented to the street. They cannot turn their backs or blank sides on it and leave it blind.

And third, the sidewalk must have users on it fairly continuously, both to add to the number of effective eyes on the street and to induce the people in buildings along the street to watch the sidewalks in sufficient numbers. Nobody enjoys sitting on a stoop or looking out a window at an empty street. Almost nobody does such a thing. Large numbers of people entertain themselves, off and on, by watching street activity.

In settlements that are smaller and simpler than big cities, controls on acceptable public behavior, if not on crime, seem to operate with greater or lesser success through a web of reputation, gossip, approval, disapproval and sanctions, all of which are powerful if people know each other and word travels. But a city's streets, which must control not only the behavior of the people of the city but also of visitors from suburbs and towns who want to have a big time away from the gossip and sanctions at home, have to operate by more direct, straightforward methods. It is a wonder cities have solved such an inherently difficult problem at all. And yet in many streets they do it magnificently.

It is futile to try to evade the issue of unsafe city streets by attempting to make some other features of a locality, say interior courtyards, or sheltered play spaces, safe instead. By definition again, the streets of a city must do most of the job of handling strangers for this is where strangers come and go. The streets must not only defend the city against predatory strangers, they must protect the many, many peaceable and well-meaning strangers who use them, insuring their safety too as they pass through. Moreover, no normal person can spend his life in some artificial haven, and this includes children. Everyone must use the streets.

On the surface, we seem to have here some simple aims: To try to secure streets where the public space is unequivocally public, physically unmixed with private or with nothing-at-all space, so that the area needing surveillance has clear and practicable limits; and to see that these public street spaces have eyes on them as continuously as possible.

But it is not so simple to achieve these objects, especially the latter. You can't make people use streets they have no reason to use. You can't make people watch streets they do not want to watch. Safety on the streets by surveillance and mutual policing of one another sounds grim, but in real life it is not grim. The safety of the street works best, most casually, and with least frequent taint of hostility or suspicion precisely where people are using and most enjoying the city streets voluntarily and are least conscious, normally, that they are policing.

The basic requisite for such surveillance is a substantial quantity of stores and other public places sprinkled along the sidewalks of a district; enterprises and public places that are used by evening and night must be among them especially. Stores, bars and restaurants, as the chief examples, work in several different and complex ways to abet sidewalk safety.

First, they give people—both residents and strangers

—concrete reasons for using the sidewalks on which these enterprises face.

Second, they draw people along the sidewalks past places which have no attractions to public use in themselves but which become traveled and peopled as routes to somewhere else; this influence does not carry very far geographically, so enterprises must be frequent in a city district if they are to populate with walkers those other stretches of street that lack public places along the sidewalk. Moreover, there should be many different kinds of enterprises, to give people reasons for crisscrossing paths.

Third, storekeepers and other small businessmen are typically strong proponents of peace and order themselves; they hate broken windows and holdups; they hate having customers made nervous about safety. They are great street watchers and sidewalk guardians if present in sufficient numbers.

Fourth, the activity generated by people on errands, or people aiming for food or drink, is itself an attraction to still other people.

This last point, that the sight of people attracts still other people, is something that city planners and city architectural designers seem to find incomprehensible. They operate on the premise that city people seek the sight of emptiness, obvious order and quiet. Nothing could be less true. People's love of watching activity and other people is constantly evident in cities everywhere. This trait reaches an almost ludicrous extreme on upper Broadway in New York, where the street is divided by a narrow central mall, right in the middle of traffic. At the cross-street intersections of this long north-south mall, benches have been placed behind big concrete buffers and on any day when the weather is even barely tolerable these benches are filled with people at block after block after block, watching the pedestrians who cross the mall in front of them, watching the traffic, watching the people on the busy sidewalks, watching each other. Eventually Broadway reaches Columbia University and Barnard College, one to the right, the other to the left. Here all is obvious order and quiet. No more stores, no more activity generated by the stores, almost no more pedestrians crossing—and no more watchers. The benches are there but they go empty in even the finest weather. I have tried them and can see why. No place could be more boring. Even the students of these institutions shun the solitude. They are doing their outdoor loitering, outdoor homework and general street watching on the steps overlooking the busiest campus crossing.

It is just so on city streets elsewhere. A lively street always has both its users and pure watchers. Last year I was on such a street in the Lower East Side of Manhattan, waiting for a bus. I had not been there longer than a minute, barely long enough to begin taking in the street's activity of errand goers, children playing, and loiterers on the stoops, when my attention was attracted by a woman who opened a window on the third floor of a tenement across the street and vigorously yoo-hooed at me. When I caught on that she wanted my attention and responded, she shouted down, "The bus doesn't run here on Saturdays!" Then by a combination of shouts and pantomime she directed me around the corner. This woman was one of thousands upon thousands of people in New York who casually take care of the streets. They notice strangers. They observe everything going on. If they need to take action, whether to direct a stranger waiting in the wrong place or to call the police, they do so. Action usually requires, to be sure, a certain self-assurance about the actor's proprietorship of the street and the support he will get if necessary, matters which will be gone into later in this book. But even more fundamental than the action and necessary to the action, is the watching itself.

Not everyone in cities helps to take care of the streets, and many a city resident or city worker is unaware of why his neighborhood is safe. The other day an incident occurred on the street where I live, and it interested me because of this point.

My block of the street, I must explain, is a small one, but it contains a remarkable range of buildings, varying from several vintages of tenements to three- and four-story houses that have been converted into low-rent flats with stores on the ground floor, or returned to single-family use like ours. Across the street there used to be mostly four-story brick tenements with stores below. But twelve years ago several buildings, from the corner to the middle of the block, were converted into one building with elevator apartments of small size and high rents.

The incident that attracted my attention was a suppressed struggle going on between a man and a little girl of eight or nine years old. The man seemed to be trying to get the girl to go with him. By turns he was directing a cajoling attention to her, and then assuming an air of nonchalance. The girl was making herself rigid, as children do when they resist, against the wall of one of the tenements across the street.

As I watched from our second-floor window, making up my mind how to intervene if it seemed advisable, I saw it was not going to be necessary. From the butcher shop beneath the tenement had emerged the woman who, with her husband, runs the shop; she was standing within earshot of the man, her arms folded and a look of determination on her face. Joe Cornacchia, who with his sons-in-law keeps the delicatessen, emerged about the same moment and stood solidly to the other side. Several heads poked out of the tenement windows above, one was withdrawn quickly and its owner reappeared a moment later in the doorway behind the man. Two men from the bar next to the butcher shop came to the doorway and waited. On my side of the street, I saw that the locksmith, the fruit man and the laundry proprietor had all come out of their shops and that the scene was also being surveyed from a number of windows besides ours. That man did not know it, but he was surrounded. Nobody was going to allow a little girl to be dragged off, even if nobody knew who she was.

I am sorry—sorry purely for dramatic purposes—to have to report that the little girl turned out to be the man's daughter.

Throughout the duration of the little drama, perhaps five minutes in all, no eyes appeared in the windows of the high-rent, small-apartment building. It was the only building of which this was true. When we first moved to our block, I used to anticipate happily that perhaps soon all the buildings would be rehabilitated like that one. I know better now, and can only anticipate with gloom and foreboding the recent news that exactly this transformation is scheduled for the rest of the block frontage adjoining the high-rent building. The high-rent tenants, most of whom are so transient we cannot even keep track of their faces,* have not the remotest idea of who takes care of their street, or how. A city neighborhood can absorb and protect a substantial number of these birds of passage, as our neighborhood does. But if and when the neighborhood finally *becomes* them, they will gradually find the streets less secure, they will be vaguely mystified about it, and if things get bad enough they will drift away to another neighborhood which is mysteriously safer.

In some rich city neighborhoods, where there is little do-it-yourself surveillance, such as residential Park Avenue or upper Fifth Avenue in New York, street watchers are hired. The monotonous sidewalks of residential Park Avenue, for example, are surprisingly little used; their putative users are populating, instead, the interesting store-, bar- and restaurant-filled sidewalks of Lexington Avenue and Madison Avenue to east and west, and the cross streets leading to these. A network of doormen and superintendents, of delivery boys and nursemaids, a form of hired neighborhood, keeps residential Park Avenue supplied with eyes. At night, with the security of the doormen as a bulwark, dog walkers safely venture forth and supplement the doormen. But this street is so blank of built-in eyes, so devoid of concrete reasons for using or watching it instead of turning the first corner off of it, that if its rents were to slip below the point where they could support a plentiful hired neighborhood of doormen and elevator men, it would undoubtedly become a woefully dangerous street.

---

*Some, according to the storekeepers, live on beans and bread and spend their sojourn looking for a place to live where all their money will not go for rent.

Once a street is well equipped to handle strangers, once it has both a good, effective demarcation between private and public spaces and has a basic supply of activity and eyes, the more strangers the merrier.

Strangers become an enormous asset on the street on which I live, and the spurs off it, particularly at night when safety assets are most needed. We are fortunate enough, on the street, to be gifted not only with a locally supported bar and another around the corner, but also with a famous bar that draws continuous troops of strangers from adjoining neighborhoods and even from out of town. It is famous because the poet Dylan Thomas used to go there, and mentioned it in his writing. This bar, indeed, works two distinct shifts. In the morning and early afternoon it is a social gathering place for the old community of Irish longshoremen and other craftsmen in the area, as it always was. But beginning in midafternoon it takes on a different life, more like a college bull session with beer, combined with a literary cocktail party, and this continues until the early hours of the morning. On a cold winter's night, as you pass the White Horse, and the doors open, a solid wave of conversation and animation surges out and hits you; very warming. The comings and goings from this bar do much to keep our street reasonably populated until three in the morning, and it is a street always safe to come home to. The only instance I know of a beating in our street occurred in the dead hours between the closing of the bar and dawn. The beating was halted by one of our neighbors who saw it from his window and, unconsciously certain that even at night he was part of a web of strong street law and order, intervened.

A friend of mine lives on a street uptown where a

church youth and community center, with many night dances and other activities, performs the same service for his street that the White Horse bar does for ours. Orthodox planning is much imbued with puritanical and Utopian conceptions of how people should spend their free time, and in planning, these moralisms on people's private lives are deeply confused with concepts about the workings of cities. In maintaining city street civilization, the White Horse bar and the church-sponsored youth center, different as they undoubtedly are, perform much the same public street civilizing service. There is not only room in cities for such differences and many more in taste, purpose and interest of occupation; cities also have a need for people with all these differences in taste and proclivity. The preferences of Utopians, and of other compulsive managers of other people's leisure, for one kind of legal enterprise over others is worse than irrelevant for cities. It is harmful. The greater and more plentiful the range of all legitimate interests (in the strictly legal sense) that city streets and their enterprises can satisfy, the better for the streets and for the safety and civilization of the city.

Bars, and indeed all commerce, have a bad name in many city districts precisely because they do draw strangers, and the strangers do not work out as an asset at all.

This sad circumstance is especially true in the dispirited gray belts of great cities and in once fashionable or at least once solid inner residential areas gone into decline. Because these neighborhoods are so dangerous, and the streets typically so dark, it is commonly believed that their trouble may be insufficient street lighting. Good lighting is important, but darkness alone does not account for the gray areas' deep, functional sickness, the Great Blight of Dullness.

The value of bright street lights for dispirited gray areas rises from the reassurance they offer to some people who need to go out on the sidewalk, or would like to, but lacking the good light would not do so. Thus the lights induce these people to contribute their own eyes to the upkeep of the street. Moreover, as is obvious, good lighting augments every pair of eyes, makes the eyes count for more because their range is greater. Each additional pair of eyes, and every increase in their range, is that much to the good for dull gray areas. But unless eyes are there, and unless in the brains behind those eyes is the almost unconscious reassurance of general street support in upholding civilization, lights can do no good. Horrifying public crimes can, and do, occur in well-lighted subway stations when no effective eyes are present. They virtually never occur in darkened theaters where many people and eyes are present. Street lights can be like that famous stone that falls in the desert where there are no ears to hear. Does it make a noise? Without effective eyes to see, does a light cast light? Not for practical purposes.

To explain the troubling effect of strangers on the streets of city gray areas, I shall first point out, for purposes of analogy, the peculiarities of another and figurative kind of street—the corridors of high-rise public housing projects, those derivatives of Radiant City. The elevators and corridors of these projects are, in a sense, streets. They are streets piled up in the sky in order to eliminate streets on the ground and permit the ground to become deserted parks like the mall at Washington Houses where the tree was stolen.

Not only are these interior parts of the buildings streets in the sense that they serve the comings and goings of residents, most of whom may not know each other or recognize, necessarily, who is a resident and who is not. They are streets also in the sense of being accessible to the public. They have been designed in an imitation of upper-class standards for apartment living without upper-class cash for doormen and elevator men. Anyone at all can go into these buildings, unquestioned, and use the traveling street of the elevator and the sidewalks that are the corridors. These interior streets, although completely accessible to public use, are closed to public view and they thus lack the checks and inhibitions exerted by eye-policed city streets

Troubled, so far as I can determine, less by the amply proved dangers to human beings in these blind-eyed streets than by the vandalism to property that occurs in them, the New York City Housing Authority some years back experimented with corridors open to public view in a Brooklyn project which I shall call Blenheim Houses although that is not its name. (I do not wish to add to its troubles by advertising it.)

Because the buildings of Blenheim Houses are sixteen stories high, and because their height permits generous expanses of shunned ground area, surveillance of the open corridors from the ground or from other buildings offers little more than psychological effect, but this psychological openness to view does appear effective to some degree. More important and effective, the corridors were well designed to induce surveillance from within the buildings themselves. Uses other than plain circulation were built into them. They were equipped as play space, and made sufficiently generous to act as narrow porches, as well as passageways. This all turned out to be so lively and interesting that the tenants added still another use and much the favorite: picnic grounds—this in spite of continual pleas and threats from the management which did not *plan* that the balcony-corridors should serve as picnic grounds. (The plan should anticipate everything and then permit no changes.) The tenants are devoted to the balcony-corridors; and as a result of being intensively used the balconies are under intense surveillance. There has been no problem of crime in these particular corridors, nor of vandalism either. Not even light bulbs are stolen or broken, although in projects of similar size with blind-eyed corridors, light bulb replacements solely because of theft or vandalism customarily run into the thousands each month.

So far so good.

A striking demonstration of the direct connection between city surveillance and city safety!

Nonetheless, Blenheim Houses has a fearsome problem of vandalism and scandalous behavior. The lighted balconies which are, as the manager puts it, "the brightest and most attractive scene in sight," draw strangers, especially teen-agers, from all over Brooklyn. But these strangers, lured by the magnet of the publicly visible corridors, do not halt at the visible corridors. They go into other "streets" of the buildings, streets that lack surveillance. These include the elevators and, more important in this case, the fire stairs and their landings. The housing police run up and down after the malefactors—who behave barbarously and viciously in the blind-eyed, six-teen-story-high stairways—and the malefactors elude them. It is easy to run the elevators up to a high floor, jam the doors so the elevators cannot be brought down, and then play hell with a building and anyone you can catch. So serious is the problem and apparently so uncontrollable, that the advantage of the safe corridors is all but canceled—at least in the harried manager's eyes.

What happens at Blenheim Houses is somewhat the same as what happens in dull gray areas of cities. The gray areas' pitifully few and thinly spaced patches of brightness and life are like the visible corridors at Blenheim Houses. They do attract strangers. But the relatively deserted, dull, blind streets leading from these places are like the fire stairs at Blenheim Houses. These are not equipped to hand!e strangers and the presence of strangers in them is an automatic menace.

The temptation in such cases is to blame the balconies—or the commerce or bars that serve as a magnet. A typical train of thought is exemplified in the Hyde Park-Kenwood renewal project now under way in Chicago. This piece of gray area adjoining the University of Chicago contains many splendid houses and grounds, but for thirty years it has been plagued with a frightening street crime problem, accompanied in latter years by considerable physical decay. The "cause" of Hyde Park-Kenwood's decline has been brilliantly identified, by the planning heirs of the bloodletting doctors, as the presence of "blight." By blight they mean that too many of the college professors and other middle-class families steadily deserted this dull and dangerous area and their places were often, quite naturally, taken by those with little economic or social choice among living places. The plan designates and removes these chunks of blight and replaces them with chunks of Radiant Garden City designed, as usual, to minimize use of the streets. The plan also adds still more empty spaces here and there, blurs even further the district's already poor distinctions between private and public space, and amputates the existing commerce, which is no great shakes. The early plans for this renewal included a relatively large imitation-suburban shopping center. But the thoughts of this brought a faint reminder of realities and a glimmer of apprehension in the course of the planning process. A large center, larger than that required for the standard shopping needs of residents in the renewal district itself, "might draw into the area extraneous people," as one of the architectural planners put it. A small shopping center was thereupon settled on. Large or small matters little.

It matters little because Hyde Park-Kenwood, like all city districts, is, in real life, surrounded by "extraneous" people. The area is an embedded part of Chicago. It cannot wish away its location. It cannot bring back its one-time condition, long gone, of semisuburbia. To plan as if it could, and to evade its deep, functional inadequacies, can have only one of two possible results.

Either extraneous people will continue to come into the area as they please, and if so they will include some strangers who are not at all nice. So far as security is concerned, nothing will have changed except that the opportunity for street crime will be a little easier, if anything, because of the added emptiness. Or the plan can be accompanied by determined, extraordinary means for keeping extraneous people out of this area, just as the adjoining University of Chicago, the institution that was the moving spirit in getting the plan under way, has itself taken the extraordinary measure, as reported in the press, of loosing police dogs every night to patrol its campus and hold at bay any human being in this dangerous unurban inner keep. The barriers formed by new projects at the edges of Hyde Park-Kenwood, plus extraordinary policing, may indeed keep out extraneous people with sufficient effectiveness. If so, the price will be hostility from the surrounding city and an ever more beleaguered feeling within the fort. And who can be sure, either, that all those thousands rightfully within the fort are trustworthy in the dark?

Again, I do not wish to single out one area, or in this case one plan, as uniquely opprobrious. Hyde Park-Kenwood is significant mainly because the diagnosis and the corrective measures of the plan are typical—just slightly more ambitious—of plans conceived for gray area renewal experiments in cities all over the country. This is City Planning, with all the stamp of orthodoxy on it, not some aberration of local willfulness.

Suppose we continue with building, and with deliberate rebuilding, of unsafe cities. How do we live with this insecurity? From the evidence thus far, there seem to be three modes of living with it; maybe in time others will be invented but I suspect these three will simply be further developed, if that is the word for it.

The first mode is to let danger hold sway, and let those unfortunate enough to be stuck with it take the consequences. This is the policy now followed with respect to low-income housing projects, and to many middle-income housing projects.

The second mode is to take refuge in vehicles. This is a technique practiced in the big wild-animal reservations of Africa, where tourists are warned to leave their cars under no circumstances until they reach a lodge. It is also the technique practiced in Los Angeles. Surprised visitors to that city are forever recounting how the police of Beverly Hills stopped them, made them prove their reasons for being afoot, and warned them of the danger. This technique of public safety does not seem to work too effectively yet in Los Angeles, as the crime rate shows, but in time it may. And think what the crime figures might be if more people without metal shells were helpless upon the vast, blind-eyed reservation of Los Angeles.

People in dangerous parts of other cities often use automobiles as protection too, of course, or try to. A letter to the editor in the *New York Post*, reads, "I live on a dark street off Utica Avenue in Brooklyn and therefore decided to take a cab home even though it was not late. The cab driver asked that I get off at the corner of Utica, saying he did not want to go down the dark street. If I had wanted to walk down the dark street, who needed him?"

The third mode, at which I've already hinted while discussing Hyde Park-Kenwood, was developed by hoodlum gangs and has been adopted widely by developers of the rebuilt city. This mode is to cultivate the institution of Turf.

Under the Turf system in its historical form, a gang appropriates as its territory certain streets or housing projects or parks—often a combination of the three. Members of other gangs cannot enter this Turf without permission from the Turf-owning gang, or if they do so it is at peril of being beaten or run off. In 1956, the New York City Youth Board, fairly desperate because of gang warfare, arranged through its gang youth workers a series of truces among fighting gangs. The truces were reported to stipulate, among other provisions, a mutual understanding of Turf boundaries among the gangs concerned and agreement not to trespass.

The city's police commissioner, Stephen P. Kennedy, thereupon expressed outrage at agreements respecting Turf. The police, he said, aimed to protect the right of every person to walk any part of the city in safety and with impunity as a basic right. Pacts about Turf, he indicated, were intolerably subversive both of public rights and public safety.

I think Commissioner Kennedy was profoundly right. However, we must reflect upon the problem facing the Youth Board workers. It was a real one, and they were trying as well as they could to meet it with whatever empirical means they could. The safety of the city, on which public right and freedom of movement ultimately depend, was missing from the unsuccessful streets, parks and projects dominated by these gangs. Freedom of the city, under these circumstances, was a rather academic ideal.

Now consider the redevelopment projects of cities: the middle- and upper-income housing occupying many acres of city, many former blocks, with their own grounds and their own streets to serve these "islands within the city," "cities within the city," and "new concepts in city living," as the advertisements for them say. The technique here is also to designate the Turf and fence the other gangs out. At first the fences were never visible. Patrolling guards were sufficient to enforce the line. But in the past few years the fences have become literal.

Perhaps the first was the high cyclone fence around a Radiant Garden City project adjoining Johns Hopkins Hospital in Baltimore (great educational institutions seem to be deplorably inventive with Turf devices). In case anyone mistakes what the fence means, the signs on the project street also say "Keep Out. No Trespassing." It is uncanny to see a city neighborhood, in a civilian city, walled off like this. It looks not only ugly, in a deep sense, but surrealistic. You can imagine how it sits with the neighbors, in spite of the antidote message on the project church's bulletin board: "Christ's Love Is The Best Tonic Of All."

New York has been quick to copy the lesson of Baltimore, in its own fashion. Indeed, at the back of Amalgamated Houses on the Lower East Side, New York has gone further. At the northern end of the project's parklike central promenade, an iron-bar gate has been permanently padlocked and is crowned not with mere metal netting but with a tangle of barbed wire. And does this defended promenade give out on depraved old megalopolis? Not at all. Its neighbor is a public playground and beyond this more project housing for a different income class.

In the rebuilt city it takes a heap of fences to make a balanced neighborhood. The "juncture" between two differently price-tagged populations, again in the rebuilt Lower East Side, that between middle-income cooperative Corlears Hook and low-income Vladeck Houses, is especially elaborate. Corlears Hook buffers its Turf against its next-door neighbors with a wide parking lot running the full width of the super-block juncture, next a spindly hedge and a six-foot-high cyclone fence, next a completely fenced-in no man's land some thirty feet wide consisting mainly of dirty blowing papers and deliberately inaccessible to anything else. Then begins the Vladeck Turf.

Similarly, on the Upper West Side, the rental agent of Park West Village, "Your Own World in the Heart of New York," on whom I have foisted myself as a prospective tenant, tells me reassuringly, "Madam, as soon as the shopping center is completed, the entire grounds will be fenced in."

"Cyclone fences?"

"That is correct, madam. And eventually"—waving his hand at the city surrounding his domain—"all that will go. Those people will go. We are the pioneers here."

I suppose it is rather like pioneer life in a stockaded village, except that the pioneers were working toward greater security for their civilization, not less.

Some members of the gangs on the new Turfs find this way of life hard to take. Such was one who wrote a letter to the *New York Post* in 1959: "The other day for the first time my pride at being a resident of Stuyvesant Town and of New York City was replaced by indignation and shame. I noticed two boys about 12 years old sitting on a Stuyvesant Town bench. They were deep in conversation, quiet, well-behaved—and Puerto Rican. Suddenly two Stuyvesant Town guards were approaching—one from the north and one from the south. The one signaled the other by pointing to the two boys. One went up to the boys and after several words, quietly spoken on both sides, the boys rose and left. They tried to look unconcerned . . . How can we expect people to have any dignity and self-respect if we rip it from them even before they reach adulthood? How really poor are we of Stuyvesant Town and of New York City, too, that we can't share a bench with two boys."

The Letters Editor gave this communication the headline, "Stay in Your Own Turf."

But on the whole, people seem to get used very quickly to living in a Turf with either a figurative or a literal fence, and to wonder how they got on without it formerly. This phenomenon was described, before the Turf fences came into the city, by the *New Yorker*, with reference not to fenced city but to fenced town. It seems that when Oak Ridge, Tennessee, was demilitarized after the war, the prospect of losing the fence that went with the militarization drew frightened and impassioned protests from many residents and occasioned town meetings of high excitement. Everyone in Oak Ridge had come, not many years before, from unfenced towns or cities, yet stockade life had become normal and they feared for their safety without the fence.

Just so, my ten-year-old nephew David, born and brought up in Stuyvesant Town, "A City Within a City," comments in wonder that anyone at all can walk on the street outside our door. "Doesn't anybody keep track whether they pay rent on this street?" he asks. "Who puts them out if they don't belong here?"

The technique of dividing the city into Turfs is not simply a New York solution. It is a Rebuilt American City solution. At the Harvard Design Conference of 1959, one of the topics pondered by city architectural designers turned out to be the puzzle of Turf, although they did not use that designation. The examples discussed happened to be the Lake Meadows middle-income project of Chicago and the Lafayette Park high-income project of Detroit. Do you keep the rest of the city out of these blind-eyed purlieus? How difficult and how unpalatable. Do you invite the rest of the city in? How difficult and how impossible.

Like the Youth Board workers, the developers and residents of Radiant City and Radiant Garden City and Radiant Garden City Beautiful have a genuine difficulty and they have to do the best they can with it by the empirical means at their disposal. They have little choice. Wherever the rebuilt city rises the barbaric concept of Turf must follow, because the rebuilt city has junked a basic function of the city street and with it, necessarily, the freedom of the city.

Under the seeming disorder of the old city, wherever the old city is working successfully, is a marvelous order for maintaining the safety of the streets and the freedom of the city. It is a complex order. Its essence is intricacy of sidewalk use, bringing with it a constant succession of eyes. This order is all composed of movement and change, and although it is life, not art, we may fancifully call it the art form of the city and liken it to the dance—not to a simple-minded precision dance with everyone kicking up at the same time, twirling in unison and bowing off en masse, but to an intricate ballet in which the individual dancers and ensembles all have distinctive parts which miraculously reinforce each other and compose an orderly whole. The ballet of the good city sidewalk never repeats itself from place to place, and in any one place is always replete with new improvisations.

The stretch of Hudson Street where I live is each day the scene of an intricate sidewalk ballet. I make my own first entrance into it a little after eight when I put out the garbage can, surely a prosaic occupation, but I enjoy my part, my little clang, as the droves of junior high school students walk by the center of the stage dropping candy wrappers. (How do they eat so much candy so early in the morning?)

While I sweep up the wrappers I watch the other rituals of morning: Mr. Halpert unlocking the laundry's handcart from its mooring to a cellar door, Joe Cornacchia's son-in-law stacking out the empty crates from the delicatessen, the barber bringing out his sidewalk folding chair, Mr. Goldstein arranging the coils of wire which proclaim the hardware store is open, the wife of the tenement's superintendent depositing her chunky three-year-old with a toy mandolin on the stoop, the vantage point from which he is learning the English his mother cannot speak. Now the primary children, heading for St. Luke's, dribble through to the south; the children for St. Veronica's cross, heading to the west, and the children for P.S. 41, heading toward the east. Two new entrances are being made from the wings: well-dressed and even elegant women and men with brief cases emerge from doorways and side streets. Most of these are heading for the bus and subways, but some hover on the curbs, stopping taxis which have miraculously appeared at the right moment, for the taxis are part of a wider morning ritual: having dropped passengers from midtown in the downtown financial district, they are now bringing downtowners up to midtown. Simultaneously, numbers of women in housedresses have emerged and as they crisscross with one another they pause for quick conversations that sound with either laughter or joint indignation, never, it seems, anything between. It is time for me to hurry to work too, and I exchange my ritual farewell with Mr. Lofaro, the short, thick-bodied, white-aproned fruit man who stands outside his doorway a little up the street, his arms folded, his feet planted, looking solid as earth itself. We nod; we each glance quickly up and down the street, then look back to each other and smile. We have done this many a morning for more than ten years, and we both know what it means: All is well.

The heart-of-the-day ballet I seldom see, because part of the nature of it is that working people who live there, like me, are mostly gone, filling the roles of strangers on other sidewalks. But from days off, I know enough of it to know that it becomes more and more intricate. Longshoremen who are not working that day gather at the White Horse or the Ideal or the International for beer and conversation. The executives and business lunchers from the industries just to the west throng the Dorgene restaurant and the Lion's Head coffee house; meat-market workers and communications scientists fill the bakery lunchroom. Character dancers come on, a strange old man with strings of old shoes over his shoulders, motor-scooter riders with big beards and girl friends who bounce on the back of the scooters and wear their hair long in front of their faces as well as behind, drunks who follow the advice of the Hat Council and are always turned out in hats, but not hats the Council would approve. Mr. Lacey, the locksmith, shuts up his shop for a while and goes to exchange the time of day with Mr. Slube at the cigar store. Mr. Koochagian, the tailor, waters the luxuriant jungle of plants in his window, gives them a critical look from the outside, accepts a compliment on them from two passers-by, fingers the leaves on the plane tree in front of our house with a thoughtful gardener's appraisal, and crosses the street for a bite at the Ideal where he can keep an eye on customers and wigwag across the message that he is coming. The baby carriages come out, and clusters of everyone from toddlers with dolls to teen-agers with homework gather at the stoops.

When I get home after work, the ballet is reaching its crescendo. This is the time of roller skates and stilts and tricycles, and games in the lee of the stoop with bottletops and plastic cowboys; this is the time of bundles and packages, zigzagging from the drug store to the fruit stand and back over to the butcher's; this is the time when teen-agers, all dressed up, are pausing to ask if their slips show or their collars look right; this is the time when beautiful girls get out of MG's; this is the time when the fire engines go through; this is the time when anybody you know around Hudson Street will go by.

As darkness thickens and Mr. Halpert moors the laundry cart to the cellar door again, the ballet goes on under lights, eddying back and forth but intensifying at the bright spotlight pools of Joe's sidewalk pizza dispensary, the bars, the delicatessen, the restaurant and the drug store. The night workers stop now at the delicatessen, to pick up salami and a container of milk. Things have settled down for the evening but the street and its ballet have not come to a stop.

I know the deep night ballet and its seasons best from

waking long after midnight to tend a baby and, sitting in the dark, seeing the shadows and hearing the sounds of the sidewalk. Mostly it is a sound like infinitely pattering snatches of party conversation and, about three in the morning, singing, very good singing. Sometimes there is sharpness and anger or sad, sad weeping, or a flurry of search for a string of beads broken. One night a young man came roaring along, bellowing terrible language at two girls whom he had apparently picked up and who were disappointing him. Doors opened, a wary semicircle formed around him, not too close, until the police came. Out came the heads, too, along Hudson Street, offering opinion, "Drunk . . . Crazy . . . A wild kid from the suburbs."*

Deep in the night, I am almost unaware how many people are on the street unless something calls them together, like the bagpipe. Who the piper was and why he favored our street I have no idea. The bagpipe just skirled out in the February night, and as if it were a signal the random, dwindled movements of the sidewalk took on direction. Swiftly, quietly, almost magically a little crowd was there, a crowd that evolved into a circle with a Highland fling inside it. The crowd could be seen on the shadowy sidewalk, the dancers could be seen, but the bagpiper himself was almost invisible because his bravura was all in his music. He was a very little man in a plain brown overcoat. When he finished and vanished, the dancers and watchers applauded, and applause came

*He turned out to be a wild kid from the suburbs. Sometimes, on Hudson Street, we are tempted to believe the suburbs must be a difficult place to bring up children.

from the galleries too, half a dozen of the hundred windows on Hudson Street. Then the windows closed, and the little crowd dissolved into the random movements of the night street.

The strangers on Hudson Street, the allies whose eyes help us natives keep the peace of the street, are so many that they always seem to be different people from one day to the next. That does not matter. Whether they are so many always-different people as they seem to be, I do not know. Likely they are. When Jimmy Rogan fell through a plate-glass window (he was separating some scuffling friends) and almost lost his arm, a stranger in an old T shirt emerged from the Ideal bar, swiftly applied an expert tourniquet and, according to the hospital's emergency staff, saved Jimmy's life. Nobody remembered seeing the man before and no one has seen him since. The hospital was called in this way: a woman sitting on the steps next to the accident ran over to the bus stop, wordlessly snatched the dime from the hand of a stranger who was waiting with his fifteen-cent fare ready, and raced into the Ideal's phone booth. The stranger raced after her to offer the nickel too. Nobody remembered seeing him before, and no one has seen him since. When you see the same stranger three or four times on Hudson Street, you begin to nod. This is almost getting to be an acquaintance, a public acquaintance, of course.

I have made the daily ballet of Hudson Street sound more frenetic than it is, because writing it telescopes it. In real life, it is not that way. In real life, to be sure, something is always going on, the ballet is never at a halt, but the general effect is peaceful and the general tenor even leisurely. People who know well such animated city streets will know how it is. I am afraid people who do not will always have it a little wrong in their heads—like the old prints of rhinoceroses made from travelers' descriptions of rhinoceroses.

On Hudson Street, the same as in the North End of Boston or in any other animated neighborhoods of great cities, we are not innately more competent at keeping the sidewalks safe than are the people who try to live off the hostile truce of Turf in a blind-eyed city. We are the lucky possessors of a city order that makes it relatively simple to keep the peace because there are plenty of eyes on the street. But there is nothing simple about that order itself, or the bewildering number of components that go into it. Most of those components are specialized in one way or another. They unite in their joint effect upon the sidewalk, which is not specialized in the least. That is its strength.

3

THE USES OF SIDEWALKS: CONTACT

Reformers have long observed city people loitering on busy corners, hanging around in candy stores and bars and drinking soda pop on stoops, and have passed a judgment, the gist of which is: "This is deplorable! If these people had decent homes and a more private or bosky outdoor place, they wouldn't be on the street!"

This judgment represents a profound misunderstanding of cities. It makes no more sense than to drop in at a testimonial banquet in a hotel and conclude that if these people had wives who could cook, they would give their parties at home.

The point of both the testimonial banquet and the social life of city sidewalks is precisely that they are public. They bring together people who do not know each other in an intimate, private social fashion and in most cases do not care to know each other in that fashion.

Nobody can keep open house in a great city. Nobody wants to. And yet if interesting, useful and significant contacts among the people of cities are confined to acquaintanceships suitable for private life, the city becomes stultified. Cities are full of people with whom, from your viewpoint, or mine, or any other individual's, a certain degree of contact is useful or enjoyable; but you do not want them in your hair. And they do not want you in theirs either.

In speaking about city sidewalk safety, I mentioned how necessary it is that there should be, in the brains behind the eyes on the street, an almost unconscious assumption of general street support when the chips are down—when a citizen has to choose, for instance, whether he will take responsibility, or abdicate it, in combating barbarism or protecting strangers. There is a short word for this assumption of support: trust. The trust of a city street is formed over time from many, many little public sidewalk contacts. It grows out of people stopping by at the bar for a beer, getting advice from the grocer and giving advice to the newsstand man, comparing opinions with other customers at the bakery and nodding hello to the two boys drinking pop on the stoop, eying the girls while waiting to be called for dinner, admonishing the children, hearing about a job from the hardware man and borrowing a dollar from the druggist, admiring the new babies and sympathizing over the way a coat faded. Customs vary: in some neighborhoods people compare notes on their dogs; in others they compare notes on their landlords.

Most of it is ostensibly utterly trivial but the sum is not trivial at all. The sum of such casual public contact at a local level—most of it fortuitous, most of it associated with errands, all of it metered by the person concerned and not thrust upon him by anyone—is a feeling for the public identity of people, a web of public respect and trust, and a resource in time of personal or neighborhood need. The absence of this trust is a disaster to a city street.

Its cultivation cannot be institutionalized. And above all, *it implies no private commitments.*

I have seen a striking difference between presence and absence of casual public trust on two sides of the same wide street in East Harlem, composed of residents of roughly the same incomes and same races. On the old-city side, which was full of public places and the sidewalk loitering so deplored by Utopian minders of other people's leisure, the children were being kept well in hand. On the project side of the street across the way, the children, who had a fire hydrant open beside their play area, were behaving destructively, drenching the open windows of houses with water, squirting it on adults who ignorantly walked on the project side of the street, throwing it into the windows of cars as they went by. Nobody dared to stop them. These were anonymous children, and the identities behind them were an unknown. What if you scolded or stopped them? Who would back you up over there in the blind-eyed Turf? Would you get, instead, revenge? Better to keep out of it. Impersonal city streets make anonymous people, and this is not a matter of esthetic quality nor of a mystical emotional effect in architectural scale. It is a matter of what kinds of tangible enterprises sidewalks have, and therefore of how people use the sidewalks in practical, everyday life.

The casual public sidewalk life of cities ties directly into other types of public life, of which I shall mention one as illustrative, although there is no end to their variety.

Formal types of local city organizations are frequently assumed by planners and even by some social workers to grow in direct, common-sense fashion out of announcements of meetings, the presence of meeting rooms, and the existence of problems of obvious public concern. Perhaps they grow so in suburbs and towns. They do not grow so in cities.

Formal public organizations in cities require an informal public life underlying them, mediating between them and the privacy of the people of the city. We catch a hint of what happens by contrasting, again, a city area possessing a public sidewalk life with a city area lacking it, as told about in the report of a settlement-house social researcher who was studying problems relating to public schools in a section of New York City:

> Mr. W—— [principal of an elementary school] was questioned on the effect of J—— Houses on the school, and the uprooting of the community around the school. He felt that there had been many effects and of these most were negative. He mentioned that the project had torn out numerous institutions for socializing. The present atmosphere of the project was in no way similar to the gaiety of the streets before the project was built. He noted that in general there seemed fewer people on the streets because there were fewer places for people to gather. He also contended that before the projects were built the Parents Association had been very strong, and now there were only very few active members.

Mr. W—— was wrong in one respect. There were not fewer places (or at any rate there was not less space) for people to gather in the project, if we count places deliberately planned for constructive socializing. Of course there were no bars, no candy stores, no hole-in-the-wall *bodegas*, no restaurants in the project. But the project

under discussion was equipped with a model comple-
ment of meeting rooms, craft, art and game rooms, outdoor benches, malls, etc., enough to gladden the heart of
even the Garden City advocates.

Why are such places dead and useless without the
most determined efforts and expense to inveigle users—
and then to maintain control over the users? What services do the public sidewalk and its enterprises fulfill that
these planned gathering places do not? And why? How
does an informal public sidewalk life bolster a more formal, organizational public life?

To understand such problems—to understand why
drinking pop on the stoop differs from drinking pop in
the game room, and why getting advice from the grocer
or the bartender differs from getting advice from either
your next-door neighbor or from an institutional lady
who may be hand-in-glove with an institutional landlord—we must look into the matter of city privacy.

Privacy is precious in cities. It is indispensable. Perhaps it is precious and indispensable everywhere, but
most places you cannot get it. In small settlements everyone knows your affairs. In the city everyone does not—
only those you choose to tell will know much about you.
This is one of the attributes of cities that is precious to
most city people, whether their incomes are high or their
incomes are low, whether they are white or colored,
whether they are old inhabitants or new, and it is a gift of
great-city life deeply cherished and jealously guarded.

Architectural and planning literature deals with privacy in terms of windows, overlooks, sight lines. The idea
is that if no one from outside can peek into where you

live—behold, privacy. This is simple-minded. Window privacy is the easiest commodity in the world to get. You just pull down the shades or adjust the blinds. The privacy of keeping one's personal affairs to those selected to know them, and the privacy of having reasonable control over who shall make inroads on your time and when, are rare commodities in most of this world, however, and they have nothing to do with the orientation of windows.

Anthropologist Elena Padilla, author of *Up from Puerto Rico*, describing Puerto Rican life in a poor and squalid district of New York, tells how much people know about each other—who is to be trusted and who not, who is defiant of the law and who upholds it, who is competent and well informed and who is inept and ignorant—and how these things are known from the public life of the sidewalk and its associated enterprises. These are matters of public character. But she also tells how select are those permitted to drop into the kitchen for a cup of coffee, how strong are the ties, and how limited the number of a person's genuine confidants, those who share in a person's private life and private affairs. She tells how it is not considered dignified for everyone to know one's affairs. Nor is it considered dignified to snoop on others beyond the face presented in public. It does violence to a person's privacy and rights. In this, the people she describes are essentially the same as the people of the mixed, Americanized city street on which I live, and essentially the same as the people who live in high-income apartments or fine town houses, too.

A good city street neighborhood achieves a marvel of balance between its people's determination to have essential privacy and their simultaneous wishes for differing degrees of contact, enjoyment or help from the people around. This balance is largely made up of small, sensitively managed details, practiced and accepted so casually that they are normally taken for granted.

Perhaps I can best explain this subtle but all-important balance in terms of the stores where people leave keys for their friends, a common custom in New York. In our family, for example, when a friend wants to use our place while we are away for a week end or everyone happens to be out during the day, or a visitor for whom we do not wish to wait up is spending the night, we tell such a friend that he can pick up the key at the delicatessen across the street. Joe Cornacchia, who keeps the delicatessen, usually has a dozen or so keys at a time for handing out like this. He has a special drawer for them.

Now why do I, and many others, select Joe as a logical custodian for keys? Because we trust him, first, to be a responsible custodian, but equally important because we know that he combines a feeling of good will with a feeling of no personal responsibility about our private affairs. Joe considers it no concern of his whom we choose to permit in our places and why.

Around on the other side of our block, people leave their keys at a Spanish grocery. On the other side of Joe's block, people leave them at the candy store. Down a block they leave them at the coffee shop, and a few hundred feet around the corner from that, in a barber shop. Around one corner from two fashionable blocks of town houses and apartments in the Upper East Side, people leave their keys in a butcher shop and a bookshop; around another corner they leave them in a cleaner's and a drug store. In unfashionable East Harlem keys are left with at least one florist, in bakeries, in luncheonettes, in Spanish and Italian groceries.

The point, wherever they are left, is not the kind of ostensible service that the enterprise offers, but the kind of proprietor it has.

A service like this cannot be formalized. Identifications . . . questions . . . insurance against mishaps. The all-essential line between public service and privacy would be transgressed by institutionalization. Nobody in his right mind would leave his key in such a place. The service must be given as a favor by someone with an unshakable understanding of the difference between a person's key and a person's private life, or it cannot be given at all.

Or consider the line drawn by Mr. Jaffe at the candy store around our corner—a line so well understood by his customers and by other storekeepers too that they can spend their whole lives in its presence and never think about it consciously. One ordinary morning last winter, Mr. Jaffe, whose formal business name is Bernie, and his wife, whose formal business name is Ann, supervised the small children crossing at the corner on the way to P.S. 41, as Bernie always does because he sees the need; lent an umbrella to one customer and a dollar to another; took custody of two keys; took in some packages for people in the next building who were away; lectured two youngsters who asked for cigarettes; gave street directions; took custody of a watch to give the repair man across the street when he opened later; gave out information on the range of rents in the neighborhood to an apartment seeker; listened to a tale of domestic difficulty and offered reassurance; told some rowdies they could not come in unless they behaved and then defined (and got) good behavior;

provided an incidental forum for half a dozen conversations among customers who dropped in for oddments; set aside certain newly arrived papers and magazines for regular customers who would depend on getting them; advised a mother who came for a birthday present not to get the ship-model kit because another child going to the same birthday party was giving that; and got a back copy (this was for me) of the previous day's newspaper out of the deliverer's surplus returns when he came by.

After considering this multiplicity of extra-merchandising services I asked Bernie, "Do you ever introduce your customers to each other?"

He looked startled at the idea, even dismayed. "No," he said thoughtfully. "That would just not be advisable. Sometimes, if I know two customers who are in at the same time have an interest in common, I bring up the subject in conversation and let them carry it on from there if they want to. But oh no, I wouldn't introduce them."

When I told this to an acquaintance in a suburb, she promptly assumed that Mr. Jaffe felt that to make an introduction would be to step above his social class. Not at all. In our neighborhood, storekeepers like the Jaffes enjoy an excellent social status, that of businessmen. In income they are apt to be the peers of the general run of customers and in independence they are the superiors. Their advice, as men or women of common sense and experience, is sought and respected. They are well known as individuals, rather than unknown as class symbols. No; this is that almost unconsciously enforced, well-balanced line showing, the line between the city public world and the world of privacy.

This line can be maintained, without awkwardness to

anyone, because of the great plenty of opportunities for public contact in the enterprises along the sidewalks, or on the sidewalks themselves as people move to and fro or deliberately loiter when they feel like it, and also because of the presence of many public hosts, so to speak, proprietors of meeting places like Bernie's where one is free either to hang around or dash in and out, no strings attached.

Under this system, it is possible in a city street neighborhood to know all kinds of people without unwelcome entanglements, without boredom, necessity for excuses, explanations, fears of giving offense, embarrassments respecting impositions or commitments, and all such paraphernalia of obligations which can accompany less limited relationships. It is possible to be on excellent sidewalk terms with people who are very different from oneself, and even, as time passes, on familiar public terms with them. Such relationships can, and do, endure for many years, for decades; they could never have formed without that line, much less endured. They form precisely because they are by-the-way to people's normal public sorties.

"Togetherness" is a fittingly nauseating name for an old ideal in planning theory. This ideal is that if anything is shared among people, much should be shared. "Togetherness," apparently a spiritual resource of the new suburbs, works destructively in cities. The requirement that much shall be shared drives city people apart.

When an area of a city lacks a sidewalk life, the people of the place must enlarge their private lives if they are to have anything approaching equivalent contact with their neighbors. They must settle for some form of "togetherness," in which more is shared with one another than in the life of the sidewalks, or else they must settle for lack of contact. Inevitably the outcome is one or the other; it has to be; and either has distressing results.

In the case of the first outcome, where people do share much, they become exceedingly choosy as to who their neighbors are, or with whom they associate at all. They have to become so. A friend of mine, Penny Kostritsky, is unwittingly and unwillingly in this fix on a street in Baltimore. Her street of nothing but residences, embedded in an area of almost nothing but residences, has been experimentally equipped with a charming sidewalk park. The sidewalk has been widened and attractively paved, wheeled traffic discouraged from the narrow street roadbed, trees and flowers planted, and a piece of play sculpture is to go in. All these are splendid ideas so far as they go.

However, there are no stores. The mothers from nearby blocks who bring small children here, and come here to find some contact with others themselves, perforce go into the houses of acquaintances along the street to warm up in winter, to make telephone calls, to take their children in emergencies to the bathroom. Their hostesses offer them coffee, for there is no other place to get coffee, and naturally considerable social life of this kind has arisen around the park. Much is shared.

Mrs. Kostritsky, who lives in one of the conveniently located houses, and who has two small children, is in the thick of this narrow and accidental social life. "I have lost the advantage of living in the city," she says, "without getting the advantages of living in the suburbs." Still more distressing, when mothers of different income or color or educational background bring their children to the street park, they and their children are rudely and pointedly ostracized. They fit awkwardly into the suburbanlike sharing of private lives that has grown in default of city sidewalk life. The park lacks benches purposely; the "togetherness" people ruled them out because they might be interpreted as an invitation to people who cannot fit in.

"If only we had a couple of stores on the street," Mrs. Kostritsky laments. "If only there were a grocery store or a drug store or a snack joint. Then the telephone calls and the warming up and the gathering could be done naturally in public, and then people would act more decent to each other because everybody would have a right to be here."

Much the same thing that happens in this sidewalk park without a city public life happens sometimes in middle-class projects and colonies, such as Chatham Village in Pittsburgh for example, a famous model of Garden City planning.

The houses here are grouped in colonies around shared interior lawns and play yards, and the whole development is equipped with other devices for close sharing, such as a residents' club which holds parties, dances, reunions, has ladies' activities like bridge and sewing parties, and holds dances and parties for the children. There is no public life here, in any city sense. There are differing degrees of extended private life.

Chatham Village's success as a "model" neighborhood where much is shared has required that the residents be similar to one another in their standards, interests and backgrounds. In the main they are middle-class professionals and their families.* It has also required that residents set themselves distinctly apart from the different people in the surrounding city; these are in the main also middle class, but lower middle class, and this is too different for the degree of chumminess that neighborliness in Chatham Village entails.

The inevitable insularity (and homogeneity) of Chatham Village has practical consequences. As one illustration, the junior high school serving the area has problems, as all schools do. Chatham Village is large enough to dominate the elementary school to which its children go, and therefore to work at helping solve this school's problems. To deal with the junior high, however, Chatham Village's people must cooperate with entirely different neighborhoods. But there is no public acquaintanceship, no foundation of casual public trust, no cross-connections with the necessary people—and no practice or ease in applying the most ordinary techniques of city public life at lowly levels. Feeling helpless, as indeed they are, some Chatham Village families move away when their children reach junior high age; others contrive to send them to private high schools. Ironically, just such neighborhood islands as Chatham Village are encouraged in orthodox planning on the specific grounds that cities need the talents and stabilizing influence of the middle class. Presumably these qualities are to seep out by osmosis.

People who do not fit happily into such colonies

---

*One representative court, for example, contains as this is written four lawyers, two doctors, two engineers, a dentist, a salesman, a banker, a railroad executive, a planning executive.

eventually get out, and in time managements become sophisticated in knowing who among applicants will fit in. Along with basic similarities of standards, values and backgrounds, the arrangement seems to demand a formidable amount of forbearance and tact.

City residential planning that depends, for contact among neighbors, on personal sharing of this sort, and that cultivates it, often does work well socially, if rather narrowly, *for self-selected upper-middle-class people*. It solves easy problems for an easy kind of population. So far as I have been able to discover, it fails to work, however, even on its own terms, *with any other kind of population.*

The more common outcome in cities, where people are faced with the choice of sharing much or nothing, is nothing. In city areas that lack a natural and casual public life, it is common for residents to isolate themselves from each other to a fantastic degree. If mere contact with your neighbors threatens to entangle you in their private lives, or entangle them in yours, and if you cannot be so careful who your neighbors are as self-selected upper-middle-class people can be, the logical solution is absolutely to avoid friendliness or casual offers of help. Better to stay thoroughly distant. As a practical result, the ordinary public jobs—like keeping children in hand—for which people must take a little personal initiative, or those for which they must band together in limited common purposes, go undone. The abysses this opens up can be almost unbelievable.

For example, in one New York City project which is designed—like all orthodox residential city planning—for sharing much or nothing, a remarkably outgoing woman prided herself that she had become acquainted, by making a deliberate effort, with the mothers of every one of the ninety families in her building. She called on them. She buttonholed them at the door or in the hall. She struck up conversations if she sat beside them on a bench.

It so happened that her eight-year-old son, one day, got stuck in the elevator and was left there without help for more than two hours, although he screamed, cried and pounded. The next day the mother expressed her dismay to one of her ninety acquaintances. "Oh, was that *your* son?" said the other woman. "I didn't know whose boy he was. If I had realized he was *your* son I would have helped him."

This woman, who had not behaved in any such insanely calloused fashion on her old public street—to which she constantly returned, by the way, for public life—was afraid of a possible entanglement that might not be kept easily on a public plane.

Dozens of illustrations of this defense can be found wherever the choice is sharing much or nothing. A thorough and detailed report by Ellen Lurie, a social worker in East Harlem, on life in a low-income project there, has this to say:

> It is . . . extremely important to recognize that for considerably complicated reasons, many adults either don't want to become involved in any friendship-relationships at all with their neighbors, or, if they do succumb to the need for some form of society, they strictly limit themselves to one or two friends, and no more. Over and over again, wives repeated their husband's warning:
>
> "I'm not to get too friendly with anyone. My husband doesn't believe in it."

"People are too gossipy and they could get us in a lot of trouble."

"It's best to mind your own business."

One woman, Mrs. Abraham, always goes out the back door of the building because she doesn't want to interfere with the people standing around in the front. Another man, Mr. Colan . . . won't let his wife make any friends in the project, because he doesn't trust the people here. They have four children, ranging from 8 years to 14, but they are not allowed downstairs alone, because the parents are afraid someone will hurt them.* What happens then is that all sorts of barriers to insure self-protection are being constructed by many families. To protect their children from a neighborhood they aren't sure of, they keep them upstairs in the apartment. To protect themselves, they make few, if any, friends. Some are afraid that friends will become angry or envious and make up a story to report to management, causing them great trouble. If the husband gets a bonus (which he decides not to report) and the wife buys new curtains, the visiting friends will see and might tell the management, who, in turn, investigates and issues a rent increase. Suspicion and fear of trouble often outweigh any need for neighborly advice and help. For these families the sense of privacy has already been extensively violated. The deepest secrets, all the family skeletons, are well known not only to management but often to other public agencies, such as the Welfare Department. To preserve any last remnants of privacy, they choose to avoid close relationships with others.

*This is very common in public projects in New York.

This same phenomenon may be found to a much lesser degree in non-planned slum housing, for there too it is often necessary for other reasons to build up these forms of self-protection. But, it is surely true that this withdrawing from the society of others is much more extensive in planned housing. Even in England, this suspicion of the neighbors and the ensuing aloofness was found in studies of planned towns. Perhaps this pattern is nothing more than an elaborate group mechanism to protect and preserve inner dignity in the face of so many outside pressures to conform.

Along with nothingness, considerable "togetherness" can be found in such places, however. Mrs. Lurie reports on this type of relationship:

> Often two women from two different buildings will meet in the laundry room, recognize each other; although they may never have spoken a single word to each other back on 99th Street, suddenly here they become "best friends." If one of these two already has a friend or two in her own building, the other is likely to be drawn into that circle and begins to make her friendships, not with women on her floor, but rather on her friend's floor.
>
> These friendships do not go into an ever-widening circle. There are certain definite well-traveled paths in the project, and after a while no new people are met.

Mrs. Lurie, who works at community organization in East Harlem, with remarkable success, has looked into the

history of many past attempts at project tenant organization. She has told me that "togetherness," itself, is one of
the factors that make this kind of organization so difficult.
"These projects are not lacking in natural leaders," she
says. "They contain people with real ability, wonderful
people many of them, but the typical sequence is that in
the course of organization leaders have found each other,
gotten all involved in each other's social lives, and have
ended up talking to nobody but each other. They have not
found their followers. Everything tends to degenerate
into ineffective cliques, as a natural course. There is no
normal public life. Just the mechanics of people learning
what is going on is so difficult. It all makes the simplest
social gain extra hard for these people."

Residents of unplanned city residential areas that
lack neighborhood commerce and sidewalk life seem
sometimes to follow the same course as residents of public projects when faced with the choice of sharing much
or nothing. Thus researchers hunting the secrets of the
social structure in a dull gray-area district of Detroit
came to the unexpected conclusion there was no social
structure.

The social structure of sidewalk life hangs partly on what
can be called self-appointed public characters. A public
character is anyone who is in frequent contact with a wide
circle of people and who is sufficiently interested to make
himself a public character. A public character need have
no special talents or wisdom to fulfill his function—
although he often does. He just needs to be present, and
there need to be enough of his counterparts. His main
qualification is that he *is* public, that he talks to lots of dif-

ferent people. In this way, news travels that is of sidewalk interest.

Most public sidewalk characters are steadily stationed in public places. They are storekeepers or barkeepers or the like. These are the basic public characters. All other public characters of city sidewalks depend on them—if only indirectly because of the presence of sidewalk routes to such enterprises and their proprietors.

Settlement-house workers and pastors, two more formalized kinds of public characters, typically depend on the street grapevine news systems that have their ganglia in the stores. The director of a settlement on New York's Lower East Side, as an example, makes a regular round of stores. He learns from the cleaner who does his suits about the presence of dope pushers in the neighborhood. He learns from the grocer that the Dragons are working up to something and need attention. He learns from the candy store that two girls are agitating the Sportsmen toward a rumble. One of his most important information spots is an unused breadbox on Rivington Street. That is, it is not used for bread. It stands outside a grocery and is used for sitting on and lounging beside, between the settlement house, a candy store and a pool parlor. A message spoken there for any teen-ager within many blocks will reach his ears unerringly and surprisingly quickly, and the opposite flow along the grapevine similarly brings news quickly in to the breadbox.

Blake Hobbs, the head of the Union Settlement music school in East Harlem, notes that when he gets a first student from one block of the old busy street neighborhoods, he rapidly gets at least three or four more and sometimes almost every child on the block. But when he gets a child from the nearby projects—perhaps through the public school or a playground conversation he has initiated—he almost never gets another as a direct sequence. Word does not move around where public characters and sidewalk life are lacking.

Besides the anchored public characters of the sidewalk, and the well-recognized roving public characters, there are apt to be various more specialized public characters on a city sidewalk. In a curious way, some of these help establish an identity not only for themselves but for others. Describing the everyday life of a retired tenor at such sidewalk establishments as the restaurant and the *bocce* court, a San Francisco news story notes, "It is said of Meloni that because of his intensity, his dramatic manner and his lifelong interest in music, he transmits a feeling of vicarious importance to his many friends." Precisely.

One need not have either the artistry or the personality of such a man to become a specialized sidewalk character—but only a pertinent specialty of some sort. It is easy. I am a specialized public character of sorts along our street, owing of course to the fundamental presence of the basic, anchored public characters. The way I became one started with the fact that Greenwich Village, where I live, was waging an interminable and horrendous battle to save its main park from being bisected by a highway. During the course of battle I undertook, at the behest of a committee organizer away over on the other side of Greenwich Village, to deposit in stores on a few blocks of our street supplies of petition cards protesting the proposed roadway. Customers would sign the cards while in the stores, and from time to time I would make my pickups.* As a result of engaging in this messenger work, I have since become automatically the sidewalk public character on petition strategy. Before long, for instance, Mr. Fox at the liquor store was consulting me, as he wrapped up my bottle, on how we could get the city to remove a long abandoned and dangerous eyesore, a closed-up comfort station near his corner. If I would undertake to compose the petitions and find the effective way of presenting them to City Hall, he proposed, he and his partners would undertake to have them printed, circulated and picked up. Soon the stores round about had comfort station removal petitions. Our street by now has many public experts on petition tactics, including the children.

Not only do public characters spread the news and learn the news at retail, so to speak. They connect with each other and thus spread word wholesale, in effect.

A sidewalk life, so far as I can observe, arises out of no mysterious qualities or talents for it in this or that type of population. It arises only when the concrete, tangible facilities it requires are present. These happen to be the same facilities, in the same abundance and ubiquity, that are required for cultivating sidewalk safety. If they are absent, public sidewalk contacts are absent too.

The well-off have many ways of assuaging needs for which poorer people may depend much on sidewalk life—from hearing of jobs to being recognized by the headwaiter. But nevertheless, many of the rich or near-

---

*This, by the way, is an efficient device, accomplishing with a fraction of the effort what would be a mountainous task door to door. It also makes more public conversation and opinion than door-to-door visits.

rich in cities appear to appreciate sidewalk life as much as anybody. At any rate, they pay enormous rents to move into areas with an exuberant and varied sidewalk life. They actually crowd out the middle class and the poor in lively areas like Yorkville or Greenwich Village in New York, or Telegraph Hill just off the North Beach streets of San Francisco. They capriciously desert, after only a few decades of fashion at most, the monotonous streets of "quiet residential areas" and leave them to the less fortunate. Talk to residents of Georgetown in the District of Columbia and by the second or third sentence at least you will begin to hear rhapsodies about the charming restaurants, "more good restaurants than in all the rest of the city put together," the uniqueness and friendliness of the stores, the pleasures of running into people when doing errands at the next corner—and nothing but pride over the fact that Georgetown has become a specialty shopping district for its whole metropolitan area. The city area, rich or poor or in between, harmed by an interesting sidewalk life and plentiful sidewalk contacts has yet to be found.

Efficiency of public sidewalk characters declines drastically if too much burden is put upon them. A store, for example, can reach a turnover in its contacts, or potential contacts, which is so large and so superficial that it is socially useless. An example of this can be seen at the candy and newspaper store owned by the housing cooperative of Corlears Hook on New York's Lower East Side. This planned project store replaces perhaps forty superficially similar stores which were wiped out (without compensation to their proprietors) on that project site and the adjoining sites. The place is a mill. Its clerks are so busy making change and screaming ineffectual imprecations at rowdies that they never hear anything except "I want that." This, or utter disinterest, is the usual atmosphere where shopping center planning or repressive zoning artificially contrives commercial monopolies for city neighborhoods. A store like this would fail economically if it had competition. Meantime, although monopoly insures the financial success planned for it, it fails the city socially.

Sidewalk public contact and sidewalk public safety, taken together, bear directly on our country's most serious social problem—segregation and racial discrimination.

I do not mean to imply that a city's planning and design, or its types of streets and street life, can automatically overcome segregation and discrimination. Too many other kinds of effort are also required to right these injustices.

But I do mean to say that to build and to rebuild big cities whose sidewalks are unsafe and whose people must settle for sharing much or nothing, *can* make it *much harder* for American cities to overcome discrimination no matter how much effort is expended.

Considering the amount of prejudice and fear that accompany discrimination and bolster it, overcoming residential discrimination is just that much harder if people feel unsafe on their sidewalks anyway. Overcoming residential discrimination comes hard where people have no means of keeping a civilized public life on a basically dignified public footing, and their private lives on a private footing.

To be sure, token model housing integration schemes here and there can be achieved in city areas handicapped

by danger and by lack of public life—achieved by applying great effort and settling for abnormal (abnormal for
cities) choosiness among new neighbors. This is an eva-
sion of the size of the task and its urgency.

The tolerance, the room for great differences among
neighbors—differences that often go far deeper than differences in color—which are possible and normal in
intensely urban life, but which are so foreign to suburbs
and pseudosuburbs, are possible and normal only when
streets of great cities have built-in equipment allowing
strangers to dwell in peace together on civilized but
essentially dignified and reserved terms.

Lowly, unpurposeful and random as they may appear,
sidewalk contacts are the small change from which a
city's wealth of public life may grow.

Los Angeles is an extreme example of a metropolis
with little public life, depending mainly instead on contacts of a more private social nature.

On one plane, for instance, an acquaintance there
comments that although she has lived in the city for ten
years and knows it contains Mexicans, she has never laid
eyes on a Mexican or an item of Mexican culture, much
less ever exchanged any words with a Mexican.

On another plane, Orson Welles has written that Hollywood is the only theatrical center in the world that has
failed to develop a theatrical bistro.

And on still another plane, one of Los Angeles' most
powerful businessmen comes upon a blank in public relationships which would be inconceivable in other cities of
this size. This businessman, volunteering that the city is
"culturally behind," as he put it, told me that he for one

was at work to remedy this. He was heading a committee to raise funds for a first-rate art museum. Later in our conversation, after he had told me about the businessmen's club life of Los Angeles, a life with which he is involved as one of its leaders, I asked him how or where Hollywood people gathered in corresponding fashion. He was unable to answer this. He then added that he knew no one at all connected with the film industry, nor did he know anyone who did have such acquaintanceship. "I know that must sound strange," he reflected. "We are glad to have the film industry here, but those connected with it are just not people one would know socially."

Here again is "togetherness" or nothing. Consider this man's handicap in his attempts to get a metropolitan art museum established. He has no way of reaching with any ease, practice or trust some of his committee's potentially best prospects.

In its upper economic, political and cultural echelons, Los Angeles operates according to the same provincial premises of social insularity as the street with the sidewalk park in Baltimore or as Chatham Village in Pittsburgh. Such a metropolis lacks means for bringing together necessary ideas, necessary enthusiasms, necessary money. Los Angeles is embarked on a strange experiment: trying to run not just projects, not just gray areas, but a whole metropolis, by dint of "togetherness" or nothing. I think this is an inevitable outcome for great cities whose people lack city public life in ordinary living and working.

4

THE USES OF SIDEWALKS:
ASSIMILATING CHILDREN

Among the superstitions of planning and housing is a fantasy about the transformation of children. It goes like this: A population of children is condemned to play on the city streets. These pale and rickety children, in their sinister moral environment, are telling each other canards about sex, sniggering evilly and learning new forms of corruption as efficiently as if they were in reform school. This situation is called "the moral and physical toll taken of our youth by the streets," sometimes it is called simply "the gutter."

If only these deprived children can be gotten off the streets into parks and playgrounds with equipment on which to exercise, space in which to run, grass to lift their souls! Clean and happy places, filled with the laughter of children responding to a wholesome environment. So much for the fantasy.

Let us consider a story from real life, as discovered by Charles Guggenheim, a documentary-film maker in St. Louis. Guggenheim was working on a film depicting the activities of a St. Louis children's day-care center. He noticed that at the end of the afternoon roughly half the children left with the greatest reluctance.

Guggenheim became sufficiently curious to investigate. Without exception, the children who left unwillingly came from a nearby housing project. And without exception again, those who left willingly came from the old "slum" streets nearby. The mystery, Guggenheim found, was simplicity itself. The children returning to the project, with its generous playgrounds and lawns, ran a gauntlet of bullies who made them turn out their pockets or submit to a beating, sometimes both. These small children could not get home each day without enduring an ordeal that they dreaded. The children going back to the old streets were safe from extortion, Guggenheim found. They had many streets to select from, and they astutely chose the safest. "If anybody picked on them, there was always a storekeeper they could run to or somebody to come to their aid," says Guggenheim. "They also had any number of ways of escaping along different routes if anybody was laying for them. These little kids felt safe and cocky and they enjoyed their trip home too." Guggenheim made the related observation of how boring the project's landscaped grounds and playgrounds were, how deserted they seemed, and in contrast how rich in interest, variety and material for both the camera and the imagination were the older streets nearby.

Consider another story from real life, an adolescent gang battle in the summer of 1959 in New York, which culminated in the death of a fifteen-year-old girl who had no connection with the battle, but happened to be standing at the grounds of the project where she lives. The events leading to the day's final tragedy, and their locales, were reported by the *New York Post* during the subsequent trial, as follows:

The first fracas occurred about noon when the Sportsmen stepped into the Forsyth St. Boys' turf in Sara Delano Roosevelt Park* . . . During the afternoon the decision was made by the Forsyth St. Boys to use their ultimate weapon, the rifle, and gasoline bombs . . . In the course of the affray, also in Sara Delano Roosevelt Park . . . a 14-year-old Forsyth St. boy was fatally stabbed and two other boys, one 11 years old, were seriously wounded . . . At about 9 P.M. [seven or eight Forsyth St. boys] suddenly descended on the Sportsmen's hangout near the Lillian Wald housing project and, from the no-man's land of Avenue D [the project grounds' boundary] lobbed their gasoline bombs into the group while Cruz crouched and triggered the rifle.

Where did these three battles occur? In a park and at the parklike grounds of the project. After outbreaks of this kind, one of the remedies invariably called for is more parks and playgrounds. We are bemused by the sound of symbols.

"Street gangs" do their "street fighting" predominately in parks and playgrounds. When the *New York Times* in September 1959 summed up the worst adolescent

---

*Forsyth St. borders Sara Delano Roosevelt Park, which extends for many blocks; the Rev. Jerry Oniki, pastor of a church on the park border, has been quoted in the *New York Times*, with reference to the park's influence on children, "Every sort of vice you can think of goes on in that park." The park has had its share of expert praise, however; among the illustrations for a 1942 article on Baron Haussmann, the rebuilder of Paris, written by Robert Moses, the rebuilder of New York, Sara Delano Roosevelt Park, then newly built, was soberly equated as an achievement with the Rue de Rivoli of Paris!

gang outbreaks of the past decade in the city, each and every one was designated as having occurred in a park. Moreover, more and more frequently, not only in New York but in other cities too, children engaged in such horrors turn out to be from super-block projects, where their everyday play has successfully been removed from the streets (the streets themselves have largely been removed). The highest delinquency belt in New York's Lower East Side, where the gang war described above occurred, is precisely the parklike belt of public housing projects. The two most formidable gangs in Brooklyn are rooted in two of the oldest projects. Ralph Whelan, director of the New York City Youth Board, reports, according to the *New York Times*, an "invariable rise in delinquency rates" wherever a new housing project is built. The worst girls' gang in Philadelphia has grown up on the grounds of that city's second-oldest housing project, and the highest delinquency belt of that city corresponds with its major belt of projects. In St. Louis the project where Guggenheim found the extortion going on is considered relatively safe compared with the city's largest project, fifty-seven acres of mostly grass, dotted with playgrounds and devoid of city streets, a prime breeding ground of delinquency in that city.* Such projects are examples, among other things, of an intent to take children off the streets. They are designed as they are partly for just this purpose.

The disappointing results are hardly strange. The

---

*This too has had its share of expert praise; it was much admired in housing and architectural circles when it was built in 1954-56 and was widely publicized as an exceptionally splendid example of housing.

same rules of city safety and city public life that apply to adults apply to children too, except that children are even more vulnerable to danger and barbarism than adults.

In real life, what significant change *does* occur if children are transferred from a lively city street to the usual park or to the usual public or project playground?

In most cases (not all, fortunately), the most significant change is this: The children have moved from under the eyes of a high numerical ratio of adults, into a place where the ratio of adults is low or even nil. To think this represents an improvement in city child rearing is pure daydreaming.

City children themselves know this; they have known it for generations. "When we wanted to do anything anti-social, we always made for Lindy Park because none of the grownups would see us there," says Jesse Reichek, an artist who grew up in Brooklyn. "Mostly we played on the streets where we couldn't get away with anything much."

Life is the same today. My son, reporting how he escaped four boys who set upon him, says, "I was scared they would catch me when I had to pass the playground. If they caught me *there* I'd be sunk!"

A few days after the murder of two sixteen-year-old boys in a playground on the midtown West Side of Manhattan, I paid a morbid visit to the area. The nearby streets were evidently back to normal. Hundreds of children, directly under the eyes of innumerable adults using the sidewalks themselves and looking from windows, were engaged in a vast variety of sidewalk games and whooping pursuits. The sidewalks were dirty, they were too narrow for the demands put upon them, and they needed shade from the sun. But here was no scene of arson, mayhem or the flourishing of dangerous weapons. In the playground where the nighttime murder had occurred, things were apparently back to normal too. Three small boys were setting a fire under a wooden bench. Another was having his head beaten against the concrete. The custodian was absorbed in solemnly and slowly hauling down the American flag.

On my return home, as I passed the relatively genteel playground near where I live, I noted that its only inhabitants in the late afternoon, with the mothers and the custodian gone, were two small boys threatening to bash a little girl with their skates, and an alcoholic who had roused himself to shake his head and mumble that they shouldn't do that. Farther down the street, on a block with many Puerto Rican immigrants, was another scene of contrast. Twenty-eight children of all ages were playing on the sidewalk without mayhem, arson, or any event more serious than a squabble over a bag of candy. They were under the casual surveillance of adults primarily visiting in public with each other. The surveillance was only seemingly casual, as was proved when the candy squabble broke out and peace and justice were re-established. The identities of the adults kept changing because different ones kept putting their heads out the windows, and different ones kept coming in and going out on errands, or passing by and lingering a little. But the numbers of adults stayed fairly constant—between eight and eleven—during the hour I watched. Arriving home, I noticed that at our end of our block, in front of the tenement, the tailor's, our house, the laundry, the pizza place and the fruit man's, twelve children were playing on the sidewalk in sight of fourteen adults.

To be sure, all city sidewalks are not under surveillance in this fashion, and this is one of the troubles of the city that planning ought properly to help correct. Underused sidewalks are not under suitable surveillance for child rearing. Nor are sidewalks apt to be safe, even with eyes upon them, if they are bordered by a population which is constantly and rapidly turning over in residence—another urgent planning problem. But the playgrounds and parks near such streets are even less wholesome.

Nor are all playgrounds and parks unsafe or under poor surveillance, as we shall see in the next chapter. But those that are wholesome are typically in neighborhoods where streets are lively and safe and where a strong tone of civilized public sidewalk life prevails. Whatever differentials exist in safety and wholesomeness between playgrounds and sidewalks in any given area are invariably, so far as I can find, in the favor of the much maligned streets.

People with actual, not theoretical, responsibility for bringing up children in cities often know this well. "You can go out," say city mothers, "but stay on the sidewalk." I say it to my own children. And by this we mean more than "Don't go into the street where the cars are."

Describing the miraculous rescue of a nine-year-old boy who was pushed down a sewer by an unidentified assailant—in a park, of course—the *New York Times* reported, "The mother had told the boys earlier in the day not to play in High Bridge Park . . . Finally she said all right." The boy's frightened companions intelligently raced out of the park and back to the evil streets where they enlisted help quickly.

Frank Havey, the settlement-house director in Boston's North End, says that parents come to him time and again with this problem: "I tell my children to play on the sidewalk after supper. But I hear children shouldn't play on the street. Am I doing wrong?" Havey tells them they are doing right. He attributes much of the North End's low delinquency rate to the excellent community surveillance of children at play where the community is at its strongest—on the sidewalks.

Garden City planners, with their hatred of the street, thought the solution to keeping children off the streets *and* under wholesome surveillance was to build interior enclaves for them in the centers of super-blocks. This policy has been inherited by the designers of Radiant Garden City. Today many large renewal areas are being replanned on the principle of enclosed park enclaves within blocks.

The trouble with this scheme, as can be seen in such already existing examples as Chatham Village in Pittsburgh and Baldwin Hills Village in Los Angeles, and smaller courtyard colonies in New York and Baltimore, is that no child of enterprise or spirit will willingly stay in such a boring place after he reaches the age of six. Most want out earlier. These sheltered, "togetherness" worlds are suitable, and in real life are used, for about three or four years of a small child's life, in many ways the easiest four years to manage. Nor do the adult residents of these places even want the play of older children in their sheltered courts. In Chatham Village and Baldwin Hills Village it is expressly forbidden. Little tots are decorative and relatively docile, but older children are noisy and energetic, and they act on their environment instead of just letting it act on them. Since the environment is already "perfect" this will not do. Furthermore, as can also be seen both in examples already existing and in plans for construction, this type of planning requires that buildings be oriented toward the interior enclave. Otherwise the enclave's prettiness goes unexploited and it is left without easy surveillance and access. The relatively dead backs of the buildings or, worse still, blank end walls, thus face on the streets. The safety of the unspecialized sidewalks is thus exchanged for a specialized form of safety for a specialized part of the population for a few years of its life. When the children venture forth, as they must and will, they are ill served, along with everyone else.

I have been dwelling on a negative aspect of child rearing in cities: the factor of protection—protection of children from their own idiocies, from adults bent on ill, and from each other. I have dwelt on it because it has been my purpose to show, by means of the most easily understood problem, how nonsensical is the fantasy that playgrounds and parks are automatically O.K. places for children, and streets are automatically not O.K. places for children.

But lively sidewalks have positive aspects for city children's play too, and these are at least as important as safety and protection.

Children in cities need a variety of places in which to play and to learn. They need, among other things, opportunities for all kinds of sports and exercise and physical skills—more opportunities, more easily obtained, than they now enjoy in most cases. However, at the same time, they need an unspecialized outdoor home base from which to play, to hang around in, and to help form their notions of the world.

It is this form of unspecialized play that the sidewalks serve—and that lively city sidewalks can serve splendidly. When this home-base play is transferred to playgrounds and parks it is not only provided for unsafely, but paid personnel, equipment and space are frittered away that could be devoted instead to more ice-skating rinks, swimming pools, boat ponds and other various and specific outdoor uses. Poor, generalized play use eats up substance that could instead be used for good specialized play.

To waste the normal presence of adults on lively sidewalks and to bank instead (however idealistically) on hiring substitutes for them, is frivolous in the extreme. It is frivolous not only socially but also economically, because cities have desperate shortages of money and of personnel for more interesting uses of the outdoors than playgrounds—and of money and personnel for other aspects of children's lives. For example, city school systems today typically have between thirty and forty children in their classes—sometimes more—and these include children with all manner of problems too, from ignorance of English to bad emotional upsets. City schools need something approaching a 50-percent increase in teachers to handle severe problems and also reduce normal class sizes to a figure permitting better education. New York's city-run hospitals in 1959 had 58 percent of their professional nursing positions unfilled, and in many another city the shortage of nurses has become alarming. Libraries, and often museums, curtail their hours, and notably the hours of their children's sections. Funds are lacking for the increased numbers of settlement houses drastically needed in the new slums and new projects of cities. Even the existing settlement houses lack funds for needed expansions and changes in their programs, in short for more staff. Requirements like these should have high priority on public and philanthropic funds—not only on funds at the present dismally inadequate levels, but on funds greatly increased.

The people of cities who have other jobs and duties, and who lack, too, the training needed, cannot volunteer as teachers or registered nurses or librarians or museum guards or social workers. But at least they can, and on lively diversified sidewalks they do, supervise the incidental play of children and assimilate the children into city society. They do it *in the course of carrying on their other pursuits.*

Planners do not seem to realize how high a ratio of adults is needed to rear children at incidental play. Nor do they seem to understand that spaces and equipment do not rear children. These can be useful adjuncts, but only people rear children and assimilate them into civilized society.

It is folly to build cities in a way that wastes this normal, casual manpower for child rearing and either leaves this essential job too much undone—with terrible consequences—or makes it necessary to hire substitutes. The myth that playgrounds and grass and hired guards or supervisors are innately wholesome for children and that city streets, filled with ordinary people, are innately evil for children, boils down to a deep contempt for ordinary people.

In real life, only from the ordinary adults of the city sidewalks do children learn—if they learn it at all—the first fundamental of successful city life: People must take a modicum of public responsibility for each other even if they have no ties to each other. This is a lesson nobody learns by being told. It is learned from the experience of having *other people without ties of kinship or close friendship or formal responsibility to you* take a modicum of public responsibility for you. When Mr. Lacey, the locksmith, bawls out one of my sons for running into the street, and then later reports the transgression to my husband as he passes the locksmith shop, my son gets more than an overt lesson in safety and obedience. He also gets, indirectly, the lesson that Mr. Lacey, with whom we have no ties other than street propinquity, feels responsible for him to a degree. The boy who went unrescued in the elevator in the "togetherness"-or-nothing project learns opposite lessons from his experiences. So do the project children who squirt water into house windows and on passers-by, and go unrebuked because they are anonymous children in anonymous grounds.

The lesson that city dwellers have to take responsibility for what goes on in city streets is taught again and again to children on sidewalks which enjoy a local public life. They can absorb it astonishingly early. They show they have absorbed it by taking it for granted that they, too, are part of the management. They volunteer (before they are asked) directions to people who are lost; they tell a man he will get a ticket if he parks where he thinks he is going to park; they offer unsolicited advice to the building superintendent to use rock salt instead of a chopper to attack the ice. The presence or absence of this kind of street bossiness in city children is a fairly good tip-off to the presence or absence of responsible adult behavior toward the sidewalk and the children who use it. The children are imitating adult attitudes. This has nothing to do with income. Some of the poorest parts of cities do the best by their children in this respect. And some do the worst.

This is instruction in city living that people hired to look after children cannot teach, because the essence of this responsibility is that you do it without being hired. It is a lesson that parents, by themselves, are powerless to teach. If parents take minor public responsibility for strangers or neighbors in a society where nobody else does, this simply means that the parents are embarrassingly different and meddlesome, not that this is the proper way to behave. Such instruction must come from society itself, and in cities, if it comes, it comes almost entirely during the time children spend at incidental play on the sidewalks.

Play on lively, diversified sidewalks differs from virtually all other daily incidental play offered American children today: It is play not conducted in a matriarchy.

Most city architectural designers and planners are men. Curiously, they design and plan to exclude men as part of normal, daytime life wherever people live. In planning residential life, they aim at filling the presumed daily needs of impossibly vacuous housewives and preschool tots. They plan, in short, strictly for matriarchal societies.

The ideal of a matriarchy inevitably accompanies all planning in which residences are isolated from other parts of life. It accompanies all planning for children in

which their incidental play is set apart in its own preserves. Whatever adult society does accompany the daily
life of children affected by such planning has to be a
matriarchy. Chatham Village, that Pittsburgh model of
Garden City life, is as thoroughly matriarchal in conception and in operation as the newest dormitory suburb. All
housing projects are.

Placing work and commerce *near* residences, but
buffering it off, in the tradition set by Garden City theory,
is fully as matriarchal an arrangement as if the residences
were miles away from work and from men. Men are not
an abstraction. They are either around, in person, or they
are not. Working places and commerce must be mingled
right in with residences if men, like the men who work
on or near Hudson Street, for example, are to be around
city children in daily life—men who are part of normal
daily life, as opposed to men who put in an occasional
playground appearance while they substitute for women
or imitate the occupations of women.

The opportunity (in modern life it has become a priv-
ilege) of playing and growing up in a daily world composed of both men and women is possible and usual for
children who play on lively, diversified city sidewalks. I
cannot understand why this arrangement should be discouraged by planning and by zoning. It ought, instead,
to be abetted by examining the conditions that stimulate
minglings and mixtures of work and commerce with residences, a subject taken up later in this book.

The fascination of street life for city children has long been
noted by recreation experts, usually with disapproval.
Back in 1928, the Regional Plan Association of New York,

in a report which remains to this day the most exhaustive American study of big-city recreation, had this to say:

> Careful checking within a radius of 1/4 mile of playgrounds under a wide range of conditions in many cities shows that about 1/7 of the child population from 5 to 15 years of age may be found on these grounds . . . The lure of the street is a strong competitor . . . It must be a well administered playground to compete successfully with the city streets, teeming with life and adventure. The ability to make the playground activity so compellingly attractive as to draw the children from the streets and hold their interest from day to day is a rare faculty in play leadership, combining personality and technical skill of a high order.

The same report then deplores the stubborn tendency of children to "fool around" instead of playing "recognized games." (Recognized by whom?) This yearning for the Organization Child on the part of those who would incarcerate incidental play, and children's stubborn preference for fooling around on city streets, teeming with life and adventure, are both as characteristic today as they were in 1928.

"I know Greenwich Village like my hand," brags my younger son, taking me to see a "secret passage" he has discovered under a street, down one subway stair and up another, and a secret hiding place some nine inches wide between two buildings, where he secretes treasures that people have put out for the sanitation truck collections along his morning route to school and that he can thus save and retrieve on his return from school. (I had such a hiding place, for the same purpose, at his age, but mine was a crack in a cliff on my way to school instead of a crack between two buildings, and he finds stranger and richer treasures.)

Why do children so frequently find that roaming the lively city sidewalks is more interesting than back yards or playgrounds? Because the sidewalks are more interesting. It is just as sensible to ask: Why do adults find lively streets more interesting than playgrounds?

The wonderful convenience of city sidewalks is an important asset to children too. Children are at the mercy of convenience more than anyone else, except the aged. A great part of children's outdoor play, especially after they start school, and after they also find a certain number of organized activities (sports, arts, handcrafts or whatever else their interests and the local opportunities provide), occurs at incidental times and must be sandwiched in. A lot of outdoor life for children adds up from bits. It happens in a small leftover interval after lunch. It happens after school while children may be pondering what to do and wondering who will turn up. It happens while they are waiting to be called for their suppers. It happens in brief intervals between supper and homework, or homework and bed.

During such times children have, and use, all manner of ways to exercise and amuse themselves. They slop in puddles, write with chalk, jump rope, roller skate, shoot marbles, trot out their possessions, converse, trade cards, play stoop ball, walk stilts, decorate soap-box scooters, dismember old baby carriages, climb on railings, run up and down. It is not in the nature of things to make a big deal out of such activities. It is not in the nature of things to go somewhere formally to do them by plan, officially. Part of their charm is the accompanying sense of freedom to roam up and down the sidewalks, a different matter from being boxed into a preserve. If it is impossible to do such things both incidentally and conveniently, they are seldom done.

As children get older, this incidental outdoor activity—say, while waiting to be called to eat—becomes less bumptious physically and entails more loitering with others, sizing people up, flirting, talking, pushing, shoving and horseplay. Adolescents are always being criticized for this kind of loitering, but they can hardly grow up without it. The trouble comes when it is done not within society, but as a form of outlaw life.

The requisite for any of these varieties of incidental play is not pretentious equipment of any sort, but rather space at an immediately convenient and interesting place. The play gets crowded out if sidewalks are too narrow relative to the total demands put on them. It is especially crowded out if the sidewalks also lack minor irregularities in building line. An immense amount of both loitering and play goes on in shallow sidewalk niches out of the line of moving pedestrian feet.

There is no point in planning for play on sidewalks unless the sidewalks are used for a wide variety of other purposes and by a wide variety of other people too. These uses need each other, for proper surveillance, for a public life of some vitality, and for general interest. If sidewalks on a lively street are sufficiently wide, play flourishes mightily right along with other uses. If the sidewalks are skimped, rope jumping is the first play casualty. Roller skating, tricycle and bicycle riding are the next casualties. The narrower the sidewalks, the more sedentary incidental play becomes. The more frequent too become sporadic forays by children into the vehicular roadways.

Sidewalks thirty or thirty-five feet wide can accommodate virtually any demand of incidental play put upon them—along with trees to shade the activities, and sufficient space for pedestrian circulation and adult public sidewalk life and loitering. Few sidewalks of this luxurious width can be found. Sidewalk width is invariably sacrificed for vehicular width, partly because city sidewalks are conventionally considered to be purely space for pedestrian travel and access to buildings, and go unrecognized and unrespected as the uniquely vital and irreplaceable organs of city safety, public life and child rearing that they are.

Twenty-foot sidewalks, which usually preclude rope jumping but can feasibly permit roller skating and the use of other wheeled toys, can still be found, although the street wideners erode them year by year (often in the belief that shunned malls and "promenades" are a constructive substitute). The livelier and more popular a sidewalk, and the greater the number and variety of its users, the greater the total width needed for it to serve its purposes pleasantly.

But even when proper space is lacking, convenience of location and the interest of the streets are both so important to children—and good surveillance so important to their parents—that children will and do adapt to skimpy sidewalk space. This does not mean we do right in taking unscrupulous advantage of their adaptability. In fact, we wrong both them and cities.

Some city sidewalks are undoubtedly evil places for rearing children. They are evil for anybody. In such neighborhoods we need to foster the qualities and facilities that make for safety, vitality and stability in city streets. This is a complex problem; it is a central problem of planning for cities. In defective city neighborhoods, shooing the children into parks and playgrounds is worse than useless, either as a solution to the streets' problems or as a solution for the children.

The whole idea of doing away with city streets, insofar as that is possible, and downgrading and minimizing their social and their economic part in city life is the most mischievous and destructive idea in orthodox city planning. That it is so often done in the name of vaporous fantasies about city child care is as bitter as irony can get.

5

THE USES OF
NEIGHBORHOOD PARKS

Conventionally, neighborhood parks or parklike open spaces are considered boons conferred on the deprived populations of cities. Let us turn this thought around, and consider city parks deprived places that need the boon of life and appreciation conferred on *them*. This is more nearly in accord with reality, for people do confer use on parks and make them successes—or else withhold use and doom parks to rejection and failure.

Parks are volatile places. They tend to run to extremes of popularity and unpopularity. Their behavior is far from simple. They can be delightful features of city districts, and economic assets to their surroundings as well, but pitifully few are. They can grow more beloved and valuable with the years, but pitifully few show this staying power. For every Rittenhouse Square in Philadelphia, or Rockefeller Plaza or Washington Square in New York, or Boston Common, or their loved equivalents in other cities, there are dozens of dispirited city vacuums called parks, eaten around with decay, little used, unloved. As a woman in Indiana said when asked if she liked the town square, "Nobody there but dirty old men who spit tobacco juice and try to look up your skirt."

In orthodox city planning, neighborhood open spaces

116

are venerated in an amazingly uncritical fashion, much as savages venerate magical fetishes.* Ask a houser how his planned neighborhood improves on the old city and he will cite, as a self-evident virtue, More Open Space. Ask a zoner about the improvements in progressive codes and he will cite, again as a self-evident virtue, their incentives toward leaving More Open Space. Walk with a planner through a dispirited neighborhood and though it be already scabby with deserted parks and tired landscaping festooned with old Kleenex, he will envision a future of More Open Space.

More Open Space for what? For muggings? For bleak vacuums between buildings? Or for ordinary people to use and enjoy? But people do not use city open space just because it is there and because city planners or designers wish they would.

In certain specifics of its behavior, every city park is a case unto itself and defies generalizations. Moreover, large parks such as Fairmount Park in Philadelphia, Central Park and Bronx Park and Prospect Park in New York, Forest Park in St. Louis, Golden Gate Park in San Francisco, Grant Park in Chicago—and even smaller Boston Common—differ much within themselves from part to part, and they also receive differing influences from the different parts of their cities which they touch. Some of the factors in the behavior of large metropolitan parks are too complex to deal with in the first part of this book; they

*E.g., "Mr. Moses conceded that some new housing might be 'ugly, regimented, institutional, identical, conformed, faceless.' But he suggested that such housing could be surrounded with parks"—from a *New York Times* story in January 1961.

will be discussed later, in Chapter Fourteen, The Curse of Border Vacuums.

Nevertheless, even though it is misleading to consider any two city parks actual or potential duplicates of one another, or to believe that generalizations can thoroughly explain all the peculiarities of any single park, it is possible to generalize about a few basic principles that deeply affect virtually all neighborhood parks. Moreover, understanding these principles helps somewhat in understanding influences working on city parks of all kinds—from little outdoor lobbies which serve as enlargements of the street, to large parks with major metropolitan attractions like zoos, lakes, woods, museums.

The reason neighborhood parks reveal certain general principles about park behavior more clearly than specialized parks do is precisely that neighborhood parks are the most generalized form of city park that we possess. They are typically intended for general bread-and-butter use as local public yards—whether the locality is predominately a working place, predominately a residential place, or a thoroughgoing mixture. Most city squares fall into this category of generalized public-yard use; so does most project land; and so does much city parkland that takes advantage of natural features like river banks or hilltops.

The first necessity in understanding how cities and their parks influence each other is to jettison confusion between real uses and mythical uses—for example, the science-fiction nonsense that parks are "the lungs of the city." It takes about three acres of woods to absorb as much carbon dioxide as four people exude in breathing, cooking and heating. The oceans of air circulating about us, not parks, keep cities from suffocating.*

Nor is more air let into the city by a given acreage of greenery than by an equivalent acreage of streets. Subtracting streets and adding their square footage to parks or project malls is irrelevant to the quantities of fresh air a city receives. Air knows nothing of grass fetishes and fails to pick and choose for itself in accordance with them.

It is necessary too, in understanding park behavior, to junk the false reassurance that parks are real estate stabilizers or community anchors. Parks are not automatically anything, and least of all are these volatile elements stabilizers of values or of their neighborhoods and districts.

Philadelphia affords almost a controlled experiment on this point. When Penn laid out the city, he placed at its center the square now occupied by City Hall, and at equal distances from this center he placed four residential

---

*Los Angeles, which needs lung help more than any other American city, also happens to have more open space than any other large city; its smog is partly owing to local eccentricities of circulation in the ocean of air, but also partly to the city's very scatter and amplitude of open space itself. The scatter requires tremendous automobile travel and this in turn contributes almost two-thirds of the chemicals to the city's smog stew. Of the thousand tons of air-polluting chemicals released each day by Los Angeles' three million registered vehicles, about 600 tons are hydrocarbons, which may be largely eliminated eventually by requiring exhaust after-burners on cars. But about 400 tons are oxides of nitrogen, and, as this is written, research has not even been started on devices for reducing this component of exhausts. The air and open land paradox, and it is obviously not a temporary paradox, is this: in modern cities generous scatters of open space promote air pollution instead of combating it. This was an effect Ebenezer Howard could hardly have foreseen. But foresight is no longer required; only hindsight.

squares. What has become of these four, all the same age, the same size, the same original use, and as nearly the same in presumed advantages of location as they could be made?

Their fates are wildly different.

The best known of Penn's four squares is Rittenhouse Square, a beloved, successful, much-used park, one of Philadelphia's greatest assets today, the center of a fashionable neighborhood—indeed, the only old neighborhood in Philadelphia which is spontaneously rehabilitating its edges and extending its real estate values.

The second of Penn's little parks is Franklin Square, the city's Skid Row park where the homeless, the unemployed and the people of indigent leisure gather amid the adjacent flophouses, cheap hotels, missions, second-hand clothing stores, reading and writing lobbies, pawnshops, employment agencies, tattoo parlors, burlesque houses and eateries. This park and its users are both seedy, but it is not a dangerous or crime park. Nevertheless, it has hardly worked as an anchor to real estate values or to social stability. Its neighborhood is scheduled for large-scale clearance.

The third is Washington Square, the center of an area that was at one time the heart of downtown, but is new specialized as a massive office center—insurance companies, publishing, advertising. Several decades ago Washington Square became Philadelphia's pervert park, to the point where it was shunned by office lunchers and was an unmanageable vice and crime problem to park workers and police. In the mid-1950s it was torn up, closed for more than a year, and redesigned. In the process its users were dispersed, which was the intent. Today it gets brief and desultory use, lying mostly empty except at lunchtime on fine days. Washington Square's district, like Franklin Square's, has failed at spontaneously maintaining its values, let alone raising them. Beyond the rim of offices, it is today designated for large-scale urban renewal.

The fourth of Penn's squares has been whittled to a small traffic island, Logan Circle, in Benjamin Franklin Boulevard, an example of City Beautiful planning. The circle is adorned with a great soaring fountain and beautifully maintained planting. Although it is discouraging to reach on foot, and is mainly an elegant amenity for those speeding by, it gets a trickle of population on fine days. The district immediately adjoining the monumental cultural center of which it is a part decayed terribly and has already been slum-cleared and converted to Radiant City.

The varying fates of these squares—especially the three that remain squares—illustrate the volatile behavior that is characteristic of city parks. These squares also happen to illustrate much about basic principles of park behavior, and I shall return to them and their lessons soon.

The fickle behavior of parks and their neighborhoods can be extreme. One of the most charming and individual small parks to be found in any American city, the Plaza in Los Angeles, ringed with immense magnolia trees, a lovely place of shade and history is today incongruously encircled on three sides with abandoned ghost buildings and with squalor so miserable the stink of it rolls over the sidewalks. (Off the fourth side is a Mexican tourist bazaar, doing fine.) Madison Park in Boston, the residential grassy square of a row-house neighborhood, a park precisely of the kind that is popping into many of today's sophisticated redevelopment plans, is the center of a neighborhood that appears to have been bombed. The houses around it—inherently no different from those in high demand at outer reaches of Philadelphia's Rittenhouse Square neighborhood—are crumbling from lack of value, with consequent neglect. As one house in a row cracks, it is demolished and the family in the next house is moved for safety; a few months later that one goes and the house beyond is emptied. No plan is involved in this, merely purposeless, gaping holes, rubble and abandonment, with the little ghost park, theoretically a good residential anchorage, at the center of the havoc. Federal Hill in Baltimore is a most beautiful and serene park and affords the finest view in Baltimore of the city and the bay. Its neighborhood, although decent, is moribund like the park itself. For generations it has failed to attract newcomers by choice. One of the bitterest disappointments in housing project history is the failure of the parks and open grounds in these establishments to increase adjacent values or to stabilize, let alone improve, their neighborhoods. Notice the rim of any city park, civic plaza or project parkland: how rare is the city open space with a rim that consistently reflects the supposed magnetism or stabilizing influence residing in parks.

And consider also the parks that go to waste most of the time, just as Baltimore's beautiful Federal Hill does. In Cincinnati's two finest parks, overlooking the river, I was able to find on a splendid, hot September afternoon a grand total of five users (three teen-age girls and one young couple); meanwhile, street after street in Cincinnati was swarming with people at leisure who lacked the slightest amenity for enjoying the city or the least kindness of shade. On a similar afternoon, with the temperature above ninety degrees, I was able to find in Corlears Hook park, a landscaped breezy river-front oasis in Manhattan's heavily populated Lower East Side, just eighteen people, most of them lone, apparently indigent, men.* The children were not there; no mother in her right mind would send a child in there alone, and the mothers of the Lower East Side are not out of their minds. A boat trip around Manhattan conveys the erroneous impression that here is a city composed largely of parkland—and almost devoid of inhabitants. Why are there so often no people where the parks are and no parks where the people are?

Unpopular parks are troubling not only because of the waste and missed opportunities they imply, but also because of their frequent negative effects. They have the same problems as streets without eyes, and their dangers spill over into the areas surrounding, so that streets along such parks become known as danger places too and are avoided.

Moreover, underused parks and their equipment suffer from vandalism, which is quite a different matter from wear. This fact was obliquely recognized by Stuart Constable, Executive Officer, at the time, of New York City's park department, when he was asked by the press what he thought of a London proposal to install television in

---

*By coincidence, when I arrived home, I found the statistical equivalent to the population of this park, eighteen people (of both sexes and all ages), gathered around the stoop of the tenement next door to us. Every parklike amenity was missing here except those that count most: enjoyment of leisure, each other and the passing city.

parks. After explaining that he did not think television a suitable park use, Constable added, "I don't think [the sets] would last half an hour before they disappeared."

Every fine summer night, television sets can be seen outdoors, used publicly, on the busy old sidewalks of East Harlem. Each machine, its extension cord run along the sidewalk from some store's electric outlet, is the informal headquarters spot of a dozen or so men who divide their attention among the machine, the children they are in charge of, their cans of beer, each other's comments and the greetings of passers-by. Strangers stop, as they wish, to join the viewing. Nobody is concerned about peril to the machines. Yet Constable's skepticism about their safety in the Parks Department's territories was amply justified. There speaks a man of experience who has presided over many, many unpopular, dangerous and ill-used parks, along with a few good ones.

Too much is expected of city parks. Far from transforming any essential quality in their surroundings, far from automatically uplifting their neighborhoods, neighborhood parks themselves are directly and drastically affected by the way the neighborhood acts upon them.

Cities are thoroughly physical places. In seeking understanding of their behavior, we get useful information by observing what occurs tangibly and physically, instead of sailing off on metaphysical fancies. Penn's three squares in Philadelphia are three ordinary, bread-and-butter types of city parks. Let us see what they tell us about their ordinary physical interactions with their neighborhoods.

Rittenhouse Square, the success, possesses a diverse

rim and diverse neighborhood hinterland. Immediately on its edges it has in sequence, as this is written, an art club with restaurant and galleries, a music school, an Army office building, an apartment house, a club, an old apothecary shop, a Navy office building which used to be a hotel, apartments, a church, a parochial school, apartments, a public-library branch, apartments, a vacant site where town houses have been torn down for prospective apartments, a cultural society, apartments, a vacant site where a town house is planned, another town house, apartments. Immediately beyond the rim, in the streets leading off at right angles and in the next streets parallel to the park sides, is an abundance of shops and services of all sorts with old houses or newer apartments above, mingled with a variety of offices.

Does anything about this physical arrangement of the neighborhood affect the park physically? Yes. This mixture of uses of buildings directly produces for the park a mixture of users who enter and leave the park at different times. They use the park at different times from one another because their daily schedules differ. The park thus possesses an intricate sequence of uses and users.

Joseph Guess, a Philadelphia newspaperman who lives at Rittenhouse Square and has amused himself by watching its ballet, says it has this sequence: "First, a few early-bird walkers who live beside the park take brisk strolls. They are shortly joined, and followed, by residents who cross the park on their way to work out of the district. Next come people from outside the district, crossing the park on their way to work within the neighborhood. Soon after these people have left the square the errand-goers start to come through, many of them lingering, and in mid-morning mothers and small children come in, along with an increasing number of shoppers. Before noon the mothers and children leave, but the square's population continues to grow because of employees on their lunch hour and also because of people coming from elsewhere to lunch at the art club and the other restaurants around. In the afternoon mothers and children turn up again, the shoppers and errand-goers linger longer, and school children eventually add themselves in. In the later afternoon the mothers have left but the homeward-bound workers come through—first those leaving the neighborhood, and then those returning to it. Some of these linger. From then on into the evening the square gets many young people on dates, some who are dining out nearby, some who live nearby, some who seem to come just because of the nice combination of liveliness and leisure. All through the day, there is a sprinkling of old people with time on their hands, some people who are indigent, and various unidentified idlers."

In short, Rittenhouse Square is busy fairly continuously for the same basic reasons that a lively sidewalk is used continuously: because of functional physical diversity among adjacent uses, and hence diversity among users and their schedules.

Philadelphia's Washington Square—the one that became a pervert park—affords an extreme contrast in this respect. Its rim is dominated by huge office buildings, and both this rim and its immediate hinterland lack any equivalent to the diversity of Rittenhouse Square—services, restaurants, cultural facilities. The neighborhood hinterland possesses a low density of dwellings.

Washington Square thus has had in recent decades only one significant reservoir of potential local users: the office workers.

Does anything about this fact affect the park physically? Yes. This principal reservoir of users all operate on much the same daily time schedule. They all enter the district at once. They are then incarcerated all morning until lunch, and incarcerated again after lunch. They are absent after working hours. Therefore, Washington Square, of necessity, is a vacuum most of the day and evening. Into it came what usually fills city vacuums—a form of blight.

Here it is necessary to take issue with a common belief about cities—the belief that uses of low status drive out uses of high status. This is not how cities behave, and the belief that it is (Fight Blight!) renders futile much energy aimed at attacking symptoms and ignoring causes. People or uses with more money at their command, or greater respectability (in a credit society the two often go together), can fairly easily supplant those less prosperous or of less status, and commonly do so in city neighborhoods that achieve popularity. The reverse seldom happens. People or uses with less money at their command, less choice or less open respectability move into already weakened areas of cities, neighborhoods that are no longer coveted by people with the luxury of choice, or neighborhoods that can draw for financing only upon hot money, exploitative money and loan-shark money. The newcomers thereupon must try to make do with something which, for one reason or another, or more typically for a complexity of reasons, has already failed to sustain popularity. Overcrowding, deterioration, crime, and other forms of blight are surface symptoms of prior and deeper economic and functional failure of the district.

The perverts who completely took over Philadelphia's Washington Square for several decades were a manifestation of this city behavior, in microcosm. They did not kill off a vital and appreciated park. They did not drive out respectable users. They moved into an abandoned place and entrenched themselves. As this is written, the unwelcome users have successfully been chased away to find other vacuums, but this act has still not supplied the park with a sufficient sequence of welcome users.

Far in the past, Washington Square did have a good population of users. But although it is still the "same" park, its use and essence changed completely when its surroundings changed. Like all neighborhood parks, it is the creature of its surroundings *and of the way its surroundings generate mutual support from diverse uses, or fail to generate such support.*

It need not have been office work that depopulated this park. Any single, overwhelmingly dominant use imposing a limited schedule of users would have had a similar effect. The same basic situation occurs in parks where residence is the overwhelmingly dominant neighborhood use. In this case, the single big daily potential reservoir of adult users is mothers. City parks or playgrounds cannot be continuously populated by mothers alone, any more than by office workers alone. Mothers, using a park in their own relatively simple sequences, can populate it significantly for about a maximum of five hours, roughly two hours in the morning and three in the afternoon, and that only if they comprise a mixture of classes.* Mothers' daily tenure of parks is not only relatively brief but is circumscribed in choice of time by meals, housework, children's naps and, very sensitively, by weather.

A generalized neighborhood park that is stuck with functional monotony of surroundings in any form is inexorably a vacuum for a significant part of the day. And here a vicious circle takes over. Even if the vacuum is protected against various forms of blight, it exerts little attraction for its limited potential reservoir of users. It comes to bore them dreadfully, for moribundity is boring. In cities, liveliness and variety attract more liveliness; deadness and monotony repel life. And this is a principle vital not only to the ways cities behave socially, but also to the ways they behave economically.

There is, however, one important exception to the rule that it takes a wide functional mixture of users to populate and enliven neighborhood park through the day. There is one group in cities which, all by itself, can enjoy and populate a park long and well—although it seldom draws other types of users. This is the group of people with total leisure, the people who lack even the responsibilities of home, and in Philadelphia these are the people of Penn's third park, Franklin Square, the Skid Row park.

There is much distaste for Skid Row parks, which is

*Blue-collar families, for example, eat supper earlier than white-collar families because the working day of the husbands, if they are on a day shift, starts and ends earlier. Thus in the playground near where I live, mothers in blue-collar families leave before four; mothers in white-collar families come in later and leave before five.

natural because human failure in such undiluted doses is hard to swallow. Customarily, too, little distinction is drawn between these and criminal parks, although they are quite different. (With time, of course, one may become the other, just as in the case of Franklin Square, an originally residential park that eventually turned into a Skid Row park after the park and its neighborhood had lost their appeal to people with choice.)

A good Skid Row park like Franklin Square has something to be said for it. Supply and demand have come together for once, and the accident is clearly appreciated among those who have been disinherited by themselves or circumstance. In Franklin Square, if the weather permits, a day-long outdoor reception holds sway. The benches at the center of the reception are filled, with a voluble standing overflow milling about. Conversational groups continually form and dissolve into one another. The guests behave respectfully to one another and are courteous to interlopers too. Almost imperceptibly, like the hand of a clock, this raggle-taggle reception creeps around the circular pool at the center of the square. And indeed, it is the hand of a clock, for it is following the sun, staying in the warmth. When the sun goes down the clock stops; the reception is over until tomorrow.*

Not all cities have well-developed Skid Row parks. New York lacks one, for example, although it has many small park fragments and playgrounds used primarily by bums, and the vicious Sara Delano Roosevelt park gets a

---

*This is not where you find drunks lying around with bottles in the morning. They are more apt to be in the city's grand Independence Mall, a new vacuum uninhabited by any recognizable form of society, even Skid Row.

lot of bums. Possibly America's biggest Skid Row park—its population vast compared with Franklin Square—is the main downtown park of Los Angeles, Pershing Square. This tells us something interesting about its surroundings too. So spattered and decentralized are the central functions of Los Angeles that the only element of its downtown that has full metropolitan dimensions and intensity is that of the leisured indigent. Pershing Square is more like a forum than a reception, a forum composed of scores of panel discussions, each with its leading monologist or moderator. The confabs extend all around the periphery of the square, where the benches and walls are, and rise to crescendos at the corners. Some benches are stenciled "Reserved for Ladies" and this nicety is observed. Los Angeles is fortunate that the vacuum of a disintegrated downtown has not been appropriated by predators but has been relatively respectably populated by a flourishing Skid Row.

But we can hardly count on polite Skid Rows to save all the unpopular parks of our cities. A generalized neighborhood park that is not headquarters for the leisured indigent can become populated naturally and casually only by being situated very close indeed to where active and different currents of life and function come to a focus. If downtown, it must get shoppers, visitors and strollers as well as downtown workers. If not downtown, it must still be where life swirls—where there is work, cultural, residential and commercial activity—as much as possible of everything different that cities can offer. The main problem of neighborhood park planning boils down to the problem of nurturing diversified neighborhoods capable of using and supporting parks.

However, many city districts do already possess precisely such ignored focal points of life which cry out for close-by neighborhood parks or public squares. It is easy to identify such centers of district life and activity, because they are where people with leaflets to hand out choose to work (if permitted by the police).

But there is no point in bringing parks to where the people are, if in the process the *reasons* that the people are there are wiped out and the park *substituted* for them. This is one of the basic errors in housing-project and civic- and cultural-center design. Neighborhood parks fail to substitute in any way for plentiful city diversity. Those that are successful never serve as barriers or as interruptions to the intricate functioning of the city around them. Rather, they help to knit together diverse surrounding functions by giving them a pleasant joint facility; in the process they add another appreciated element to the diversity and give something back to their surroundings, as Rittenhouse Square or any other good park gives back.

You can neither lie to a neighborhood park, nor reason with it. "Artist's conceptions" and persuasive renderings can put *pictures* of life into proposed neighborhood parks or park malls, and verbal rationalizations can conjure up users who ought to appreciate them, but in real life only diverse surroundings have the practical power of inducing a natural, continuing flow of life and use. Superficial architectural variety may look like diversity, but only a genuine content of economic and social diversity, resulting in people with different schedules, has meaning to the park and the power to confer the boon of life upon it.

Given good location, a bread-and-butter neighborhood park can make much of its assets, but it can also fritter them away. It is obvious that a place that looks like a jail yard will neither attract users nor reciprocate with its surroundings in the same fashion as a place that looks like an oasis. But there are all kinds of oases too, and some of their salient characteristics for success are not so obvious.

Outstandingly successful neighborhood parks seldom have much competition from other open spaces. This is understandable, because people in cities, with all their other interests and duties, can hardly enliven unlimited amounts of local, generalized park. City people would have to devote themselves to park use as if it were a business (or as the leisured indigent do) to justify, for example, the plethora of malls, promenades, playgrounds, parks and indeterminate land oozes afforded in typical Radiant Garden City schemes, and enforced in official urban rebuilding by stringent requirements that high percentages of land be left open.

We can already see that city districts with relatively large amounts of generalized park, like Morningside Heights or Harlem in New York, seldom develop intense community focus on a park and intense love for it, such as the people of Boston's North End have for their little Prado or the people of Greenwich Village have for Washington Square, or the people of the Rittenhouse Square district have for their park. Greatly loved neighborhood parks benefit from a certain rarity value.

The ability of a neighborhood park to stimulate passionate attachment or, conversely, only apathy, seems to have little or nothing to do with the incomes or occupations of a population in a district. This is an inference which can be drawn from the widely differing income, occupational and cultural groups who are simultaneously deeply attached to a park like New York's Washington Square. The relationship of differing income classes to given parks can also sometimes be observed in sequence over time, either positively or negatively. Over the years, the economic condition of people in Boston's North End has risen appreciably. Both in time of poverty and in time of prosperity, the Prado, a minute but central park, has been the heart of the neighborhood. Harlem in New York affords an illustration of consistent reverse behavior. Over the course of years Harlem has changed from a fashionable upper-middle-class residential district, to a lower-middle-class district, to a district predominantly of the poor and the discriminated against. During all this sequence of different populations, Harlem, with a wealth of local parks as compared to Greenwich Village, for example, has never seen a period in which one of its parks was a vital focus of community life and identity. The same sad observation can be made of Morningside Heights. And it is also true typically of project grounds, even including those carefully designed.

This inability of a neighborhood or district to attach itself with affection—and with the immense resulting power of symbolism—to a neighborhood park is due, I think, to a combination of negative factors: first, parks that are possible candidates are handicapped because of insufficient diversity in their immediate surroundings, and consequent dullness; and second, what diversity and life are available are dispersed and dissipated among too many different parks, too similar in purpose to each other.

Certain qualities in design can apparently make a difference too. For if the object of a generalized bread-and-butter neighborhood park is to attract as many different kinds of people, with as many different schedules, interests, and purposes as possible, it is clear that the design of the park should abet this generalization of patronage rather than work at cross-purposes to it. Parks intensely used in generalized public-yard fashion tend to have four elements in their design which I shall call intricacy, centering, sun and enclosure.

Intricacy is related to the variety of reasons for which people come to neighborhood parks. Even the same person comes for different reasons at different times; sometimes to sit tiredly, sometimes to play or to watch a game, sometimes to read or work, sometimes to show off, sometimes to fall in love, sometimes to keep an appointment, sometimes to savor the hustle of the city from a retreat, sometimes in the hope of finding acquaintances, sometimes to get closer to a bit of nature, sometimes to keep a child occupied, sometimes simply to see what offers, and almost always to be entertained by the sight of other people.

If the whole thing can be absorbed in a glance, like a good poster, and if every place looks like every other place in the park and also feels like every other place when you try it, the park affords little stimulation to all these differing uses and moods. Nor is there much reason to return to it again and again.

An intelligent and able woman who lives beside Rittenhouse Square remarks, "I've used it almost every day for fifteen years, but the other night I tried to draw a plan of it from memory and couldn't. It was too complicated for me." The same phenomenon is true of Washington Square in New York. In the course of a community battle to protect it from a highway, the strategists frequently tried to sketch the park roughly during meetings, to illustrate a point. Very difficult.

Yet neither of these parks is so complex in plan as all that. Intricacy that counts is mainly intricacy at eye level, change in the rise of ground, groupings of trees, openings leading to various focal points—in short, subtle expressions of difference. The subtle differences in setting are then exaggerated by the differences in use that grow up among them. Successful parks always look much more intricate in use than when they are empty.

Even very small squares that are successful often get ingenious variation into the stage sets they provide for their users. Rockefeller Center does it by making drama out of four changes in level. Union Square in downtown San Francisco has a plan that looks deadly dull on paper or from a high building; but it is bent onto such changes in ground level, like Dali's painting of the wet watches, that it appears remarkably various. (This is, of course, exactly the transformation that happens, on a larger scale, to San Francisco's straight, regular gridiron street patterns as they tumble up and down the hills.) Paper plans of squares and parks are deceptive—sometimes they are crammed full of apparent differences that mean almost nothing because they are all below eye level, or are discounted by the eye because they are too often repeated.

Probably the most important element in intricacy is centering. Good small parks typically have a place somewhere within them commonly understood to be the center—at the very least a main crossroads and pausing point, a climax. Some small parks or squares are virtually all center, and get their intricacy from minor differences at their peripheries.

People try hard to create centers and climaxes to a park, even against odds. Sometimes it is impossible. Long strip parks, like the dismally unsuccessful Sara Delano Roosevelt park in New York and many riverside parks, are frequently designed as if they were rolled out from a die stamper. Sara Delano Roosevelt park has four identical brick "recreation" barracks stamped along it at intervals. What can users make of this? The more they move back and forth, the more they are in the same place. It is like a trudge on a treadmill. This too is a common failing in project design, and almost unavoidable there, because most projects are essentially die-stamped design for die-stamped functions.

People can be inventive in their use of park centers. The fountain basin in New York's Washington Square is used inventively and exuberantly. Once, beyond memory, the basin possessed an ornamental iron centerpiece with a fountain. What remains is the sunken concrete circular basin, dry most of the year, bordered with four steps ascending to a stone coping that forms an outer rim a few feet above ground level. In effect, this is a circular arena, a theater in the round, and that is how it is used, with complete confusion as to who are spectators and who are the show. Everybody is both, although some are more so: guitar players, singers, crowds of darting children, impromptu dancers, sunbathers, conversers, show-offs, photographers, tourists, and mixed in with them all a bewildering sprinkling of absorbed readers—not there for lack of choice, because quiet benches to the east are half-deserted.

The city officials regularly concoct improvement schemes by which this center within the park would be sown to grass and flowers and surrounded by a fence. The invariable phrase used to describe this is, "restoring the land to park use."

That is a different form of park use, legitimate in places. But for neighborhood parks, the finest centers are stage settings for people.

Sun is part of a park's setting for people, shaded, to be sure, in summer. A high building effectively cutting the sun angle across the south side of a park can kill off a lot of it. Rittenhouse Square, for all its virtues, has this misfortune. On a good October afternoon, for example, almost a third of the square lies completely empty; the great building shadow across it from a new apartment house is a great eraser of human beings within its pall.

Although buildings should not cut sun from a park—if the object is to encourage full use—the presence of buildings around a park is important in design. They enclose it. They make a definite shape out of the space, so that it appears as an important event in the city scene, a positive feature, rather than a no-account leftover. Far from being attracted by indefinite leftovers of land oozing around buildings, people behave as if repelled by them. They even cross streets as they meet up with them, a phenomenon that can be watched wherever a housing project, for example, breaks into a busy street. Richard Nelson, a Chicago real estate analyst who watches the behavior of people in cities as a clue to economic values, reports, "On a warm September afternoon, Mellon Square in downtown Pittsburgh contained too many users to count. But that same afternoon, during a period of two hours, only three people—one old lady knitting, one bum, one unidentifiable character asleep with a newspaper over his face—used the park of the downtown Gateway Center."

Gateway Center is a Radiant City office and hotel project with the buildings set here and there in empty land. It lacks the degree of diversity of Mellon Square's surroundings, but its diversity is not low enough to account for only four users (counting Nelson himself) during the heart of a good afternoon. City park users simply do not seek settings for buildings; they seek settings for themselves. To them, parks are foreground, buildings background, rather than the reverse.

Cities are full of generalized parks that can hardly be expected to justify themselves, even if their districts are successfully enlivened. This is because some parks are basically unfitted, whether by location, size or shape, to serve successfully in the public-yard fashion I have been discussing. Nor are they fitted by size or inherent variety of scene to become major metropolitan parks. What can be done with them?

Some of these, if sufficiently small, can do another job well: simply pleasing the eye. San Francisco is good at this. A tiny triangular street intersection leftover, which in most cities would either be flattened into asphalt or else have a hedge, a few benches and be a dusty nonentity, in San Francisco is a fenced miniature world of its own, a deep, cool world of water and exotic forest, populated by the birds that have been attracted. You cannot go in yourself. You do not need to, because your eyes go in and take you farther into this world than feet could

ever go. San Francisco gives an impression of much ver-
dure and relief from city stoniness. Yet San Francisco is
a crowded city and little ground is used to convey this
impression. The effect arises mainly from small bits of
intensive cultivation, and it is multiplied because so
much of San Francisco's greenery is vertical—window
boxes, trees, vines, thick ground cover on little patches
of "waste" slopes.

Gramercy Park in New York overcomes an awkward
situation by pleasing the eye. This park happens to be a
fenced private yard in a public place; the property goes
with the residential buildings across the surrounding
streets. It must be entered with a key. Since it is blessed
with splendid trees, excellent maintenance and an air of
glamor, it successfully provides for the passing public a
place to please the eye, and so far as the public is concerned this is its justification.

But parks primarily to please the eye, uncombined
with other uses, are by definition where eyes will see
them; and again by definition they are best small because
to do their job well they must do it beautifully and intensively, not perfunctorily.

The worst problem parks are located precisely where
people do not pass by and likely never will. A city park
in this fix, afflicted (for in such cases it is an affliction)
with a good-sized terrain, is figuratively in the same position as a large store in a bad economic location. If such a
store can be rescued and justified, it will be by dint of
heavy concentration on what merchants call "demand
goods" instead of reliance on "impulse sales." If the
demand goods do bring enough customers, a certain
gravy from impulse sales may follow.

From the standpoint of a park, what is demand goods?

We can get some hints by looking at a few such problem parks. Jefferson Park in East Harlem is an example. It consists of a number of parts, the ostensibly principal one intended for general neighborhood use—equivalent to impulse sales in merchandising vocabulary. But everything about it thwarts this purpose. Its location is at the far edge of its community, bounded on one side by the river. It is further isolated by a wide, heavy traffic street. Its internal planning runs largely to long, isolated walks without effective centers. To an outsider it looks weirdly deserted; to insiders, it is a focus of neighborhood conflict, violence and fear. Since a brutal evening murder of a visitor by teen-agers in 1958, it has been more than ever shunned and avoided.

However, among Jefferson Park's several separate sections, one does redeem itself handsomely. This is a big outdoor swimming pool, obviously not big enough. Sometimes it contains more people than water.

Consider Corlears Hook, the portion of the East River parklands where I could find only eighteen people amid the lawns and benches on a good day. Corlears Hook possesses, off to a side, a ball field, nothing special, and yet on that same day most of the park's life, such as it was, was in the ball field. Corlears Hook also contains, among its meaningless acres of lawns, a band shell. Six times a year, on summer evenings, thousands of people from the Lower East Side pour into the park to hear a concert series. For a total of some eighteen hours in the year, Corlears Hook park comes alive and is vastly enjoyed.

Here we see demand goods operating, although obviously too limited in quantity and too desultory in time. It is clear, however, that people do come to these parks for certain special demand goods, although they simply do not come for generalized or impulse park use. In short, if a generalized city park cannot be supported by uses arising from natural, nearby intense diversity, it must convert from a generalized park to a specialized park. Effective diversity of use, drawing deliberately a sequence of diversified users, must be deliberately introduced into the park itself.

Only experience and trial and error can indicate what diverse combinations of activities can operate effectively as demand goods for any specific problem park. But we can make some useful generalized guesses about components. First, a negative generalization: Magnificent views and handsome landscaping fail to operate as demand goods; maybe these "should," but demonstrably they do not. They can work as adjuncts only.

On the other hand, swimming operates as demand goods. So does fishing, especially if there is bait buying and boating along with it. Sports fields do. So do carnivals, or carnival-like activities.*

*   *   *

*Dr. Karl Menninger, director of the Menninger Psychiatric Clinic of Topeka, addressing a meeting devoted to city problems, in 1958, discussed the types of activities that appear to combat the will to destruction. He listed these as (1) plentiful contacts with plenty of other people; (2) work, including even drudgery; and (3) violent play. It is Menninger's belief that cities afford disastrously little opportunity for violent play. The types he singled out as having proved useful were active outdoor sports, bowling and shooting galleries like those found in carnivals and amusement parks but only occasionally (Times Square, for instance) in cities.

Music (including recorded music) and plays also serve as demand goods. It is curious that relatively little is done with these in parks, because the casual introduction of cultural life is part of the historic mission of cities. It is a mission that can still operate full force, as the *New Yorker* indicated in this comment on the free Shakespeare season of 1958 in Central Park:

> The ambiance, the weather, the color and lights, and simple curiosity brought them out; some had never seen any sort of play in the flesh. Hundreds came back again and again; a fellow we know says he met a group of Negro children who told him they had been to *Romeo and Juliet* five times. The lives of a lot of these converts have been enlarged and enriched; so has the audience for the American theater of the future. But spectators like them, new to the theater, are the very ones who won't show up, a dollar or two dollars in hand, to pay for an experience that they do not even know to be pleasant.

This suggests, for one thing, that universities with drama departments (and, so often, with dead, problem parks in their vicinities) might try putting two and two together, rather than cultivating hostile policies of defended Turf. Columbia University in New York is taking a constructive step by planning sports facilities—for both the university and the neighborhood—in Morningside Park, which has been shunned and feared for decades. Adding a few other activities too, like music or shows, could convert a dreadful neighborhood liability into an outstanding neighborhood asset.

Cities lack minor park activities that could serve as

minor "demand goods." Some are discoverable by observation of what people try to do if they can get away with it. For instance, the manager of a shopping center near Montreal found his ornamental pool mysteriously filthy every morning. Spying after closing hours he found that children were sneaking in and washing and polishing their bikes there. Places to wash bikes (where people have bikes), places to hire and to ride bikes, places to dig in the ground, places to build ramshackle wigwams and huts out of old lumber, are activities usually crowded out of cities. The Puerto Ricans who come to our cities today have no place to roast pigs outdoors unless they can find a private yard for the purpose, but outdoor pig roasts and the parties that follow can be as much fun as the Italian street festivals many city dwellers have learned to love. Kite flying is a minor activity but there are those who love it, and it suggests kite-flying places where materials for making kites are sold too, and where there are terraces on which to work at them. Ice skating used to be enjoyed on many ponds within northern cities until it was crowded out. Fifth Avenue in New York used to have five fashionable skating ponds between Thirty-first and Ninety-eighth streets, one only four blocks from the present rink at Rockefeller Plaza. Artificial rinks have permitted the rediscovery of city ice skating in our time, and in cities at the latitudes of New York, Cleveland, Detroit and Chicago artificial rinks extend the skating season to include almost half the year. Every city district could probably enjoy and use an outdoor park ice rink if it had one, and provide a population of entranced watchers too. Indeed, relatively small rinks placed at more numerous locations are much more civilized and pleasant than huge centralized rinks.

All this takes money. But American cities today, under the illusions that open land is an automatic good and that quantity is equivalent to quality, are instead frittering away money on parks, playgrounds and project land-oozes too large, too frequent, too perfunctory, too ill-located, and hence too dull or too inconvenient to be used.

City parks are not abstractions, or automatic repositories of virtue or uplift, any more than sidewalks are abstractions. They mean nothing divorced from their practical, tangible uses, and hence they mean nothing divorced from the tangible effects on them—for good or for ill—of the city districts and uses touching them.

Generalized parks can and do add great attraction to neighborhoods that people find attractive for a great variety of other uses. They further depress neighborhoods that people find unattractive for a wide variety of other uses, for they exaggerate the dullness, the danger, the emptiness. The more successfully a city mingles everyday diversity of uses and users in its everyday streets, the more successfully, casually (and economically) its people thereby enliven and support well-located parks that can thus give back grace and delight to their neighborhoods instead of vacuity.

6

THE USES OF
CITY NEIGHBORHOODS

Neighborhood is a word that has come to sound like a
Valentine. As a sentimental concept, "neighborhood" is
harmful to city planning. It leads to attempts at warping
city life into imitations of town or suburban life. Sentimentality plays with sweet intentions in place of good
sense.

A successful city neighborhood is a place that keeps
sufficiently abreast of its problems so it is not destroyed
by them. An unsuccessful neighborhood is a place that is
overwhelmed by its defects and problems and is progressively more helpless before them. Our cities contain all
degrees of success and failure. But on the whole we
Americans are poor at handling city neighborhoods, as
can be seen by the long accumulations of failures in our
great gray belts on the one hand, and by the Turfs of
rebuilt city on the other hand.

It is fashionable to suppose that certain touchstones of
the good life will create good neighborhoods—schools,
parks, clean housing and the like. How easy life would
be if this were so! How charming to control a complicated
and ornery society by bestowing upon it rather simple
physical goodies. In real life, cause and effect are not so
simple. Thus a Pittsburgh study, undertaken to show the
supposed clear correlation between better housing and

improved social conditions, compared delinquency records in still uncleared slums to delinquency records in new housing projects, and came to the embarrassing discovery that the delinquency was higher in the improved housing. Does this mean improved shelter increases delinquency? Not at all. It means other things may be more important than housing, however, and it means also that there is no direct, simple relationship between good housing and good behavior, a fact which the whole tale of the Western world's history, the whole collection of our literature, and the whole fund of observation open to any of us should long since have made evident. Good shelter is a useful good in itself, as shelter. When we try to justify good shelter instead on the pretentious grounds that it will work social or family miracles we fool ourselves. Reinhold Niebuhr has called this particular self-deception, "The doctrine of salvation by bricks."

It is even the same with schools. Important as good schools are, they prove totally undependable at rescuing bad neighborhoods and at creating good neighborhoods. Nor does a good school building guarantee a good education. Schools, like parks, are apt to be volatile creatures of their neighborhoods (as well as being creatures of larger policy). In bad neighborhoods, schools are brought to ruination, physically and socially; while successful neighborhoods improve their schools by fighting for them.*

Nor can we conclude, either, that middle-class fami-

---

* In the Upper West Side of Manhattan, a badly failed area where social disintegration has been compounded by ruthless bulldozing, project building and shoving people around, annual pupil turnover in schools

lies or upper-class families build good neighborhoods, and poor families fail to. For example, within the poverty of the North End in Boston, within the poverty of the West Greenwich Village waterfront neighborhoods, within the poverty of the slaughterhouse district in Chicago (three areas, incidentally, that were all written off as hopeless by their cities' planners), good neighborhoods were created: neighborhoods whose internal problems have grown less with time instead of greater. Meantime, within the once upper-class grace and serenity of Baltimore's beautiful Eutaw Place, within the one-time upper-class solidity of Boston's South End, within the culturally privileged purlieus of New York's Morningside Heights, within miles upon miles of dull, respectable middle-class gray area, bad neighborhoods were created, neighborhoods whose apathy and internal failure grew greater with time instead of less.

To hunt for city neighborhood touchstones of success in high standards of physical facilities, or in supposedly competent and nonproblem populations, or in nostalgic memories of town life, is a waste of time. It evades the meat of the question, which is the problem of what city neighborhoods do, if anything, that may be socially and economically useful in cities themselves, and how they do it.

---

was more than 50 percent in 1959-60. In 16 schools, it reached an average of 92 percent. It is ludicrous to think that with any amount of effort, official or unofficial, even a tolerable school is possible in a neighborhood of such extreme instability. Good schools are impossible in any unstable neighborhoods with high pupil turnover rates, and this includes unstable neighborhoods which *also* have good housing.

We shall have something solid to chew on if we think of city neighborhoods as mundane organs of self-government. Our failures with city neighborhoods are, ultimately, failures in localized self-government. And our successes are successes at localized self-government. I am using self-government in its broadest sense, meaning both the informal and formal self-management of society.

Both the demands on self-government and the techniques for it differ in big cities from the demands and techniques in smaller places. For instance, there is the problem of all those strangers. To think of city neighborhoods as organs of city self-government or self-management, we must first jettison some orthodox but irrelevant notions about neighborhoods which may apply to communities in smaller settlements but not in cities. We must first of all drop any ideal of neighborhoods as self-contained or introverted units.

Unfortunately orthodox planning theory is deeply committed to the ideal of supposedly cozy, inward-turned city neighborhoods. In its pure form, the ideal is a neighborhood composed of about 7,000 persons, a unit supposedly of sufficient size to populate an elementary school and to support convenience shopping and a community center. This unit is then further rationalized into smaller groupings of a size scaled to the play and supposed management of children and the chitchat of housewives. Although the "ideal" is seldom literally reproduced, it is the point of departure for nearly all neighborhood renewal plans, for all project building, for much modern zoning, and also for the practice work done by today's architectural-planning students, who will be inflicting their adaptations of it on cities tomorrow. In New York City alone, by 1959, more than half a million people were already living in adaptations of this vision of planned neighborhoods. This "ideal" of the city neighborhood as an island, turned inward on itself, is an important factor in our lives nowadays.

To see why it is a silly and even harmful "ideal" for cities, we must recognize a basic difference between these concoctions grafted into cities, and town life. In a town of 5,000 or 10,000 population, if you go to Main Street (analogous to the consolidated commercial facilities or community center for a planned neighborhood), you run into people you also know at work, or went to school with, or see at church, or people who are your children's teachers, or who have sold or given you professional or artisan's services, or whom you know to be friends of your casual acquaintances, or whom you know by reputation. Within the limits of a town or village, the connections among its people keep crossing and recrossing and this can make workable and essentially cohesive communities out of even larger towns than those of 7,000 population, and to some extent out of little cities.

But a population of 5,000 or 10,000 residents in a big city has no such innate degree of natural cross-connections within itself, except under the most extraordinary circumstances. Nor can city neighborhood planning, no matter how cozy in intent, change this fact. If it could, the price would be destruction of a city by converting it into a parcel of towns. As it is, the price of trying, and not even succeeding at a misguided aim is conversion of a city into a parcel of mutually suspicious and hostile

Turfs. There are many other flaws in this "ideal" of the planned neighborhood and its various adaptations.*

Lately a few planners, notably Reginald Isaacs of Harvard, have daringly begun to question whether the conception of neighborhood in big cities has any meaning at all. Isaacs points out that city people are mobile. They can and do pick and choose from the entire city (and beyond) for everything from a job, a dentist, recreation, or friends, to shops, entertainment, or even in some cases their children's schools. City people, says Isaacs, are not stuck with the provincialism of a neighborhood, and why should they be? Isn't wide choice and rich opportunity the point of cities?

This is indeed the point of cities. Furthermore, this very fluidity of use and choice among city people is precisely the foundation underlying most city cultural activ-

---

*Even the old reason for settling on an ideal population of about 7,000—sufficient to populate an elementary school—is silly the moment it is applied to big cities, as we discover if we merely ask the question: Which school? In many American cities, parochial-school enrollment rivals or surpasses public-school enrollment. Does this mean there should be two schools as presumed neighborhood glue, and the population should be twice as large? Or is the population right, and should the schools be half as large? And why the elementary school? If school is to be the touchstone of scale, why not the junior high school, an institution typically far more troublesome in our cities than the elementary school? The question "Which school?" is never asked because this vision is based on no more realism about schools than about anything else. The school is a plausible, and usually abstract, excuse for defining *some* size for a unit that comes out of dreams about imaginary cities. It is necessary as a formal framework, to preserve designers from intellectual chaos, and it has no other reason for being. Ebenezer Howard's model towns are the ancestors of the idea, to be sure, but its durability comes from the need to fill an intellectual vacuum.

ities and special enterprises of all kinds. Because these can draw skills, materials, customers or clienteles from a great pool, they can exist in extraordinary variety, and not only downtown but in other city districts that develop specialties and characters of their own. And in drawing upon the great pool of the city in this way, city enterprises increase, in turn, the choices available to city people for jobs, goods, entertainment, ideas, contacts, services.

Whatever city neighborhoods may be, or may not be, and whatever usefulness they may have, or may be coaxed into having, their qualities cannot work at cross-purposes to thoroughgoing city mobility and fluidity of *use*, without economically weakening the city of which they are a part. The lack of either economic or social self-containment is natural and necessary to city neighborhoods—simply because they are parts of cities. Isaacs is right when he implies that the conception of neighborhood in cities is meaningless—so long as we think of neighborhoods as being self-contained units to any significant degree, modeled upon town neighborhoods.

But for all the innate extroversion of city neighborhoods, it fails to follow that city people can therefore get along magically without neighborhoods. Even the most urbane citizen does care about the atmosphere of the street and district where he lives, no matter how much choice he has of pursuits outside it; and the common run of city people do depend greatly on their neighborhoods for the kind of everyday lives they lead.

Let us assume (as is often the case) that city neighbors have nothing more fundamental in common with each other than that they share a fragment of geography. Even so, if they fail at managing that fragment decently, the fragment will fail. There exists no inconceivably energetic and all-wise "They" to take over and substitute for localized self-management. Neighborhoods in cities need not supply for their people an artificial town or village life, and to aim at this is both silly and destructive. But neighborhoods in cities do need to supply some means for civilized self-government. This is the problem.

Looking at city neighborhoods as organs of self-government, I can see evidence that only three kinds of neighborhoods are useful: (1) the city as a whole; (2) street neighborhoods; (and 3) districts of large, subcity size, composed of 100,000 people or more in the case of the largest cities.

Each of these kinds of neighborhoods has different functions, but the three supplement each other in complex fashion. It is impossible to say that one is more important than the others. For success with staying power at any spot, all three are necessary. But I think that other neighborhoods than these three kinds just get in the way, and make successful self-government difficult or impossible.

The most obvious of the three, although it is seldom called a neighborhood, is the city as a whole. We must never forget or minimize this parent community while thinking of a city's smaller parts. This is the source from which most public money flows, even when it comes ultimately from the federal or state coffers. This is where most administrative and policy decisions are made, for good or ill. This is where general welfare often comes into direst conflict, open or hidden, with illegal or other destructive interests.

Moreover, up on this plane we find vital special-interest communities and pressure groups. The neighbor-hood of the entire city is where people especially inter-ested in the theater or in music or in other arts find one another and get together, no matter where they may live. This is where people immersed in specific professions or businesses or concerned about particular problems exchange ideas and sometimes start action. Professor P. Sargant Florence, a British specialist on urban economics, has written,"My own experience is that, apart from the special habitat of intellectuals like Oxford or Cambridge, a city of a million is required to give me, say, the twenty or thirty congenial friends I require!" This sounds rather snooty, to be sure, but Professor Florence has an impor-tant truth here. Presumably he likes his friends to know what he is talking about. When William Kirk of Union Settlement, and Helen Hall of Henry Street Settlement, miles apart in New York City, get together with *Con-sumers' Union,* a magazine located still other miles away, and with researchers from Columbia University, and with the trustees of a foundation, to consider the personal and community ruin wrought by loan shark–installment ped-dlers in low-income projects, they know what each is talk-ing about and, what is more, can put their peculiar kinds of knowledge together with a special kind of money to learn more about the trouble and find ways to fight it. When my sister, Betty, a housewife, helps devise a scheme in the Manhattan public school which one of her children attends, whereby parents who know English give homework help to the children of parents who do not, and the scheme works, this knowledge filters into a special-interest neighborhood of the city as a whole; as a result, one evening Betty finds herself away over in the

Bedford-Stuyvesant section of Brooklyn, telling a district group of ten P-TA presidents there how the scheme works, and learning some new things herself.

A city's very wholeness in bringing together people with communities of interest is one of its greatest assets, possibly the greatest. And, in turn, one of the assets a city district needs is people with access to the political, the administrative, and the special-interest communities of the city as a whole.

In most big cities, we Americans do reasonably well at creating useful neighborhoods belonging to the whole city. People with similar and supplementing interests do find each other fairly well. Indeed, they typically do so most efficiently in the largest cities (except for Los Angeles which does miserably at this, and Boston which is pretty pathetic). Moreover, big-city governments, as Seymour Freedgood of *Fortune* magazine so well documented in *The Exploding Metropolis,* are able and energetic at the top in many instances, more so than one would surmise from looking at social and economic affairs in the endless failed neighborhoods of the same cities. Whatever our disastrous weakness may be, it is hardly sheer incapability for forming neighborhoods at the top, out of cities as a whole.

At the other end of the scale are a city's streets, and the minuscule neighborhoods they form, like our neighborhood of Hudson Street for example.

In the first several chapters of this book I have dwelt heavily upon the self-government functions of city streets: to weave webs of public surveillance and thus to protect strangers as well as themselves; to grow networks of small-scale, everyday public life and thus of trust and social control, and to help assimilate children into reasonably responsible and tolerant city life.

The street neighborhoods of a city have still another function in self-government, however, and a vital one: they must draw effectively on help when trouble comes along that is too big for the street to handle. This help must sometimes come from the city as a whole, at the other end of the scale. This is a loose end I shall leave hanging, but ask you to remember.

The self-government functions of streets are all humble, but they are indispensable. In spite of much experiment, planned and unplanned, there exists no substitute for lively streets.

How large is a city street neighborhood that functions capably? If we look at successful street-neighborhood networks in real life, we find this is a meaningless question, because wherever they work best, street neighborhoods have no beginnings and ends setting them apart as distinct units. The size even differs for different people from the same spot, because some people range farther, or hang around more, or extend their street acquaintance farther than others. Indeed, a great part of the success of these neighborhoods of the streets depends on their overlapping and interweaving, turning the corners. This is one means by which they become capable of economic and visual variation for their users. Residential Park Avenue in New York appears to be an extreme example of neighborhood monotony, and so it would be if it were an isolated strip of street neighborhood. But the street neighborhood of a Park Avenue resident only begins on Park, quickly turns a corner off it, and then another corner. It is part of a set of interweaving neighborhoods containing great diversity, not a strip.

Isolated street neighborhoods that do have definite boundaries can be found in plenty, to be sure. They are typically associated with long blocks (and hence with infrequent streets), because long blocks tend almost always to be physically self-isolating. Distinctly separate street neighborhoods are nothing to aim for; they are generally characteristic of failure. Describing the troubles of an area of long, monotonous, self-isolating blocks on Manhattan's West Side, Dr. Dan W. Dodson of New York University's Center for Human Relations Studies, notes: "Each [street] appears to be a separate world of its own with a separate culture. Many of those interviewed had no conception of the neighborhood other than the street on which they resided."

Summing up the incompetence of the area, Dr. Dodson comments, "The present state of the neighborhood indicates that the people there have lost the capacity for collective action, or else they would long since have pressured the city government and the social agencies into correcting some of the problems of community living." These two observations by Dr. Dodson on street isolation and incompetence are closely related.

Successful street neighborhoods, in short, are not discrete units. They are physical, social and economic continuities—small scale to be sure, but small scale in the sense that the lengths of fibers making up a rope are small scale.

Where our city streets do have sufficient frequency of commerce, general liveliness, use and interest, to cultivate continuities of public street life, we Americans do prove fairly capable at street self-government. This capability is most often noticed and commented on in districts of poor, or one-time poor people. But casual street neighborhoods, good at their functions, are also characteristic of high-income areas that maintain a persistent popularity—rather than ephemeral fashion—such as Manhattan's East Side from the Fifties to the Eighties, or the Rittenhouse Square district in Philadelphia, for example.

To be sure, our cities lack sufficient streets equipped for city life. We have too much area afflicted with the Great Blight of Dullness instead. But many, many city streets perform their humble jobs well and command loyalty too, unless and until they are destroyed by the impingement of city problems too big for them, or by neglect for too long a time of facilities that can be supplied only from the city as a whole, or by deliberate planning policies that the people of the neighborhood are too weak to defeat.

And here we come to the third kind of city neighborhood that is useful for self-government: the district. This, I think, is where we are typically most weak and fail most disastrously. We have plenty of city districts in name. We have few that function.

The chief function of a successful district is to mediate between the indispensable, but inherently politically powerless, street neighborhoods, and the inherently powerful city as a whole.

Among those responsible for cities, at the top, there is much ignorance. This is inescapable, because big cities are just too big and too complex to be comprehended in detail from any vantage point—even if this vantage point is at the top—or to be comprehended by any human; yet detail is of the essence. A district citizens' group from East Harlem, in anticipation of a meeting it had arranged with the Mayor and his commissioners, prepared a document recounting the devastation wrought in the district by remote decisions (most of them well meant, of course), and they added this comment: "We must state how often we find that those of us who live or work in East Harlem, coming into daily contact with it, see it quite differently from . . . the people who only ride through on their way to work, or read about it in their daily papers or, too often, we believe, make decisions about it from desks downtown." I have heard almost these same words in Boston, in Chicago, in Cincinnati, in St. Louis. It is a complaint that echoes and re-echoes in all our big cities.

Districts have to help bring the resources of a city down to where they are needed by street neighborhoods, and they have to help translate the experiences of real life, in street neighborhoods, into policies and purposes of their city as a whole. And they have to help maintain an area that is usable, in a civilized way, not only for its own residents but for other users—workers, customers, visitors—from the city as a whole.

To accomplish these functions, an effective district has to be large enough to count as a force in the life of the city as a whole. The "ideal" neighborhood of planning theory is useless for such a role. A district has to be big and powerful enough to fight city hall. Nothing less is to any purpose. To be sure, fighting city hall is not a district's only function, or necessarily the most important. Nevertheless, this is a good definition of size, in functional terms, because sometimes a district has to do exactly this, and also because a district lacking the power and will to fight city hall—and to win—when its people feel deeply threatened, is unlikely to possess the power and will to contend with other serious problems.

Let us go back to the street neighborhoods for a moment, and pick up a loose end I left dangling: the job, incumbent upon good street neighborhoods, to get help when too big a problem comes along.

Nothing is more helpless than a city street alone, when its problems exceed its powers. Consider, as an illustration, what happened with respect to a case of narcotics pushing on a street in uptown West Side Manhattan in 1955. The street on which this case occurred had residents who worked all over the city and had friends and acquaintances outside the street as well as on it. On the street itself they had a reasonably flourishing public life centered around the stoops, but they had no neighborhood stores and no regular public characters. They also had no connection with a district neighborhood; indeed, their area has no such thing, except in name.

When heroin began to be sold from one of the apartments, a stream of drug addicts filtered into the street—not to live, but to make their connections. They needed money to buy the drugs. An epidemic of holdups and robberies on the street was one answer. People became afraid to come home with their pay on Fridays. Sometimes at night terrible screaming terrorized the residents. They were ashamed to have friends visit them. Some of the adolescents on the street were addicts, and more were becoming so.

The residents, most of whom were conscientious and respectable, did what they could. They called the police many times. Some individuals took the initiative of finding that the responsible outfit to talk with was the Narcotics Squad. They told the detectives of the squad where the heroin was being sold, and by whom, and when, and what days supplies seemed to come.

Nothing happened except that things continued to get worse.

Nothing much ever happens when one helpless little street fights alone some of the most serious problems of a great city.

Had the police been bribed? How is anybody to know?

Lacking a district neighborhood, lacking knowledge of any other persons who cared about this problem in this place and could bring weight to bear on it, the residents had gone as far as they knew how to go. Why didn't they at least call their local assemblyman, or get in touch with the political club? Nobody on the street knew those people (an assemblyman has about 115,000 constituents) or knew anybody who did know them. In short, this street simply had no connections of any kind with a district neighborhood, let alone effective connections with an effective district neighborhood. Those on the street who could possibly manage it moved away when they saw that the street's situation was evidently hopeless. The street plunged into thorough chaos and barbarism.

New York had an able and energetic police commissioner during these events, but he could not be reached by everyone. Without effective intelligence from the streets and pressure from districts, he too must become to a degree helpless. Because of this gap, so much good intent at the top comes to so little purpose at the bottom, and vice-versa.

Sometimes the city is not the potential helper, but the antagonist of a street, and again, unless the street contains extraordinarily influential citizens, it is usually helpless alone. On Hudson Street we recently had this problem. The Manhattan Borough engineers decided to cut ten feet off our sidewalks. This was part of a mindless, routinized city program of vehicular road widening.

We people on the street did what we could. The job printer stopped his press, took off of it work on which he had an urgent deadline, and printed emergency petitions on a Saturday morning so the children, out of school, could help get them around. People from overlapping street neighborhoods took petitions and spread them farther. The two parochial schools, Episcopal and Catholic, sent petitions home with their children. We gathered about a thousand signatures from the street and the tributaries off it; these signatures must have represented most of the adults directly affected. Many businessmen and residents wrote letters, and a representative group formed a delegation to visit the Borough President, the elected official responsible.

But by ourselves, we would still hardly have had a chance. We were up against a sanctified general policy on street treatment, and were opposing a construction job that would mean a lot of money for somebody, on which arrangements were already far advanced. We had learned of the plan in advance of the demolition purely by luck. No public hearing was required, for technically this was merely an adjustment in the curb line.

We were told at first that the plans would not be changed; the sidewalk must go. We needed power to back up our pipsqueak protest. This power came from our district—Greenwich Village. Indeed, a main purpose of our petitions, although not an ostensible purpose, was to dramatize to the district at large that an issue had erupted. The swift resolutions passed by district-wide organizations counted more for us than the street-neighborhood expressions of opinion. The man who got our delegation its appointment, Anthony Dapolito, the president of the citizens' Greenwich Village Association, and the people on our delegation who swung the most weight were from other streets than ours entirely; some from the other side of the district. They swung weight precisely because they represented opinion, and opinion makers, at district scale. With their help, we won.

Without the possibility of such support, most city streets hardly try to fight back—whether their troubles emanate from city hall or from other drawbacks of the human condition. Nobody likes to practice futility.

The help we got puts some individuals on our street under obligation, of course, to help other streets or aid more general district causes when help is wanted. If we neglect this, we may not get help next time we need it.

Districts effective at carrying the intelligence from the streets upward sometimes help translate it into city policy. There is no end to such examples, but this will do for illustration: As this is written, New York City is supposedly somewhat reforming its treatment for drug addicts, and simultaneously city hall is pressuring the federal government to expand and reform its treatment work, and to increase its efforts at blocking narcotics smuggling from abroad. The study and agitation that have helped push these moves did not originate with some mysterious "They." The first public agitation for reform and expansion of treatment was stirred not by officials at all, but by district pressure groups from districts like East Harlem and Greenwich Village. The disgraceful way in which arrest rolls are padded with victims while sellers operate openly and untouched is exposed and publicized by just these pressure groups, not by officials and least of all by the police. These pressure groups studied the problem and have pressed for changes and will continue to, precisely because they are in direct touch with experiences in street neighborhoods. The experience of an orphaned street like that on the Upper West Side, on the other hand, never teaches anybody anything—except to get the hell out.

It is tempting to suppose that districts can be formed federally out of distinct separate neighborhoods. The Lower East Side of New York is attempting to form an effective district today, on this pattern, and has received large philanthropic grants for the purpose. The formalized federation system seems to work fairly well for purposes on which virtually everyone is agreed, such as applying pressure for a new hospital. But many vital questions in local city life turn out to be controversial. In the Lower East Side, for example, the federated district organizational structure includes, as this is written, people trying to defend their homes and neighborhoods from obliteration by the bulldozers; and it also contains the developers of cooperative projects and various other business interests who wish the governmental powers of condemnation to be used to wipe out these residents. These are genuine conflicts of interest—in this case, the ancient conflict between predator and prey. The people trying to save themselves spend much of their effort, futilely, trying to get resolutions adopted and letters approved by boards of directors that contain their chief enemies!

Both sides in hot fights on important local questions need to bring their full, consolidated, district-scale strength (nothing less is effective) to bear on the city policy they want to shape or the decisions they want to influence. They have to fight it out with each other, and with officials, on the plane where the effective decisions are made, because this is what counts in winning. Anything that diverts such contenders into fragmenting their power and watering their efforts by going through "decision-making" motions with hierarchies and boards at ineffectual levels where no responsible government powers of decision reside, vitiates political life, citizen effectiveness and self-government. This becomes play at self-government, not the real thing.

When Greenwich Village fought to prevent its park, Washington Square, from being bisected by a highway, for example, majority opinion was overwhelmingly against the highway. But not unanimous opinion; among those for the highway were numerous people of prominence, with leadership positions in smaller sections of the district. Naturally they tried to keep the battle on a level of sectional organization, and so did the city government. Majority opinion would have frittered itself away in these tactics, instead of winning. Indeed, it was frittering itself away until this truth was pointed out by Raymond Rubinow, a man who happened to work in the district, but did not live there. Rubinow helped form a *Joint* Emergency Committee, a true district organization cutting through other organizational lines. Effective districts operate as Things in their own right, and most particularly must their citizens who are in agreement with each other on controversial questions act together at district scale, or they get nowhere. Districts are not groups of petty principalities, working in federation. If they work, they work as integral units of power and opinion, large enough to count.

Our cities possess many islandlike neighborhoods too small to work as districts, and these include not only the project neighborhoods inflicted by planning, but also many unplanned neighborhoods. These unplanned, too small units have grown up historically, and often are enclaves of distinctive ethnic groups. They frequently perform well and strongly the neighborhood functions of streets and thus keep marvelously in hand the kinds of neighborhood social problems and rot that develop from within. But also, just such too small neighborhoods are helpless, in the same way streets are helpless, against the problems and rot that develop from without. They are shortchanged on public improvements and services because they lack power to get them. They are helpless to reverse the slow-death warrants of area credit-blacklisting by mortgage lenders, a problem terribly difficult to fight even with impressive district power. If they develop conflicts with people in adjoining neighborhoods, both they and the adjoining people are apt to be helpless at improving relationships. Indeed, insularity makes these relationships deteriorate further.

Sometimes, to be sure, a neighborhood too small to function as a district gets the benefit of power through possessing an exceptionally influential citizen or an important institution. But the citizens of such a neighborhood pay for their "free" gift of power when the day comes that their interests run counter to those of Papa Bigwheel or Papa Institution. They are helpless to defeat Papa in the government offices, up where the decisions are made, *and therefore they are helpless also to teach him or influence him.* Citizens of neighborhoods that include a university, for example, are often in this helpless fix.

Whether a district of sufficient potential power does become effective and useful as an organ of democratic self-government depends much on whether the insularity of too small neighborhoods within it is overcome. This is principally a social and political problem for a district and the contenders within it, but it is also a physical problem. To plan deliberately, and physically, on the premise that separated city neighborhoods of less than district size are a worthy ideal, is to subvert self-government; that the motives are sentimental or paternalistic is no help. When the physical isolation of too small neighborhoods is abetted by blatant social distinctions, as in projects whose populations are price-tagged, the policy is savagely destructive to effective self-government and self-management in cities.

The value of city districts that swing real power (but in which street neighborhoods are not lost as infinitesimal units) is no discovery of mine. Their value is rediscovered and demonstrated empirically over and over. Nearly every large city has at least one such effective district. Many more areas struggle sporadically to function like districts in time of crisis.

Not surprisingly, a reasonably effective district usually accrues to itself, with time, considerable political power. It eventually generates, too, whole series of individuals able to operate simultaneously at street scale and district scale, and on district scale and in neighborhoods of the city as a whole.

To correct our general disastrous failure to develop functional districts is in great part a problem of city administrative change, which we need not go into at this point. But we also need, among other things, to abandon conventional planning ideas about city neighborhoods. The "ideal" neighborhood of planning and zoning theory, too large in scale to possess any competence or meaning as a street neighborhood, is at the same time too small in scale to operate as a district. It is unfit for anything. It will not serve as even a point of departure. Like the belief in medical bloodletting, it was a wrong turn in the search for understanding.

If the only kinds of city neighborhoods that demonstrate useful functions in real-life self-government are the city as a whole, streets, and districts, then effective neighborhood physical planning for cities should aim at these purposes:

First, to foster lively and interesting streets.

Second, to make the fabric of these streets as continuous a network as possible *throughout* a district of potential subcity size and power.

Third, to use parks and squares and public buildings as part of this street fabric; use them to intensify and knit together the fabric's complexity and multiple use. They should not be used to island off different uses from each other, or to island off subdistrict neighborhoods.

Fourth, to emphasize the functional identity of areas large enough to work as districts.

If the first three aims are well pursued, the fourth will

follow. Here is why: Few people, unless they live in a world of paper maps, can identify with an abstraction called a district, or care much about it. Most of us identify with a place in the city because we use it, and get to know it reasonably intimately. We take our two feet and move around in it and come to count on it. The only reason anyone does this much is that useful or interesting or convenient differences fairly nearby exert an attraction.

Almost nobody travels willingly from sameness to sameness and repetition to repetition, even if the physical effort required is trivial.*

Differences, *not duplications,* make for cross-use and hence for a person's identification with an area greater than his immediate street network. Monotony is the enemy of cross-use and hence of functional unity. As for Turf, planned or unplanned, nobody outside the Turf can possibly feel a natural identity of interest with it or with what it contains.

Centers of use grow up in lively, diverse districts, just as centers of use occur on a smaller scale in parks, and such centers count especially in district identification if

*Thus it was discovered in Jefferson Houses, in East Harlem, that many people who had lived in the project four years had never laid eyes on the community center. It is at the dead end of the project (dead end, in the sense that no city life, only more park, lies beyond). People from other portions of the project had no normal reason for traveling to it from their portions and every normal reason not to. It looked, over there, like more of the same. A settlement-house director in the Lower East Side, Dora Tannenbaum of Grand Street Settlement, says of people in different building groupings of an adjacent project: "These people cannot seem to get the idea they have anything in common with one another. They act as if the other parts of the project were on a different planet." Visually these projects are units. Functionally they are no such thing. The appearance tells a lie.

they contain also a landmark that comes to stand for the place symbolically and, in a way, for the district. But centers cannot carry the load of district identification by themselves; differing commercial and cultural facilities, and different-looking scenes, must crop up all through. Within this fabric, physical barriers, such as huge traffic arteries, too large parks, big institutional groupings, are functionally destructive because they block cross-use.

How big, in absolute terms, must an effective district be? I have given a functional definition of size: big enough to fight city hall, but not so big that street neighborhoods are unable to draw district attention and to count.

In absolute terms, this means different sizes in different cities, depending partly on the size of the city as a whole. In Boston, when the North End had a population upward of 30,000 people, it was strong in district power. Now its population is about half that, partly from the salutary process of uncrowding its dwellings as its people have unslummed, and partly from the unsalutary process of being ruthlessly amputated by a new highway. Cohesive though the North End is, it has lost an important sum of district power. In a city like Boston, Pittsburgh or possibly even Philadelphia, as few as 30,000 people may be sufficient to form a district. In New York or Chicago, however, a district as small as 30,000 amounts to nothing. Chicago's most effective district, the Back-of-the-Yards, embraces about 100,000 people, according to the director of the district Council, and is building up its population further. In New York, Greenwich Village is on the small side for an effective district, but is viable because it manages to make up for this with other advantages. It contains approximately 80,000 residents, along with a working population (perhaps a sixth of them the same people) of approximately 125,000. East Harlem and the Lower East Side of New York, both struggling to create effective districts, each contain about 200,000 residents, and need them.

Of course other qualities than sheer population size count in effectiveness—especially good communication and good morale. But population size is vital because it represents, if most of the time only by implication, votes. There are only two ultimate public powers in shaping and running American cities: votes and control of the money. To sound nicer, we may call these "public opinion" and "disbursement of funds," but they are still votes and money. An effective district—and through its mediation, the street neighborhoods—possesses one of these powers: the power of votes. Through this, and this alone, can it effectively influence the power brought to bear on it, for good or for ill, by public money.

Robert Moses, whose genius at getting things done largely consists in understanding this, has made an art of using control of public money to get his way with those whom the voters elect and depend on to represent their frequently opposing interests. This is, of course, in other guises, an old, sad story of democratic government. The art of negating the power of votes with the power of money can be practiced just as effectively by honest public administrators as by dishonest representatives of purely private interests. Either way, seduction or subversion of the elected is easiest when the electorate is fragmented into ineffectual units of power.

On the maximum side, I know of no district larger than 200,000 which operates like a district. Geographical size imposes empirical population limits in any case. In real life, the maximum size of naturally evolved, effective districts seems to be roughly about a mile and a half square.* Probably this is because anything larger gets too inconvenient for sufficient local cross-use and for the functional identity that underlies district political identity. In a very big city, populations must therefore be dense to achieve successful districts; otherwise, sufficient political power is never reconciled with viable geographic identity.

This point on geographic size does not mean a city can be mapped out in segments of about a square mile, the segments defined with boundaries, and districts thereby brought to life. It is not boundaries that make a district, but the cross-use and life. The point in considering the physical size and limits of a district is this: the kinds of objects, natural or man-made, that form physical barriers to easy cross-use must be somewhere. It is better that they be at the edges of areas large enough to work as districts than that they cut into the continuity of otherwise feasible districts. The fact of a district lies in what it *is* internally, and in the internal continuity and overlapping with which it is used, not in the way it ends or in how it looks in an air view. Indeed, in many cases very popular city districts spontaneously extend their edges, unless prevented from doing so by physical barriers. A district too thoroughly buffered off also runs the danger of losing economically stimulating visitors from other parts of the city.

*The Back-of-the-Yards in Chicago is the only significant exception to this rule that I know of. It is an exception with perhaps useful implications in some cases, which need not concern us here but will be dealt with later in this book as an administrative question.

Neighborhood planning units that are significantly defined only by their fabric and the life and intricate cross-use they generate, rather than by formalistic boundaries, are of course at odds with orthodox planning conceptions. The difference is the difference between dealing with living, complex organisms, capable of shaping their own destinies, and dealing with fixed and inert settlements, capable merely of custodial care (if that) of what has been bestowed upon them.

In dwelling on the necessity for districts, I do not want to give the impression that an effective city district is self-contained either economically, politically or socially. Of course it is not and cannot be, any more than a street can be. Nor can districts be duplicates of one another; they differ immensely, and should. A city is not a collection of repetitious towns. An interesting district has a character of its own and specialties of its own. It draws users from outside (it has little truly urban economic variety unless it does), and its own people go forth.

Nor is there necessity for district self-containment. In Chicago's Back-of-the-Yards, most of the breadwinners used to work, until the 1940's, at the slaughterhouses within the district. This did have a bearing on district formation in this case, because district organization here was a sequel to labor union organization. But as these residents and their children have graduated from the slaughterhouse jobs, they have moved into the working life and public life of the greater city. Most, other than teen-agers with after-school jobs, now work outside the district. This movement has not weakened the district; coincident with it, the district has grown stronger.

The constructive factor that has been operating here meanwhile is time. Time, in cities, is the substitute for self-containment. Time, in cities, is indispensable.

The cross-links that enable a district to function as a Thing are neither vague nor mysterious. They consist of working relationships among specific people, many of them without much else in common than that they share a fragment of geography.

The first relationships to form in city areas, given any neighborhood stability, are those in street neighborhoods and those among people who do have something else in common and belong to organizations with one another—churches, P-TA's, businessmen's associations, political clubs, local civic leagues, fund-raising committees for health campaigns or other public causes, sons of such-and-such a village (common clubs among Puerto Ricans today, as they have been with Italians), property owners' associations, block improvement associations, protesters against injustices, and so on, ad infinitum.

To look into almost any relatively established area of a big city turns up so many organizations, mostly little, as to make one's head swim. Mrs. Goldie Hoffman, one of the commissioners of Philadelphia's redevelopment agency, decided to try the experiment of casing the organizations, if any, and the institutions in a dear little Philadelphia section of about ten thousand people, which was up for renewal. To her astonishment and everyone else's, she found nineteen. Small organizations and special-interest organizations grow in our cities like leaves on the trees, and in their own way are just as awesome a manifestation of the persistence and doggedness of life.

The crucial stage in the formation of an effective district goes much beyond this, however. An interweaving, but different, set of relationships must grow up; these are working relationships among people, usually leaders, who enlarge their local public life beyond the neighborhoods of streets and specific organizations or institutions and form relationships with people whose roots and backgrounds are in entirely different constituencies, so to speak. These hop-and-skip relationships are more fortuitous in cities than are the analogous, almost enforced, hop-and-skip links among people from different small groupings within self-contained settlements. Perhaps because we are typically more advanced at forming whole-city neighborhoods of interest than at forming districts, hop-skip district relationships sometimes originate fortuitously among people from a district who meet in a special-interest neighborhood of the whole city, and then carry over this relationship into their district. Many district networks in New York, for instance, start in this fashion.

It takes surprisingly few hop-skip people, relative to a whole population, to weld a district into a real Thing. A hundred or so people do it in a population a thousand times their size. But these people must have time to find each other, time to try expedient cooperation—as well as time to have rooted themselves, too, in various smaller neighborhoods of place or special interest.

When my sister and I first came to New York from a small city, we used to amuse ourselves with a game we called Messages. I suppose we were trying, in a dim way, to get a grip on the great, bewildering world into which we had come from our cocoon. The idea was to pick two wildly dissimilar individuals—say a headhunter in the

Solomon Islands and a cobbler in Rock Island, Illinois—
and assume that one had to get a message to the other by
word of mouth; then we would each silently figure out a
plausible, or at least possible, chain of persons through
whom the message could go. The one who could make the
shortest plausible chain of messengers won. The headhunter would speak to the headman of his village, who
would speak to the trader who came to buy copra, who
would speak to the Australian patrol officer when he came
through, who would tell the man who was next slated to
go to Melbourne on leave, etc. Down at the other end, the
cobbler would hear from his priest, who got it from the
mayor, who got it from a state senator, who got it from
the governor, etc. We soon had these close-to-home messengers down to a routine for almost everybody we could
conjure up, but we would get tangled in long chains at the
middle until we began employing Mrs. Roosevelt. Mrs.
Roosevelt made it suddenly possible to skip whole chains
of intermediate connections. She knew the most unlikely
people. The world shrank remarkably. It shrank us right
out of our game, which became too cut and dried.

A city district requires a small quota of its own Mrs.
Roosevelts—people who know unlikely people, and
therefore eliminate the necessity for long chains of communication (which in real life would not occur at all).

Settlement-house directors are often the ones who
begin such systems of district hop-skip links, but they can
only begin them and work at opportune ways to extend
them; they cannot carry the load. These links require the
growth of trust, the growth of cooperation that is, at least
at first, apt to be happenstance and tentative; and they
require people who have considerable self-confidence, or

sufficient concern about local public problems to stand them in the stead of self-confidence. In East Harlem, where, after terrible disruption and population turnover, an effective district is slowly re-forming against great odds, fifty-two organizations participated in a 1960 pressure meeting to tell the Mayor and fourteen of his commissioners what the district wants. The organizations included P-TA's, churches, settlements and welfare groups, civic clubs, tenant associations, businessmen's associations, political clubs, and the local congressman, assemblyman and councilman. Fifty-eight individuals had specific responsibilities in getting up the meeting and setting its policy; they included people of all sorts of talents and occupations, and a great ethnic range—Negroes, Italians, Puerto Ricans, and undefinables. This represents a lot of hop-skip district links. It has taken years and skill on the part of half a dozen people to achieve this amount of network, and the process is only starting to reach the stage of being effective.

Once a good, strong network of these hop-skip links does get going in a city district, the net can enlarge relatively swiftly and weave all kinds of resilient new patterns. One sign that it is doing so, sometimes, is the growth of a new kind of organization, more or less district-wide, but impermanent, formed specifically for *ad hoc* purposes.* But to get going, a district network needs

---

* In Greenwich Village, these frequency run to long, explicit names: e.g., the Joint Emergency Committee to Close Washington Square Park to All but Emergency Traffic; the Cellar Dwellers' Tenant Emergency Committee; the Committee of Neighbors to Get the Clock on Jefferson Market Courthouse Started, the Joint Village Committee to Defeat the West Village Proposal and Get a Proper One.

these three requisites: a start of some kind; a physical area with which sufficient people can identify as users; and Time.

The people who form hop-skip links, like the people who form the smaller links in streets and special-interest organizations, are not at all the statistics that are presumed to represent people in planning and housing schemes. Statistical people are a fiction for many reasons, one of which is that they are treated as if infinitely interchangeable. Real people are unique, they invest years of their lives in significant relationships with other unique people, and are not interchangeable in the least. Severed from their relationships, they are destroyed as effective social beings—sometimes for a little while, sometimes forever.*

In city neighborhoods, whether streets or districts, if too many slowly grown public relationships are disrupted at once, all kinds of havoc can occur—so much havoc, instability and helplessness, that it sometimes seems time will never again get in its licks.

Harrison Salisbury, in a series of *New York Times* articles, "The Shook-Up Generation," put well this vital point about city relationships and their disruption.

"Even a ghetto [he quoted a pastor as saying], after it has remained a ghetto for a period of time

---

*There are people who seemingly can behave like interchangeable statistics and take up in a different place exactly where they left off, but they must belong to one of our fairly homogeneous and ingrown nomad societies, like Beatniks, or Regular Army officers and their families, or the peripatetic junior executive families of suburbia, described by William H. Whyte, Jr., in *The Organization Man*.

builds up its social structure and this makes for
more stability, more leadership, more agencies for
helping the solution of public problems."

But when slum clearance enters an area [Salis-
bury went on], it does not merely rip out slatternly
houses. It uproots the people. It tears out the
churches. It destroys the local business man. It sends
the neighborhood lawyer to new offices downtown
and it mangles the tight skein of community friendships and group relationships beyond repair.

It drives the old-timers from their broken-down
flats or modest homes and forces them to find new
and alien quarters. And it pours into a neighborhood hundreds and thousands of new faces . . .

Renewal planning, which is largely aimed at saving
buildings, and incidentally some of the population, but
at strewing the rest of a locality's population, has much
the same result. So does too heavily concentrated private
building, capitalizing in a rush on the high values created
by a stable city neighborhood. From Yorkville, in New
York, an estimated 15,000 families have been driven out
between 1951 and 1960 by this means; virtually all of
them left unwillingly. In Greenwich Village, the same
thing is happening. Indeed, it is a miracle that our cities
have any functioning districts, not that they have so few.
In the first place, there is relatively little city territory at
present which is, by luck, well suited physically to forming districts with good cross-use and identity. And within
this, incipient or slightly too weak districts are forever
being amputated, bisected and generally shaken up by
misguided planning policies. The districts that are effective enough to defend themselves from planned disrup-

tion are eventually trampled in an unplanned gold rush by those who aim to get a cut of these rare social treasures.

To be sure, a good city neighborhood can absorb newcomers into itself, both newcomers by choice and immigrants settling by expediency, and it can protect a reasonable amount of transient population too. But these increments or displacements have to be gradual. If self-government in the place is to work, underlying any float of population must be a continuity of people who have forged neighborhood networks. These networks are a city's irreplaceable social capital. Whenever the capital is lost, from whatever cause, the income from it disappears, never to return until and unless new capital is slowly and chancily accumulated.

Some observers of city life, noting that strong city neighborhoods are so frequently ethnic communities—especially communities of Italians, Poles, Jews or Irish—have speculated that a cohesive ethnic base is required for a city neighborhood that works as a social unit. In effect, this is to say that only hyphenated-Americans are capable of local self-government in big cities. I think this is absurd.

In the first place, these ethnically cohesive communities are not always as naturally cohesive as they may look to outsiders. Again citing the Back-of-the-Yards as an example, its backbone population is mainly Central European, but all kinds of Central European. It has, for example, literally dozens of national churches. The traditional enmities and rivalries among these groups were a most severe handicap. Greenwich Village's three main parts derive from an Italian community, an Irish community and a Henry Jamesian patrician community. Ethnic cohe-

siveness may have played a part in the formation of these
sections, but it has been no help in welding district cross-
links—a job that was begun many years ago by a remarkable settlement-house director, Mary K. Simkhovich.
Today many streets in these old ethnic communities have
assimilated into their neighborhoods a fantastic ethnic
variety from almost the whole world. They have also
assimilated a great sprinkling of middle-class professionals and their families, who prove to do very well at city
street and district life, in spite of the planning myth that
such people need protective islands of pseudosuburban
"togetherness." Some of the streets that functioned best in
the Lower East Side (before they were wiped out) were
loosely called "Jewish," but contained, as people actually
involved in the street neighborhoods, individuals of more
than forty differing ethnic origins. One of New York's
most effective neighborhoods, with an internal communication that is a marvel, is the midtown East Side of predominately high-income people, utterly undefinable
except as Americans.

In the second place, wherever ethnically cohesive
neighborhoods develop and are stable, they possess
another quality besides ethnic identity. They contain
many individuals who stay put. This, I think, more than
sheer ethnic identity, is the significant factor. It typically
takes many years after such groups have settled in for
time to work and for the inhabitants to attain stable, effective neighborhoods.

Here is a seeming paradox: To maintain in a neighborhood sufficient people who stay put, a city must have the
very fluidity and mobility of use that Reginald Isaacs

noted, as mentioned early in this chapter, when he speculated whether neighborhoods can therefore mean anything very significant to cities.

Over intervals of time, many people change their jobs
and the locations of their jobs, shift or enlarge their outside friendships and interests, change their family sizes,
change their incomes up or down, even change many of
their tastes. In short they live, rather than just exist. If they
live in diversified, rather than monotonous, districts—in
districts, particularly, where many details of physical
change can constantly be accommodated—and if they like
the place, they can stay put despite changes in the locales
or natures of their other pursuits or interests. Unlike the
people who must move from a lower-middle to a middle-
middle to an upper-middle suburb as their incomes and
leisure activities change (or be very outré indeed), or the
people of a little town who must move to another town
or to a city to find different opportunities, city people
need not pull up stakes for such reasons.

A city's collection of opportunities of all kinds, and the
fluidity with which these opportunities and choices can be
used, is an asset—not a detriment—for encouraging city-
neighborhood stability.

However, this asset has to be capitalized upon. It is
thrown away where districts are handicapped by sameness and are suitable, therefore, to only a narrow range of
incomes, tastes and family circumstances. Neighborhood
accommodations for fixed, bodiless, statistical people are
accommodations for instability. The people in them, as
statistics, may stay the same. But the people in them, as
people, do not. Such places are forever way stations.

*   *   *

In the first section of this book, of which this is the close, I have been emphasizing assets and strengths peculiar to big cities, and weaknesses peculiar to them also. Cities, like anything else, succeed only by making the most of their assets. I have tried to point out the kinds of places in cities that do this, and the way they work. My idea, however, is not that we should therefore try to reproduce, routinely and in a surface way, the streets and districts that do display strength and success as fragments of city life. This would be impossible, and sometimes would be an exercise in architectural antiquarianism. Moreover, even the best streets and districts can stand improvement, especially amenity.

But if we understand the principles behind the behavior of cities, we can build on potential assets and strengths, instead of acting at cross-purposes to them. First we have to know the general results we want—and know because of knowing how life in cities works. We have to know, for instance, that we want lively, well-used streets and other public spaces, and why we want them. But knowing what to want, although it is a first step, is far from enough. The next step is to examine some of the workings of cities at another level: the economic workings that produce those lively streets and districts for city users.

PART TWO

THE CONDITIONS
FOR CITY DIVERSITY

7

THE GENERATORS OF DIVERSITY

Classified telephone directories tell us the greatest single fact about cities: the immense numbers of parts that make up a city, and the immense diversity of those parts. Diversity is natural to big cities.

"I have often amused myself," wrote James Boswell in 1791, "with thinking how different a place London is to different people. They, whose narrow minds are contracted to the consideration of some one particular pursuit, view it only through that medium . . . But the intellectual man is struck with it, as comprehending the whole of human life in all its variety, the contemplation of which is inexhaustible."

Boswell not only gave a good definition of cities, he put his finger on one of the chief troubles in dealing with them. It is so easy to fall into the trap of contemplating a city's uses one at a time, by categories. Indeed, just this—analysis of cities, use by use—has become a customary planning tactic. The findings on various categories of use are then put together into "broad, overall pictures."

The overall pictures such methods yield are about as useful as the picture assembled by the blind men who felt the elephant and pooled their findings. The elephant lumbered on, oblivious to the notion that he was a leaf, a snake, a wall, tree trunks and a rope all somehow stuck together. Cities, being our own artifacts, enjoy less defense against solemn nonsense.

To understand cities, we have to deal outright with combinations or mixtures of uses, not separate uses, as the essential phenomena. We have already seen the importance of this in the case of neighborhood parks. Parks can easily—too easily—be thought of as phenomena in their own right and described as adequate or inadequate in terms, say, of acreage ratios to thousands of population. Such an approach tells us something about the methods of planners, but it tells us nothing useful about the behavior or value of neighborhood parks.

A mixture of uses, if it is to be sufficiently complex to sustain city safety, public contact and cross-use, needs an enormous diversity of ingredients. So the first question—and I think by far the most important question—about planning cities is this: How can cities generate enough mixture among uses—enough diversity—throughout enough of their territories, to sustain their own civilization?

It is all very well to castigate the Great Blight of Dullness and to understand why it is destructive to city life, but in itself this does not get us far. Consider the problem posed by the street with the pretty sidewalk park in Baltimore, which I mentioned back in Chapter Three. My friend from the street, Mrs. Kostritsky, is quite right when she reasons that it needs some commerce for its users' convenience. And as might be expected, inconvenience and lack of public street life are only two of the by-products of residential monotony here. Danger is another—fear of the streets after dark. Some people fear to be alone in their houses by day since the occurrence of two nasty daytime assaults. Moreover, the place lacks commercial choices as well as any cultural interest. We can see very well how fatal is its monotony.

But having said this, then what? The missing diversity, convenience, interest and vitality do not spring forth because the area needs their benefits. Anybody who started a retail enterprise here, for example, would be stupid. He could not make a living. To wish a vital urban life might somehow spring up here is to play with daydreams. The place is an economic desert.

Although it is hard to believe, while looking at dull gray areas, or at housing projects or at civic centers, the fact is that big cities *are* natural generators of diversity and prolific incubators of new enterprises and ideas of all kinds. Moreover, big cities are the natural economic homes of immense numbers and ranges of small enterprises.

The principal studies of variety and size among city enterprises happen to be studies of manufacturing, notably those by Raymond Vernon, author of *Anatomy of a Metropolis,* and by P. Sargant Florence, who has examined the effect of cities on manufacturing both here and in England.

Characteristically, the larger a city, the greater the variety of its manufacturing, and also the greater both the number and the proportion of its small manufacturers. The reasons for this, in brief, are that big enterprises have greater self-sufficiency than small ones, are able to maintain within themselves most of the skills and equipment they need, can warehouse for themselves, and can sell to a broad market which they can seek out wherever it may be. They need not be in cities, and although sometimes it is advantageous for them to be there, often it is more advantageous not to. But for small manufacturers, everything is reversed. Typically they must draw on many and varied supplies and skills outside themselves, they must serve a narrow market at the point where a market exists, and they must be sensitive to quick changes in this market. Without cities, they would simply not exist. Dependent on a huge diversity of other city enterprises, they can add further to that diversity. This last is a most important point to remember. City diversity itself permits and stimulates more diversity.

For many activities other than manufacturing, the situation is analogous. For example, when Connecticut General Life Insurance Company built a new headquarters in the countryside beyond Hartford, it could do so only by dint of providing—in addition to the usual working spaces and rest rooms, medical suite and the like—a large general store, a beauty parlor, a bowling alley, a cafeteria, a theater and a great variety of games space. These facilities are inherently inefficient, idle most of the time. They require subsidy, not because they are kinds of enterprises which are necessarily money losers, but because here their use is so limited. They were presumed necessary, however, to compete for a working force, and to hold it. A large company can absorb the luxury of such inherent inefficiencies and balance them against other advantages it seeks. But small offices can do nothing of the kind. If they want to compete for a work force on even terms or better, they must be in a lively city setting where their employees find the range of subsidiary conveniences and choices that they want and need. Indeed, one reason, among many others, why the much-heralded postwar exodus of big offices from cities turned out to be mostly talk is that the differentials in cost of suburban land and space are typically canceled by the greater amount of space per worker required for facilities that in cities no single employer need provide, nor any one corps of workers or customers support. Another reason why such enterprises have stayed in cities, along with small firms, is that many of their employees, especially executives, need to be in close, face-to-face touch and communication with people outside the firm—including people from small firms.

The benefits that cities offer to smallness are just as marked in retail trade, cultural facilities and entertainment. This is because city populations are large enough to support wide ranges of variety and choice in these things. And again we find that bigness has all the advantages in smaller settlements. Towns and suburbs, for instance, are natural homes for huge supermarkets and for little else in the way of groceries, for standard movie houses or drive-ins and for little else in the way of theater. There are simply not enough people to support further variety, although there may be people (too few of them) who would draw upon it were it there. Cities, however, are the natural homes of supermarkets and standard movie houses *plus* delicatessens, Viennese bakeries, foreign groceries, art movies, and so on, all of which can be found coexisting, the standard with the strange, the large with the small. Wherever lively and popular parts of cities are found, the small much outnumber the large.* Like the

* In retail trade, this tendency has been growing stronger, if anything. Richard Nelson, the Chicago real estate analyst, examining the postwar trend of retail sales in some twenty city downtowns, has discovered that the large department stores have typically lost trade; the chain variety

small manufacturers, these small enterprises would not exist somewhere else, in the absence of cities. Without cities, they would not exist.

The diversity, of whatever kind, that is generated by cities rests on the fact that in cities so many people are so close together, and among them contain so many different tastes, skills, needs, supplies, and bees in their bonnets.

Even quite standard, but small, operations like proprietor-and-one-clerk hardware stores, drug stores, candy stores and bars can and do flourish in extraordinary numbers and incidence in lively districts of cities because there are enough people to support their presence at short, convenient intervals, and in turn this convenience and neighborhood personal quality are big parts of such enterprises' stock in trade. Once they are unable to be supported at close, convenient intervals, they lose this advantage. In a given geographical territory, half as many people will not support half as many such enterprises spaced at twice the distance. When distance inconvenience sets in, the small, the various and the personal wither away.

As we have transformed from a rural and small-town country into an urban country, business enterprises have

---

stores have stayed about even; and the small and special stores have increased their business and usually have also increased in number. There is no real competition outside the cities for these small and various city enterprises; but it is relatively easy for the big and standardized, in their natural homes outside the city, to compete with what is big and standardized within. This happens, incidentally, to be exactly what has occurred in the neighborhood where I live. Wanamaker's, the big department store formerly located in Greenwich Village, has gone out of business here and established itself in a suburb instead, at the same time that small and special stores in its immediate former vicinity have increased by the score and flourished mightily.

thus become more numerous, not only in absolute terms, but also in proportionate terms. In 1900 there were 21 independent nonfarm businesses for each 1,000 persons in the total U.S. population. In 1959, in spite of the immense growth of giant enterprises during the interval, there were 26 $1/2$ independent nonfarm businesses for each 1,000 persons in the population. With urbanization, the big get bigger, but the small also get more numerous.

Smallness and diversity, to be sure, are not synonyms. The diversity of city enterprises includes all degrees of size, but great variety does mean a high proportion of small elements. A lively city scene is lively largely by virtue of its enormous collection of small elements.

Nor is the diversity that is important for city districts by any means confined to profit-making enterprises and to retail commerce, and for this reason it may seem that I put an undue emphasis on retail trade. I think not, however. Commercial diversity is, in itself, immensely important for cities, socially as well as economically. Most of the uses of diversity on which I dwelt in Part I of this book depend directly or indirectly upon the presence of plentiful, convenient, diverse city commerce. But more than this, wherever we find a city district with an exuberant variety and plenty in its commerce, we are apt to find that it contains a good many other kinds of diversity also, including variety of cultural opportunities, variety of scenes, and a great variety in its population and other users. This is more than coincidence. The same physical and economic conditions that generate diverse commerce are intimately related to the production, or the presence, of other kinds of city variety.

But although cities may fairly be called natural economic generators of diversity and natural economic incubators of new enterprises, this does not mean that cities *automatically* generate diversity just by existing. They generate it because of the various efficient economic pools of use that they form. Wherever they fail to form such pools of use, they are little better, if any, at generating diversity than small settlements. And the fact that they need diversity socially, unlike small settlements, makes no difference. For our purposes here, the most striking fact to note is the extraordinary unevenness with which cities generate diversity.

On the one hand, for example, people who live and work in Boston's North End, or New York's Upper East Side or San Francisco's North Beach-Telegraph Hill, are able to use and enjoy very considerable amounts of diversity and vitality. Their visitors help immensely. But the visitors did not create the foundations of diversity in areas like these, nor in the many pockets of diversity and economic efficiency scattered here and there, sometimes most unexpectedly, in big cities. The visitors sniff out where something vigorous exists already, and come to share it, thereby further supporting it.

At the other extreme, huge city settlements of people exist without their presence generating anything much except stagnation and, ultimately, a fatal discontent with the place. It is not that they are a different kind of people, somehow duller or unappreciative of vigor and diversity. Often they include hordes of searchers, trying to sniff out these attributes somewhere, anywhere. Rather, something is wrong with their districts; something is lacking to catalyze a district population's ability to interact economically and help form effective pools of use.

Apparently there is no limit to the numbers of people in a city whose potentiality as city populations can thus be wasted. Consider, for instance, the Bronx, a borough of New York containing some one and a half million people. The Bronx is woefully short of urban vitality, diversity and magnetism. It has its loyal residents, to be sure, mostly attached to little bloomings of street life here and there in "the old neighborhood," but not nearly enough of them.

In so simple a matter of city amenity and diversity as interesting restaurants, the 1,500,000 people in the Bronx cannot produce. Kate Simon, the author of a guidebook, *New York Places and Pleasures,* describes hundreds of restaurants and other commercial establishments, particularly in unexpected and out-of-the-way parts of the city. She is not snobbish, and dearly likes to present her readers with inexpensive discoveries. But although Miss Simon tries hard, she has to give up the great settlement of the Bronx as thin pickings at any price. After paying homage to the two solid metropolitan attractions in the borough, the zoo and the Botanical Gardens, she is hard put to recommend a single place to eat outside the zoo grounds. The one possibility she is able to offer, she accompanies with this apology: "The neighborhood trails off sadly into a no man's land, and the restaurant can stand a little refurbishing, but there's the comfort of knowing that . . . the best of Bronx medical skill is likely to be sitting all around you."

Well, that is the Bronx, and it is too bad it is so; too bad for the people who live there now, too bad for the people who are going to inherit it in future out of their lack of economic choice, and too bad for the city as a whole.

And if the Bronx is a sorry waste of city potentialities, as it is, consider the even more deplorable fact that it is possible for whole cities to exist, whole metropolitan areas, with pitifully little city diversity and choice. Virtually all of urban Detroit is as weak on vitality and diversity as the Bronx. It is ring superimposed upon ring of failed gray belts. Even Detroit's downtown itself cannot produce a respectable amount of diversity. It is dispirited and dull, and almost deserted by seven o'clock of an evening.

So long as we are content to believe that city diversity represents accident and chaos, of course its erratic generation appears to represent a mystery.

However, the conditions that generate city diversity are quite easy to discover by observing places in which diversity flourishes and studying the economic reasons why it can flourish in these places. Although the results are intricate, and the ingredients producing them may vary enormously, this complexity is based on tangible economic relationships which, in principle, are much simpler than the intricate urban mixtures they make possible.

To generate exuberant diversity in a city's streets and districts, four conditions are indispensable:

1. The district, and indeed as many of its internal parts as possible, must serve more than one primary function; preferably more than two. These must insure the presence of people who go outdoors on different schedules and are in the place for different purposes, but who are able to use many facilities in common.

2. Most blocks must be short; that is, streets and opportunities to turn corners must be frequent.

3. The district must mingle buildings that vary in age and condition, including a good proportion of old ones so

that they vary in the economic yield they must produce. This mingling must be fairly close-grained.

4. There must be a sufficiently dense concentration of people, for whatever purposes they may be there. This includes dense concentration in the case of people who are there because of residence.

The necessity for these four conditions is the most important point this book has to make. In combination, these conditions create effective economic pools of use. Given these four conditions, not all city districts will produce a diversity equivalent to one another. The potentials of different districts differ for many reasons; but, given the development of these four conditions (or the best approximation to their full development that can be managed in real life), a city district should be able to realize its best potential, wherever that may lie. Obstacles to doing so will have been removed. The range may not stretch to African sculpture or schools of drama or Rumanian tea houses, but such as the possibilities are, whether for grocery stores, pottery schools, movies, candy stores, florists, art shows, immigrants' clubs, hardware stores, eating places, or whatever, they will get their best chance. And along with them, city life will get its best chances.

In the four chapters that follow, I shall discuss each of these four generators of diversity, one at a time. The purpose of explaining them one at a time is purely for convenience of exposition, not because any one—or even any three—of these necessary conditions is valid alone. *All* four in combination are necessary to generate city diversity; the absence of any one of the four frustrates a district's potential.

8

THE NEED FOR
MIXED PRIMARY USES

CONDITION 1: *The district, and indeed as many of its internal parts as possible, must serve more than one primary function; preferably more than two. These must insure the presence of people who go outdoors on different schedules and are in the place for different purposes, but who are able to use many facilities in common.*

On successful city streets, people must appear at different times. This is time considered on a small scale, hour by hour through the day. I have already explained this necessity in social terms while discussing street safety and also neighborhood parks. Now I shall point out its economic effects.

Neighborhood parks, you will recall, need people who are in the immediate vicinity for different purposes from one another, or else the parks will be used only sporadically.

Most consumer enterprises are just as dependent as parks on people going to and fro throughout the day, but with this difference: If parks lie idle, it is bad for them and their neighborhoods but they do not disappear as a consequence. If consumer enterprises lie idle for much of the day they may disappear. Or, to be more accurate, in most such cases they never appear in the first place. Stores, like parks, need users.

For a humble example of the economic effects of people spread through time of day, I will ask you to think back to a city sidewalk scene: the ballet of Hudson Street. The continuity of this movement (which gives the street its safety) depends on an economic foundation of basic mixed uses. The workers from the laboratories, meat-packing plants, warehouses, plus those from a bewildering variety of small manufacturers, printers and other little industries and offices, give all the eating places and much of the other commerce support at midday. We residents on the street and on its more purely residential tributaries could and would support a modicum of commerce by ourselves, but relatively little. We possess more convenience, liveliness, variety and choice than we "deserve" in our own right. The people who work in the neighborhood also possess, on account of us residents, more variety than they "deserve" in their own right. We support these things together by unconsciously cooperating economically. If the neighborhood were to lose the industries, it would be a disaster for us residents. Many enterprises, unable to exist on residential trade by itself, would disappear. Or if the industries were to lose us residents, enterprises unable to exist on the working people by themselves would disappear.*

As it is, workers and residents together are able to produce *more* than the sum of our two parts. The enter-

*Please remember, however, that this factor of users spread through time of day is only one of four necessary factors for generating diversity. Do not think it explains everything by itself, even though it is an essential factor.

prises we are capable of supporting, mutually, draw out onto the sidewalk by evening many more residents than would emerge if the place were moribund. And, in a modest way, they also attract still another crowd in addition to the local residents or local workers. They attract people who want a change from their neighborhoods, just as we frequently want a change from ours. This attraction exposes our commerce to a still larger and more diverse population, and this in turn has permitted a still further growth and range of commerce living on all *three* kinds of population in varying proportions: a shop down the street selling prints, a store that rents diving equipment, a dispensary of first-rate pizza, a pleasant coffee house.

Sheer numbers of people using city streets, and the way those people are spread through the hours of the day, are two different matters. I shall deal with sheer numbers in another chapter; at this stage it is important to understand that numbers, in themselves, are not an equivalent for people distributed through time of day.

The significance of time spread can be seen especially clearly at the downtown tip of Manhattan, because this is a district suffering from extreme time unbalance among its users. Some 400,000 persons are employed here, in a district embracing Wall Street, the adjoining law and insurance complexes, the city's municipal offices, some federal and state offices, groups of docks and shipping offices, and a number of other work complexes. An undetermined but considerable additional number of people visit the district during working hours, mostly on office or government business.

This is an immense number of users for a territory

sufficiently compact so that any part of it is readily accessible on foot from almost any other part. Among them,
these users represent a tremendous daily demand for
meals and other goods, to say nothing of cultural services.

Yet the district is miserable at providing services and
amenities proportionate to the need. Its eating places
and clothing shops are pitifully inadequate in number
and variety for the demands on them. The district used
to have one of the best hardware stores in New York, but
a few years ago it could no longer make ends meet, and
closed. It had one of the finest, largest and longest established food specialty stores in the city; it too has recently
closed down. Once upon a time it had a few movies but
they became sleeping places for the leisured indigent and
eventually disappeared. The district's cultural opportunities are nil.

All these lacks, which may seem on the surface to be
frivolous, are a handicap. Firm after firm has left for
mixed-use midtown Manhattan (which has become the
city's main downtown). As one real estate broker put it,
otherwise their personnel departments can't get or keep
people who can spell "molybdenum." These losses, in
turn, have badly undermined the district's once supreme
convenience for face-to-face business contacts, so that
now law firms and banks are moving out, to be closer to
clients who have already moved. The district has become
second-rate in its very function—providing managerial
headquarters—which is the foundation of its prestige and
usefulness and its reason for being.

Meantime, outside of the big offices that form the
breathtaking skyline of lower Manhattan is a ring of stagnation, decay, vacancies and vestigial industries. Con-

sider this paradox: Here are plenty of people, and people moreover who want and value city diversity badly enough so it is difficult or sometimes impossible to keep them from scooting away elsewhere to get it. And here, cheek-by-jowl with the demand, are plenty of convenient and even empty places for diversity to grow in. What can be wrong?

To see what is wrong, it is only necessary to drop in at any ordinary shop and observe the contrast between the mob scene at lunch and the dullness at other times. It is only necessary to observe the deathlike stillness that settles on the district after five-thirty and all day Saturday and Sunday.

"They come in like a tide," the *New York Times* quoted a saleswoman in a clothing store. "I always know when it's a few minutes after noon." "The first group floods the store from noon to just before 1 P.M.," the *Times* reporter went on to explain. "Then there is a short breathing spell. A few minutes after 1 P.M. a second group spills in." And then, although the paper did not say so, a few minutes before 2 P.M. the store goes dead.

The business done by consumers' enterprises here must be mainly crammed into some two or three hours a day, some ten or fifteen hours a week. This degree of underuse is a miserable inefficiency for any plant. A certain number of enterprises can cover their overhead and make a profit by exploiting the midday mob operation to the hilt. But there must be few enough so that each reaps a capacity mob at that time. Restaurants too can live on lunch and coffee breaks, instead of lunch and dinner, if there are relatively so few that they do a quick-turnover business in their too few bonanza hours. How does this add up to general convenience and amenity for those 400,000 workers? Badly.

It is no accident that the New York Public Library gets more anguished telephone calls from this district than from any other—at lunchtime, of course—asking, "Where is the library branch down here? I can't find it." There is none, typically enough. If there were, it could hardly be built big enough for the queues at lunchtime and perhaps at five o'clock and hardly small enough for the trade at other times.

Aside from the mob-scene enterprises, other retail services can and do manage by keeping their overhead abnormally low. This is how most of the interesting and civilized and unusual places which have not yet gone out of business manage to exist, and the reason why they are in singularly decrepit and decaying lodgings.

The business and financial interests represented in lower Manhattan have for several years, in cooperation with the city, been working hard at preparing plans and starting work to regenerate this area. They have proceeded according to orthodox planning beliefs and principles.

The first step in their reasoning is good. They face the fact of trouble, and also face its general nature. The planning brochure prepared by the Downtown-Lower Manhattan Association says: "To ignore the factors that threaten the economic health of lower Manhattan is to accept a continuing exodus of long-established businesses and activities to areas in which they can find better working conditions and a more agreeable and convenient environment for their employees."

The brochure indicates, moreover, a glimmer of

understanding about the need to spread people through time of day, for it states, "A residential population would stimulate the development of shopping facilities, restaurants, places of entertainment and garage facilities which would prove highly desirable for use by the daytime working population as well."

But it is only a poor glimmer of understanding and the plans themselves are an exercise in cures irrelevant to the disease.

A residential population is, to be sure, introduced in the proposed plans. It will take up a lot of territory, in the form of project buildings, parking lots and empty land, but in people—as the brochure itself states—it will amount to only about 1 percent of the number of persons in the daytime population. What Herculean economic power that little band is to exert! What amazing feats of hedonism must it accomplish to support "the development of shopping facilities, restaurants, places of entertainment . . . highly desirable for use by the daytime working population as well"!

The new residential population is to be, of course, only part of the plan. The other parts will intensify the present trouble. They will do so in two ways. First, they are aimed at bringing in still more daytime work uses—manufacturing, international trade offices and a huge new federal office building, among others. Second, the land clearance planned for these additional working places and for the housing projects and the associated highways will clear out—along with empty buildings and decayed work uses—much of the low-overhead service and commerce that does still exist to serve the working population. Facilities already too meager in range (and number) for the working population will be further sub-tracted, as a by-product to adding *more* working popula-tion and an utterly meaningless number of residents. Conditions already inconvenient will become intolerable. The plans, moreover, will foreclose the chance of reason-ably adequate services ever being developed, because no room, at economical rents for the incubation of new enter-prise, will exist for them.

Lower Manhattan is in really serious trouble, and the routine reasoning and remedies of orthodox planning merely compound the trouble. What could be done to ameliorate *effectively* the district's extreme time unbalance of users, which is the root of its trouble?

Residence, no matter how introduced, cannot help effectively. The daytime use of the district is so intensive that residents, even at the highest densities possible, would always be ineffectually small in their proportion-ate numbers, and would preempt territories of a size utterly disproportionate to the economic contribution they could render here.

The first step in planning the infusion of new poten-tial uses is to have a practical idea of what the infusion must accomplish if it is to overcome the district's root trouble.

The infusion would obviously have to result in the presence of maximum numbers of persons at the times when the district needs them most for time balance: midafternoons (between two and five o'clock), evenings, Saturdays and Sundays. The only possible concentrations large enough to make any difference would consist of great numbers of visitors at those times, and this in turn has to mean tourists together with many people of the city itself, coming back over and over again in their leisure time.

Whatever it is that attracts this infusion of new people must also be attractive to people who work in the district. At least its presence cannot bore or repel them.

This new putative use (or uses) cannot, furthermore, replace wholesale the very buildings and territories in which new, spontaneous enterprises and facilities, stimulated by the new time spread of people, can grow with the freedom and flexibility of accommodations they will need.

And finally, this new use (or uses) ought to be in accord with the district's character, certainly not at cross-purposes to it. It is the character of lower Manhattan to be intensive, to be exciting, to be dramatic, and this is one of its greatest assets. What is more dramatic, even romantic, than the tumbled towers of lower Manhattan, rising suddenly to the clouds like a magic castle girdled by water? Its very touch of jumbled jaggedness, its towering-sided canyons, are its magnificence. What vandalism it would represent (what vandalism the present project plans represent!) to dilute this magnificent city presence with the humdrum and the regimented.

What does exist here to draw visitors at leisure hours, for instance on week ends? Over the years, unfortunately, almost every unique appeal to visitors that could possibly be rooted out of this district by plan has been rooted out. The aquarium, which used to sit in Battery Park at the tip of the island and was the main attraction of that park, has been removed and rebuilt in Coney Island, the last place it was needed. A strange and vital little Armenian neighborhood (*there* was residence that counted because of its uniqueness as a tourist and visitor attraction) was rooted out lock, stock and barrel for a tunnel approach, and now the guidebooks and the women's pages of the newspapers send visitors over to Brooklyn to find its transplanted remnants and extraordinary shops. The excursion boats, the trip to the Statue of Liberty, have been surrounded by less glamour than the checkout line in a supermarket. The Parks Department snack bar at the Battery is about as appealing as a school cafeteria. Battery Park itself, in the most stirring location of the city, riding into the harbor like a prow, has been made to resemble the grounds of an old people's home. Everything thus far inflicted on this district by plan (and everything more which has been proposed by plan) says in the plainest terms to human beings, "Go away! Leave me alone!" Nothing says, "Come on! "

So much could be done.

The waterfront itself is the first wasted asset capable of drawing people at leisure. Part of the district's waterfront should become a great marine museum—the permanent anchorage of specimen and curiosity ships, the best collection to be seen and boarded anywhere. This would bring into the district tourists in the afternoon, tourists and people of the city, both, on week ends and holidays, and in summertime it should be a great thing for the evening. Other features of the shoreline should be the embarkation points for pleasure voyages in the harbor and around the island; these embarkation points should be as glamorous and salty as art can make them. If new sea-food restaurants and much else would not start up nearby, I will eat my lobster shell.

There should be related attractions, set not at the shoreline itself but inland a little, within the matrix of streets, deliberately to carry visitors farther in easy steps. A new aquarium should be built, for example, and it ought to be admission-free, unlike the one at Coney. A city of almost eight million can support two aquariums and can afford to show off its fish free. That public-library branch which is needed so badly should be built, and it should be not only the usual circulating branch, but also the specialized library center for all marine and financial lore.

Special events based on all these attractions should be concentrated in evenings and week ends; inexpensive theater and opera ought to be added. Jason Epstein, a publisher and student of cities, who has thoughtfully considered the experiments of European cities for clues helpful to lower Manhattan, suggests a permanent one-ring circus, like the one in Paris. This, if it were done well, would be far more effective as sheer economic support to the long-term business value of this district than the dreary additions of more manufacturing plants, taking up the room, contributing nothing the district needs to maintain its strength (and depriving of their presence other parts of the city that really need manufacturing plants).

As the district livened up during evenings and week ends, we could expect some new residential use to appear spontaneously. Lower Manhattan does contain numerous old houses, run down but fundamentally attractive, of just the kind that have been rehabilitated elsewhere when life broke out. People in search of what is both unique and alive would ferret them out. However, residence in such an area as this must necessarily be a manifestation of district vitality, rather than a cause of it.

Do my suggestions for additional uses based on leisure-time attraction seem frivolous and expensive?

Consider, then, the expected cost of the plans prepared by the Downtown-Lower Manhattan Association and the city for more working places still, for the housing projects and parking lots, and for the highways to take the project people out of the district on week ends.

These things are to cost, their planners estimate, *one billion dollars* of public and private money!

The extreme condition of currently unbalanced spread of people through time of day in lower Manhattan illustrates a number of sobering principles that apply equally to other city districts:

No neighborhood or district, no matter how well established, prestigious or well heeled, and no matter how intensely populated for one purpose, can flout the necessity for spreading people through time of day without frustrating its potential for generating diversity.

Furthermore, a neighborhood or district perfectly calculated, it seems, to fill one function, whether work or any other, and with everything ostensibly necessary to that function, cannot actually provide what is necessary if it is confined to that one function.

Unless a plan for a district which lacks spread of people through time of day gets at the cause of the trouble, the best that can be done is to replace old stagnation with new. It may look cleaner for a while, but that is not much to buy with a lot of money.

It should be clear by now that I am discussing two different kinds of diversity. The first, primary uses, are those which, in themselves, bring people to a specific place because they are anchorages. Offices and factories are primary uses. So are dwellings. Certain places of entertainment, education and recreation are primary uses. To a degree (that is, for an appreciable proportion of their users), so are many museums, libraries and galleries, but not all.

Primary uses can be unusual sometimes. In Louisville, since the war a great sample shoe market, for bargain, odd-lot shoes, has gradually grown up in about thirty stores concentrated on four blocks of one street. Grady Clay, real estate editor of the *Louisville Courier-Journal,* and a leading city design and planning critic, reports that the group has about a half-million pairs of shoes on display and in warehouses. "This is in the inner gray area," Mr. Clay writes me, "but as soon as the word got around, customers began flocking in from all over, so that you see Indianapolis, Nashville, Cincinnati shoppers, plus a good Cadillac trade. I have been thinking a bit about it. Nobody could have planned this growth. Nobody has encouraged it. The biggest threat, in fact, is the expressway which will cut diagonally across. Nobody at City Hall seems at all concerned about it. I hope to stir up some interest . . ."

As this suggests, you cannot tell from outward impressiveness or other signs of putative importance how effective a primary use is, as an attractor of people. Some of the most impressive *looking* are ineffectual in performance. For instance, the main building of Philadelphia's public library, stuck in a monumental cultural center, draws fewer users than three of the library's branches, including an attractive but unostentatious establishment inserted among the downtown shops of Chestnut Street. Like many cultural enterprises, libraries are a combination of primary use and convenience use, and work best as either when they combine these attributes. In size and appearance then, and in its stock of books, the main library building is more significant; but in its role as an element of city use, the small branch is more significant, belying appearances. It is always necessary to think of performance in terms of users when trying to understand how primary mixtures work.

Any primary use whatever, by itself is relatively ineffectual as a creator of city diversity. If it is combined with another primary use that brings people in and out and puts them on the street at the same time, nothing has been accomplished. In practical terms, we cannot even call these differing primary uses. However, when a primary use is combined, effectively, with another that puts people on the street at different times, then the effect can be economically stimulating: a fertile environment for secondary diversity.

Secondary diversity is a name for the enterprises that grow in response to the presence of primary uses, to serve the people the primary uses draw. If this secondary diversity serves single primary uses, no matter what the type of use, it is innately inefficient.* Serving mixed primary uses, it can be innately efficient and—if the other three condi-

---

*Shopping centers that serve only residential primary use, for example, have a trouble similar to that of lower Manhattan, but in reverse so far as time is concerned. Thus many such shopping centers have been closing up in the mornings and staying open in the evenings. "The way things are now," said a shopping center executive quoted in the *New York Times,* "you could shoot a cannon down the mall of any shopping center at midday and not hit a soul." The innate inefficiency of serving a single primary use is one reason (in combination with several others) why so few shopping centers are able to support any but standardized, high-turnover enterprises.

tions for generating diversity are favorable also—it can be exuberant.

If this spread of street use spreads a variety of consumer needs or tastes through time of day, all sorts of uniquely urban and specialized services and shops can make out, and this is a process that builds upon itself. The more intricately mixed, and therefore efficient, the pools of users are, the more services and shops there can be that need to sift their clienteles from all sorts of population, and in turn the more people are drawn. So it is necessary here to make still another distinction.

If secondary diversity flourishes sufficiently and contains enough that is unusual or unique, it seemingly can and does become, in its accumulation, a primary use itself. People come specifically for it. This is what happens in good shopping districts or even, to a humble extent, on Hudson Street. I do not wish to minimize this occurrence; it is vital to the economic health of city streets and districts, and to cities as a whole. It is vital to city fluidity of use, to great choice, and to interesting and useful differences in character among streets and districts.

Nevertheless, secondary diversity seldom becomes quite a primary use fully "in its own right." If it is to have staying power, and the vitality to grow and change, it must retain its basic foundation of mixed primary uses—people spread through time of day because of fixed reasons. This is true even of downtown shopping, which is there, basically, because of other mixed primary uses, and which withers (even if slowly) when these become seriously unbalanced.

I have mentioned several times in passing that primary use mixtures must be *effective* if they are to generate diversity. What makes them effective? They must, of course, be combined with the other three conditions that stimulate diversity. But in addition, the primary mixture has to perform effectively itself.

Effectiveness means, first, that the people using the streets at different times must actually use the *same* streets. If their paths are separated from one another's, or buffered from one another's, there is no mixture in reality. In terms of city-street economics, mutual support among differences is then a fiction, or something to be seen merely as an abstraction of adjoining different uses, with no meaning except on a map.

Effectiveness means, second, that the people using the same streets at differing times must include, among them, people who will use some of the same facilities. All kinds of people can be present, but those who turn up for one reason at one time must not be sorted out in some totally incompatible fashion from those who turn up for another reason. As an extreme example, where the new home of the Metropolitan Opera in New York is to share a street with a low-income public housing project across the way, the juncture is meaningless—even if there were a place here for mutually supported diversity to grow. This type of hopeless economic contretemps seldom turns up naturally in a city, but it is frequently introduced by plan.

And finally, effectiveness means that the mixture of people on a street at one time of day must bear some reasonably proportionate relationship to people there at other times of day. I have already made this point in discussing the plans for the lower tip of Manhattan. It has often been observed that lively downtowns are apt to have dwellings fingering into them and close beside them, and night uses these residents enjoy and help support. This is an accurate observation so far as it goes, and on the strength of it many cities are expecting miracles from residential projects downtown, in the fashion of the lower Manhattan plan. But in real life, where such combinations have vitality the residents are part of a very complex pool of downtown day, night and week-end uses in reasonable balance.

Similarly, a few thousand workers dribbled in among tens or hundreds of thousands of residents make no appreciable balance either in sum or at any particular spot of any significance. Or a lone office building amid a large grouping of theaters amounts to little or nothing in practical terms. In short, with primary mixtures, it is everyday, ordinary performance in mixing people, as pools of economic mutual support, that counts. This is the point, and it is a tangible, concrete economic matter, not a vaguely "atmospheric" effect.

I have been dwelling upon downtowns. This is not because mixtures of primary uses are unneeded elsewhere in cities. On the contrary they are needed, and the success of mixtures downtown (or in the most intensive portions of cities, whatever they are called) is related to the mixture possible in other parts of cities.

I have been dwelling on downtowns for two reasons in particular. First, insufficient primary mixture is typically the principal fault in our downtowns, and often the only disastrous basic fault. Most big-city downtowns fulfill—or in the past did fulfill—all four of the necessary conditions for generating diversity. That is why they were able to become downtowns. Today, typically, they still do fulfill three of the conditions. But they have become (for reasons that will be discussed in Chapter Thirteen) too predominately devoted to work and contain too few people after working hours. This condition has been more or less formalized in planning jargon, which no longer speaks of "downtowns" but instead of "CBD's"—standing for Central Business Districts. A Central Business District that lives up to its name and is truly described by it, is a dud. Few downtowns have reached (yet) the degree of unbalance to be found at the lower tip of Manhattan. Most have, in addition to their working people, a good many daytime shoppers during working hours and on Saturdays. But most are on their way toward this unbalance, and have fewer potential assets than lower Manhattan has for retrieving themselves.

The second reason for emphasizing primary mixtures downtown is the direct effect on other parts of cities. Probably everyone is aware of certain general dependencies by a city on its heart. When a city heart stagnates or disintegrates, a city as a social neighborhood of the whole begins to suffer: People who ought to get together, by means of central activities that are failing, fail to get together. Ideas and money that ought to meet, and do so often only by happenstance in a place of central vitality, fail to meet. The networks of city public life develop gaps they cannot afford. Without a strong and *inclusive* central heart, a city tends to become a collection of interests isolated from one another. It falters at producing something greater, socially, culturally and economically, than the sum of its separated parts.

All these considerations are important, but I have in

mind here a more specific economic effect exerted by a strong city heart upon other districts.

The peculiar benefits that cities afford to incubation operate, as I have pointed out, most efficiently and surely where the most complex pools of use form. From such incubators of enterprise spring economic youngsters that may—and in real life do—later transfer their power to other parts of a city.

This movement has been well described by Richard Ratcliff, professor of land economics at the University of Wisconsin. "Decentralization is a symptom of degeneration and decay," says Ratcliff, "only if it leaves a vacuum behind. Where decentralization is the product of centripetal forces, it is healthy. Much of the outward movement of certain urban functions occurs as they are pushed out of the center, rather than as they respond to a pull toward outlying locations."

In a healthy city, notes Professor Ratcliff, there is a constant replacement of less intensive uses by more intensive uses.* "Artificially induced dispersion is another question. It holds the danger of loss in total efficiency and productivity."

In New York, as Raymond Vernon has noted in *Anatomy of a Metropolis*, the intensive developments of parts of Manhattan Island for white-collar work have been pushing manufacturers out into the other boroughs. (When city manufacturers get big and self-sufficient enough they may go to suburbs or little towns, which

---

*This process can go to extremes and destroy itself, but that is another aspect of the question, which I shall deal with in Part III of this book. We can ignore it for the time being.

depend economically too on the powerful incubating effects of those wonderfully productive places, intensive big cities.)

Uses crowded out from incubators of diversity and enterprise are of two kinds, like other city diversity. If they are crowded-out secondary diversity, serving people drawn by mixtures of primary uses, they must find other places in which secondary diversity can flourish—other places with mixtures of primary uses among other factors—or else languish and probably die. Their movement, if they are able to find congenial places, can represent opportunity for a city. They help heighten and speed the formation of further complex city. This is one of the influences, for example, from outside Hudson Street that has been affecting us. This is where the skin-diver equipment people come from, and the print and framing people, and the sculptor who took over an empty store. They are enterprises bubbling over from more intensive generators of diversity.

Although this movement is valuable (if it is not lost for lack of sufficient economically fertile ground), it is less significant and basic than the movement of primary diversity crowded out from intensive centers. For when primary uses, such as manufacturing, for instance, boil over and outward from pools of use that can no longer contain everything they generate, these can become ingredients of primary mixture in places where the primary use of work is desperately needed. Their presence can help create new pools of primary mixed use.

One land-use economist, Larry Smith, has aptly called office buildings chess pieces. "You have used up those chess pieces already," he is said to have told a planner who was trying to revitalize an unrealistic number of spots with dreamy plans for new office buildings. All primary uses, whether offices, dwellings or concert halls, are a city's chessmen. Those that move differently from one another must be employed *in concert* to accomplish much. And as in chess, a pawn can be converted to a queen. But city building has this difference from chess: The number of pieces is not fixed by the rules. If well deployed, the pieces multiply.

In city downtowns, public policy cannot inject directly the entirely private enterprises that serve people after work and enliven and help invigorate the place. Nor can public policy, by any sort of fiat, hold these uses in a downtown. But indirectly, public policy can encourage their growth by using its own chessmen, and those susceptible to public pressure, in the right places as primers.

Carnegie Hall, on West Fifty-seventh Street in New York, is a striking example of such a primer. It has worked remarkably well for its street in spite of the serious handicap of too-long blocks. The presence of Carnegie Hall, which brings intensive use to the street by night, generated in time the presence of another use that needs night business—two motion-picture theaters. And because Carnegie Hall is a music center, it generated the presence of many small music, dance and drama studios and recital rooms. All this is mixed and woven with residences—two hotels and many apartments close by, which have all kinds of tenants, but notably a great many who are musicians and teachers of music. The street works by day because of small office buildings, and large office buildings to east and west, and finally because the double-shift use is able to support secondary diversity that has, in time, become an attraction too. The time spread of users is of course stimulating to restaurants, and here is a whole gamut: a fine Italian restaurant, a glamorous Russian restaurant, a sea-food restaurant, an espresso house, several bars, an Automat, a couple of soda fountains, a hamburger house. Between and among the restaurants you can buy rare coins, old jewelry, old or new books, very nice shoes, art supplies, remarkably elaborate hats, flowers, gourmet foods, health foods, imported chocolates. You can buy or sell thrice-worn Dior dresses and last year's minks, or rent an English sports car.

In this case, Carnegie Hall is a vital chessman, working in concert with other chessmen. The most ruinous plan that could be devised for this entire neighborhood would be to destroy Carnegie Hall and replace it with another office building. This was precisely what was about to happen, as an accompaniment to New York's decision to take all its most impressive, or potentially impressive, cultural chessmen out of play and segregate them in a planning island called the Lincoln Center for the Performing Arts. Carnegie Hall was saved by a hair, owing to stubborn citizen pressure politics, although it will no longer be the home of the New York Philharmonic, which is going to decontaminate itself from the ordinary city.

Now this is a pitiful kind of planning, which would blindly destroy a city's existing pools of use and automatically foster new problems of stagnation, as a thoughtless by-product to pushing through new dreams. Chessmen—and in downtowns night-use chessmen that can be located by public policy or public pressure—should be placed to fortify and extend existing vitality, and also to help balance up, in strategic places, existing time unbalances. New York's midtown has many places with intensive daytime use that go ominously dead at night, that need precisely the chessmen being taken out of play at Lincoln Center. The stretch of new office building centering on Park Avenue between Grand Central Station and Fifty-ninth Street is such a territory. The area just south of Grand Central is another. The shopping district centering on Thirty-fourth Street is another. Many a once vital district, having lost in the past a mixture of primary uses which brought attraction, popularity and high economic value, has declined sadly.

This is why projects such as cultural or civic centers, besides being woefully unbalanced themselves as a rule, are tragic in their effects on their cities. They isolate uses—and too often intensive night uses too—from the parts of cities that must have them or sicken.

Boston was the first American city to plan for itself a decontaminated cultural district. In 1859, a Committee of Institutes called for a "Cultural Conservation," setting aside a tract to be devoted "solely to institutions of an educational, scientific and artistic character," a move that coincided with the beginning of Boston's long, slow decline as a live cultural leader among American cities. Whether the deliberate segregation and decontamination of numerous cultural institutions from the ordinary city and ordinary life was part of the cause of Boston's cultural decline, or whether it was simply a symptom and seal of a decadence already inevitable from other causes, I do not know. One thing is sure: Boston's downtown has suffered miserably from lack of good mixtures in its primary uses, particularly good mixing in of night uses and of live (not museum-piece and once-upon-a-time) cultural uses.

It is said, by those who have the problem of raising money for large cultural enterprises, that rich people will contribute much more readily and heavily for large, decontaminated islands of monuments than for single cultural buildings set in a city's matrix. This was one of the rationalizations which resulted in the plans for New York's Lincoln Center for the Performing Arts. Whether this is true about fund raising I do not know; it would not be surprising, however, since the well-off who are also enlightened have been informed by experts for years that project building is the only worthwhile city building.

Among downtown planners and the businessmen's groups who work with them, there is a myth (or alibi) that Americans all stay home at night watching TV or else attend the P-TA meeting. This is what they tell you in Cincinnati when you ask about their downtown, which is dead by evening and consequently half-alive by day. Yet Cincinnatians pay some half-million visits a year to the generally expensive night life across the river in Covington, Kentucky, which has its own kind of morbid unbalance. "People don't go out," is one of the alibis also used in Pittsburgh to explain its dead downtown.*

Downtown, the Pittsburgh Parking Authority's garages are operating at only between 10 and 20 percent of capacity by eight o clock in the evening, except for the central Mellon Square garage which may reach 50 percent

---

*The other alibi, offered rather proudly by businessmen, is that "We've got a downtown something like Wall Street." Apparently they haven't heard Wall Street's neighborhood news about its difficulties.

if something is doing at the hotels. (Like parks and consumer shops, parking and traffic facilities are innately inefficient and wasteful without time spread of users.) Meantime, the parking problem three miles from downtown in a section called Oakland is something fierce. "No sooner does one crowd move out of that place than another moves in," explains an Authority official. "It's a headache." It is also easy to understand. Oakland contains the Pittsburgh symphony, the civic light opera, the little-theater group, the most fashionable restaurant, the Pittsburgh Athletic Association, two other major clubs, the main Carnegie library, museum and art galleries, the Historical Society, the Shriners' Mosque, the Mellon Institute, a favorite hotel for parties, the Y.M.H.A., headquarters of the Board of Education, and all the major hospitals.

Because Oakland contains a high disproportion of leisure-time, after-work uses, it is unbalanced too, and Pittsburgh has no good place, either in Oakland or in the working downtown, for generating intensively its principal metropolitan secondary diversity. The standard stores and the lowbrow diversity, such as it is, are downtown. What higher-brow commercial diversity does exist has mostly chosen Oakland as apparently the better bet of the two places; but it is bloodless and marginal because Oakland is far from the effective pool of use that a metropolitan heart should be.

Pittsburgh's instrument for getting into this twofold unbalance was a real estate operator, the late Frank Nicola, who fifty years ago, in the City Beautiful era, began promoting a cultural center on the pristine meadows of a dairy farm. He had a good start because the Carnegie library and art center had already accepted a gift site from the Schenley land holdings. Downtown Pittsburgh in those days was not, in any case, an attractive place for such establishments because it was unrelievedly grim, smoky and sooty.

Now, however, downtown Pittsburgh is potentially attractive for leisure use, thanks to the massive cleaning up led by the businessmen's Allegheny Conference. And theoretically, the downtown's one-shift unbalance should soon be partly remedied by a civic auditorium and the later addition of a symphony hall and apartments, all immediately adjoining downtown. But the spirit of the dairy farm and of culture decontaminated from the city still reigns. Every device—arterial highways, belts of park, parking lots—severs these projects from the working downtown, insures that their juncture will remain an abstraction on maps instead of a living economic reality of people appearing at different times on the same streets. American downtowns are not declining mysteriously, because they are anachronisms, nor because their users have been drained away by automobiles. They are being witlessly murdered, in good part by deliberate policies of sorting out leisure uses from work uses, under the misapprehension that this is orderly city planning.

Primary-use chessmen cannot be strewn hither and yon in a city, of course, taking into account only the need of spreading people through time of day, and ignoring the particular needs of the uses themselves—what will be good locations for *them*.

However, such arbitrariness is unnecessary. I have spoken admiringly from time to time about the intricate, underlying order of cities. It is part of the beauty of this order that success for the mixture in itself, and success for the peculiar and specific elements of the mixture, are apt to be in harmony rather than contradiction. I have given some examples of this identity (or correspondence) of interest already in this chapter, and have touched on others by implication: e.g., the new work uses planned for lower Manhattan will not only increase that district's fundamental trouble, but at the same time will burden the new employees and officials with an economically dull and an inconvenient city environment. Now I shall give an illustrative example of the quite complex ill effects that can arise when this innate order of city vitality is flouted.

We might call this the case of the courts and the opera. Forty-five years ago, San Francisco began building a civic center, which has given trouble ever since. This particular center, placed near the downtown and intended to pull the downtown toward it, has of course repelled vitality and gathered around itself instead the blight that typically surrounds these dead and artificial places. The center includes, among the other arbitrary objects in its parks, the opera house, the city hall, the public library and various municipal offices.

Now, considering the opera house and the library as chessmen, how could they have best helped the city? Each would have been used, separately, in *close* conjunction with high-intensity downtown offices and shops. This, and the secondary diversity they would help anchor, would *also* have been a more congenial environment for either of these two buildings themselves. The opera, as it is, stands related to nothing, enjoying the irrelevant convenience of its nearest neighboring facility, the Civil Service Employment waiting room at the back of City Hall. And the library, as it is, is the leaning wall of Skid Row.

Unfortunately, in affairs of this kind, one mistake leads on and on. In 1958, a location had to be picked for a criminal courts building. The logical spot, it was well recognized, would be some place near the other municipal offices, for the convenience of lawyers and of the services that attach to lawyers' neighborhoods. But it was also recognized that the courts building would be bound to catalyze, somewhere in its vicinity, a secondary diversity of bail-bond houses and un-chic bars. What to do? Put the courts close to the civic center or in it, so they would be near some of the buildings with which they need to work? But the environment of the criminal courts is nothing to encourage near the opera! The nondescript rattiness nearby is already unsuitable enough.

Every alternative solution to such a ludicrous dilemma must be poor. The solution chosen was to place the courts at an inconvenient distance, but the opera was saved from further contamination by life other than "civic," whatever that may mean.

This tiresome muddle arises not in the least from contradictions between demands by the city as an organism and demands by various specific uses, nor do most planning muddles arise from any such contradictions. They arise chiefly from theories which are in arbitrary contradiction with *both* the order of cities and the needs of individual uses.

This point of unsuitable theory—in this case esthetic theory—is so important and so consistently frustrating in one form and another to proper city primary mixtures,

that I shall pursue the implications of this case a little further here.

Elbert Peets, an architect who for many years was a
consistently dissenting member of the Washington, D. C.,
Fine Arts Commission, has stated the conflict well, and
although he is speaking of Washington his remarks apply
to this trouble in San Francisco and to troubles in many
other places too:

> It is my feeling that wrong principles motivate
> important aspects [of current Washington town
> planning]. These principles have developed histori-
> cally and have acquired so much support of habit
> and vested interest that the busy people guiding
> Washington's architectural growth doubtless accept
> them without question—which, however, we must
> not do.
>
> Briefly, what is happening is this: the govern-
> ment capital is turning away from the city; the gov-
> ernment buildings are being concentrated together
> and separated from the buildings of the city. This
> was not L'Enfant's idea. On the contrary, he made
> every effort to amalgamate the two, to make them
> serve each other. He distributed government build-
> ings, markets, seats of national societies, academies,
> and State memorials at points of architectural
> advantage throughout the city, as if with the defi-
> nite purpose of putting the impress of the national
> capital on every part. This was sound sentiment and
> sound architectural judgment.
>
> From the Chicago Fair of 1893 came the archi-
> tectural ideology that sees a city as a monumental
> court of honor sharply set off from a profane and
> jumbled area of "concessions." . . . There is no evi-

dence, in this procedure, of feeling for the city as an organism, a matrix that is worthy of its monuments and friendly with them . . . The loss is social, as well as esthetic . . .

Here, one might say offhand, are two opposed esthetic visions, a matter of taste, and who can quarrel with taste? But this goes deeper than taste. One of these visions—the sorted-out "courts of honor"—contradicts the functional and economic needs of cities and of their specific uses too. The other vision—the mingled city with individual architectural focal points intimately surrounded by the everyday matrix—is in harmony with the economic and other functional behavior of cities.*

Every city primary use, whether it comes in monumental and special guise or not, needs its intimate matrix of "profane" city to work to best advantage. The courts building in San Francisco needs one kind of matrix with its secondary diversity. The opera needs another kind of matrix with its secondary diversity. And the matrices of the city need these uses themselves, for the influence of their presence helps form a city's matrices. Furthermore, a city matrix needs its own less spectacular internal minglings ("jumbles" to the simple-minded). Else it is not a matrix but, like housing projects, it is "profane" monotony, working no more sensibly than the "sacred" monotony of civic centers like San Francisco's.

*The New York Public Library at Fifth Avenue and Forty-second Street is an example of such an architectural focal point; the old Jefferson Market Courthouse in the center of Greenwich Village is another. Every reader, I am sure, is familiar with individual monumental focal points in a city matrix.

To be sure, any principle can be applied arbitrarily and destructively by people who fail to understand its workings. L'Enfant's esthetic theory of focal points interdependent with the everyday city matrix surrounding them could be applied by trying to strew primary uses—especially those capable of monumental appearance—without regard for the economic or other working relationships that they require. But L'Enfant's theory is admirable, not as an abstract visual good in isolation from function, but rather because it is capable of being applied and adapted in harmony with the needs of real establishments in real cities. If these functional needs are considered and respected, esthetic theories that glorify sorted-out and isolated uses, either "sacred" or "profane," are impossible to apply.

In city districts that are predominately or heavily residential, the more complexity and variety of primary uses that can be cultivated, the better, just as in downtowns. But the chief chessman that is needed in these districts is the primary use of work. As we have seen in the examples of the park at Rittenhouse Square, or Hudson Street, these two primary uses can dovetail nicely with one another, the streets livening up with workers at midday when they go dead from the dwellings, livening up from the dwellings in the evening when they go dead from the work.

The desirability of segregating dwellings from work has been so dinned into us that it takes an effort to look at real life and observe that residential districts lacking mixture with work do not fare well in cities. In an article on Negro ghettos by Harry S. Ashmore in the *New York Herald Tribune*, a Harlem political leader was quoted as saying, "The whites are likely to ease back in here, and take Harlem away from us. After all, [Harlem is] the most attractive piece of real estate in the whole area. We've got hills and views of both rivers, and transportation is good, and it's the only close-in area that doesn't have any industry."

Only in planning theory does this make Harlem an "attractive piece of real estate." From the time of its white middle- and upper-class beginnings, Harlem never was a workable, economically vigorous residential district of a city, and it probably never will be, no matter who lives there, until it gets, among other physical improvements, a good, healthy mixture of work stirred alongside and among its stretches of dwellings.

Primary work uses in residential districts cannot be produced by wishing for them, any more than secondary diversity can be. Public policy can do relatively little that is positive to get working uses woven in where they are absent and needed in cities, other than to *permit* and indirectly encourage them.

But attempts at positive lures are not the most pressing first need in any case, nor the most fruitful way to spend efforts in gray areas that need vitality. The first problem is to make the most of any work and other primary-use chessmen where they already do exist in failing residential districts. The sample-shoe market in Louisville, although it is a strange example, cries out for such opportunism. Much of the borough of Brooklyn does, and some of the Bronx, and indeed, inner gray areas in almost all big cities.

How do you use the existing presence of working places opportunistically, and build from this? How do you weld them in to help form, with dwellings, effective pools of street use? Here we must make a distinction between the typical downtown and the usual residential district in trouble. In downtowns, lack of sufficient primary mixture is usually the most serious basic handicap. In most residential districts, and especially most gray areas, lack of primary mixture is usually only one handicap, and sometimes not the most severe. Indeed, it is easy to find instances in which work is mixed with dwellings, yet to little avail in helping generate diversity or vigor. This is because most city residential districts also have blocks that are too large, or they were built up all at once and have never overcome this original handicap even as their buildings have aged, or very commonly they lack sufficient population in sheer numbers. In short, they are deficient in several of the four conditions for generating diversity.

Instead of worrying about where enough work is to come from, the first problem is to identify where, in residential districts, it does exist and is being wasted as an element of primary use. In cities you have to build from existing assets, to make more assets. To think how to make the most of work and dwelling mixtures, where they exist or give promise of existing, it is necessary to understand the parts played by the three other generators of diversity too.

However, I shall anticipate the discussion in the next three chapters to say this: Of the four generators of diversity, two represent easy problems to deal with in curing the troubles of gray areas—aged buildings are usually already present to do their potential share; and additional streets where they are needed are not innately difficult to acquire. (They are a minor problem compared with the large-scale land clearance we have been taught to waste our money on.)

The two other necessary conditions, however—mixtures of primary diversity and sufficient concentration of dwellings—are more difficult to create if they are lacking. The sensible thing is to begin where at least *one* of these two conditions already exists or can be fostered relatively easily.

The hardest city districts to deal with will be residential gray areas that lack infusions of work to build upon, and that also lack high densities of dwellings. Failing or failed city areas are in trouble not so much because of what they have (which can always be regarded as a base to build upon), but because of what they lack. Gray areas with the most severe and the most difficult-to-supply lacks can hardly be helped toward vigor unless other gray-area districts that do have at least a start toward primary mixture are nurtured, and unless downtowns are reinvigorated with better spread of people through time of day. The more successfully a city generates diversity and vitality in any of its parts, of course, the better become its chances for building success, ultimately, in still other parts—including, eventually, those most discouraging to begin with.

It should go without saying that streets or districts which do have good primary mixtures and are successful at generating city diversity should be treasured, rather than despised for their mixture and destroyed by attempts to sort out their components from one another. But unfortunately, conventional planners seem to see in just such popular and attractive places only an irresistible invitation to employ the destructive and simple-minded purposes of orthodox city planning. Given enough federal funds and enough power, planners can easily destroy city primary mixtures faster than these can grow in unplanned districts, so that there is a net loss of basic primary mixture. Indeed, this is happening today.

9

THE NEED FOR
SMALL BLOCKS

CONDITION 2: *Most blocks must be short; that is, streets and opportunities to turn corners must be frequent.*

The advantages of short blocks are simple.

Consider, for instance, the situation of a man living on a long street block, such as West Eighty-eighth Street in Manhattan, between Central Park West and Columbus Avenue. He goes westward along his 800-foot block to reach the stores on Columbus Avenue or take the bus, and he goes eastward to reach the park, take the subway or another bus. He may very well never enter the adjacent blocks on Eighty-seventh Street and Eighty-ninth Street for years.

This brings grave trouble. We have already seen that isolated, discrete street neighborhoods are apt to be helpless socially. This man would have every justification for disbelieving that Eighty-seventh and Eighty-ninth streets or their people have anything to do with him. To believe it, he has to go beyond the ordinary evidence of his everyday life.

So far as his neighborhood is concerned, the *economic* effect of these self-isolating streets is equally constricting. The people on this street, and the people on the adjacent

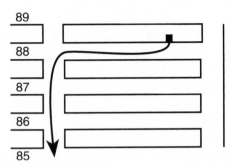

streets can form a pool of economic use only where their long, separated paths meet and come together in one stream. In this case, the nearest place where that can happen is Columbus Avenue.

And because Columbus Avenue is the only nearby place where tens of thousands of people from these stagnant, long, backwater blocks meet and form a pool of use, Columbus Avenue has its own kind of monotony—endless stores and a depressing predominance of commercial standardization. In this neighborhood there is geographically so little street frontage on which commerce can live,

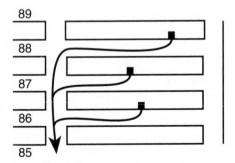

that it must all be consolidated, regardless of its type or the scale of support it needs or the scale of convenience (distance from users) that is natural to it. Around about stretch the dismally long strips of monotony and darkness—the Great Blight of Dullness, with an abrupt garish gash at long intervals. This is a typical arrangement for areas of city failure.

This stringent physical segregation of the regular users of one street from the regular users of the next holds, of course, for visitors too. For instance, I have been going to a dentist on West Eighty-sixth Street just off Columbus Avenue for more than fifteen years. In all that time, although I have ranged north and south on Columbus, and north and south on Central Park West, I have never used West Eighty-fifth Street or West Eighty-seventh Street. It would be both inconvenient and pointless to do so. If I take the children, after the dentist, to the planetarium on West Eighty-first Street between Columbus and Central Park West, there is only one possible direct route: down Columbus and then into Eighty-first.

Let us consider, instead, the situation if these long east-west blocks had an extra street cut across them—not a sterile "promenade" of the kind in which super-block projects abound, but a street containing buildings where things could start up and grow at spots economically viable: places for buying, eating, seeing things, getting a drink. With the extra street, the Eighty-eighth Street man would no longer need to walk a monotonous, always-the-same path to a given point. He would have various alternative routes to choose. The neighborhood would literally have opened up to him.

The same would be true of people living on other

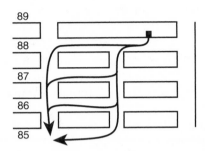

streets, and for those nearer Columbus heading toward a point in the park or toward the subway. Instead of mutual isolation of paths, these paths would now be mixed and mingled with one another.

The supply of feasible spots for commerce would increase considerably, and so could the distribution and convenience of their placement. If among the people on West Eighty-eighth there are a third enough people to support a newspaper and neighborhood oddment place somewhat like Bernie's around the corner from us, and the same might be said of Eighty-seventh and Eighty-ninth, now there would be a possibility that they might do so around one of their additional corners. As long as these people can never pool their support nearby except in one stream only, such distribution of services, economic opportunity and public life is an impossibility.

In the case of these long blocks, even people who are present in the neighborhood for the same primary reasons are kept too much apart to permit them to form reasonably intricate pools of city cross-use. Where differing primary uses are involved, long blocks are apt to thwart effective mixture in exactly the same way. They automatically sort people into paths that meet too infrequently,

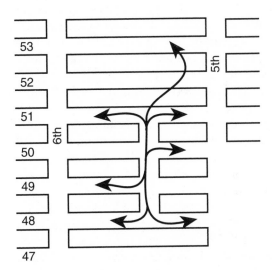

so that different uses very near each other geographically are, in practical effect, literally blocked off from one another.

To contrast the stagnation of these long blocks with the fluidity of use that an extra street could bring is not a far-fetched supposition. An example of such a transformation can be seen at Rockefeller Center, which occupies three of the long blocks between Fifth and Sixth avenues. Rockefeller Center has that extra street.

I ask those readers who are familiar with it to imagine it without its extra north-south street, Rockefeller Plaza. If the center's buildings were continuous along each of its side streets all the way from Fifth to Sixth Avenue, it would no longer be a center of use. It could not be. It would be a group of self-isolated streets pooling only at Fifth and Sixth avenues. The most artful design in other respects could not tie it together, because it is fluidity of use, and the mixing of paths, not homogeneity of architecture, that ties together city neighborhoods into pools of city use, whether those neighborhoods are predominately for work or predominately for residence.

To the north, Rockefeller Center's street fluidity extends in diminished form, as far as Fifty-third Street, because of a block-through lobby and an arcade that people use as a further extension of the street. To the south, its fluidity as a pool of use ends abruptly along Forty-eighth Street. The next street down, Forty-seventh, is self-isolated. It is largely a wholesaling street (the center of gem wholesaling), a surprisingly marginal use for a street that lies geographically next to one of the city's greatest attractions. But just like the users of Eighty-seventh and Eighty-eighth streets, the users of Forty-seventh and Forty-eighth streets can go for years without ever mixing into one another's streets.

Long blocks, in their nature, thwart the potential advantages that cities offer to incubation, experimentation, and many small or special enterprises, insofar as these depend upon drawing their customers or clients from among much larger cross-sections of passing public. Long blocks also thwart the principle that if city mixtures of use are to be more than a fiction on maps, they must result in different people, bent on different purposes, appearing at different times, but using the *same* streets.

Of all the hundreds of long blocks in Manhattan, a bare eight or ten are spontaneously enlivening with time or exerting magnetism.

It is instructive to watch where the overflow of diversity and popularity from Greenwich Village has spilled and where it has halted. Rents have steadily gone up in Greenwich Village, and predictors have regularly been predicting, for at least twenty-five years now, a renascence of once fashionable Chelsea directly to the north. This prediction may seem logical because of Chelsea's location, because its mixtures and types of buildings and densities of dwelling units per acre are almost identical with those of Greenwich Village, and also because it even has a mixture of work with its dwellings. But the renascence has never happened. Instead, Chelsea languishes behind its barriers of long, self-isolating blocks, decaying in most of them faster than it is rehabilitated in others. Today it is being extensively slum-cleared, and in the process endowed with even bigger and more monotonous blocks. (The pseudoscience of planning seems almost neurotic in its determination to imitate empiric failure and ignore empiric success.) Meantime, Greenwich Village has extended itself and its diversity and popularity far to the east, working outward through a little neck between industrial concentrations, following unerringly the direction of short blocks and fluid street use even though the buildings in that direction are not so attractive or seemingly suitable as those in Chelsea. This movement in one direction and halt in another is neither capricious nor mysterious nor "a chaotic accident." It is a down-to-earth response to what works well economically for city diversity and what does not.

Another perennial "mystery" raised in New York is why the removal of the elevated railway along Sixth Avenue on the West Side stimulated so little change and added so little to popularity, and why the removal of the

elevated railway along Third Avenue on the East Side
stimulated so much change and added so greatly to popularity. But long blocks have made an economic monstrosity of the West Side, the more so because they occur
toward the center of the island, precisely where the West
Side's most effective pools of use would and should form,
had they a chance. Short blocks occur on the East Side
toward the center of the island, exactly where the most
effective pools of use have had the best chance of forming and extending themselves.*

Theoretically, almost all the short side streets of the
East Side in the Sixties, Seventies and Eighties are residential only. It is instructive to notice how frequently and
how nicely special shops like bookstores or dressmakers
or restaurants have inserted themselves, usually, but not
always, near the corners. The equivalent West Side does
not support bookstores and never did. This is not because
its successive discontented and deserting populations all
had an aversion to reading nor because they were too
poor to buy books. On the contrary the West Side is full of
intellectuals and always has been. It is probably as good
a "natural" market for books as Greenwich Village and
possibly a better "natural" market than the East Side.

---

*Going west from Fifth Avenue, the first three blocks, and in some
places four, are 800 feet long, except where Broadway, on a diagonal,
intersects. Going east from Fifth Avenue, the first four blocks vary
between 400 and 420 feet in length. At Seventieth Street, to pick a random point where the two sides of the island are divided by Central Park,
the 2,400 linear feet of building line between Central Park West and
West End Avenue are intersected by *only two* avenues. On the east side,
an equivalent length of building line extends from Fifth Avenue to a little beyond Second Avenue and is intersected by *five* avenues. The stretch
of East Side with its five intersecting avenues is immensely more popular than the West Side with its two.

Because of its long blocks, the West Side has never been physically capable of forming the intricate pools of fluid street use necessary to support urban diversity.

A reporter for the *New Yorker*, observing that people *try* to find an extra north-south passage in the too-long blocks between Fifth and Sixth avenues, once attempted to see if he could amalgamate a makeshift mid-block trail from Thirty-third Street to Rockefeller Center. He discovered reasonable, if erratic, means for short-cutting through nine of the blocks, owing to block-through stores and lobbies and Bryant Park behind the Forty-second Street Library. But he was reduced to wiggling under fences or clambering through windows or coaxing superintendents, to get through four of the blocks, and had to evade the issue by going into subway passages for two.

In city districts that become successful or magnetic, streets are virtually never made to disappear. Quite the contrary. Where it is possible, they multiply. Thus in the Rittenhouse Square district of Philadelphia and in Georgetown in the District of Columbia, what were once back alleys down the centers of blocks have become streets with buildings fronting on them, and users using them like streets. In Philadelphia, they often include commerce.

Nor do long blocks possess more virtue in other cities than they do in New York. In Philadelphia there is a neighborhood in which buildings are simply being let fall down by their owners, in an area between the downtown and the city's major belt of public housing projects. There are many reasons for this neighborhood's hopelessness, including the nearness of the rebuilt city with its social disintegration and danger, but obviously the neighborhood has not been helped by its own physical structure. The standard Philadelphia block is 400 feet square (halved by the alleys-become-streets where the city is most successful). In this falling-down neighborhood some of that "street waste" was eliminated in the original street layout; its blocks are 700 feet long. It stagnated, of course, beginning from the time it was built up. In Boston, the North End, which is a marvel of "wasteful" streets and fluidity of cross-use, has been heroically unslumming itself against official apathy and financial opposition.

The myth that plentiful city streets are "wasteful," one of the verities of orthodox planning, comes of course from the Garden City and Radiant City theorists who decried the use of land for streets because they wanted that land consolidated instead into project prairies. This myth is especially destructive because it interferes intellectually with our ability to see one of the simplest, most unnecessary, and most easily corrected reasons for much stagnation and failure.

Super-block projects are apt to have all the disabilities of long blocks, frequently in exaggerated form, and this is true even when they are laced with promenades and malls, and thus, in theory, possess streets at reasonable intervals through which people can make their way. These streets are meaningless because there is seldom any active reason for a good cross-section of people to use them. Even in passive terms, simply as various alternative changes of scene in getting from here to yonder, these paths are meaningless because all their scenes are essentially the same. The situation is the opposite from that the *New Yorker* reporter noticed in the blocks between Fifth and Sixth avenues. There people try to hunt out streets which they need but which are missing. In projects, people are apt to avoid malls and cross-malls which are there, but are pointless.

I bring up this problem not merely to berate the anomalies of project planning again, but to indicate that frequent streets and short blocks are valuable because of the fabric of intricate cross-use that they permit among the users of a city neighborhood. Frequent streets are not an end in themselves. They are a means toward an end. If that end—generating diversity and catalyzing the plans of many people besides planners—is thwarted by too repressive zoning, or by regimented construction that precludes the flexible growth of diversity, nothing significant can be accomplished by short blocks. Like mixtures of primary use, frequent streets are effective in helping to generate diversity *only because of the way they perform.* The means by which they work (attracting mixtures of users along them) and the results they can help accomplish (the growth of diversity) are inextricably related. The relationship is reciprocal.

10

THE NEED FOR
AGED BUILDINGS

CONDITION 3: *The district must mingle buildings that vary in age and condition, including a good proportion of old ones.*

Cities need old buildings so badly it is probably impossible for vigorous streets and districts to grow without them. By old buildings I mean not museum-piece old buildings, not old buildings in an excellent and expensive state of rehabilitation—although these make fine ingredients—but also a good lot of plain, ordinary, low-value old buildings, including some rundown old buildings.

If a city area has only new buildings, the enterprises that can exist there are automatically limited to those that can support the high costs of new construction. These high costs of occupying new buildings may be levied in the form of rent, or they may be levied in the form of an owner's interest and amortization payments on the capital costs of the construction. However the costs are paid off, they have to be paid off. And for this reason, enterprises that support the cost of new construction must be capable of paying a relatively high overhead—high in comparison to that necessarily required by old buildings. To support such high overheads, the enterprises must be either (a) high profit or (b) well subsidized.

If you look about, you will see that only operations that are well established, high-turnover, standardized or heavily subsidized can afford, commonly, to carry the costs of new construction. Chain stores, chain restaurants and banks go into new construction. But neighborhood bars, foreign restaurants and pawn shops go into older buildings. Supermarkets and shoe stores often go into new buildings; good bookstores and antique dealers seldom do. Well-subsidized opera and art museums often go into new buildings. But the unformalized feeders of the arts—studios, galleries, stores for musical instruments and art supplies, backrooms where the low earning power of a seat and a table can absorb uneconomic discussions—these go into old buildings. Perhaps more significant, hundreds of ordinary enterprises, necessary to the safety and public life of streets and neighborhoods, and appreciated for their convenience and personal quality, can make out successfully in old buildings, but are inexorably slain by the high overhead of new construction.

As for really new ideas of any kind—no matter how ultimately profitable or otherwise successful some of them might prove to be—there is no leeway for such chancy trial, error and experimentation in the high-overhead economy of new construction. Old ideas can sometimes use new buildings. New ideas must use old buildings.

Even the enterprises that can support new construction in cities need old construction in their immediate vicinity. Otherwise they are part of a total attraction and total environment that is economically too limited—and therefore functionally too limited to be lively, interesting and convenient. Flourishing diversity anywhere in a city means the mingling of high-yield, middling-yield, low-yield and no-yield enterprises.

The only harm of aged buildings to a city district or street is the harm that eventually comes of *nothing but* old age—the harm that lies in everything being old and everything becoming worn out. But a city area in such a situation is not a failure because of being all old. It is the other way around. The area is all old because it is a failure. For some other reason or combination of reasons, all its enterprises or people are unable to support new construction. It has, perhaps, failed to hang on to its own people or enterprises that do become successful enough to support new building or rehabilitation; they leave when they become this successful. It has also failed to attract newcomers with choice; they see no opportunities or attractions here. And in some cases, such an area may be so infertile economically that enterprises which might grow into successes in other places, and build or rebuild their shelter, never make enough money in this place to do so.*

A successful city district becomes a kind of ever-normal granary so far as construction is concerned. Some of the old buildings, year by year, are replaced by new ones—or rehabilitated to a degree equivalent to replacement. Over the years there is, therefore, constantly a mix-

---

*These are all reasons having to do with inherent, built-in handicaps. There is another reason, however, why some city districts age unremittingly, and this other reason has nothing to do, necessarily, with inherent flaws. The district may have been blacklisted, in a concerted way, by mortgage lenders, the way Boston's North End has been. This means of dooming a neighborhood to inexorable wearing out is both common and destructive. But for the moment we are dealing with the conditions that affect a city area's inherent economic ability to generate diversity and staying power.

ture of buildings of many ages and types. This is, of course, a dynamic process, with what was once new in the mixture eventually becoming what is old in the mixture.

We are dealing here again, as we were in the case of mixed primary uses, with the economic effects of time. But in this case we are dealing with the economics of time not hour by hour through the day, but with the economics of time by decades and generations.

Time makes the high building costs of one generation the bargains of a following generation. Time pays off original capital costs, and this depreciation can be reflected in the yields required from a building. Time makes certain structures obsolete for some enterprises, and they become available to others. Time can make the space efficiencies of one generation the space luxuries of another generation. One century's building commonplace is another century's useful aberration.

The economic necessity for old buildings mixed with new is not an oddity connected with the precipitous rise in building costs since the war, and especially throughout the 1950's. To be sure, the difference between the yield most postwar building must bring and the yield that pre-Depression buildings must bring is especially sharp. In commercial space, the difference between carrying costs per square foot can be as much as 100 or 200 percent, even though the older buildings may be better built than the new, and even though the maintenance costs of all buildings, including old ones, have risen. Old buildings were a necessary ingredient of city diversity back in the 1920's and the 1890's. Old buildings will still be a necessity when today's new buildings are the old ones. This has been, still is, and will be, true no matter how erratic or how steady construction costs themselves are, because a depreciated building requires less income than one which has not yet paid off its capital costs. Steadily rising construction costs simply accentuate the need for old buildings. Possibly they also make necessary a higher *proportion* of old buildings in the total street or district mixture, because rising building costs raise the general threshold of pecuniary success required to support the costs of new construction.

A few years ago, I gave a talk at a city design conference about the social need for commercial diversity in cities. Soon my words began coming back at me from designers, planners and students in the form of a slogan (which I certainly did not invent): "We must leave room for the corner grocery store!"

At first I thought this must be a figure of speech, the part standing for the whole. But soon I began to receive in the mail plans and drawings for projects and renewal areas in which, literally, room had been left here and there at great intervals for a corner grocery store. These schemes were accompanied by letters that said, "See, we have taken to heart what you said."

This corner-grocery gimmick is a thin, patronizing conception of city diversity, possibly suited to a village of the last century, but hardly to a vital city district of today. Lone little groceries, in fact, do badly in cities as a rule. They are typically a mark of stagnant and undiverse gray area.

Nevertheless, the designers of these sweetly meant inanities were not simply being perverse. They were doing, probably, the best they could under the economic conditions set for them. A suburban-type shopping center at some place in the project, and this wan spotting of corner groceries, were the most that could be hoped for. For these were schemes contemplating either great blankets of new construction, or new construction combined with extensive, prearranged rehabilitation. Any vigorous range of diversity was precluded in advance by the consistently high overhead. (The prospects are made still poorer by insufficient primary mixtures of uses and therefore insufficient spread of customers through the day.)

Even the lone groceries, if they were ever built,* could hardly be the cozy enterprises envisioned by their designers. To carry their high overhead, they must either be (a) subsidized—by whom and why?—or (b) converted into routinized, high-turnover mills.

Large swatches of construction built at one time are inherently inefficient for sheltering wide ranges of cultural, population, and business diversity. They are even inefficient for sheltering much range of mere commercial diversity. This can be seen at a place like Stuyvesant Town in New York. In 1959, more than a decade after operation began, of the 32 store fronts that comprise Stuyvesant Town's commercial space, seven were either empty or were being used uneconomically (for storage, window advertising only, and the like). This represented disuse or underuse of 22 percent of the fronts. At the same time, across the bordering streets, where buildings of every age and condition are mingled, were 140 store fronts, of which 11 were empty or used uneconomically, representing a

---

*They are usually dropped from the plans, or indefinitely postponed, at the time when the economic realities of rents must be faced.

disuse or underuse of only 7 percent. Actually, the disparity is greater than this would appear, because the empty fronts in the old streets were mostly small, and in linear feet represented less than 7 percent, a condition which was not true of the project stores. The good business side of the street is the age-mingled side, even though a great share of its customers are Stuyvesant Town people, and even though they must cross wide and dangerous traffic arteries to reach it. This reality is acknowledged by the chain stores and supermarkets too, which have been building new quarters in the age-mingled setting instead of filling those empty fronts in the project.

One-age construction in city areas is sometimes protected nowadays from the threat of more efficient and responsive commercial competition. This protection—which is nothing more or less than commercial monopoly—is considered very "progressive" in planning circles. The Society Hill renewal plan for Philadelphia will, by zoning, prevent competition to its developer's shopping centers throughout a whole city district. The city's planners have also worked out a "food plan" for the area, which means offering a monopolistic restaurant concession to a single restaurant chain for the whole district. Nobody else's food allowed! The Hyde Park-Kenwood renewal district of Chicago reserves a monopoly on almost all commerce for a suburban-type shopping center to be the property of that plan's principal developer. In the huge Southwest redevelopment district of Washington, the major housing developer seems to be going so far as to eliminate competition with himself. The original plans for this scheme contemplated a central, suburban-type shopping center plus a smattering of convenience stores—our old friend, the lonely corner grocery gimmick. A shopping center economist predicted that these convenience stores might lead to diminished business for the main, suburban-type center which, itself, will have to support high overhead. To protect it, the convenience stores were dropped from the scheme. It is thus that routinized monopolistic packages of substitute city are palmed off as "planned shopping."

Monopoly planning can make financial successes of such inherently inefficient and stagnant one-age operations. But it cannot thereby create, in some magical fashion, an equivalent to city diversity. Nor can it substitute for the inherent efficiency, in cities, of mingled age and inherently varied overhead.

Age of buildings, in relation to usefulness or desirability, is an extremely relative thing. Nothing in a vital city district seems to be too old to be chosen for use by those who have choice—or to have its place taken, finally, by something new. And this usefulness of the old is not simply a matter of architectural distinction or charm. In the Back-of-the-Yards, Chicago, no weather-beaten, undistinguished, run-down, presumably obsolete frame house seems to be too far gone to lure out savings and to instigate borrowing—because this is a neighborhood that people are not leaving as they achieve enough success for choice. In Greenwich Village, almost no old building is scorned by middle-class families hunting a bargain in a lively district, or by rehabilitators seeking a golden egg. In successful districts, old buildings "filter up."

At the other extreme, in Miami Beach, where novelty is the sovereign remedy, hotels ten years old are considered aged and are passed up because others are newer.

Newness, and its superficial gloss of well-being, is a very perishable commodity.

Many city occupants and enterprises have no need for new construction. The floor of the building in which this book is being written is occupied also by a health club with a gym, a firm of ecclesiastical decorators, an insurgent Democratic party reform club, a Liberal party political club, a music society, an accordionists' association, a retired importer who sells maté by mail, a man who sells paper and who also takes care of shipping the maté, a dental laboratory, a studio for watercolor lessons, and a maker of costume jewelry. Among the tenants who were here and gone shortly before I came in, were a man who rented out tuxedos, a union local and a Haitian dance troupe. There is no place for the likes of us in new construction. And the last thing we need is new construction.* What we need, and a lot of others need, is old construction in a lively district, which some among us can help make livelier.

Nor is new residential building in cities an unadulterated good. Many disadvantages accompany new residential city building; and the value placed on various advantages, or the penalties accruing from certain disadvantages, are given different weights by different people. Some people, for instance, prefer more space for the money (or equal space for less money) to a new dinette designed for midgets. Some people like walls they don't hear through. This is an advantage they can get with

---

*No, the *last* thing we need is some paternalist weighing whether we are sufficiently noncontroversial to be admitted to subsidized quarters in a Utopian dream city.

many old buildings but not with new apartments, whether they are public housing at $14 a room per month or luxury housing at $95 a room per month.* Some people would rather pay for improvements in their living conditions partly in labor and ingenuity, and by selecting which improvements are most important to them, instead of being indiscriminately improved, and all at a cost of money. In spontaneously unslumming slums, where people are staying by choice, it is easy to observe how many ordinary citizens have heard of color, lighting and furnishing devices for converting deep or dismal spaces into pleasant and useful rooms, have heard of bedroom air-conditioning and of electric window fans, have learned about taking out non-bearing partitions, and have even learned about throwing two too small flats into one. Minglings of old buildings, with consequent minglings in living costs and tastes, are essential to get diversity and stability in residential populations, as well as diversity in enterprises.

Among the most admirable and enjoyable sights to be found along the sidewalks of big cities are the ingenious adaptations of old quarters to new uses. The town-house parlor that becomes a craftsman's showroom, the stable that becomes a house, the basement that becomes an immigrants' club, the garage or brewery that becomes a theater, the beauty parlor that becomes the ground floor of a duplex, the warehouse that becomes a factory for Chi-

---

*"Dear, are you sure the stove is one of the 51 exciting reasons we're living in Washington Square Village?" asks the wife in a cartoon issued by protesting tenants in an expensive New York redevelopment project. "You'll have to speak up, honey," replies the husband. "Our neighbor just flushed his toilet."

nese food, the dancing school that becomes a pamphlet printer's, the cobbler's that becomes a church with lovingly painted windows—the stained glass of the poor—the butcher shop that becomes a restaurant: these are the kinds of minor changes forever occurring where city districts have vitality and are responsive to human needs.

Consider the history of the no-yield space that has recently been rehabilitated by the Arts in Louisville Association as a theater, music room, art gallery, library, bar and restaurant. It started life as a fashionable athletic club, outlived that and became a school, then the stable of a dairy company, then a riding school, then a finishing and dancing school, another athletic club, an artist's studio, a school again, a blacksmith's, a factory, a warehouse, and it is now a flourishing center of the arts. Who could anticipate or provide for such a succession of hopes and schemes? Only an unimaginative man would think he could; only an arrogant man would want to.

These eternal changes and permutations among old city buildings can be called makeshifts only in the most pedantic sense. It is rather that a form of raw material has been found in the right place. It has been put to a use that might otherwise be unborn.

What is makeshift and woebegone is to see city diversity outlawed. Outside the vast, middle-income Bronx project of Parkchester, where the standardized, routinized commerce (with its share of empty fronts) is protected from unauthorized competition or augmentation within the project, we can see such an outcast huddle, supported by Parkchester people. Beyond a corner of the project, hideously clumped on a stretch of pocked asphalt left over from a gas station, are a few of the other things the project people apparently need: quick loans, musical instruments, camera exchange, Chinese restaurant, odd-lot clothing. How many other needs remain unfilled? What is wanted becomes academic when mingled building age is replaced by the economic rigor mortis of one-age construction, with its inherent inefficiency and consequent need for forms of "protectionism."

Cities need a mingling of old buildings to cultivate primary diversity mixtures, as well as secondary diversity. In particular, they need old buildings to incubate new primary diversity.

If the incubation is successful enough, the yield of the buildings can, and often does, rise. Grady Clay reports that this is already observable, for instance, in the Louisville sample-shoe market. "Rents were very low when the market began to attract shoppers," he says. "For a shop about twenty feet by forty feet, they were $25 to $50 a month. They have already gone up to about $75." Many a city's enterprises which become important economic assets start small and poor, and become able, eventually, to afford carrying costs of rehabilitation or new construction. But this process could not occur without that low-yield space in the right place, in which to start.

Areas where better mixtures of primary diversity must be cultivated will have to depend heavily on old buildings, especially at the beginning of deliberate attempts to catalyze diversity. If Brooklyn, New York, as an example, is ever to cultivate the quantity of diversity and degree of attraction and liveliness it needs, it must take maximum economic advantage of combinations of residence and work. Without these primary combinations, in effective and concentrated proportions, it is hard to see how Brooklyn can begin to catalyze its potential for secondary diversity.

Brooklyn cannot well compete with suburbs for capturing big and well-established manufacturers seeking a location. At least it cannot at present, certainly not by trying to beat out the suburbs at *their* game, on their terms. Brooklyn has quite different assets. If Brooklyn is to make the most of work-residence primary mixtures, it must depend mainly on incubating work enterprises, and then holding on to them as long as it can. While it has them, it must combine them with sufficiently high concentrations of residential population, and with short blocks, to make the most of their presence. The more it makes of their presence, the more firmly it is apt to hold work uses.

But to incubate those work uses, Brooklyn needs old buildings, needs them for exactly the task they fulfill there. For Brooklyn is quite an incubator. Each year, more manufacturing enterprises leave Brooklyn for other locations than move into Brooklyn from elsewhere. Yet the number of factories in Brooklyn has been constantly growing. A thesis prepared by three students at Brooklyn's Pratt Institute * explains this paradox well:

> The secret is that Brooklyn is an incubator of industry. Small businesses are constantly being started there. A couple of machinists, perhaps, will get tired of working for someone else and start out for themselves in the back of a garage. They'll prosper and grow; soon they will get too big for the

*Stuart Cohen, Stanley Kogan and Frank Marcellino.

garage and move to a rented loft; still later they buy a building. When they outgrow that, and have to build for themselves, there is a good chance they will move out to Queens, or Nassau or New Jersey. But in the meantime, twenty or fifty or a hundred more like them will have started up.

Why do they move when they build for themselves? For one thing, Brooklyn offers too few attractions aside from those a new industry finds are necessities—old buildings and nearness to the wide range of other skills and supplies a small enterprise must have. For another, little or no effort has been made to plan for working needs—e.g., great sums of money are spent on highways choked with private automobiles rushing into the city and out of it; no comparable thought or money is spent on trucking expressways for manufacturers who use the city's old buildings, its docks and its railways.*

Brooklyn, like most of our city areas in decline, has more old buildings than it needs. To put it another way, many of its neighborhoods have for a long time lacked

---

*Cost of land, conventionally assumed to be a significant deterrent today to building in the city for expanding businesses, has been steadily diminishing in ratio to construction costs, and to almost all other costs. When Time, Inc., decided to build on an expensive plot of ground near the center of Manhattan, for example, instead of on much cheaper ground near the edge, it based its decision on a host of reasons, among which was the fact that taxi fares alone for employees' business trips from the inconvenient site would come to more, per year, than the difference in land carrying costs! Stephen G. Thompson of *Architectural Forum* has made the (unpublished) observation that redevelopment subsidies frequently bring the cost of city land lower than the cost of carpet for the buildings. To justify land costs higher than carpet costs, a city has to be a *city*, not a machine or a desert.

gradual increments of new buildings. Yet if Brooklyn is ever to build upon its inherent assets and advantages—which is the only way successful city building can be done—many of those old buildings, well distributed, will be essential to the process. Improvement must come by supplying the conditions for generating diversity that are missing, not by wiping out old buildings in great swathes.

We can see around us, from the days preceding project building, many examples of decaying city neighborhoods built up all at once. Frequently such neighborhoods have begun life as fashionable areas; sometimes they have had instead a solid middle-class start. Every city has such physically homogeneous neighborhoods.

Usually just such neighborhoods have been handicapped in every way, so far as generating diversity is concerned. We cannot blame their poor staying power and stagnation entirely on their most obvious misfortune: being built all at once. Nevertheless, this is one of the handicaps of such neighborhoods, and unfortunately its effects can persist long after the buildings have become aged.

When such an area is new, it offers no economic possibilities to city diversity. The practical penalties of dullness, from this and other causes, stamp the neighborhood early. It becomes a place to leave. By the time the buildings have indeed aged, their only useful city attribute is low value, which by itself is not enough.

Neighborhoods built up all at once change little physically over the years as a rule. The little physical change that does occur is for the worse—gradual dilapidation, a few random, shabby new uses here and there. People look at these few, random differences and regard them as evidence, and perhaps as cause, of drastic change. Fight blight! They regret that the neighborhood has changed. Yet the fact is, physically it has changed remarkably little. People's feelings about it, rather, have changed. The neighborhood shows a strange inability to update itself, enliven itself, repair itself, or to be sought after, out of choice, by a new generation. It is dead. Actually it was dead from birth, but nobody noticed this much until the corpse began to smell.

Finally comes the decision, after exhortations to fix up and fight blight have failed, that the whole thing must be wiped out and a new cycle started. Perhaps some of the old buildings will be left if they can be "renewed" into the economic equivalent of new buildings. A new corpse is laid out. It does not smell yet, but it is just as dead, just as incapable of the constant adjustments, adaptations and permutations that make up the processes of life.

There is no reason why this dismal, foredoomed cycle need be repeated. If such an area is examined to see which of the other three conditions for generating diversity are missing, and then those missing conditions are corrected as well as they can be, some of the old buildings must go: extra streets must be added, the concentration of people must be heightened, room for new primary uses must be found, public and private. But a good mingling of the old buildings must remain, and in remaining they will have become something more than mere decay from the past or evidence of previous failure. They will have become the shelter which is necessary, and valuable to the district, for many varieties of middling-, low- and no-yield diversity. The economic value of new buildings is replaceable in cities. It is replaceable by the spending of more construction money. But the economic value of old buildings is irreplaceable at will. It is created by time. This economic requisite for diversity is a requisite that vital city neighborhoods can only inherit, and then sustain over the years.

11

THE NEED FOR
CONCENTRATION

CONDITION 4: *The district must have a sufficiently dense concentration of people, for whatever purpose they may be there. This includes people there because of residence.*

For centuries, probably everyone who has thought about cities at all has noticed that there seems to be some connection between the concentration of people and the specialties they can support. Samuel Johnson, for one, remarked on this relationship back in 1785. "Men, thinly scattered," he said to Boswell, "make a shift, but a bad shift, without many things . . . It is being concentrated which produces convenience."

Observers are forever rediscovering this relationship in new times and places. Thus in 1959, John H. Denton, a professor of business at the University of Arizona, after studying American suburbs and British "new towns" came to the conclusion that such places must rely on ready access to a city for protection of their cultural opportunities. "He based his findings," reported the *New York Times*, "on the lack of a sufficient density of population to support cultural facilities. Mr. Denton . . . said that decentralization produced such a thin population spread that the only effective economic demand that could exist in suburbs was that of the majority. The only goods and cultural activities available will be those that the majority requires, he observed," and so on.

Both Johnson and Professor Denton were speaking about the economic effects of large numbers of people, but not numbers loosely added up indefinitely from thinly spread populations. They were making the point that it seems to matter greatly how thinly or how thickly people are concentrated. They were comparing the effects of what we call high and low densities.

This relationship of concentration—or high density—to conveniences and to other kinds of diversity is generally well understood as it applies to downtowns. Everyone is aware that tremendous numbers of people concentrate in city downtowns and that, if they did not, there would be no downtown to amount to anything—certainly not one with much downtown diversity.

But this relationship between concentration and diversity is very little considered when it comes to city districts where residence is a chief use. Yet dwellings form a large part of most city districts. The people who live in a district also form a large share, usually, of the people who use the streets, the parks and the enterprises of the place. Without help from the concentration of the people who live there, there can be little convenience or diversity where people live, and where they require it.

To be sure, the dwellings of a district (like any other use of the land) need to be supplemented by other primary uses so people on the streets will be well spread through the hours of the day, for the economic reasons explained in Chapter Eight. These other uses (work, entertainment, or whatever) must make intensive use of city land if they are to contribute effectively to concentration. If they simply take up physical room and involve few people, they will do little or nothing for diversity or liveliness. I think it is hardly necessary to belabor that point.

This same point is just as important, however, about dwellings. City dwellings have to be intensive in their use of the land too, for reasons that go much deeper than cost of land. On the other hand, this does not mean that everyone can or should be put into elevator apartment houses to live—or into any other one or two types of dwellings. That kind of solution kills diversity by obstructing it from another direction.

Dwelling densities are so important for most city districts, and for their future development, and are so little considered as factors in vitality, that I shall devote this chapter to that aspect of city concentration.

High dwelling densities have a bad name in orthodox planning and housing theory. They are supposed to lead to every kind of difficulty and failure.

But in our cities, at least, this supposed correlation between high densities and trouble, or high densities and slums, is simply incorrect, as anyone who troubles to look at real cities can see. Here are a few illustrations:

In San Francisco, the district of highest dwelling densities—and highest coverage of residential land with buildings too—is North Beach-Telegraph Hill. This is a popular district that has spontaneously and steadily unslummed itself in the years following the Depression and the Second World War. San Francisco's chief slum problem, on the other hand, is a district called the Western Addition, a place that has steadily declined and is now being extensively cleared. The Western Addition (which at one time, when it was new, was a good address) has a dwelling-unit density considerably lower than North Beach-Telegraph Hill's, and, for that matter, lower than the still fashionable Russian Hill's and Nob Hill's.

In Philadelphia, Rittenhouse Square is the only district that has been spontaneously upgrading and extending its edges, and is the only inner city area that has not been designated for either renewal or clearance. It has the highest dwelling density in Philadelphia. The North Philadelphia slums currently display some of the city's most severe social problems. They have dwelling densities averaging at most half those of Rittenhouse Square. Vast territories of additional decay and social disorder in Philadelphia have dwelling densities less than half those of Rittenhouse Square.

In Brooklyn, New York, the most generally admired, popular and upgrading neighborhood is Brooklyn Heights; it has much the highest density of dwellings in Brooklyn. Tremendous expanses of failed or decaying Brooklyn gray area have densities half those of Brooklyn Heights or less.

In Manhattan, the most fashionable pocket of the midtown East Side, and the most fashionable pocket of Greenwich Village have dwelling densities in the same high range as the heart of Brooklyn Heights. But an interesting difference can be observed. In Manhattan, very popular areas, characterized by high degrees of vitality and diversity, surround these most fashionable pockets. In these surrounding popular areas, dwelling densities go still higher. In Brooklyn Heights, on the other hand, the fashionable pocket is surrounded by neighborhoods where dwelling unit densities drop off; vitality and popularity drop off too.

In Boston, as already mentioned in the introduction to this book, the North End has unslummed itself and is one of the city's healthiest areas. It has much the highest dwelling densities in Boston. The Roxbury district, which has been steadily declining for a generation, has a dwelling density about a ninth that of the North End's.*

The overcrowded slums of planning literature are teeming areas with a high density of dwellings. The overcrowded slums of American real life are, more and more typically, dull areas with a low density of dwellings. In Oakland, California, the worst and most extensive slum problem is an area of some two hundred blocks of

---

*Here are the density figures for these examples. They are given in numbers of dwelling units per net acre of residential land. When two figures are given, they represent a range into which the average or averages for the place concerned fall (which is the way this data is often tabulated or mapped). In San Francisco: North Beach-Telegraph Hill, 80-140, about the same as Russian Hill and Nob Hill, but the buildings cover more of the residential ground in North Beach-Telegraph Hill; the Western Addition, 55-60. In Philadelphia: Rittenhouse Square, 80-100; North Philadelphia slums, about 40; row-house neighborhoods in trouble, typically 30-45. In Brooklyn: Brooklyn Heights, 125-174 at heart and 75-124 in most of the remainder; drop-offs to 45-74 beyond; as examples of Brooklyn areas in decline or trouble, Bedford-Stuyvesant, about half at 75-124 and half at 45-74; Red Hook, mostly 45-74; some Brooklyn spots in decay as low as 15-24. In Manhattan: most fashionable pocket of midtown East Side, 125-174, rising in Yorkville to 175-254; Greenwich Village, most fashionable pocket, 124-174, rising to 175-254 for most of remainder with pocket containing stable, old, unslummed Italian community rising above 255. In Boston, North End, 275; Roxbury, 21-40.

For Boston and New York, these figures are from planning commission measurements and tabulations; for San Francisco and Philadelphia they are estimates by planning or redevelopment staff members.

detached, one- and two-family houses which can hardly be called dense enough to qualify as real city densities at all. Cleveland's worst slum problem is a square mile of much the same thing. Detroit is largely composed, today, of seemingly endless square miles of low-density failure. The East Bronx of New York, which might almost stand as a symbol of the gray belts that have become the despair of cities, has low densities for New York; in most parts of the East Bronx, densities are well below the whole city averages. (New York's average dwelling density is 55 units per net residential acre.)

However, it will not do to jump to the conclusion that all areas of high dwelling density in cities do well. They do not, and to assume that this is "the" answer would be to oversimplify outrageously. For instance, Chelsea, much of the badly failed uptown West Side, and much of Harlem, all in Manhattan, have dwelling densities in the same high ranges as those of Greenwich Village, Yorkville and the midtown East Side. Once-ultrafashionable River-

---

Although all cities make a fetish of minute density analysis in project planning, surprisingly few have much accurate data on nonproject densities. (One planning director told me he could see no reason for studying them except as light on how big the relocation problem would be if they were knocked down!) No city that I know of has studied just what localized, building-by-building variations in density go into the makeup of density averages in successful and popular neighborhoods. "It's too hard to generalize about districts like that," complained a planning director when I asked him about specific density variations, at small scale, in one of his city's most successful districts. It is hard, or impossible, to generalize about such districts precisely because they are, themselves, so little "generalized" or standardized in their groupings. This very capriciousness and diversity of the components is one of the most important, and most ignored, facts about density averages in successful districts.

side Drive, plagued by trouble today, has still higher dwelling densities.

We cannot understand the effects of high and low densities if we assume that the relationship between concentrations of people and production of diversity is a simple, straight mathematical affair. The results of this relationship (which Dr. Johnson and Professor Denton both spoke of in its simple, crude form), are drastically influenced by other factors too; three of these occupy the three preceding chapters.

No concentration of residents, however high it may be, is "sufficient" if diversity is suppressed or thwarted by other insufficiencies. As an extreme example, no concentration of residence, however high, is "sufficient" to generate diversity in regimented projects, because diversity has been regimented out in any case. And much the same effects, for different reasons, can occur in unplanned city neighborhoods, where the buildings are too standardized or the blocks are too long, or there is no mixture of other primary uses besides dwellings.

However, it still remains that dense concentrations of people are *one* of the necessary conditions for flourishing city diversity. And it still follows that in districts where people live, this means there must be a dense concentration of their dwellings on the land preempted for dwellings. The other factors that influence how much diversity is generated, and where, will have nothing much to influence if enough people are not there.

One reason why low city densities conventionally have a good name, unjustified by the facts, and why high city densities have a bad name, equally unjustified, is that high densities of dwellings and overcrowding of dwellings are often confused. High densities mean large numbers of dwellings per acre of land. Overcrowding means too many people in a dwelling for the number of rooms it contains. The census definition of overcrowding is 1.5 persons per room or more. It has nothing to do with the number of dwellings on the land, just as in real life high densities have nothing to do with overcrowding.

This confusion between high densities and over-crowding, which I will go into briefly because it so much interferes with understanding the role of densities, is another of the obfuscations we have inherited from Garden City planning. The Garden City planners and their disciples looked at slums which had both many dwelling units on the land (high densities) and too many people within individual dwellings (overcrowding), and failed to make any distinction between the fact of overcrowded rooms and the entirely different fact of densely built up land. They hated both equally, in any case, and coupled them like ham and eggs, so that to this day housers and planners pop out the phrase as if it were one word, "high-densityandovercrowding."

Adding further to the confusion came a statistical monstrosity much used by reformers to aid their housing-project crusades—a raw figure of numbers of persons per acre. These menacing figures never tell how many dwellings or how many rooms there are to the acre, and if the figure is given for a badly troubled area—as it almost invariably is—the implication is deafening that there is something dreadful, on the face of it, in such heavy concentrations of people. The fact that the people may be living four to a room, or may be a distillation of misery in every guise, becomes all but irrelevant. It happens that Boston's North End, with 963 persons per net residential acre, has a death rate (1956 figures) of 8.8 per thousand population and a TB death rate of 0.6 per ten thousand. Boston's South End, meantime, has 361 persons per residential acre, a death rate of 21.6 per thousand population, and a TB death rate of 12 per ten thousand. It would be ridiculous to say that these indications of something very wrong in the South End come of having 361 persons per residential acre instead of almost 1,000. The facts are more complicated. But it is equally ridiculous to take the case of a miserable population at 1,000 persons to the acre and imply that that figure is therefore villainous.

It is typical of this confusion between high densities and overcrowding that one of the great Garden City planners, Sir Raymond Unwin, titled a tract which had nothing to do with overcrowding, but instead with super-block arrangements of low-density dwellings, *Nothing Gained by Overcrowding.* By the 1930's, overcrowding of dwellings with people and supposed "overcrowding" of land with buildings (i.e., city dwelling densities and land coverage) were taken to be practically identical in meaning and results, insofar as the distinction was thought about at all. When observers like Lewis Mumford and Catherine Bauer could not avoid noticing that some very successful areas of cities had high densities of dwellings and high ground coverages, but not too many persons in a dwelling or a room, they took the tack (Mumford still takes it) that the fortunate people living in comfort in these popular places are living in slums, but are too insensitive to know it or resent it.

Overcrowding of dwellings and high densities of

dwellings are always being found one without the other. The North End and Greenwich Village and Rittenhouse Square and Brooklyn Heights have high densities for their cities, but with few exceptions their dwellings are not overcrowded. The South End and North Philadelphia and Bedford-Stuyvesant have much lower densities, but their dwellings frequently are overcrowded, with too many persons in a dwelling. Today we are much more apt to find overcrowding at low densities than at high densities.

Nor does slum clearance as practiced in our cities usually have anything to do with solving the problem of overcrowding. Instead, slum clearance and renewal typically add to that problem. When old buildings are replaced with new projects, the dwelling densities are often made lower than they were, so there are fewer dwellings in a district than before. Even if the same dwelling densities are repeated, or lifted a little, fewer people are accommodated than were put out, because the people who were displaced were often overcrowded. The result is that overcrowding increases somewhere else, especially if colored people, who can find few areas in which to live, have been displaced. All cities carry laws against overcrowding on their books, but these laws cannot be enforced when the city's own rebuilding plans force overcrowding in new places.

In theory, one might suppose that the dense concentrations of people necessary to help generate diversity in a city neighborhood can live in either a sufficiently high density of dwellings or in an overcrowded lower density of dwellings. The number of people in a given area could be the same under these two conditions. But in real life the results are different. In the case of enough people in enough dwellings, the diversity can be generated and people can develop attachment and loyalty to their unique neighborhood mixture of things, without a built-in destructive force—overcrowding of dwellings with too many people per room—necessarily working at cross-purposes. Diversity and its attractions are combined with tolerable living conditions in the case of enough dwellings for enough people, and so more people who develop choice are apt to stay put.

Overcrowding within dwellings or rooms, in our country, is almost always a symptom of poverty or of being discriminated against, and it is one (but only one) of many infuriating and discouraging liabilities of being very poor or of being victimized by residential discrimination, or both. Indeed, overcrowding at low densities may be even more depressing and destructive than over-crowding at high densities, because at low densities there is less public life as a diversion and escape, and as a means, too, for fighting back politically at injustices and neglect.

Everybody hates overcrowding and those who must endure it hate it worst. Almost nobody overcrowds by choice. But people often do live in high-density neigh-borhoods by choice. Overcrowded neighborhoods, low-density or high-density, are usually neighborhoods that did not work out when they were inhabited in uncrowded fashion by people who had choice. The people with choice left. Neighborhoods that have uncrowded them-selves with time, or have maintained uncrowding over several generations, are apt to be neighborhoods that have been working out and that both hold and attract the loyalty of people who do have choice. The tremendous gray belts of relatively low density that ring our cities, decaying and being deserted, or decaying and being over-crowded, are significant signals of the typical failure of *low* densities in big cities.

What are proper densities for city dwellings?

The answer to this is something like the answer Lincoln gave to the question, "How long should a man's legs be?" Long enough to reach the ground, Lincoln said.

Just so, proper city dwelling densities are a matter of performance. They cannot be based on abstractions about the quantities of land that ideally should be allotted for so-and-so many people (living in some docile, imaginary society).

Densities are too low, or too high, when they frustrate city diversity instead of abetting it. This flaw in performance is *why* they are too low or too high. We ought to look at densities in much the same way as we look at calories and vitamins. Right amounts are right amounts because of how they perform. And what is right differs in specific instances.

Let us begin at the low end of the density scale to understand, broadly, why a density that may perform well in one place is poor in another.

Very low densities, six dwellings or fewer to the net acre, can make out well in suburbs. Lots at such densities average, say, 70 by 100 feet or more. Some suburban densities go higher, of course; lots at ten dwellings to the acre average just under, say, 50 by 90 feet, which is a squeeze for suburban living but, with clever site planning, good design and genuine suburban location, can yield a suburb or a reasonable facsimile.

Between ten and twenty dwellings to the acre yields a kind of semisuburb,* consisting either of detached or two-family houses on handkerchief plots, or else of generously sized row houses with relatively generous yards or greens. These arrangements, although they are apt to be dull, can be viable and safe if they are secluded from city life; for example if they lie toward the outer edges of a big city. They will not generate city liveliness or public life—their populations are too thin—nor will they help maintain city sidewalk safety. But there may be no need for them to do so.

However, densities of this kind ringing a city are a bad long-term bet, destined to become gray area. As the city continues to grow, the character that makes these semisuburbs reasonably attractive and functional is lost. As they are engulfed and embedded deep in a city, they lose, of course, their former geographical closeness to true suburbs or countryside. But more than that, they lose their protection from people who do not "fit in" to each other's private lives economically or socially, and they lose their aloofness from the peculiar problems of city life. Swallowed into a city and its ordinary problems, they possess no city vitality to contend with these problems.

In short, there is a justification for densities averaging twenty dwellings or less to the acre, and there may be good reasons for these densities, so long as their dwellings and neighborhoods are not everyday part and parcel of a big city.

---

*The classic ideal of strict Garden City planning has been in this range: twelve dwellings to the acre.

Above these semisuburban densities, the realities of city life can seldom be evaded, even for a short time.

In cities (which you will recall have not the local self-containment of towns), densities at twenty dwellings to the acre and above mean that many people who live near each other geographically are strangers to one another and always will be strangers. Not only that, but strangers from elsewhere find it easy to be present because other neighborhoods of this same density or higher are close by.

Rather abruptly, once a semisuburban density is exceeded, or a suburban location engulfed, an entirely different kind of city settlement exists—a settlement which now has different kinds of everyday jobs to handle and a need for different ways of handling them, a settlement which lacks assets of one kind but potentially has assets of another kind. From this point on, a city settlement needs city vitality and city diversity.

Unfortunately, however, densities high enough to bring with them innate city problems are not by any means necessarily high enough to do their share in producing city liveliness, safety, convenience and interest. And so, between the point where semisuburban character and function are lost, and the point at which lively diversity and public life can arise, lies a range of big-city densities that I shall call "in-between" densities. They are fit neither for suburban life nor for city life. They are fit, generally, for nothing but trouble.

The "in-between" densities extend upward to the point, by definition, at which genuine city life can start flourishing and its constructive forces go to work. This point varies. It varies in different cities, and it varies within the same city depending on how much help the dwellings are getting from other primary uses, and from users attracted to liveliness or uniqueness from outside the district.

Districts like Rittenhouse Square in Philadelphia and North Beach-Telegraph Hill in San Francisco, both of which enjoy great good fortune in mixtures of uses and attractions to outside users, can demonstrably maintain vitality at densities of approximately 100 dwelling units to the net acre. On the other hand, in Brooklyn Heights this is evidently not enough. Where the average there falls off to 100 dwellings to the net acre, vitality falls off.*

I can find only one city district with vitality that has well under 100 dwellings per acre, and this is the Back-of-the-Yards in Chicago. It is able to be an exception because politically this district gets the benefits that ordinarily come only with dense concentration. At "in-between" densities it nevertheless has enough people to swing weight in a big city because its functioning district territory extends much farther geographically than other

* Some planning theorists call for urban variety and liveliness, and simultaneously prescribe "in-between" densities. For example, in the Winter 1960-61 issue of *Landscape* magazine, Lewis Mumford writes, "Now the great function of the city is . . . to permit, indeed to encourage and incite, the greatest potential number of meetings, encounters, challenges, between all persons, classes and groups, providing, as it were, a stage upon which the drama of social life may be enacted, with the actors taking their turn as spectators and the spectators as actors." In the next paragraph, however, he castigates city areas occupied at densities of 200 to 500 *persons* (italics mine) per acre, and recommends "housing that will permit parks and gardens as an integral part of the design, at densities not higher than a hundred, or at most, in quarters for childless people, of 125 *persons* per acre." Densities of 100 *persons* per acre mean dwelling-unit densities in the range of 25-50 per acre. Urbanity and "in-between" densities like this can be combined only theoretically; they are incompatible because of the economics of generating city diversity.

districts manage except in name, and it uses this full political weight with extraordinary skill and steel to get what it needs. But even the Back-of-the-Yards shares some of the liabilities of visual monotony, small, everyday inconvenience, and fear of strangers who look too alien, that go virtually always with "in-between" densities. The Back-of-the-Yards is gradually raising its densities, to take care of the district population's natural increase. To increase densities gradually, as is being done here, is by no means undercutting this district's social and economic assets. On the contrary, it is strengthening them.

To fix upon a functional answer as to where the "in-between" densities end, we can say that a district escapes from them when its land devoted to dwellings is dense enough to do a good primary-diversity job of helping to generate flourishing secondary city diversity and liveliness. A density figure that accomplishes this in one place may be much too low in another.

A numerical answer means less than a functional answer (and unfortunately can even deafen the dogmatic to the truer and more subtle reports that come in from life). But I should judge that numerically the escape from "in-between" densities probably lies somewhere around the figure of 100 dwellings to an acre, under circumstances *most congenial in all other respects* to producing diversity. As a general rule, I think 100 dwellings per acre will be found to be too low.

Assuming that an escape has been made from the trouble-creating "in-between" densities, let us return to consideration of viable city densities. How high "should" city dwelling densities go? How high can they go?

Obviously, if the object is vital city life, the dwelling densities should go as high as they need to go to stimulate the maximum potential diversity in a district. Why waste a city district's and a city population's potential for creating interesting and vigorous city life?

It follows, however, that densities can get too high if they reach a point at which, for any reason, they begin to repress diversity instead of to stimulate it. Precisely this can happen, and it is the main point in considering how high is too high.

The reason dwelling densities can begin repressing diversity if they get too high is this: At some point, to accommodate so many dwellings on the land, standardization of the buildings must set in. This is fatal, because great diversity in age and types of buildings has a direct, explicit connection with diversity of population, diversity of enterprises and diversity of scenes.

Among all the various kinds of buildings (old or new) in a city, some kinds are always less efficient than others in adding dwellings to the land. A three-story building will get fewer dwellings onto a given number of square feet of land than a five-story building; a five-story building, fewer than a ten-story building. If you want to go up far enough, the number of dwellings that can go onto a given plot of land is stupendous—as Le Corbusier demonstrated with his schemes for a city of repetitive skyscrapers in a park.

But in this process of packing dwellings on given acreages of land, it does not do to get too efficient, and it never did. There must be leeway for variety among buildings. All those variations that are of less than maximum efficiency get crowded out. Maximum efficiency, or anything approaching it, means standardization.

At any particular place and time, under the given circumstances of regulations, technology and financing,
some particular way of packing dwellings onto the land is
apt to be the most efficient way. At some places and
times, for example, narrow three-story row houses were
apparently the answer for maximum efficiency at getting
city dwellings on the land. Where these crowded out all
other dwelling types they brought a pall of monotony. At
another period, wider five- or six-story walk-up tenements were the most efficient. When Riverside Drive in
Manhattan was built up, twelve- and fourteen-story elevator apartments were apparently the answer for maximum packing efficiency, and with this particular
standardization as a base the highest dwelling density
belt in Manhattan has been produced

Elevator apartments are today the most efficient way
of packing dwellings on a given amount of building land.
And within this type are certain most efficient subtypes
such as those of maximum height for low-speed elevators,
usually considered today as twelve stories, and those of
maximum economic height for pouring reinforced concrete. (Such height in turn depends on the technological
improvement of cranes, so this figure increases every few
years. As this is written, it is twenty-two stories.) Elevator apartments are not only the most efficient way of
packing people on a given amount of land. They can,
under unfavorable circumstances, also be probably the
most dangerous way of doing it, as experience in many a
low-income housing project shows. In some circumstances, they are excellent.

Elevator apartments do not produce standardization
by virtue of being elevator apartments, any more than

three-story houses produce standardization by virtue of
being three-story houses. But elevator apartments do produce standardization when they are almost the only way
a neighborhood is housed—just as three-story houses
produce monotonous standardization when they are
almost the only way in which a neighborhood is housed.

No one way is a good way to house a city neighborhood; no mere two or three ways are good. The more variations there can be, the better. As soon as the range and
number of variations in buildings decline, the diversity
of population and enterprises is too apt to stay static or
decline, instead of increasing.

It is not easy to reconcile high densities with great
variety in buildings, yet it must be attempted. Anti-city
planning and zoning virtually prevent it, as we shall see.

Popular high-density city areas have considerable
variation among their buildings—sometimes immense
variation. Greenwich Village is such a place. It manages to
house people at densities ranging from 125 to above 200
dwelling units per acre, without standardization of buildings. These averages are obtained from mixtures of everything from single-family houses, houses with flats,
tenements and all kinds of small apartment houses and
flats, on up to elevator apartments of many different ages
and sizes.

The reason Greenwich Village can reconcile such high
densities with such great variety is that a high proportion
of the land which is devoted to residences (called net residential acres) is covered with buildings. Relatively little
is left open and unbuilt upon. In most parts, the buildings
cover the residential land at averages estimated as ranging from 60 percent to 80 percent of the land, leaving the

other 40 percent to 20 percent of the land unbuilt on as yards, courts and the like. This is a high ratio of ground coverage. It is so efficient a use of the *land* itself, that it permits a good deal of "inefficiency" in buildings. Most of them need not be highly efficient at packing, but even so, high average densities are reached.

Now, suppose that only 15 percent to 25 percent of the residential land is built upon, and the other 75 percent to 85 percent is left open and unbuilt on. These are common figures for housing projects, with their expanses of open land which are so hard to control in city life and produce so much vacuity and trouble. More open land means remarkably less building space. If open land is doubled from 40 percent and becomes 80 percent, the amount of land that can be built upon is cut by two thirds! Instead of having 60 percent of the land to build on, you have only 20 percent to build on.

When so much land is left open, the land itself is being used "inefficiently" so far as packing dwellings on it is concerned. The strait jacket is very tight when only 20 percent or 25 percent can be built upon. The density of dwellings must be very low, or, alternatively, dwellings must be packed with great efficiency onto the fraction of the ground that can take the buildings. Under these circumstances, it is impossible to reconcile high densities with variety. Elevator apartments, and often very high ones, are unavoidable.

The Stuyvesant Town project in Manhattan has a density of 125 dwellings per net acre, a density that would be on the low side for Greenwich Village. Yet to accommodate so many dwellings as this in Stuyvesant Town, where the ground coverage is only 25 percent (75 percent left open), the dwellings must be most rigidly standardized in rank upon rank of virtually identical, massive elevator apartment houses. More imaginative architects and site planners might have arranged the buildings differently, but no possible difference could be more than superficial. Mathematical impossibility would defy genius itself to introduce genuine substantial variety at these low ground coverages with these densities.

Henry Whitney, an architect and project housing expert, has worked out many theoretically possible combinations of elevator buildings with lower buildings, using the low ground coverages required for public housing and for nearly all federally subsidized renewal. Mr. Whitney found that no matter how you slice it, it is physically impossible to get above low city densities (40 to an acre or thereabouts) without standardizing all but a minute token of the dwellings—*unless ground coverages are increased,* which is to say unless open space is decreased. One hundred dwellings to the acre at low ground coverages yield not even token variety—and yet this density is a probable minimum if the unfit "in-between" densities are to be avoided.

Low ground coverages—no matter by what means they are imposed, from local zoning to federal fiat—and diversity of buildings, and viable city densities are thus conditions that are incompatible with one another. At low coverages, if the densities are high enough to help engender city diversity, they are automatically too high to *permit* diversity. The thing is a built-in contradiction.

Assuming that ground coverages are high, however, just how high can a neighborhood's densities go without sacrificing the neighborhood to standardization? This depends a good deal on how many variations, and what variations, already exist in a neighborhood from the past. Variations from the past are a foundation to which new variations of the present (and eventually the future) are added. A neighborhood already standardized, from the past, at three-story houses or five-story tenements is not going to get a full, good range of variation by adding one more type in the present, thereby creating a higher density and letting it go at that. The worst case possible is no foundation from the past at all: empty land.

It is hardly possible to expect that many really different types of dwellings or their buildings can be added *at any one time.* To think they can be is wishful thinking. There are fashions in building. Behind the fashions lie economic and technological reasons, and these fashions exclude all but a few genuinely different possibilities in city dwelling construction *at any one time.*

In districts where densities are too low, they can be raised and variation increased by adding new buildings simultaneously in different, separated spots only. In short, densities should be raised—and new buildings introduced for this purpose—gradually rather than in some sudden, cataclysmic upheaval to be followed by nothing more for decades. The very process of increasing densities gradually but continually can result in increasing variety too, and thus can permit high ultimate densities without standardization.

How high ultimate densities can go without standardization is limited finally, of course, by the land, even when the coverage of the ground is very high. In the North End of Boston, the high densities, averaging 275 dwellings per acre, include considerable variation; but this good combination has been partly obtained at the expense of ground coverages which reach too high a proportion of the land behind some buildings. Too much building has occurred, in the past, as a second layer in the back yards and courts within the little blocks. Actually, these interior buildings add a relatively small share to the density, for they are small and usually low. And they are not a fault in every case either; as occasional oddities they are charming. The trouble comes from too many. With the addition to the district of a few elevator apartment houses—variety of accommodation the North End lacks—open spaces inside blocks could be somewhat increased without lowering district densities. At the same time the district's variety of accommodations would be increased, rather than lessened. But this could not be done if pseudo-city low ground coverages had to accompany the elevator buildings.

I doubt that it is possible, without drastic standardization, to go higher than the North End's density of 275 dwellings per net acre. For most districts—lacking the North End's peculiar and long heritage of different building types—the ultimate danger mark imposing standardization must be considerably lower; I should guess, roughly, that it is apt to hover at about 200 dwellings to the net acre.

Now we must bring the streets into this.

High ground coverages, necessary as they are for variety at high densities, can become intolerable, particularly as they approach 70 percent. They become intolerable if the land is not interlaced with frequent streets. Long blocks with high ground coverages are oppressive. Frequent streets, because they are openings between build-ings, compensate for high coverage of ground off the streets.

Frequent streets are necessary to city districts in any case, if diversity is to be generated. So their importance as an accompaniment to high ground coverage merely reinforces the need.

However, it is obvious that if streets are numerous, instead of scarce, open land in the form of streets has been added. If we add public parks in lively places, we are also adding another kind of open land. And if nonresidential buildings are well mingled into dwelling areas (as they must be if primary uses are well mixed), a similar effect is achieved, in that dwellings and residents of the district as a sum total are thinned to that extent.

The combination of these devices—more numerous streets, lively parks in lively places, and various nonresi-dential uses mingled in, together with great variations among the dwellings themselves—creates totally differ-ent effects from grimly unrelieved high densities and high ground coverages. But this combination also creates a number of effects totally different from high densities "relieved" by quantities of open residential grounds. The results are so different because each of these other devices I have mentioned provides far more than "relief" from high ground coverages. Each contributes, in its own dis-tinctive and indispensable way, to the diversity and vital-ity of an area, so that something constructive, instead of merely inert, can result from the high densities.

To say that cities need high dwelling densities and high net ground coverages, as I am saying they do, is conventionally regarded as lower than taking sides with the man-eating shark.

But things have changed since the days when Ebenezer Howard looked at the slums of London and concluded that to save the people, city life must be abandoned. Advances in fields less moribund than city planning and housing reform, fields such as medicine, sanitation and epidemiology, nutrition and labor legislation, have profoundly revolutionized dangerous and degrading conditions that were once inseparable from high-density city life.

Meantime, populations in metropolitan areas (central cities, together with their suburbs and dependent towns) have continued to grow, to the point where they now absorb 97 percent of our total population increases.

"The trend may be expected to continue," says Dr. Philip M. Hauser, director of the University of Chicago's population research center, ". . . because such agglomerations of population represent the most efficient producer and consumer units that our society has yet devised. The very size, density and congestion of our Standard Metropolitan Areas, to which some city planners object, are among our most precious economic assets."

Between 1958 and 1980, Dr. Hauser points out, the U.S. population is going to increase by an amount somewhere between 57 million (assuming a decline to the low 1942-44 birth rate) and 99 million (assuming an increase in birth rate 10 percent above the 1958 level). If the birth rate continues at the 1958 level, the increase will be 86 million.

Virtually all this growth will go into metropolitan areas. Much of the increase, of course, will come directly from big cities themselves, because big cities are no longer eaters of people as they were not so long ago. They have become suppliers of people.

The increase can be dribbled out in suburbs, semi-suburbs and dull new "in-between" belts—spreading from dull, inner cities of predominately low-vitality, "in-between" densities.

Or we can take advantage of this metropolitan area growth and, with at least part of it, we can begin building up currently unfit city districts, limping along at "in-between" densities—build them up to the point where (in conjunction with other conditions for generating diversity) these concentrations of population can support city life possessing character and liveliness.

Our difficulty is no longer how to contain people densely in metropolitan areas and avoid the ravages of disease, bad sanitation and child labor. To go on thinking in these terms is anachronistic. Our difficulty today is rather how to contain people in metropolitan areas and avoid the ravages of apathetic and helpless neighborhoods.

The solution cannot lie in vain attempts to plan new, self-sufficient towns or little cities throughout metropolitan regions. Our metropolitan areas are already dotted with amorphous, disintegrated places that *once* were relatively self-sufficient and integrated towns or little cities. The day they are pulled into the intricate economy of a metropolitan area, with its multiplicity of choices in places of work, recreation and shopping, they begin to lose their integrity, their relative completeness, socially, economically and culturally. We cannot have it both ways: our twentieth-century metropolitan economy combined with nineteenth-century, isolated town or little-city life.

Because we are faced with the fact of big-city and metropolitan populations, big ones that will get bigger, we are faced with the job of intelligently developing genuine city life and increasing city economic strength. It is silly to try to deny the fact that we Americans are a city people, living in a city economy—and in the process of denying this lose all the true countryside of metropolitan areas too, as we have been steadily losing it at about 3,000 acres a day for the past ten years.

However, reason does not rule this world, and it will not necessarily rule here. The unreasoning dogma that healthy areas like the high-density North End of Boston *must* be slums, or *must* be bad, because they are high-density, would not have been accepted by modern planners as it has if there were not two fundamentally different ways of looking at the question of people in dense concentrations—and if those two ways were not, at bottom, emotional.

People gathered in concentrations of big-city size and density can be felt to be an automatic—if necessary—evil. This is a common assumption: that human beings are charming in small numbers and noxious in large numbers. Given this point of view, it follows that concentrations of people should be physically minimized in every way: by thinning down the numbers themselves insofar as this is possible, and beyond that by aiming at illusions of suburban lawns and small-town placidity. It follows that the exuberant variety inherent in great numbers of people, tightly concentrated, should be played down, hidden, hammered into a semblance of the thinner, more tractable variety or the outright homogeneity often represented in thinner populations. It follows that these confusing creatures—so many people gathered together—should be sorted out and stashed away as decently and quietly as possible, like chickens on a modern egg-factory farm.

On the other hand, people gathered in concentrations of city size and density can be considered a positive good, in the faith that they are desirable because they are the source of immense vitality, and because they do represent, in small geographic compass, a great and exuberant richness of differences and possibilities, many of these differences unique and unpredictable and all the more valuable because they are. Given this point of view, it follows that the presence of great numbers of people gathered together in cities should not only be frankly accepted as a physical fact. It follows that they should also be enjoyed as an asset and their presence celebrated: by raising their concentrations where it is needful for flourishing city life, and beyond that by aiming for a visibly lively public street life and for accommodating and encouraging, economically and visually, as much variety as possible.

Systems of thought, no matter how objective they may purport to be, have underlying emotional bases and values. The development of modern city planning and housing reform has been emotionally based on a glum reluctance to accept city concentrations of people as desirable, and this negative emotion about city concentrations of people has helped deaden planning intellectually.

No good for cities or for their design, planning, economics or people, can come of the emotional assumption that dense city populations are, per se, undesirable. In my view, they are an asset. The task is to promote the city life of city people, housed, let us hope, in concentrations both dense enough *and* diverse enough to offer them a decent chance at developing city life.

12

SOME MYTHS ABOUT DIVERSITY

"Mixed uses look ugly. They cause traffic congestion. They invite ruinous uses."

These are some of the bugbears that cause cities to combat diversity. These beliefs help shape city zoning regulations. They have helped rationalize city rebuilding into the sterile, regimented, empty thing it is. They stand in the way of planning that could deliberately encourage spontaneous diversity by providing the conditions necessary to its growth.

Intricate minglings of different uses in cities are not a form of chaos. On the contrary, they represent a complex and highly developed form of order. Everything in this book so far has been directed toward showing how this complex order of mingled uses works.

Nevertheless, even though intricate mixtures of buildings, uses and scenes are necessary for successful city districts, does diversity carry, too, the disadvantages of ugliness, warring uses and congestion that are conventionally attributed to it by planning lore and literature?

These supposed disadvantages are based on images of unsuccessful districts which have not too much, but too little diversity. They call up visions of dull, down-at-heel residential areas, pocked with a few shabby, shoestring enterprises. They call up visions of low-value land uses, like junk yards or used-car lots. They call up visions of garish, sprawling, unremitting commerce. None of these conditions, however, represents flourishing city diversity. On the contrary, these represent precisely the senility that befalls city neighborhoods in which exuberant diversity has either failed to grow or has died off with time. They represent what happens to semisuburbs which are engulfed by their cities but fail, themselves, to grow up and behave economically like successful city districts.

Flourishing city diversity, of the kind that is catalyzed by the combination of mixed primary uses, frequent streets, mixture of building ages and overheads, and dense concentration of users, does not carry with it the disadvantages of diversity conventionally assumed by planning pseudoscience. I now intend to show why it does not carry them, and why these disadvantages are fantasies which, like all fantasies that are taken too seriously, interfere with handling reality.

Let us consider, first, the belief that diversity looks ugly. Anything looks ugly, to be sure, if it is done badly. But this belief implies something else. It implies that city diversity of uses is inherently messy in appearance; and it also implies that places stamped with homogeneity of uses look better, or at any rate are more amenable to pleasant or orderly esthetic treatment.

But homogeneity or close similarity among uses, in real life, poses very puzzling esthetic problems.

If the sameness of use is shown candidly for what it is—sameness—it looks monotonous. Superficially, this monotony might be thought of as a sort of order, however dull. But esthetically, it unfortunately also carries with it a deep disorder: the disorder of conveying no direction. In places stamped with the monotony and repetition of sameness you move, but in moving you seem to have gotten nowhere. North is the same as south, or east as west. Sometimes north, south, east and west are all alike, as they are when you stand within the grounds of a large project. It takes differences—many differences—cropping up in different directions to keep us oriented. Scenes of thoroughgoing sameness lack these natural announcements of direction and movement, or are scantly furnished with them, and so they are deeply confusing. This is a kind of chaos.

Monotony of this sort is generally considered too oppressive to pursue as an ideal by everybody but some project planners or the most routine-minded real estate developers.

Instead, where uses are in actual fact homogeneous, we often find that deliberate distinctions and differences are contrived among the buildings. But these contrived differences give rise to esthetic difficulties too. Because inherent differences—those that come from genuinely differing uses—are lacking among the buildings and their settings, the contrivances represent the desire merely to *appear* different.

Some of the more blatant manifestations of this phenomenon were well described, back in 1952, by Douglas Haskell, editor of *Architectural Forum*, under the term "googie architecture." Googie architecture could then be seen in its finest flowering among the essentially homogeneous and standardized enterprises of roadside commercial strips: hot-dog stands in the shape of hot dogs, ice-cream stands in the shape of ice-cream cones. These are obvious examples of virtual sameness trying, by dint of exhibitionism, to appear unique and different from

their similar commercial neighbors. Mr. Haskell pointed
out that the same impulses to look special (in spite of not
being special) were at work also in more sophisticated
construction: weird roofs, weird stairs, weird colors,
weird signs, weird anything.

Recently Mr. Haskell has observed that similar signs
of exhibitionism have been appearing in supposedly dignified establishments.

Indeed they have: in office buildings, shopping centers, civic centers, airline terminals. Eugene Raskin, professor of architecture at Columbia University, commented
on this same phenomenon in an essay, "On the Nature of
Variety," in the Summer 1960 issue of the *Columbia University Forum.* Genuine architectural variety, Raskin
pointed out, does not consist in using different colors or
textures.

> Can it be in using contrasting forms? [he asked].
> A visit to one of the larger shopping centers (the
> Cross County Shopping Center in New York's
> Westchester County comes to mind, but pick your
> own) will make the point: though slabs, towers, cir-
> cles and flying stairs bound and abound all over the
> lot, the result has the appalling sameness of the tor-
> tures of hell. They may poke you with different
> instruments, but it's all pain . . .
>
> When we build, say, a business area in which
> all (or practically all) are engaged in earning their
> livings, or a residential area in which everyone is
> deep in the demands of domesticity, or a shopping
> area dedicated to the exchange of cash and com-
> modities—in short, where the pattern of human
> activity contains only one element, it is impossible

for the architecture to achieve a convincing variety
—convincing of the known facts of human variation. The designer may vary color, texture and form
until his drawing instruments buckle under the
strain, proving once more that art is the one
medium in which one cannot lie successfully.

The more homogeneity of use in a street or a neighborhood, the greater is the temptation to be different in
the only way left to be different. Wilshire Boulevard in
Los Angeles is an example of one grand exercise after
another in superficially contrived distinction, for several
miles of innately monotonous office buildings.

But Los Angeles is not unique in presenting us with
such vistas. San Francisco, for all its scorn of this kind of
thing in Los Angeles, looks much the same at its new outskirts of sorted-out shopping centers and housing developments, and for the same basic reasons. Euclid Avenue in
Cleveland, which used to be considered by many critics
one of the most beautiful of American avenues (it was, in
those days, essentially a suburban avenue of large, fine
houses with large, fine grounds), has now been excoriated,
with justice, by critic Richard A. Miller in *Architectural
Forum*, as one of the ugliest and most disorganized of city
streets. In converting to outright urban use, Euclid Avenue
has converted to homogeneity: office buildings again, and
again a chaos of shouted, but superficial, differences.

Homogeneity of uses poses an unavoidable esthetic
dilemma: Shall the homogeneity look as homogeneous as
it is, and be frankly monotonous? Or shall it try not to
look as homogeneous as it is and go in for eye-catching,
but meaningless and chaotic differences? This, in city

guise, is the old, familiar esthetic zoning problem of homogeneous suburbs: Shall they zone to require conformity in appearance, or shall they zone to prohibit sameness? If to prohibit sameness, where must the line be drawn against what is too nonconforming in design?

Wherever a city area is functionally homogeneous in its uses, this also becomes an esthetic dilemma for the city, and in more intensive form than in the suburbs, because buildings are so much more dominant in the general scene of cities. It is a ridiculous dilemma for cities, and it has no decent answer.

Diversity of uses, on the other hand, while it is too often handled poorly, does offer the decent possibility of displaying genuine differences of content. Therefore these can become interesting and stimulating differences to the eye, without phoniness, exhibitionism or belabored novelty.

Fifth Avenue in New York between Fortieth Street and Fifty-ninth Street is tremendously diverse in its large and small shops, bank buildings, office buildings, churches, institutions. Its architecture expresses these differences in use, and differences accrue from the varying ages of the buildings, differences in technology and historical taste. But Fifth Avenue does not look disorganized, fragmented or exploded.* Fifth Avenue's architectural

---

* Its only blatant eyesore and element of disorganization is a group of billboards on the northeast corner of Forty-second Street. These are presumably well meant because, as this is written, they are fatuously exhorting the passing throngs to pray in family groups, to save for a rainy day, and to fight delinquency. Their power to reform is questionable. Their power to blight the view up Fifth Avenue from the library is unquestionable.

contrasts and differences arise mainly out of differences in content. They are sensible and natural contrasts and differences. The whole hangs together remarkably well, without being monotonous either.

The new office stretch of New York's Park Avenue is far more standardized in content than Fifth Avenue. Park Avenue has the advantage of containing among its new office buildings several which, in themselves, are masterpieces of modern design.* But does homogeneity of use or homogeneity of age help Park Avenue esthetically? On the contrary, the office blocks of Park Avenue are wretchedly disorganized in appearance, and far more given than Fifth Avenue to a total effect of chaotic architectural willfulness, overlaid on boredom.

There are many instances of city diversity that include the use of residences and come off well. The Rittenhouse Square area in Philadelphia, Telegraph Hill in San Francisco, parts of the North End in Boston, afford examples. Small groups of residential buildings can be similar or even identical to each other without imposing a pall of monotony, so long as the grouping takes in no more than a short street block, and is not thereupon immediately repeated. In such a case, we look at the grouping as a unit, and see it as differing, in content and appearance, from whatever the next use or residential type may be.

Sometimes diversity of uses, combined with diversity of age, can even take the curse of monotony off blocks that are far too long—and again without the need for exhibitionism because differences of real substance exist. An example of this kind of diversity is Eleventh Street

*Lever House, Seagram, Pepsi-Cola, Union Carbide.

between Fifth and Sixth Avenues in New York, a street admired as both dignified and interesting to walk on. Along its south side it contains, going west, a fourteen-story apartment house, a church, seven three-story houses, a five-story house, thirteen four-story houses, a nine-story apartment, five four-story houses with a restaurant and bar at the street level, a five-story apartment, a little graveyard, and a six-story apartment house with a restaurant at street level; on the north side, again going west, it contains a church, a four-story house with a nursery school in it, a nine-story apartment house, three five-story houses, a six-story apartment house, an eight-story apartment house, five four-story houses, a six-story residence club, two five-story apartment houses, another five-story apartment house of very different vintage, a nine-story apartment house, a new addition to the New School for Social Research with a library at street level and a public view to the interior courtyard, a four-story house, a five-story apartment house with a restaurant at street level, a mean- and cheap-looking one-story laundry and cleaner, a three-story apartment house with a candy and newspaper store at street level. While these are nearly all residential buildings, they are broken into by instances of ten other uses. Even the purely residential buildings themselves embrace many different periods of technology and taste, many different modes and costs of living. They have an almost fantastic array of matter-of-fact, modestly stated differences: different heights at first-floor levels, differing arrangements for entrances and sidewalk access. These arise directly out of the fact that the buildings actually are different in kind and age. The effect is both serene and unselfconscious.

Still more interesting visual effects, and again without any need for exhibitionism or other phoniness, can and do arise in cities from mixtures in building types far more radical than those of Eleventh Street—more radical because they are based on more radical inherent differences. Most landmarks and focal points in cities—of which we need more, not fewer—come from the contrast of a use radically different from its surroundings, and therefore inherently special-looking, happily located to make some drama and contrast of the inherent difference. This, of course, was what Peets was talking about (see Chapter Eight) when he advocated that monumental or noble buildings be set within the matrix of the city, instead of being sorted out and withdrawn into "courts of honor" with other inherently similar neighbors there.

Nor are the innate radical differences of humbler elements in city mixtures to be scorned esthetically. They too can convey the pleasures of contrast, movement and direction, without forced superficialities: the workshops that turn up mingled with residences, the manufacturing buildings, the art gallery next to the fish market that delights me every time I go to buy fish, the hoity-toity gourmet shop in another part of town that peacefully contrasts and coexists with a robust bar of the kind where new Irish immigrants come to hear about jobs.

Genuine differences in the city architectural scene express, as Raskin says so excellently,

> . . . the interweaving of *human* patterns. They are full of people doing different things, with different reasons and different ends in view, and the

architecture reflects and expresses this difference—which is one of content rather than form alone. Being human, human beings are what interest us most. In architecture as in literature and the drama, it is the richness of human variation that gives vitality and color to the human setting . . .

Considering the hazard of monotony . . . the most serious fault in our zoning laws lies in the fact that they *permit* an entire area to be devoted to a single use.

In seeking visual order, cities are able to choose among three broad alternatives, two of which are hopeless and one of which is hopeful. They can aim for areas of homogeneity which look homogeneous, and get results depressing and disorienting. They can aim for areas of homogeneity which try not to look homogeneous, and get results of vulgarity and dishonesty. Or they can aim for areas of great diversity and, because real differences are thereby expressed, can get results which, at worst, are merely interesting, and at best can be delightful.

How to accommodate city diversity well in visual terms, how to respect its freedom while showing visually that it is a form of order, is the central esthetic problem of cities. I shall deal with it in Chapter Nineteen of this book. For the moment, the point is this: City diversity is not innately ugly. That is a misconception, and a most simple-minded one. But lack of city diversity is innately either depressing on the one hand, or vulgarly chaotic on the other.

*   *   *

Is it true that diversity causes traffic congestion?

Traffic congestion is caused by vehicles, not by people in themselves.

Wherever people are thinly settled, rather than densely concentrated, or wherever diverse uses occur infrequently, any specific attraction does cause traffic congestion. Such places as clinics, shopping centers or movies bring with them a concentration of traffic—and what is more, bring traffic heavily along the routes to and from them. A person who needs or wants to use them can do so only by car. Even a grade school can mean traffic congestion in such a milieu, because children must be carried to school. Lack of wide ranges of concentrated diversity can put people into automobiles for almost all their needs. The spaces required for roads and for parking spread everything out still farther, and lead to still greater uses of vehicles.

This is tolerable where the population is thinly spread. It becomes an intolerable condition, destructive of all other values and all other aspects of convenience, where populations are heavy or continuous.

In dense, diversified city areas, people still walk, an activity that is impractical in suburbs and in most gray areas. The more intensely various and close-grained the diversity in an area, the more walking. Even people who come into a lively, diverse area from outside, whether by car or by public transportation, walk when they get there.

Is it true that city diversity invites ruinous uses? Is permissiveness for all (or almost all) kinds of uses in an area destructive?

To consider this, we need to consider several different

kinds of uses—some of which actually are harmful, and some of which are conventionally considered to be harmful but are not.

One destructive category of uses, of which junk yards are an example, contributes nothing to a district's general convenience, attraction, or concentration of people. In return for nothing, these uses make exorbitant demands upon the land—and upon esthetic tolerance. Used-car lots are in this category. So are buildings which have been abandoned or badly underused.

Probably everyone (except possibly the owners of such objects) is agreed that this category of uses is blighting.

But it does not follow that junk yards and their like are therefore threats which accompany city diversity. Successful city districts are never dotted with junk yards, but that is not *why* these districts are successful. It is the other way around. They lack junk yards *because* they are successful.

Deadening and space-taking low economic uses like junk yards and used-car lots grow like pigweed in spots which are *already* uncultivated and unsuccessful. They sprout in places that have low concentrations of foot traffic, too little surrounding magnetism, and no high-value competition for the space. Their natural homes are gray areas and the dwindled-off edges of downtowns, where the fires of diversity and vitality burn low. If all controls were lifted from housing-project malls, and these dead, underused places found their natural economic level, junk yards and used-car lots are exactly what would sprout in many of them.

The trouble represented by junk yards goes deeper

than the Blight Fighters can plumb. It achieves nothing to cry "Take them away! They shouldn't be there!" The problem is to cultivate an economic environment in the district which makes more vital uses of the land profitable and logical. If this is not done, the land might as well be used for junk yards, which after all have *some* use. Little else is apt to be successful, and this includes public uses, like parks or school yards, which fail catastrophically precisely where the economic environment is too poor for other uses that depend on magnetism and surrounding vitality. The kind of problem symbolized by junk yards, in short, is not solved by fearing diversity, or by suppression, but rather by catalyzing and cultivating a fertile economic environment for diversity.

A second category of uses is conventionally considered, by planners and zoners, to be harmful, especially if these uses are mingled into residential areas. This category includes bars, theaters, clinics, businesses and manufacturing. It is a category which is not harmful; the arguments that these uses are to be tightly controlled derive from their effects in suburbs and in dull, inherently dangerous gray areas, not from their effects in lively city districts.

Thin smatterings of nonresidential uses do little good in gray areas, and can do harm, because gray areas are unequipped to handle strangers—or to protect them either, for that matter. But again, this is a problem that arises from too feeble a diversity in the prevailing dullness and darkness.

In lively city districts, where abundant diversity has been catalyzed, these uses do not do harm. They are positively necessary, either for their direct contributions to safety, public contact and cross-use, or because they help support other diversity which has these direct effects.

Work uses suggest another bugaboo: reeking smokestacks and flying ash. Of course reeking smokestacks and flying ash are harmful, but it does not follow that intensive city manufacturing (most of which produces no such nasty by-products) or other work uses must be segregated from dwellings. Indeed, the notion that reek or fumes are to be combated by zoning and land-sorting classifications at all is ridiculous. The air doesn't know about zoning boundaries. Regulations specifically aimed at the smoke or the reek itself are to the point.

Among planners and zoners, the great shibboleth in land use was formerly the glue factory. "Would you want a glue factory in your neighborhood?" was the clincher. Why a glue factory I do not know, except possibly that glue then meant dead horses and old fish, and the reference could be counted upon to make nice people shudder and stop thinking. There used to be a glue factory near us. It was in a small, attractive brick building and was one of the cleanest-looking places on its block.

Nowadays, the glue factory has been replaced by a different bogy, the "mortuary," which is trotted out as a crowning example of the horrors that insinuate their way into neighborhoods which lack tight controls on uses. Yet mortuaries, or funeral parlors as we call them in the city, seem to do no harm. Perhaps in vital, diversified city neighborhoods, in the midst of life, the reminder of death is not the pall it may be on waning suburban streets. Curiously, the proponents of rigid use controls, who object so firmly to death in the city, seem to object equally firmly to life breaking out in the city.

One of the blocks of Greenwich Village which happens to be spontaneously upgrading itself in attractiveness, interest and economic value, happens also to have a funeral parlor on it as this is written, and has had for years. Is this objectionable? Obviously it has been no deterrent to the families who have put money into the rehabilitation of town houses on the street, nor to the businessmen who have been investing money in opening or refurbishing quarters there, nor to the builder erecting a new high-rent apartment.*

The strange idea that death should be an unnoticeable or unmentionable part of city life was apparently debated in Boston a century ago, when city improvers advocated the removal of the small old graveyards of Boston's downtown churches. One Bostonian, Thomas Bridgman, whose views prevailed, had this to say, "The burial place of the dead, so far as it has any influence, is on the side of virtue and religion . . . Its voice is one of perpetual rebuke to folly and sin."

The only clue I can find to the presumed harm wrought by funeral parlors in cities is contained in *The Selection of Retail Locations*, by Richard Nelson. Nelson proves statistically that people visiting funeral parlors do not customarily combine this call with shopping errands.

---

*This particular block, incidentally, is always spoken of locally as a nice residential street, and residence is indeed its predominant use, both in fact and in appearance. But consider what else it has, as this is written, tucked among its residences: the funeral parlor of course, a real estate office, two laundries, an antiques shop, a savings and loan office, three doctors' offices, a church and synagogue (combined), a little theater in the rear behind the church and synagogue, a hairdresser, a vocal studio, five restaurants, and a mysterious building that could be anything from a school to a craft-factory to a rehabilitation center, and isn't telling.

Therefore, it is of no extra retail advantage to locate next to a funeral parlor.

In low-income neighborhoods of big cities, such as New York's East Harlem, funeral parlors can, and often do, operate as positive and constructive forces. This is because a funeral parlor presupposes an undertaker. Undertakers, like druggists, lawyers, dentists and clergymen, are representatives, in these neighborhoods, of such qualities as dignity, ambition and knowledgeability. They are typically well-known public characters, active in local civic life. Quite often, they eventually go into politics too.

Like so much of orthodox planning, the presumed harm done by this use and that use has been somehow accepted without anyone's asking the questions, "Why is it harmful? Just how does it do harm, and what is this harm?" I doubt that there is any legal economic use (and few illegal ones) which can harm a city district as much as lack of abundant diversity harms it. No special form of city blight is nearly so devastating as the Great Blight of Dullness.

Having said this, I shall bring up a final category of uses which, unless their location is controlled, are harmful in abundantly diversified city districts. They can be numbered on one hand: parking lots, large or heavy trucking depots, gas stations, gigantic outdoor advertising* and enterprises which are harmful not because of their nature, exactly, but because *in certain streets* their scale is wrong.

All five of these problem uses are apt to be profitable enough (unlike junk yards) to afford, and to seek, space in

---

*Usually, but not always. What would Times Square be without its huge outdoor advertising?

vital, diversified areas. But at the same time they usually act as street desolators. Visually, they are disorganizing to streets, and are so dominating that it is hard—sometimes impossible—for any countering sense of order in either street use or street appearance to make much impression.

The visual effects of the first four of these problem uses are easily seen and often thought about. The uses themselves are the problem because of the *kinds* of uses they are.

However, the fifth problem use I have mentioned is different, because in this case the problem is *size* of use rather than *kind* of use. On certain streets, any disproportionately large occupant of street frontage is visually a street disintegrator and desolator, although exactly the same *kinds* of uses, at small scale, do no harm and are indeed an asset.

For example, many city "residential" streets shelter, along with their dwellings, all kinds of commercial and working uses, and these can and do fit in well so long as the street frontage which each one occupies is no greater, say, than that taken up by the typical residence. Literally, as well as figuratively, the uses fit in. The street has a visual character which is consistent and basically orderly as well as various.

But on just such a street, a use that abruptly takes street frontage on a large scale can appear to explode the street—make it fly apart in fragments.

This problem has nothing to do with use, in the usual zoning sense of use. A restaurant or snack place, a grocery, a cabinetmaker, a printer's shop, for instance, can fit well into such a street. But exactly the same *kind* of use— say, a big cafeteria, a supermarket, a large woodworking factory or a printing plant—can wreak visual havoc (and sometimes auditory havoc) because it is on a different *scale*.

Such streets need controls to defend them from the ruin that completely permissive diversity might indeed bring them. But the controls needed are not controls on kinds of uses. The controls needed are controls on the scale of street frontage permitted to a use.

This is so obvious and so ubiquitous a city problem that one would think its solution must be among the concerns of zoning theory. Yet the very existence of the problem is not even recognized in zoning theory. As this is written, the New York City Planning Commission has been holding hearings on a new, progressive, up-to-the-minute comprehensive zoning resolution. Interested organizations and individuals in the city have been invited to study, among other things, the proposed zoning categories into which streets fall and to make recommendations for shifts from one category to another if that seems desirable. There are several dozen use categories, each differentiated most carefully and thoughtfully—and all of them are irrelevant to the real-life problems of use in diverse city districts.

What can you recommend, when the very theory behind such a zoning resolution—not merely its detail—needs drastic overhaul and rethinking? This sad circumstance has given rise to many a ludicrous strategy session, for instance, in the civic organizations of Greenwich Village. Many well-loved and popular residential side streets contain mixtures and sprinklings of small establishments. These are generally present by exemption from existing residential zoning, or are in violation of the zoning.

Everybody likes their presence, and no arguments arise over their desirability. The arguments, rather, revolve around the question of what kind of categories in the new zoning will be least at odds with the needs of real life. The drawbacks of each offered category are formidable. The argument against a commercial category for such streets is that, although it will permit the small-scale uses that are an asset, it will also permit uses purely as uses, without regard to scale; for instance, large supermarkets will be permitted and these are greatly feared by residents as explosive to such streets and destructive to residential street character—as they are. Ask for residential categories, this argument continues, and then small establishments can infiltrate in violation of the zoning as they have in the past. The argument against a residential category is that somebody might actually take it seriously and the zoning against "nonconforming" small-scale uses might be enforced! Upright citizens, with the civic interests of their neighborhoods genuinely at heart, sit soberly plotting as to what regulation will offer the most constructive circumvention of itself.

The dilemma posed is urgent and real. One Greenwich Village street, for example, recently came up against a version of precisely this problem because of a case in the Board of Standards and Appeals. A bakery on this street, at one time mainly retail and small, has grown vigorously into a substantial wholesaler, and was applying for a zoning exemption to expand considerably farther (taking over the quarters of a former wholesale laundry next door). The street, which has long been zoned "residential," has been upgrading itself recently, and many of its property owners and renting residents, in their growing pride and concern with their street, decided to fight the exemption request. They lost. It is no wonder they lost, for their case was blurry. Some of the leaders of the fight, who owned property or lived in property with small-scale nonresidential uses on the ground floors, were themselves in conflict, actual or sympathetic, with the "residential" zoning—just as surely as the relatively big bakery was. However, precisely the many small-scale nonresidential uses on the street, which have been increasing, are responsible for much of the increased attractiveness and value of the street for residence. They are acquisitions, and the people on the street know it, for they make the street interesting and safe. They include a real estate office, a small publishing company, a book-shop, a restaurant, a picture framer, a cabinetmaker, a shop that sells old posters and prints, a candy store, a cof-fee house, a laundry, two groceries, and a small experi-mental theater.

I asked a leader of the fight against the bakery exemp-tion, a man who is also the principal owner of rehabili-tated residential property on the street, which alternative in his opinion would do greater harm to his residential property values: the gradual elimination of all "nonresi-dential" uses on the street, or the expansion of the bakery. The first alternative would be more destructive, he answered, but added, "Isn't an implied choice of that kind absurd!"

It is absurd. A street like this is a puzzle and an anom-aly under conventional use-zoning theory. It is a puzzle even as a commercial zoning problem. As city commercial zoning has become more "progressive" (i.e., imitative of suburban conditions) it has begun to emphasize distinctions between "local convenience shops," "district shopping," and the like. The up-to-the-minute New York resolution has all this too. But how do you classify such a street as this one with the bakery? It combines the most purely localized conveniences (like the laundry and the candy store) with district-wide attractions (like the cabinetmaker, the picture framer, the coffee house) and with city-wide attractions (like the theater, the art galleries, the poster shop). Its mixture is unique, but the pattern of unclassifiable diversity which it represents is not in the least unique. All lively, diversified city areas, full of vitality and surprises, exist in another world from that of suburban commerce.

By no means all city streets need zoning for scale of street frontage. Many streets, particularly where large or wide buildings predominate, whether for residential or for other uses or both, can contain enterprises of large street frontages, and mix them with small ones too, without appearing to explode and disintegrate, and without being functionally overwhelmed by one use. Fifth Avenue has such mixtures of large and small scale. But those city streets that do need scale zoning need it badly, not just for their own sake but because the presence of streets with consistent character adds diversity to the city scene itself.

Raskin, in his essay on variety, suggested that the greatest flaw in city zoning is that it *permits* monotony. I think this is correct. Perhaps the next greatest flaw is that it ignores *scale* of use, where this is an important consideration, or confuses it with *kind* of use, and this leads, on the one hand, to visual (and sometimes functional) disintegration of streets, or on the other hand to indiscriminate

attempts to sort out and segregate kinds of uses no matter
what their size or empiric effect. Diversity itself is thus
unnecessarily suppressed, rather than one limited manifestation of it, unfortunate in certain places.

To be sure, city areas with flourishing diversity sprout
strange and unpredictable uses and peculiar scenes. But
this is not a drawback of diversity. This is the point, or
part of it. That this should happen is in keeping with one
of the missions of cities.

Paul J. Tillich, professor of theology at Harvard,
observes:

> By its nature, the metropolis provides what other-
> wise could be given only by traveling; namely, the
> strange. Since the strange leads to questions and
> undermines familiar tradition, it serves to elevate
> reason to ultimate significance . . . There is no bet-
> ter proof of this fact than the attempts of all totali-
> tarian authorities to keep the strange from their
> subjects . . . The big city is sliced into pieces, each of
> which is observed, purged and equalized. The mys-
> tery of the strange and the critical rationality of men
> are both removed from the city.

This is an idea familiar to those who appreciate and
enjoy cities, although it is usually expressed more lightly.
Kate Simon, author of *New York Places and Pleasures,* is
saying much the same thing when she suggests, "Take the
children to Grant's [restaurant] . . . they may bump into
people whose like they may never see elsewhere and may
possibly never forget."

The very existence of popular city guidebooks, with their emphases on the discovery, the curious, the different, are an illustration of Professor Tillich's point. Cities have the capability of providing something for everybody, only because, and only when, they are created by everybody.

PART THREE

FORCES OF DECLINE AND REGENERATION

13

THE SELF-DESTRUCTION OF DIVERSITY

My observations and conclusions thus far sum up to this: In our American cities, we need all kinds of diversity, intricately mingled in mutual support. We need this so city life can work decently and constructively, and so the people of cities can sustain (and further develop) their society and civilization. Public and quasi-public bodies are responsible for some of the enterprises that help make up city diversity—for instance, parks, museums, schools, most auditoriums, hospitals, some offices, some dwellings. However, most city diversity is the creation of incredible numbers of different people and different private organizations, with vastly differing ideas and purposes, planning and contriving outside the formal framework of public action. The main responsibility of city planning and design should be to develop—insofar as public policy and action can do so—cities that are congenial places for this great range of unofficial plans, ideas and opportunities to flourish, along with the flourishing of the public enterprises. City districts will be economically and socially congenial places for diversity to generate itself and reach its best potential if the districts possess good mixtures of primary uses, frequent streets, a close-grained mingling of different ages in their buildings, and a high concentration of people.

In this group of chapters on decline and regeneration, I intend to dwell on several powerful forces that can influence, for good or for ill, the growth of diversity and vitality in cities, once an area is not crippled by lack of one or more of the four conditions necessary for generating diversity.

These forces, in the form that they work for ill, are: the tendency for outstandingly successful diversity in cities to destroy itself; the tendency for massive single elements in cities (many of which are necessary and otherwise desirable) to cast a deadening influence; the tendency for population instability to counter the growth of diversity; and the tendency for both public and private money either to glut or to starve development and change.

These forces are interrelated, to be sure; all factors in city changes are interrelated with all other factors. Nevertheless, it is possible and useful to look at each of these forces in its own right. The purpose of recognizing and understanding them is to try to combat them or—better yet—convert them into constructive forces. Besides influencing the growth of diversity itself, these forces also sometimes affect the ease or difficulty with which the basic conditions for generating diversity can be introduced. Leaving them out of account, even the best planning for vitality would fall a step back for every two steps forward.

The first of these powerful forces is the tendency for outstanding success in cities to destroy itself—purely as a result of being successful. In this chapter I shall discuss the self-destruction of diversity, a force which, among its other effects, causes our downtowns continually to shift their centers and move. This is a force that creates has-

been districts, and is responsible for much inner-city stagnation and decay.

The self-destruction of diversity can happen in streets, at
small nodes of vitality, in groupings of streets, or in whole
districts. The last case is the most serious.

Whichever form the self-destruction takes, this, in
broad strokes, is what happens: A diversified mixture of
uses at some place in the city becomes outstandingly popular and successful as a whole. Because of the location's
success, which is invariably based on flourishing and
magnetic diversity, ardent competition for space in this
locality develops. It is taken up in what amounts to the
economic equivalent of a fad.

The winners in the competition for space will represent only a narrow segment of the many uses that
together created success. Whichever one or few uses have
emerged as the most profitable in the locality will be
repeated and repeated, crowding out and overwhelming
less profitable forms of use. If tremendous numbers of
people, attracted by convenience and interest, or charmed
by vigor and excitement, choose to live or work in the
area, again the winners of the competition will form a narrow segment of population of users. Since so many want
to get in, those who get in or stay in will be self-sorted by
the expense.

Competition based on retail profitability is most apt
to affect streets. Competition based on working- or living-
space attraction is most apt to affect whole groupings of
streets, or even whole districts.

Thus, from this process, one or few dominating uses
finally emerge triumphant. But the triumph is hollow. A

most intricate and successful organism of economic mutual support and social mutual support has been destroyed by the process.

From this point on, the locality will gradually be deserted by people using it for purposes other than those that emerged triumphant from the competition—because the other purposes are no longer there. Both visually and functionally, the place becomes more monotonous. All the economic disadvantages of people being spread insufficiently through time of day are likely to follow. The locality's suitability even for its predominant use will gradually decline, as the suitability of downtown Manhattan for managerial offices has declined because of this reason. In time, a place that was once so successful and once the object of such ardent competition, wanes and becomes marginal.

Many streets which have already gone through this process and are at rest in their moribundity can be seen in our cities. Others, caught in the process now, can be watched in action. Among those in the neighborhood where I live is Eighth Street, the principal commercial street of Greenwich Village. Thirty-five years ago, this was a nondescript street. Then one of its principal property owners, Charles Abrams (who happens also to be an exceptionally enlightened planning and housing expert), built on the street a small night club and a motion-picture theater unusual for its time. (The narrow auditorium for good screen viewing, the coffee lounge and the intimate atmosphere have since been widely copied.) These enterprises proved popular. They brought more people into the street during evening hours and week ends, to supplement the day people passing through, and thus helped stimulate the growth of convenience and special shops. These, in their own right, began to bring still more people, day and evening. As I have mentioned previously, a two-shift street like this is an economically sound place for restaurants. The history of Eighth Street began to bear this out. It acquired an interesting growth and range of restaurants.

Among all the enterprises of Eighth Street, it happened that restaurants became the largest money-earners per square foot of space. Naturally it followed that Eighth Street went more and more to restaurants. Meantime, at its Fifth Avenue corner, a diversity of clubs, galleries and some small offices were crowded out by blank, monolithic, very high-rent apartments. The only unusual factor in this history is Abrams himself. Unlike most property owners, who might not have pondered the implications of what was occurring, or have seen reason for worry in the face of success, Abrams watched, with dismay, bookstores, galleries, clubs, craftsmen and one-of-a-kind shops being pushed out. He watched new ideas starting up in other streets, and fewer new ideas coming to Eighth Street. He could see that some of this movement was helping to enliven and diversify other streets, but he could also see that Eighth Street was slowly but steadily starting to undiversify itself. He realized that if the process ran its full and logical course, Eighth Street would eventually be left beached, in the wake of popularity that had moved away. For much of his own property, in a strategic stretch of the street, Abrams has thus deliberately searched out tenants who will add something other than restaurants to the mixture. But sometimes he has to search hard for them because they must reasonably approach the current high earning power of restaurants. This narrows down the possibilities—even purely commercial possibilities. Eighth Street's worst potential threat to its diversity and its long-term success is, in short, the force let loose by outstanding success.

Another nearby street, Third Street, is far advanced in a similar trouble, because of another kind of sorting. This street, for a stretch of several blocks, has become immensely popular with tourists, drawn first by the local bohemian life of coffee houses and neighborhood bars, with—at first—a light sprinkling of night clubs, all mingled with the interesting neighborhood shops and residential life of a stable old Italian and artists' district. In their proportions of fifteen years ago, the evening visitors were a constructive part of the area's mixture. The general liveliness they helped create was part of the residential appeal, as well as an appeal to visitors. Night spots are today overwhelming the street, and are also overwhelming the very life of the area. Into a district excellent at handling and protecting strangers they have concentrated too many strangers, all in too irresponsible a mood, for any conceivable city society to handle naturally. The duplication of the most profitable use is undermining the base of its own attraction, as disproportionate duplication and exaggeration of some single use always does in cities.

We are accustomed to thinking of streets, or neighborhoods of streets, as divided into functional uses—entertainment, offices, residence, shopping or the like. And so they are, but only to a degree if they maintain their success. For example, streets which become so profitable for such secondary diversity as clothing shopping that clothing shopping becomes almost their exclusive use, decline as they are progressively deserted and ignored by people with other secondary purposes in mind. If such a street has long blocks, which further degenerate it as a pool of intricate cross-use, the sorting out of its users, and the resulting stagnation, is emphasized. And if such a street belongs in a district which, in general, is sorting into one primary use—such as work—there is seldom hope for any spontaneous turn for the better.

The self-destruction of diversity can be seen at outstandingly successful little nodes of activity, as well as along street stretches. The process is the same. As an example, consider the crossing of Chestnut and Broad Streets in Philadelphia, a spot which a few years ago was a climax of Chestnut Street's varied shopping and other activities. The corners of this crossing were what real estate men call a "100 percent location." It was an enviable place to be. One of the corner occupants was a bank. Three other banks bought themselves into the three other corners, apparently to be at the 100 percent location too. From that moment, it was no longer the 100 percent location. The crossing is today a dead barrier along Chestnut Street, and the tumble of diversity and activity has been pushed beyond.

These banks were making the same mistake as a family I know who bought an acre in the country on which to build a house. For many years, while they lacked the money to build, they visited the site regularly and picnicked on a knoll, the site's most attractive feature. They liked so much to visualize themselves as always there, that when they finally built they put the house on the knoll. But then the knoll was gone. Somehow they had

not realized they would destroy it and lose it by sup-
planting it with themselves.

Streets (especially if their blocks are short) sometimes can
weather much duplication of successful uses, or else can
regenerate themselves spontaneously after declining and
stagnating for a time. These escapes are possible if the surrounding district sustains a strong and vigorous mixture
of diversity—especially a strong, underlying base of primary diversity.

However, when whole neighborhoods of streets, and
entire districts, embark on excessive duplication of the
most profitable or prestigious uses, the problem is far
more serious.

Striking evidences of this disastrous sorting-out can
be seen in many city downtowns. The successive historical centers of Boston's downtown, like so many archeo-
logical layers, are fossilized as stratum after stratum of
sorted-out uses, each stratum lacking primary mixture,
each stratum stagnated. The Boston Planning Board, analyzing downtown uses, mapped them by color—one color
to designate managerial and financial offices, another for
government, another for shopping, another for entertainment, and so on. The stagnant areas all show on the map
as a series of virtually solid swatches of a single color
each. On the other hand, at one end of the downtown,
where the Back Bay meets a corner of the Public Gardens,
is a swatch of map marked with a different kind of legend, designated in red and yellow stripes. This swatch
was too complex to map according to specific uses, so it
was given an appropriate representational legend, standing for "mixed." This is the only part of Boston's down-

town that is at present spontaneously changing, growing, acting like a live city.

Such successions of sorted-out downtown neighborhoods as those in Boston are generally thought of, vaguely, as the residue left by a moving downtown center. They are regarded as a result of the center's movement elsewhere. But they are not. These clumps of excessive duplication are the *cause* of the center's movement. Diversity is crowded out by the duplication of success. Unless they are handsomely financed to start with, or instantly successful (which is seldom the case), new ideas tumble into second-best locations; thereby second-best becomes first-rate, flourishes for a time, and eventually it too is destroyed by the duplication of its own greatest successes.

In New York, the sorting-out of downtown was already being memorialized back in the 1880's, in a jingle of the time:

> From Eighth Street down, the men are earning it.
> From Eighth Street up, the women are spending it.
> That is the manner of this great town,
> From Eighth Street up and Eighth Street down.

Willa Cather, writing in *My Mortal Enemy* of Madison Square as its turn arrived to become an intense center of diversity, described it thus: "Madison Square was then at the parting of the ways; had a double personality, half commercial, half social, with shops to the south and residences on the north."

Miss Cather put her finger on the characteristic of mixture and "double personality" that always marks an outstandingly successful center as it approaches its crest and poises there. But the mixture hardly represents a "parting of the ways." It is a coming together and mingling of the ways.

Madison Square, now a glum, has-been district of massive office buildings and a commerce very marginal in comparison to that it once enjoyed, was remarkable at its crest for possessing the old Madison Square Garden (now supplanted by an office building). Never since has New York had such an urbane, glamorous and magnetic assembly hall, because never since has New York had a major assembly hall at the magnetic, expensive center of a good mixture.

The eventual sorting out and long decline of Madison Square was not, of course, an isolated event. It was part of a larger movement, made up of many accumulations of economic pressure upon successful mixtures of uses. On a larger scale than Madison Square, these pressures of competition for space were continually unsorting diversity throughout the entire middle of downtown, and tumbling diversity out at the upper end of downtown; downtown itself was moving as a result, leaving its beached districts behind.

A moving downtown usually leaves, along with its clumps of excessive duplication, pockets of nothing much at all, places which the most intensive new combinations of diversity have bypassed or over which they have leapfrogged. These pockets or side strips are apt to remain nothing much at all thenceforth, because the sorted-out clumps adjoining them provide so poor a spread of people through time of day. There is space here, but nothing to catalyze uses for it.

Apparently the self-destruction of district diversity by excessive duplication occurs in London too, because of the same forces that move American downtowns. An article on the planning problems of Central London, in the January 1959 *Journal of the Town Planning Institute*, a British periodical, has this to say:

> For many years now variety has gone from the City [the bank and financial office center]. There the teeming daytime population contrasts with a 5,000 night population. What has happened in the City is happening to the West End. The claim of many who have offices in the West End is that for their clients and customers they have the amenities of the hotels, the clubs, the restaurants and for their staff the shops and the parks. If the process goes on, these very advantages will be gobbled up and the West End will become one dreary sea of office blocks.

We have pitifully few outstandingly successful residential districts in our American cities; most city residential districts have never possessed the four fundamental conditions for generating exuberant diversity in the first place. Therefore, examples of the self-destruction that follows outstanding success are more usual in downtowns. But the relatively few city residential districts that do become outstandingly magnetic and successful at generating diversity and vitality are subjected ultimately to the same forces of self-destruction as downtowns. In this case, so many people want to live in the locality that it becomes profitable to build, in excessive and devastating quantity, for those who can pay the most. These are usually childless people, and today they are not simply people who can pay the most in general, but people who can or will pay the most for the smallest space. Accommodations for this narrow, profitable segment of population multiply, at the expense of all other tissue and all other population. Families are crowded out, variety of scene is crowded out, enterprises unable to support their share of the new construction costs are crowded out. This process is now occurring, very rapidly, in much of Greenwich Village, Yorkville and the midtown East Side of Manhattan. The uses duplicated excessively are different from those duplicated excessively at centers of downtowns, but the process is the same, the reason why it occurs is the same, and the ultimate effects are the same. The admired and magnetic knoll is destroyed by its own new occupants, by the act of occupation.

The process I have described occurs only in small areas at a time, because it is a sequel only to outstanding success. Nevertheless, the destructive power of this process is larger and more serious than its geographical scope at any one time suggests. The very fact that the process does occur in localities of outstanding success makes it difficult for our cities to build further upon outstanding success. It too often slips into decline.

Furthermore, the very means by which outstanding success declines make the process doubly destructive to cities. At the same time new construction and narrow multiplications of uses are destroying mutual support in one locality, they are, in effect, depriving other localities of their presence, localities where they would *add* to diversity and strengthen mutual support, rather than subtract these qualities.

For some reason, banks, insurance companies and prestige offices are consistently the most voracious double-destroyers in this way. Look to see where banks or insurance companies are clustered, and you will too often see where a center of diversity has been supplanted, a knoll of vitality leveled. You will see a place that is already a has-been or is becoming so. I suspect that this curious circumstance is owing to two facts. Such organizations are conservative. Conservatism, applied to the choice of city locations, means investing where success is already a well-established fact. To see that investment may destroy success requires looking too far ahead for those who value most what is already achieved—and are perhaps mystified by localities with a potential for success, or are insecure about them, because of not understanding why some places in cities should be successful, and others not. In the second place, such organizations have money, and thus are able to supplant most rivals for the space they want. The wish and the ability to settle on the knoll are thus combined most effectively in banks and insurance companies, and in prestige offices—which borrow readily from banks and insurance companies. To a certain extent, the convenience of being very close to one another is important, as it is in many other city activities. But this hardly accounts for the accuracy and degree with which such powerful organizations supplant successful combinations of diversity. Once a locality has been stagnated by their excessive duplication of work uses (at the expense of other tissue), the more prosperous among them readily leave the nest of convenience which is no longer so appealing.

However, it would be misleading to fix upon particular culprits among differing city uses, even outstanding culprits. Too many other uses exert the same economic pressures and end with the same hollow triumphs.

It is more fruitful, I think, to approach this as a problem of malfunction in cities themselves.

First, we must understand that self-destruction of diversity is caused by success, not by failure.

Second, we must understand that the process is a continuation of the same economic processes that led to the success itself, and were indispensable to it. Diversity grows in a city area because of economic opportunity and economic attraction. During the process of diversity growth, rival users of space are crowded out. All city diversity grows, in part at least, at the expense of some other tissue. During this growth period even some unique uses may be crowded out because they give such low economic return for the land they occupy. This we think of as salutary if the unique uses are junk yards, used-car lots or abandoned buildings; and it *is* salutary. During the growth period, much of the new diversity occurs not merely at the expense of uniquely low-value tissue, but also at the expense of already existing duplications of use. Sameness is being subtracted at the same time diversity is being added. This result of economic competition for space is net increase in diversity.

At some point the diversity growth has proceeded so far that the addition of new diversity is mainly in competition with already existing diversity. Relatively little sameness is being subtracted, perhaps none. This is the case when a center of activity and diversity has reached a peak. If the addition is really something different (as the first bank on the corner in Philadelphia was), there is still no net loss in diversity.

Here is a process, then, that operates for a time as a healthy and salutary function, but by failing to modify itself at a critical point becomes a malfunction. The analogy that comes to mind is faulty feedback.

The conception of electronic feedback has become familiar with the development of computers and automated machinery, where one of the end products of an act or series of acts by the machine is a signal which modifies and guides the next act. A similar feedback process, regulated chemically rather than electronically, is now believed to modify some of the behavior of cells. A report in the *New York Times* explains it thus:

> The presence of an end product in the milieu of a cell causes the machinery that produces the end product to slow down or to stop. This form of cell behavior Dr. [Van R.] Potter [of the University of Wisconsin Medical School] characterized as "intelligent." In contrast, a cell that has changed or mutated behaves like an "idiot" in that it continues without feedback regulation to produce even materials that it does not require.

I think that last sentence is a fair description of the behavior of city localities where the success of diversity destroys itself.

Suppose we think of successful city areas, for all their extraordinary and intricate economic and social order, as faulty in this fashion. In creating city success, we human beings have created marvels, but we left out feedback. What can we do with cities to make up for this omission?

*   *   *

I doubt that we can provide for cities anything equivalent to a true feedback system, working automatically and with perfection. But I think we can accomplish much with imperfect substitutes.

The problem is to hamper excess duplications at one place, and divert them instead to other places in which they will not be excess duplications, but healthy additions. The other places may be at some distance, or very close by indeed. But in any case they cannot be fixed on arbitrarily. They *must* be places where the use concerned will have an excellent opportunity for sustained success— a better opportunity, in fact, than in a locality that is doomed to destroy itself.

I think this diversion can be encouraged by a combination of three means, which I shall call: zoning for diversity; staunchness of public buildings; and competitive diversion. I shall touch on each of these briefly.

Zoning for diversity must be thought of differently from the usual zoning for conformity, but like all zoning it is suppressive. One form of zoning for diversity is already familiar in certain city districts: controls against demolition of historically valuable buildings. Already different from their surroundings, these are zoned to stay different from them. A slightly advanced development of this concept was proposed by Greenwich Village civic groups for their area, and adopted by the city, in 1959. On certain streets, the height limitations for buildings were drastically reduced. Most of the streets affected already contain numerous buildings in excess of the new height limitations. This is not evidence of illogic, but is precisely why the new limitations were asked: so that the lower buildings remaining could not be further replaced by excessive duplication of the more valuable high buildings. Again, sameness was being zoned out—or in effect, differences zoned in—even though in a most limited fashion and on relatively few streets.

The purpose of zoning for deliberate diversity should not be to freeze conditions and uses as they stand. That would be death. Rather, the point is to insure that changes or replacements, as they do occur, cannot be overwhelmingly of one kind. This means, often, constraints on too rapid a replacement of too many buildings. I think the specific scheme of diversity zoning, or the specific combination of schemes, that an outstandingly successful city locality requires is likely to differ with the locality and with the particular form of self-destruction that threatens it. However, in principle, zoning aimed directly at building ages and building sizes is a logical tool, because variety in types of accommodations is reflected, usually, in variety of uses and populations. A park being surrounded by intensive duplications of tall offices or apartments might well be zoned for lower buildings along its south side in particular, thus accomplishing two useful purposes at one stroke: protecting the park's supply of winter sun, and protecting indirectly, to some extent at least, its diversity of surrounding uses.

All such zoning for diversity—since the deliberate intent is to prevent excessive duplication of the most profitable uses—needs to be accompanied by tax adjustments. Land hampered from conversion to its most immediately profitable potential use needs to have this fact reflected in its taxes. It is unrealistic to put a ceiling on a property's development (whether the tool is control of height, bulk, historical or esthetic value, or some other device) and then let the assessment on such a property reflect the irrelevant values of more profitably developed properties nearby. Indeed, raising the assessments on city property because of increased profitability of the neighbors, is a powerful means today of forcing excess duplications. This pressure would continue to force them, even in the face of controls overtly intended to hamper duplications. The way to raise the tax base of a city is not at all to exploit to the limit the short-term tax potential of every site. This undermines the long-term tax potential of whole neighborhoods. The way to raise a city's tax base is to expand the city's territorial quantity of successful areas. A strong city tax base is a by-product of strong city magnetism, and one of its necessary ingredients—once the object is to sustain success—is a certain amount of close-grained, deliberate, calculated variation in localized tax yields to anchor diversity and forestall its self-destruction.

The second potential tool for hampering unbridled duplication of uses is what I call staunchness of public buildings. By this I mean that public and quasi-public bodies should adopt, for their properties, a policy some-what like Charles Abrams' private policy for his property on Eighth Street. Abrams combats the excessive duplica-tion of restaurants on his property by seeking other kinds of uses. Public and quasi-public bodies should establish their buildings and facilities at points where these will add effectively to diversity in the first place (rather than duplicate their neighbors). Then, in their role as uses, these should stand staunch, no matter how valuable the property becomes because of surrounding success (which they have helped create if they located well), and no matter how large the offers from those who would supplant them to duplicate surrounding successful uses. This is a penny-foolish but pound-wise policy for municipalities and for bodies having an enlightened stake in municipal success—analogous to penny-foolish but pound-wise taxation policy for enforcing diversity zoning devices. The New York Public Library, on an immensely valuable site, contributes more of value to the locality than any possible profitable duplication of nearby uses—because it is so different, visually and functionally. When pressure from citizens persuaded New York's city government to lend funds to a quasi-public body, so it could buy Carnegie Hall from its private owner who was going to sell it for duplication of nearby uses, and Carnegie Hall was thus retained as a concert hall and auditorium, a continuing effective mixture of primary uses in the neighborhood was thereby anchored. In short, public and public-spirited bodies can do much to anchor diversity by standing staunch in the midst of *different* surrounding uses, while money rolls around them and begs to roll over them.

Both of these tools, zoning for diversity and staunchness of public uses, are defensive actions against self-destruction of diversity. They are windbreaks, so to speak, which can stand against the gusts of economic pressures, but can hardly be expected to stand fast against sustained gales. Any forms of zoning, any forms of public building policy, any forms of tax assessment policy, no matter how enlightened, give eventually under sufficiently powerful economic pressure. They usually have, and probably they usually will.

Along with defensive tools must therefore go another: competitive diversion.

There is a widespread belief that Americans hate cities. I think it is probable that Americans hate city failure, but, from the evidence, we certainly do not hate successful and vital city areas. On the contrary, so many people want to make use of such places, so many people want to work in them or live in them or visit in them, that municipal self-destruction ensues. In killing successful diversity combinations with money, we are employing perhaps our nearest equivalent to killing with kindness.

In short, the demand for lively and diversified city areas is too great for the supply.

If outstandingly successful city localities are to withstand the forces of self-destruction—and if the nuisance value of defense against self-destruction is to be an effective nuisance value—the sheer supply of diversified, lively, economically viable city localities must be increased. And with this, we are back to the basic need to supply *more* city streets and districts with the four conditions economically necessary to city diversity.

To be sure, there will always be some districts, at any particular moment in time, which are most exuberantly diversified, most popular and most tempting for destruction by momentarily most profitable duplications. If other localities are not far behind in opportunities and interest, however, and still others are coming along, these can offer competitive diversion from the most popular. Their pull would be reinforced by the obstacles to duplications introduced in the most popular districts, which are a necessary adjunct to competitive diversion. But the competitive pull would have to be there, even though it could be a lesser pull.

If and when competing localities, in their turn, should

become sufficiently successful to need city substitutes for feedback signals, they should ask and get defenses against excessive duplication.

The time at which a city locality starts to act like an "idiot" cell is not hard to discover. Anyone intimate with an outstandingly successful city district knows when this qualitative turn is in process of occurring. Those who use the facilities that are starting to disappear, or view them with pleasure, know full well when the diversity and interest of the locality to which they are attached are on the downgrade. They know full well when segments of the population are being crowded out, and diversity of population is narrowing—especially if they are being crowded out themselves. They even know many of these results in advance of their fulfillment, by projecting proposed or imminent physical changes into changes in everyday life and the everyday scene. The people in a district talk about it, they register both the fact and effect of diversity's self-destruction long before slowpoke maps and statistics tell, too late, the misfortune of what happened.

At bottom, this problem of the self-destruction of outstanding success is the problem of getting the supply of vital, diversified city streets and districts into a saner relationship with demand.

14

THE CURSE OF
BORDER VACUUMS

Massive single uses in cities have a quality in common
with each other. They form borders, and borders in cities
usually make destructive neighbors.

A border—the perimeter of a single massive or
stretched-out use of territory—forms the edge of an area
of "ordinary" city. Often borders are thought of as passive
objects, or matter-of-factly just as edges. However, a border exerts an active influence.

Railroad tracks are the classic examples of borders, so
much so that they came to stand, long ago, for social borders too—"the other side of the tracks"—a connotation,
incidentally, associated with small towns rather than with
big cities. Here we shall be concerned not with the social
connotations of areas demarcated by borders, but rather
with the physical and functional effects of borders on
their immediate city surroundings.

In the case of a railroad track, the district lying to one
side may do better or worse than the district lying to the
other side. But the places that do worst of all, physically,
are typically the zones directly beside the track, on both
sides. Whatever lively and diverse growth occurs to either
side, whatever replacement of the old or worn-out occurs,
is likely to happen beyond these zones, inward, away
from the tracks. The zones of low value and decay which

we are apt to find beside the tracks in our cities appear to afflict everything within the zones except the buildings that make direct, practical use of the track itself or its sidings. This is curious, because we can often see, looking at the ingredients in the decline and decay, that at one time some people did see fit to put new buildings, even ambitious buildings, in this zone of decline.

The blight-proneness of zones along the tracks has usually been explained as a result of the noise, the soot of steam locomotive days, and the general undesirability of railroad tracks as an environment. However, I think these disadvantages are only part of the cause, and perhaps a minor part. Why did they not discourage development there in the first place?

Furthermore, we can see that the same sort of blight typically occurs along city waterfronts. Usually it is worse and there is more of it along the waterfronts than along the tracks. Yet waterfronts are not inherently noisy, dirty or disagreeable environments.

It is curious, too, how frequently the immediate neighborhoods surrounding big-city university campuses, City Beautiful civic centers, large hospital grounds, and even large parks, are extraordinarily blight-prone, and how frequently, even when they are not smitten by physical decay, they are apt to be stagnant—a condition that precedes decay.

Yet if conventional planning and land-use theory were true, and if quiet and cleanliness had as much positive effect as they are supposed to, exactly these disappointing zones should be outstandingly successful economically, and vital socially.

Different as railroad tracks, waterfronts, campuses,

expressways, large parking areas and large parks are from each other in most ways, they also have much in common with each other—so far as their tendency to exist amid moribund or declining surroundings is concerned. And if we look at the parts of cities most literally attractive—i.e., those that literally attract people, in the flesh— we find that these fortunate localities are seldom in the zones immediately adjoining massive single uses.

The root trouble with borders, as city neighbors, is that they are apt to form dead ends for most users of city streets. They represent, for most people, most of the time, barriers.

Consequently, the street that adjoins a border is a terminus of generalized use. If this street, which is the end of the line for people in the area of "ordinary" city, also gets little or no use from people inside the single-use border-forming territory, it is bound to be a deadened place, with scant users. This deadness can have further repercussions. Because few people use the immediate border street, the side streets (and in some cases the parallel street) adjoining it are also less used as a result. They fail to get a by-the-way circulation of people going beyond them in the direction of the border, because few are going to that Beyond. If those adjoining streets, therefore, become too empty and therefore in turn are shunned, their adjoining streets may also be less used. And so it goes, until the forces of heavy use from an area of strong attraction come into counterplay.

Borders can thus tend to form vacuums of use adjoining them. Or to put it another way, by oversimplifying the use of the city at one place, on a large scale, they tend to simplify the use which people give to the adjoining territory too, and this simplification of use—meaning fewer users, with fewer different purposes and destinations at hand—feeds upon itself. The more infertile the simplified territory becomes for economic enterprises, the still fewer the users, and the still more infertile the territory. A kind of unbuilding, or running-down process is set in motion.

This is serious, because literal and continuous mingling of people, present because of different purposes, is the only device that keeps streets safe. It is the only device that cultivates secondary diversity. It is the only device that encourages districts to form in place of fragmented, self-isolated neighborhoods or backwaters.

Abstract or more indirect support among differing city uses (helpful though this may be on another plane) does not serve such purposes.

Sometimes visible evidence of the running-down process is almost as graphic as a diagram. This is the case in some parts of the Lower East Side of New York; it is especially striking at night. At the borders of the dark and empty grounds of the massive, low-income housing projects, the streets are dark and empty of people too. Stores, except for a few sustained by the project dwellers themselves, have gone out of business, and many quarters stand unused and empty. Street by street, as you move away from the project borders, a little more life is to be found, progressively a little more brightness, but it takes many streets before the gradual increase of economic activity and movement of people become strong. And each year the vacuum seems to eat a little farther in. Neighborhoods or streets caught between two such borders close together can be utterly deadened, border to border.

Sometimes a newspaper account describes some vivid incident of the running-down process—for example, this account of an event in February 1960 from the *New York Post:*

> The slaying in Cohen's butcher shop at 164 E. 174th St. Monday night was no isolated incident, but the culmination of a series of burglaries and holdups along the street . . . Ever since work started on the Cross-Bronx Expressway across the street some two years ago, a grocer said, trouble has plagued the area . . . Stores which once stayed open to 9 or 10 o'clock are shutting down at 7 P.M. Few shoppers dare venture out after dark, so storekeepers feel the little business they lose hardly justifies the risk in remaining open late . . . The slaying had the greatest impact on the owner of a nearby drug store, which remains open to 10 P.M. "We're scared to death," he commented. "We're the only store that stays open that late."

Sometimes we can infer the formation of such vacuums, as when a newspaper advertisement lists an amazing bargain—a ten-room brick house, recently rehabilitated, with new copper plumbing, to be sold for $12,000—and the address pins down its location: between the borders of a huge project and an expressway.

Sometimes the main effect is the gradual, progressive spread, from street to street, of simple sidewalk insecurity. Morningside Heights in New York contains a long, narrow strip of neighborhood edged on one side by a campus and on the other side by a long waterfront park. This strip is further interrupted by the barriers of intervening institutions. Every place you go in this strip brings you quickly to a border. The most shunned of these borders by evening, for decades, has been that of the park. But gradually and almost imperceptibly, the common consent that insecurity exists has affected more and more of the territory, until today there is only one side of one street that carries more than solitary footfalls at night. This one-sided street, a stretch of Broadway, is across from the deadened perimeter of the big campus; and even it dies off through much of the strip, where it becomes preempted by another border.

But in most cases, there is nothing dramatic in any way about a border vacuum. Rather, vitality just appears absent and the condition is apt to be taken for granted. Here is a good characterization of a vacuum, in *The Wapshot Chronicle*, a novel by John Cheever: "North of the park you come into a neighborhood that seems blighted—not persecuted, but only unpopular, as if it suffered acne or bad breath, and it has a bad complexion—colorless and seamed and missing a feature here and there."

The exact reasons for scantness of use at a border vary.

Some borders damp down use by making travel across them a one-way affair. Housing projects are examples of this. The project people cross back and forth across the border (usually, in any appreciable numbers, at only one side of the project or at most two sides). The adjoining people, for the most part, stay strictly over on their side of the border and treat the line as a dead end of use.

Some borders halt cross-use from both sides. Open railroad tracks or expressways or water barriers are common examples.

Some borders have cross-use from both directions, but it is limited, in appreciable amounts, to daylight or it falls off drastically at certain times of year. Large parks are common examples.

Still other borders have scant use along them because the massive single elements that form them possess such a low intensity of land use, relative to the great perimeters they possess. Civic centers with large grounds are common examples. The New York City Planning Commission is trying, as this is written, to institute an industrial park in Brooklyn, and has announced that this will consist of 100 acres, and will accommodate firms employing about 3,000 workers. Thirty workers to an acre is so low-intensity a use of city land, and 100 acres affords such an immense perimeter, that this enterprise will create scant use all along its borders.

From whichever cause the effect is produced, the pertinent effect is scant use (few users, there in the flesh) along a large-scale or stretched-out perimeter.

The phenomenon of border vacuums is baffling to city designers, especially to those who sincerely value urban liveliness and variety and dislike both deadness and nondescript sprawl. Borders, they sometimes reason, are a feasible means of heightening intensity, and of giving a city a sharp, clear form, as medieval town walls apparently did with medieval towns. This is a plausible idea, because some borders undoubtedly do serve to concentrate, and thereby intensify, city areas. The water barriers of San Francisco and of Manhattan have both had this effect.

And yet, even when a major border has concentrated city intensity, as in those cases, the zone along the border itself seldom reflects that intensity, or garners a fair share of it.

It helps to understand this "perverse" behavior if, in our minds, we divide all of the land of a city into two types. The first type, which can be called general land, is used for general public circulation by people on foot. It is land over which people move freely, and by choice, on their way from here to yonder, and from yonder back again. It includes the streets, many of the smaller parks, and sometimes it includes the lobbies of buildings when they are used freely as streets.

The second type of land, which can be called special land, is not commonly used as public thoroughfare by people on foot. It can be built on or not; it can be publicly owned or not; it can be physically accessible to people or not. This is beside the point. The point is that people walk around it, or alongside it, but not through it.

Let us consider this special land, for the moment, as something that is in the way, so far as the general public on foot is concerned. It is a geographic obstacle, either because it is barred to them or because it contains so little of concern to them.

Looked at in this way, all the special land of a city is an interference with the use of the general land.

But looked at in another way, this special land contributes greatly to the use of the general land. It contributes people. Special land provides whatever people there are to circulate. It provides them either by housing them at home or at work, or by attracting them to it for other purposes. If you have no city buildings, you have no use for city streets.

Both kinds of land thus contribute to circulation. But

there is always a certain tension in their relationship. There is always a pull and a counterpull between the special land's two roles: as a contributor to the use of general land on the one hand, and an interference with its use on the other.

This is a principle long and well understood by downtown merchants, and as a principle it is easiest to explain in their terms. Wherever a significant "dead place" appears on a downtown street, it causes a drop in the intensity of foot circulation there, and in the use of the city at that point. Sometimes the drop is so serious economically that business declines to one side or the other of the dead place. Such a dead place may be an actual vacancy, or it may be a little-used monument of some sort, or it may be a parking lot, or it may simply be a group of banks that go dead after three o'clock in the afternoon. Whatever it may be specifically, the role of the dead place as a geographic obstacle to the general land has overcome its role as a contributor of users to the general land. The tension has gone slack.

The general land can absorb and elide most of the effects of special-land dead spots, especially when these are physically small in scale. Variations in intensity of the special land's give-and-take with the general land are needed, because small quiet spots and crescendos of busy spots are necessary results and aspects of street and district diversity.

However, the tension between the two kinds of land can go completely slack, and cannot normally be elided or compensated, if the special land becomes an immense obstacle. How much does it take away from the general land as a physical obstacle (or as a block to use by choice)? How much does it give back to the general land in concentration of users? A poor answer to this equation usually means a vacuum in the general land. The question is not why intensity of use should be so perverse that it fails to come up to the nice sharp border. The question, rather, is why we should expect it to be so perverse as to do so.

Besides tending to produce these vacuums in the nearby general land (and hence abnormally poor places for diversity or social vitality to grow), borders divide up cities into pieces. They set asunder the neighborhoods of "ordinary" city lying to either side of them. In this respect, they behave in a fashion opposite from small parks. Small parks, if they are popular, knit together their neighborhoods from different sides, and mingle the people from them. Borders also behave in a fashion opposite from city streets, for these too ordinarily knit together territory and uses lying to either side, and mingle users. Borders behave in a fashion opposite from many impressive but smaller-scale uses which otherwise have something in common with borders. For instance, a railroad station interacts with its surroundings differently from a railroad track; a single government building interacts differently with its neighborhood from the way a large civic center interacts with its neighborhoods.

This sundering, or city-carving, effect of borders is not in itself always detrimental. If each of the localities separated from one another by a border is large enough to form a strong city district, with a sufficiently large and diverse pool of uses and users, the separation effect is apt to be harmless. Indeed, it can be positively useful, as a means by which people help orient themselves, help carry a map of the city in their minds, and understand a district as a place.

The trouble arises when districts (as described back in Chapter Six) are bisected or fragmented by borders so that the neighborhoods sundered are weak fragments and a district of subcity size cannot functionally exist. Frequent borders, whether formed by arterial highways, institutions, projects, campuses, industrial parks, or any other massive uses of special land, can in this way tear a city to tatters.

Understanding the drawbacks of borders should help rescue us from producing unnecessary borders, as we do today, under the misapprehension that gratuitous border building represents an advanced form of order in cities.

However, it does not follow that all institutions or other facilities that cleave cities with borders and tend to ring themselves with vacuums are to be considered enemies of city life. On the contrary, many of them are obviously desirable and most important to cities. A big city needs universities, large medical centers, large parks containing metropolitan attractions. A city needs railroads; it can use waterfronts for economic advantage and for amenity; it needs some expressways (especially for trucking).

The point is hardly to disdain such facilities as these, or to minimize their value. Rather, the point is to recognize that they are mixed blessings.

If we can counter their destructive effects, these facilities will themselves be better served. It is no blessing to most of them, or to those who use them, to be surrounded by dullness or vacuity, let alone decay.

*   *   *

The simplest cases to correct, I think, are borders that could logically encourage much greater use of their perimeters.

Consider, for example, Central Park in New York City. Along the east side, it has several examples of intensive use (mostly daytime use) at its perimeter or close inside—the zoo, the Metropolitan Museum of Art, the model boat pond. On the west side there is a curious penetration of the perimeter, especially notable because it operates at night and because it has been created by users themselves. This is a particular cross walk into the park which, by common consent, has become the path for evening and night walking of dogs, hence for other strollers, hence for anyone who wishes to go into the park and still feel safe.

However, the park's perimeter—especially on its west side—contains great vacuous stretches, and it exerts a bad vacuum effect along a lot of border. Meantime, the park is full of objects, deep inside, that can be used only during daylight hours, not because of their nature but because of their location. They are also hard to reach for many of their putative users. The chess house (which looks like a dreary garage) is an example. The carousel is another. The guards shepherd people away from these places, for their own safety, as early as four-thirty on midwinter afternoons. Moreover, these facilities, aside from their heavy and ugly architecture, are formidably out of spirit in their deep, interior park locations. It is quite an achievement to make a splendid carousel seem lost and gloomy, but this has been achieved in Central Park.

Park uses like these should be brought right up to the borders of big parks, and designed as links between the park and its bordering street. They can belong to the world of the street and, on their other side, to the world of the park, and be charming in their double life. They should be calculated, not as rims shutting off a park (that would be terrible) but as spots of intense and magnetic border activity. Their use by night should be encouraged. They need not be huge. Three or four chess and checker pavilions, each with its own architectural character and setting, disposed at perimeter points around a very large park count, for this purpose, far more than one chess and checker house four times as large.

It is up to the other side of the street also—the city side—to combat park vacuums. We are always hearing suggestions for injecting dubious uses into large city parks. There is always pressure for commercialization. Some of these suggestions are puzzling, such as the question of the gift of a new café for Central Park, which has aroused much controversy in New York. This is figuratively a border-line case, and it is also literally a border-line case. Many such semicommercial or commercial uses belong on the city side of a park border, placed deliberately to dramatize and intensify cross-use (and cross-surveillance) to and fro. They ought generally to work in partnership with border uses on the park side: an example would be a park skating rink brought *immediately* up to a park border, and across the street, on the city side, a café where the skaters could get refreshments and where watchers could observe the skating across the way from enclosed or open raised terraces. Again there is no reason why both rink and café could not be used all evening and into the night. Bicycle riding is fine in a large park; but bicycle renting could be over on the city side of the line.

The point, in short, would be to seek out border-line cases and invent new ones too, keeping the city as city and the park as park, but making the partnership connections between them explicit, lively and sufficiently frequent.

The principle here has been brilliantly stated, in another connection, by Kevin Lynch, associate professor of planning at Massachusetts Institute of Technology, and the author of *The Image of the City*. "An edge may be more than simply a dominant barrier," writes Lynch, "if some visual or motion penetration is allowed through it—if it is, as it were, structured to some depth with the regions on either side. It then becomes a seam rather than a barrier, a line of exchange along which two areas are sewn together."

Lynch was speaking of visual and esthetic problems concerning borders, and the same principle, exactly, applies to many functional problems caused by borders.

Universities could make portions, at least, of their campuses more like seams and less like barriers if they placed their uses intended for the public at strategic points on their perimeters, and if they also put at their perimeters, and opened up as scenes, their elements congenial to public view and interest—instead of hiding them. On a very small scale, because it is a relatively small institution, the New School for Social Research in New York has done this with a new building containing a library. The library is a link between the street and the school's little "campus," an attractive interior courtyard. Both the library and the view are visually opened up and dramatized and they are a delight and an enlivener on their street. Big universities in cities, so far as I can see, have given no thought or imagination to the unique establishments they are. Typically they either pretend to be cloistered or countrified places, nostalgically denying their transplantation, or else they pretend to be office buildings. (Of course they are neither.)

Waterfronts, too, can be made to act much more like seams than they ordinarily do today. The usual form of rescue for a decayed waterfront vacuum is to replace it with a park, which in turn becomes a border element—usually appallingly underused, as might be expected—and this moves the vacuum effect inland. It is more to the point to grasp the problem where it originates, at the shoreline, and aim at making the shore a seam. Waterfront work uses, which are often interesting, should not be blocked off from ordinary view for interminable stretches, and the water itself thereby blocked off from city view too at ground level. Such stretches should be penetrated by small, and even casual, public openings calculated for glimpsing or watching work and water traffic. Near where I live is an old open dock, the only one for miles, next to a huge Department of Sanitation incinerator and scow anchorage. The dock is used for eel fishing, sunbathing, kite flying, car tinkering, picnicking, bicycle riding, ice-cream and hot-dog vending, waving at passing boats, and general kibitzing. (Since it does not belong to the Parks Department nobody is forbidden anything.) You could not find a happier place on a hot summer evening or a lazy summer Sunday. From time to time, a great slushing and clanking fills the air as a sanitation truck dumps its load into a waiting garbage scow. This is not pretty-pretty, but it is an event greatly enjoyed on the dock. It fascinates everybody. Penetrations into working waterfronts need to be right where the work (loading, unloading, docking) goes on to either side, rather than segregated where there is nothing much to see. Boating, boat visiting, fishing, and swimming where it is practicable, all help make a seam, instead of a barrier, of that troublesome border between land and water.

It is hopeless to try to convert some borders into seams. Expressways and their ramps are examples. Moreover, even in the case of large parks, campuses or waterfronts, the barrier effects can likely be overcome well only along portions of perimeters.

The only way, I think, to combat vacuums in these cases is to rely on extraordinarily strong counterforces close by. This means that population concentration ought to be made deliberately high (and diverse) near borders, that blocks close to borders should be especially short and potential street use extremely fluid, and that mixtures of primary uses should be abundant; so should mixtures in age of buildings. This may not bring much intensity of use right up to the very borders themselves, but it can help confine the vacuum to a small zone. Near New York's Central Park, much of Madison Avenue to the east operates thus as a counterforce to the park's border vacuum. On the west, there is no such close counterforce. On the south side, the counterforce operates as far as the sidewalk opposite the park. In Greenwich Village, the counterforce has the waterfront vacuum in gradual retreat, partly because the blocks are so very short—160 feet in some cases—that it is easy for liveliness to take another little jump.

To employ counterforce against *necessary* city borders means this: as many city elements as possible must be used to build lively, mixed territory, and as few as possible must be used to compose borders unnecessarily.

Dwellings, whether subsidized or unsubsidized, major halls, auditoriums, government buildings, most schools, most city industry, all city commerce, work congenially in mingled settings, as part and parcel of the intricate mixed city fabric itself. When such elements are withdrawn from the mixture and segregated in the form of massive single uses, they not only result in gratuitous borders but, by being subtracted from other elements of city mixtures, they leave less material for creating counterforces.

Planned pedestrian street schemes, *if* they throw formidable borders for moving and parked cars around inherently weak and fragmentary preserves, *can introduce more problems than they solve.* Yet this is a fashionable planning idea for downtown shopping streets and for the "town centers" of renewal areas. One of the dangers of devising city traffic schemes and arterial systems without understanding, first, how cities themselves work, is just this: The schemes, with the best intents behind them, can inject no end of border vacuums and discontinuities of use, and in places where these may do the greatest and most gratuitous harm.

15

UNSLUMMING AND SLUMMING

Slums and their populations are the victims (and the perpetuators) of seemingly endless troubles that reinforce each other. Slums operate as vicious circles. In time, these vicious circles enmesh the whole operations of cities. Spreading slums require ever greater amounts of public money—and not simply more money for publicly financed improvement or to stay even, but more money to cope with ever widening retreat and regression. As needs grow greater, the wherewithal grows less.

Our present urban renewal laws are an attempt to break this particular linkage in the vicious circles by forthrightly wiping away slums and their populations, and replacing them with projects intended to produce higher tax yields, or to lure back easier populations with less expensive public requirements. The method fails. At best, it merely shifts slums from here to there, adding its own tincture of extra hardship and disruption. At worst, it destroys neighborhoods where constructive and improving communities exist and where the situation calls for encouragement rather than destruction.

Like Fight Blight and Conservation campaigns in neighborhoods declining into slums, slum shifting fails because it tries to overcome causes of trouble by diddling with symptoms. Sometimes even the very symptoms that preoccupy the slum shifters are, in the main, vestiges of former troubles rather than significant indications of current or future ills.

Conventional planning approaches to slums and slum dwellers are thoroughly paternalistic. The trouble with paternalists is that they want to make impossibly profound changes, and they choose impossibly superficial means for doing so. To overcome slums, we must regard slum dwellers as people capable of understanding and acting upon their own self-interests, which they certainly are. We need to discern, respect and build upon the forces for regeneration that exist in slums themselves, and that demonstrably work in real cities. This is far from trying to patronize people into a better life, and it is far from what is done today.

Vicious circles, to be sure, are hard to follow. Cause and effect become confused precisely because they do link and relink with one another in such complicated ways.

Yet there is one particular link that is crucial. If it is broken (and to break it is no simple matter of supplying better housing), a slum spontaneously unslums.

The key link in a perpetual slum is that too many people move out of it too fast—and in the meantime dream of getting out. This is the link that has to be broken if any other efforts at overcoming slums or slum life are to be of the least avail. This is the link that actually was broken and has stayed broken in places like the North End, or the Back-of-the-Yards in Chicago, or North Beach in San Francisco, or the unslummed former slum in which I live. If only a handful of American city slums had ever managed to break this link, we might regard it skeptically as grounds for hope. These places might be freaks. More significant are the great number of slum neighborhoods in which unslumming starts, goes unrecognized, and too often is discouraged or destroyed. The portions of East Harlem in New York which had proceeded far along in unslumming were first discouraged by unavailability of necessary money; then where this slowed the unslumming process but still did not bring regression to slum conditions, most of these neighborhoods were destroyed outright—to be replaced by projects which became almost pathological displays of slum troubles. Many areas in the Lower East Side which had started unslumming have been destroyed. My own neighborhood, as recently as the early 1950's, was saved from disastrous amputation only because its citizens were able to fight city hall—and even at that, only because the officials were confronted with embarrassing evidence that the area was drawing in newcomers with money, although this symptom of its unslummed status was possibly the least significant of the constructive changes that had occurred unnoticed.*

Herbert Gans, a sociologist at the University of Pennsylvania, has given, in the February 1959 journal of the American Institute of Planners, a sober but poignant portrait of an unrecognized unslumming slum, the West End of Boston, on the eve of its destruction. The West End, he points out, although regarded officially as a "slum," would have been more accurately described as "a stable, low-rent area." If, writes Gans, a slum is defined as an area which "because of the nature of its social environ-

---

*In 1961, the city is actually trying again for authority and federal funds to "renew" us into an inane pseudosuburb. Of course the neighborhood is fighting this bitterly.

ment can be proved to create problems and pathologies," then the West End was not a slum. He speaks of the intense attachment of residents to the district, of its highly developed informal social control, of the fact that many residents had modernized or improved the interiors of their apartments—all typical characteristics of an unslumming slum.

Unslumming hinges, paradoxically, on the retention of a very considerable part of a slum population within a slum. It hinges on whether a considerable number of the residents and businessmen of a slum find it both desirable and practical to make and carry out their own plans right there, or whether they must virtually all move elsewhere.

I shall use the designation "perpetual slums" to describe slums which show no signs of social or economic improvement with time, or which regress after a little improvement. However, if the conditions for generating city diversity can be introduced into a neighborhood while it is a slum, and if any indications of unslumming are encouraged rather than thwarted, I believe there is no reason that any slum need be perpetual.

The inability of a perpetual slum to hold enough of its population for unslumming is a characteristic that starts before the slum itself starts. There is a fiction that slums, in forming, malignantly supplant healthy tissue. Nothing could be farther from the truth.

The first sign of an incipient slum, long before visible blight can be seen, is stagnation and dullness. Dull neighborhoods are inevitably deserted by their more energetic, ambitious or affluent citizens, and also by their young people who can get away. They inevitably fail to draw newcomers by choice. Furthermore, aside from these selective desertions and the selective lack of vigorous new blood, such neighborhoods eventually are apt to undergo rather sudden wholesale desertions by their nonslum populations. The reasons why this is so have already been stated; there is no need to reiterate the sheer impracticality of the Great Blight of Dullness for city life.

Nowadays, the wholesale desertions by nonslum populations which give a slum its initial opportunity to form, are sometimes blamed on the proximity of another slum (especially if it is a Negro slum) or on the presence of a few Negro families, much as in the past slum formation was sometimes blamed on the presence or proximity of Italian or Jewish or Irish families. Sometimes the desertion is blamed on the age and obsolescence of dwellings, or on vague, general disadvantages such as lack of playgrounds or proximity of factories.

However, all such factors are immaterial. In Chicago, you can see neighborhoods only a block and two blocks in from the lakefront parkland, far from the settlements of minority groups, well endowed with greenery, quiet enough to make one's flesh creep, and composed of substantial, even pretentious, buildings. On these neighborhoods are the literal signs of desertion: "For Rent," "To Let," "Vacancy," "Rooms for Permanent and Transient Guests," "Guests Welcome," "Sleeping Rooms," "Furnished Rooms," "Unfurnished Rooms," "Apartments Available." These buildings have trouble drawing occupants in a city where the colored citizens are cruelly overcrowded in their shelter and cruelly overcharged for it. The buildings are going begging because they are being rented or sold only to whites—and whites, who have so much more choice, do not care to live here. The beneficiaries of this particular impasse, at least for the moment, turn out to be the immigrating hillbillies, whose economic choice is small and whose familiarity with city life is still smaller. It is a dubious benefit they receive: inheritance of dull and dangerous neighborhoods whose unfitness for city life finally repelled residents more sophisticated and competent than they.

Sometimes, to be sure, a deliberate conspiracy to turn over the population of a neighborhood does exist—on the part of real estate operators who make a racket of buying houses cheaply from panicked white people and selling them at exorbitant prices to the chronically housing-starved and pushed-around colored population. But even this racket works only in already stagnated and low-vitality neighborhoods. (Sometimes the racket perversely improves a neighborhood's upkeep, when it brings in colored citizens more competent in general and more economically able than the whites they replaced; but the exploitative economics sometimes results instead in replacement of an uncrowded, apathetic neighborhood with an overcrowded neighborhood in considerable turmoil.)

If there were no slum dwellers or poor immigrants to inherit city failures, the problem of low-vitality neighborhoods abandoned by those with choice would still remain and perhaps would be even more troubling. This condition can be found in parts of Philadelphia where "decent, safe and sanitary" dwellings go empty in stagnated neighborhoods, while their former populations move outward into new neighborhoods which are little different, intrinsically, from the old except that they are not yet embedded by the city.

It is easy to see where new slums are spontaneously forming today, and how dull, dark and undiverse are the streets in which they typically form, because the process is happening now. What is harder to realize, because it lies in the past, is the fact that lack of lively urbanity has usually been an original characteristic of slums. The classic reform literature about slums does not tell us this. Such literature—Lincoln Steffens' *Autobiography* is a good example—focused on slums that had already overcome their dull beginnings (but had acquired other troubles in the meantime). A teeming, bustling slum was pinpointed at a moment in time, with the deeply erroneous implication that as a slum is, so it was—and as it is, so it shall be, unless it is wiped away root and branch.

The unslummed former slum in which I live was just such a teeming place by the early decades of this century, and its gang, the Hudson Dusters, was notorious throughout the city, but its career as a slum did not begin in any such bustle. The history of the Episcopal chapel a few blocks down the street tells the tale of the slum's formation, almost a century ago in this case. The neighborhood had been a place of farms, village streets and summer homes which evolved into a semisuburb that became embedded in the rapidly growing city. Colored people and immigrants from Europe were surrounding it; neither physically nor socially was the neighborhood equipped to handle their presence—no more, apparently, than a semisuburb is so equipped today. Out of this quiet residential area—a charming place, from the evidence of old pictures—there were at first many random desertions by congregation families; those of the congregation who remained eventually panicked and departed en masse. The church building was abandoned to Trinity parish, which took it over as a mission chapel to minister to the influx of the poor who inherited the semisuburb. The former congregation re-established the church far uptown, and colonized in its neighborhood a new quiet residential area of unbelievable dullness; it is now a part of Harlem. The records do not tell where the next preslum was built by these wanderers.

The reasons for slum formation, and the processes by which it happens, have changed surprisingly little over the decades. What is new is that unfit neighborhoods can be deserted more swiftly, and slums can and do spread thinner and farther, than was the case in the days before automobiles and government-guaranteed mortgages for suburban developments, when it was less practical for families with choice to flee neighborhoods that were displaying some of the normal and inevitable conditions that accompany city life (such as presence of strangers), but none of the natural means for converting these conditions into assets.

At the time a slum first forms, its population may rise spectacularly. This is not a sign of popularity, however. On the contrary, it means the dwellings are becoming overcrowded; this is happening because people with the least choice, forced by poverty or discrimination to overcrowd, are coming into an unpopular area.

The density of the dwelling units themselves may or may not increase. In old slums, they customarily did increase because of the construction of tenements. But the rise in dwelling density typically did not cut down the overcrowding. Total population increased greatly instead, with overcrowding superimposed on the high dwelling densities.

Once a slum has formed, the pattern of emigration that made it is apt to continue. Just as in the case of the preslum emigration, two kinds of movement occur. Successful people, including those who achieve very modest gains indeed, keep moving out. But there are also apt to be periodic wholesale migrations, as a whole population begins to achieve modest gains. Both movements are destructive, the second apparently more so than the first.

Overcrowding, which is one symptom of the population instability, continues. It continues, not because the overcrowded people remain, but because they leave. Too many of those who overcome the economic necessity to overcrowd get out, instead of improving their lot within the neighborhood. They are quickly replaced by others who currently have little economic choice. The buildings, naturally, wear out with disproportionate swiftness under these conditions.

Residents of a perpetual slum constantly change in this fashion. Sometimes the change is considered noteworthy because the economic emigrations and immigrations entail an ethnic change. But the movement occurs in all perpetual slums, even those that remain ethnically constant. For instance, a Negro slum in a big city, such as central Harlem in New York, may remain a Negro slum for a long period, but undergo huge, selective turnovers in population.

The constant departures leave, of course, more than housing vacancies to be filled. They leave a community in a perpetually embryonic stage, or perpetually regressing to helpless infancy. The age of buildings is no index to the age of a community, which is formed by a continuity of people.

In this sense, a perpetual slum is always going backward instead of forward, a circumstance that reinforces most of its other troubles. In some drastic cases of wholesale turnover, it seems that what is getting a start again is hardly a community but a jungle. This happens when the new people flooding in have little in common to begin with, and those who are most ruthless and bitter begin to set what tone there is. Anyone who does not like that jungle—which is evidently nearly everyone, for turnover is tremendous in such places—either gets out as fast as he can or dreams of getting out. Even in such seemingly irreparable milieus, however, if the population can be held, a slow improvement starts. I know one such street in New York where this is true, but it is terribly hard to get sufficient people anchored.

The perpetual slum's progress backward occurs in planned slums, just as it does in unplanned slums. The main difference is that perpetual overcrowding is not one of the symptoms in planned slums, because the number of occupants in dwellings is regulated. Harrison Salisbury, in his series of articles on delinquency in the *New York Times*, has described the crucial link of the vicious circle as it operates, in this case, in low-income projects:

> . . . In only too many instances . . . the slums have been shut up within new brick and steel. The horror and deprivation has been immured behind

those cold new walls. In a well-intended effort to solve one social ill, the community succeeded in intensifying other evils and in creating new ones. Admission to low-rent housing projects basically is controlled by income levels . . . Segregation is imposed not by religion or color but by the sharp knife of income or lack of income. What this does to the social fabric of the community must be witnessed to be appreciated. The able, rising families are constantly driven out . . . At the intake end the economic and social levels tend to drop lower and lower . . . A human catch-pool is formed that breeds social ills and requires endless outside assistance.

It is the constant hope of the builders of these planned slums that they will surely improve as "a community has time to form." But time here, as in an unplanned perpetual slum, is an eternal disrupter instead of a builder. As might be expected, therefore, the worst examples of the immured slums, such as Salisbury was describing, are almost invariably the oldest low-income projects, where the perpetual sliding backward of the perpetual slum has had longest to operate.

However, an ominous modification in this pattern has started to appear. With the increase in planned slum shifting, and the rising proportions of "relocated" people in new projects, these new projects are sometimes starting off today with the sullenness and discouragement typical of old projects or of old perpetual unplanned slums— as if they had already, in their youth, been subjected to the vicissitudes of many disruptions and disintegrations. This is probably because so many of their residents have already lived with such experiences, and of course take them along as emotional baggage. Mrs. Ellen Lurie, of Union Settlement, describing conditions in a new project, comments:

> One observation can easily be made as a result of all the visits with site tenants [families placed in public housing because their old homes were taken for city rebuilding]. As difficult a job as management has in running a large project, a bulk of initially unhappy people, angry at the Housing Authority for forcibly uprooting them, not fully understanding all the reasons for the move, lonely and insecure in a strange new environment—such families must make project management all the more overwhelming a task.

Neither slum shifting nor slum immuring breaks that key link in the perpetuation of slums—the tendency (or necessity) for too many people to leave too fast. Both these devices merely aggravate and intensify the processes of perpetual movement backward. Only unslumming overcomes American city slums, or ever has overcome them. If unslumming did not exist, we would have to invent it. However, since it does exist, and does work, the point is to help it happen faster and in more places.

The foundation for unslumming is a slum lively enough to be able to enjoy city public life and sidewalk safety. The worst foundation is the dull kind of place that makes slums, instead of unmaking them.

Why slum dwellers should stay in a slum by choice, after it is no longer economically necessary, has to do with the most personal content of their lives, in realms which planners and city designers can never directly reach and manipulate—nor should want to manipulate. The choice has much to do with the slum dwellers' personal attachments to other people, with the regard in which they believe they are held in the neighborhood, and with their sense of values as to what is of greater and what is of lesser importance in their lives.

Indirectly, however, the wish to stay is obviously influenced by physical factors in the neighborhood. The treasured "security" of the home base is, in part, a literal security from physical fear. Slums where the streets are empty and frightening, and one is unsafe, simply do not spontaneously unslum. And beyond this, people who do stay in an unslumming slum, and improve their lot within the neighborhood, often profess an intense attachment to their street neighborhood. It is a big part of their life. They seem to think that their neighborhood is unique and irreplaceable in all the world, and remarkably valuable in spite of its shortcomings. In this they are correct, for the multitude of relationships and public characters that make up an animated city street neighborhood are always unique, intricate and have the value of the unreproducible original. Unslummed or unslumming neighborhoods are complex places, very different from the simpler, physically stereotyped places in which slums typically form.

I do not mean to imply, however, that every slum which gets itself enough diversity and a sufficiently interesting and convenient life automatically unslums. Some do not—or what is more usual, they do start to unslum for a time, the process proves impractical because there are too many obstacles (mostly financial) in the way of the needed changes, and the place regresses, or is perhaps destroyed.

In any case, where attachment to a slum becomes strong enough to stimulate unslumming, that attachment begins before the unslumming. If people are going to stay by choice when they have choice, they must have become attached before that time. Later is too late.

One of the early symptoms that people are staying by choice is apt to be a drop in population, accompanied neither by an increase in dwelling vacancies nor by a decrease in dwelling densities. In short, a given number of dwellings is being occupied by fewer people. Paradoxically, this is a signal of popularity. It means that formerly overcrowded inhabitants who have become economically able to uncrowd are doing so in their old neighborhood instead of abandoning it to a new wave of the overcrowded.

To be sure, the population drop also represents people who have deserted, and this is important too, as we shall see. But the significant factor to note at this point is that the places of those leaving are, to a notable degree, being preempted by people who are staying by choice.

In the neighborhood where I live, which happens to have been an Irish slum, unslumming was obviously well started as early as 1920, when the population in our census tract was down to 5,000 from 6,500 in 1910 (the population peak). In the Depression, population rose a little as families recrowded, but by 1940 it was down to 2,500 and stayed at about that in 1950. During this period there were few demolitions in this census tract, but some rehabilitation; there were few apartment vacancies at any time; and in the main the population was composed of those who had been there in the old 1910 days, and of their children and grandchildren. The drop to less than half of the peak slum population was, in the main, a measure of the degree of uncrowding that occurred in a neighborhood with a high dwelling unit density on the residential land. Indirectly, it also represented an increase in income and choice characterizing the people who remained.

Similar population drops occurred in all the unslumming neighborhoods of Greenwich Village. In the once unbelievably overpacked tenements of the South Village, which was an Italian slum, population dropped in an illustrative census tract from almost 19,000 in 1910 to about 12,000 in 1920, rose again to almost 15,000 in the Depression, and then with prosperity dropped and stayed at about 9,500. As in my neighborhood, this unslumming drop did not represent a replacement of the old slum population by a new and different middle-class population. It represented much of the old population moving into the middle class. In both these illustrative tracts, which I have chosen as examples of the degree of uncrowding because the number of dwelling units themselves remained very stable, child population dropped slightly less, proportionately, than total population; these were, in the main, families that were staying.*

The uncrowding that has occurred in the North End

*In those Greenwich Village census tracts which were always middle-class or high-income, never having become slums, populations did not drop during these same years, because there was no overcrowded figure for it to drop from. Typically, in these census tracts, population has risen, in some cases mightily, owing to increases in dwelling units themselves—mainly apartment houses. In these tracts, however, child population, *always low*, failed to rise proportionately.

of Boston is fully comparable to that which occurred in the unslumming of Greenwich Village.

To know whether uncrowding has occurred, or is occurring, and whether a drop in population is a sign of the popularity of the neighborhood with those who know it best, one must know whether or not the drop is accompanied by appreciable dwelling vacancies. For instance, in some parts of the Lower East Side (by no means all), population drops during the 1930's were only in part from uncrowding. They represented also large numbers of vacancies. When these vacancies filled up again, they filled with an overcrowded population, as might be expected. They had been abandoned by those with choice.

When sufficient people begin to stay in a slum by choice, several other important things also begin to happen.

The community itself gains competence and strength, partly from practice and growth of trust, and finally (this takes much longer) from becoming less provincial. These matters were gone into in Chapter Six, the discussion of neighborhoods.

At this point I would like to emphasize a third change that occurs—and that is implied in the eventual decrease of provincialism. This change is a gradual self-diversification within the population itself. The degree of financial and educational advancement among those who remain in an unslumming slum varies. The majority make modest gains, some make considerable gains, and some make virtually no gains at all. The different skills, interests, activities and acquaintanceships outside the neighborhood vary and diverge with time.

City officials today prate about "bringing back the

middle class," as if nobody were in the middle class until he had left the city and acquired a ranch house and a barbecue and thereby become precious. To be sure, cities are losing their middle class populations. However, cities need not "bring back" a middle class, and carefully protect it like an artificial growth. Cities grow the middle class. But to keep it as it grows, to keep it as a stabilizing force in the form of a self-diversified population, means considering the city's people valuable and worth retaining, right where they are, before they become middle class.

Even those who remain poorest in an unslumming slum are gainers from the process of unslumming—and therefore they make the city a gainer too. In our neighborhood, these most unlucky or least ambitious of the original slum population, who might otherwise be permanent slum dwellers, have happily escaped that fate. Furthermore, although these people at the bottom are hardly successes by most standards, in their street neighborhoods most of them are successes. They make up a vital part of the web of casual public life. The amount of time they devote to street watching and street management makes some of the rest of us parasites upon them.

Into an unslumming or unslummed slum customarily come new increments of poor or ignorant immigrants from time to time. The Boston banker whom I quoted in the introduction to this book derided the North End because "it is still getting some immigrants." So is our neighborhood. This too is one of the great services of unslumming. People are accommodated and assimilated, not in undigestible floods, but as gradual additions, in neighborhoods capable of accepting and handling strangers in a civilized fashion. The immigrants—ours happen to be mostly Puerto Ricans and they are going to make a fine middle class which the city cannot afford to lose—do not escape most of the problems of being immigrants, but at least they do escape the ordeal and demoralization of the perpetual slum. They quickly assimilate into the public street life, and are lively and competent at holding up their end. These very same people could hardly act as they do within the community, nor would they be likely to stay put as long, were they part of a tumultuous replacement throng in a perpetual slum.

Other gainers from unslumming are newcomers who have choice. They can find in the city a place to live which is fit for city life.

Both kinds of newcomers add to the population diversification of an unslumming or unslummed neighborhood. But the indispensable foundation for this added population diversity is the self-diversification and stability of the former slum population itself.

At the beginning of the process of unslumming, few if any of the slum's most outstandingly successful residents—or their most successful and ambitious children—are apt to stay. Unslumming begins with those who make modest gains, and with those to whom personal attachments overshadow their individual achievement. Later, with improvement, the threshold of success or ambition among those who stay may rise appreciably.

The losses of the most successful or most daring are, in peculiar fashion, also necessary to the unslumming, I think. For some of those who leave are overcoming one of the terrible problems of most slum populations—the onus of discrimination.

The discrimination which operates most drastically

today is, of course, discrimination against Negroes. But it is an injustice with which all our major slum populations have had to contend to some degree.

A ghetto, by the very fact that it is a ghetto, is a place in which most people of spirit, especially the young who have not learned resignation, will not stay entirely willingly. This is true no matter how objectively good their physical accommodations and social surroundings may otherwise be. They may have to stay. They may diversify within the ghetto considerably. But this is far from the same as acceptance and glad attachment. It is fortunate, in my opinion, that so many of our ghetto dwellers do not feel resigned or defeatist; we would have far more to worry about as a society if we could easily get away with our tendencies toward master-race psychology. But be that as it may, the fact is that in our ghettos live people of spirit, and they don't like ghettos.

When discrimination is appreciably broken down outside a ghetto by its more successful progeny, then the old neighborhood has a great burden lifted from it. Then it is no longer, necessarily, a mark of inferiority to stay there. It can be a mark of genuine choice. In the North End, as an example of what I mean, a young butcher explained carefully to me that it no longer "downgraded" a person to live there. To illustrate his point, he took me to the door of his shop, pointed out a three-story row house down the block, told me that the family who lived there just spent $20,000 modernizing it (out of saved earnings!), and added, "That man could live anywhere. Today, he could move into a high-class suburb if he wanted to. He wants to stay here. People who stay here don't have to, you know. They like it."

The effective breaking down of residential discrimination outside a slum, and the less dramatic self-diversification within an unslumming slum, proceed concurrently. If America has now, in the case of Negroes, reached an effective halt in this process and in general entered a stage of arrested development—a thought I find both highly improbable and quite intolerable—then it may be that Negro slums cannot effectively unslum in the fashion demonstrated by slums formed by other ethnic populations and population mixtures. In this case, the damage to our cities might be the least of our worries; unslumming is a by-product of other kinds of vigor and other forms of economic and social change.

When an area has unslummed, it is easy to forget how bad it once was and how helpless both the area and its population were thought to be. This supposed utter worthlessness of the neighborhood was once the case of the area where I live. I see no reason to believe that Negro slums cannot unslum too, and more swiftly than the old slums at that, if the processes at work are understood and helped. As in the case of other slums, overcoming of discrimination outside the slum, and unslumming within the slum, must proceed concurrently. Neither can wait for the accomplishment of the other. Every relaxation of discrimination outside can help unslumming within. Progress in unslumming within helps outside. The two go together.

The inherent resources necessary for unslumming—advancement and self-diversification in a population—demonstrably exist among colored people, including the colored people who are in slums or who have passed through slums, as strikingly as these resources exist among white people. In a way the proved and obvious possession of these resources is more striking among the colored, because they emerge in spite of disproportionate obstacles against their emergence. Indeed, because of the very facts that colored populations advance, self-diversify and have too much spirit to like ghettos, our inner cities have already lost far more of the Negro middle class than they can afford to lose.

I think inner cities will go on losing too much of the Negro middle class almost as fast as it forms until, in actual fact, the choice of remaining there no longer means, for a colored person, an implied acceptance of ghetto citizenship and status. In short, unslumming is at the very least directly—as well as indirectly—inhibited by discrimination. Here I want to remind readers, without repeating it, of a point made near the beginning of this book, on pages 94 and 95, drawing a connection between an urban quality of street use and street life, and the feasibility of overcoming residential discrimination.

Although we Americans talk much about the rapidity with which we accept change, this does not apply to rapidity of intellectual change, I am afraid. Generation after generation, nonslum dwellers stick to the same foolish ideas about slums and slum dwellers. The pessimists always seem to feel that there is something inferior about the current crops of slum dwellers themselves, and can point out supposedly dire differences that distinguish them from previous immigrants. The optimists always seem to feel that there is nothing wrong with slums that could not be fixed by housing and land-use reform and enough social workers. It is hard to say which oversimplification is the sillier.

* * *

Self-diversification of a population is reflected in diversification of commercial and cultural enterprises. Diversification of income alone makes a difference in the range of possible commercial diversification, often in the humblest ways. Consider, as an illustrative example, the case of a New York cobbler who hung on while most of the adjoining neighborhood was cleared of its population and a new low-income project constructed. After his long and hopeful wait for his new customers, he is going out of business at this location. As he explains it, "I used to get good strong working boots to do, good shoes worth working on. But those new people, even the working men, are *all* so poor. Their shoes are so cheap and flimsy they fall to pieces. They bring them in—look. Shoes like this can't be repaired. What can I do to them—remake them? Even so, they can't pay for the work. There's no use for me here." The old neighborhood would have been characterized as predominately poor too, but it had people who had made modest gains. It was not a sorting of all the poorest.

In unslumming slums where great population drops have occurred with uncrowding, this event has been accompanied by a directly related increase in diversity of incomes—and sometimes by a considerable increase in visitors and cross-use from other neighborhoods and other districts. Under these conditions, tremendous drops in population (which of course occurred gradually rather than as a cataclysm) have not resulted in commercial decimation. On the contrary, the range and prosperity of enterprises typically increases in unslumming slums.

With the *uniformly* very poor, it takes very concentrated densities to produce a genuine exuberance and interesting range of diversity, as some of our old slums did by dint of fantastic overcrowding superimposed on top of very high dwelling densities—combined, of course, with the other three basic conditions for generating diversity.

Successful unslumming means that enough people must have an attachment to the slum that they wish to stay, and it also means that it must be practical for them to stay. Impracticality is the rock on which many an unslumming slum is wrecked. Impracticality has mostly to do with unavailability of money for improvements, for new buildings, and for commercial enterprises at a time when these needs become urgent and their discouragement crucial. Impracticality has to do with the difficulty of making, with time, many changes in detail in the unslumming slum. I shall deal with this problem in the course of the next two chapters.

Aside from these more subtle (but powerful) discouragements, unslumming today is frequently halted by the ultimate discouragement—destruction.

The very fact that a slum has uncrowded itself makes it an extremely tempting site for whole or partial urban "renewal" clearance. The relocation problem looks so simple in comparison with that of horrendously overcrowded perpetual slums. Also the area's comparative social health makes it tempting to clear for a higher-income population. It seems a feasible place for "bringing back the middle class." Unlike a perpetual slum, it is "ripe for redevelopment," as if some mysterious virtue of civilization resided in the very ground here and would be transferred. Describing the destruction of the lively, stable, low-rent West End in Boston, Gans made an observation which applies also to other big cities engaged in redevelopment: "Meanwhile, other areas which have older, more deteriorated and even harmful housing have a lower priority for renewal, because of the lack of interest among potential developers or other powerful interests."

Nothing in the training of planners, architects or government officials contradicts these temptations to destroy unslumming slums. On the contrary, everything that makes these men experts reinforces the temptation; for a slum which has been successfully unslumming displays—inevitably—features of layout, use, ground coverage, mixture and activities that are diametrically opposed to the ideals of Radiant Garden City. Otherwise it would never have been able to unslum.

An unslumming slum is peculiarly vulnerable in still another respect. Nobody is making a fortune out of it. The two great moneymakers in cities are, on the one hand, unsuccessful, perpetual slums and, on the other hand, high-rent or high-cost areas. An unslumming neighborhood is no longer paying off excessively, as it may once have paid, to exploiting slum landlords who do best with greenhorns, nor is it so lush or concentrated a field for policy, drug, vice or protection rackets as is a perpetual slum. On the other hand, neither is it rendering the premium land and building prices associated with the self-destruction of diversity. It is just providing a decent, animated place to live for people who are predominately of modest circumstances, and providing an unspectacular livelihood to the owners of many small enterprises.

Thus the only people who object to destruction of an unslumming neighborhood—especially if it has not yet begun drawing newcomers with choice—are those who have businesses there or who live there. If they try to explain to the uncomprehending experts that this is a good place and growing better, nobody pays attention. In every city, such protests are discounted as the howls of people of narrow vision standing in the way of progress and higher tax receipts.

The processes that occur in unslumming depend on the fact that a metropolitan economy, if it is working well, is constantly transforming many poor people into middle-class people, many illiterates into skilled (or even educated) people, many greenhorns into competent citizens.

In Boston, the improvement of the North End was explained to me by several people outside the district as a peculiar, a freakish thing, based on the circumstance that "North Enders are Sicilians." When I was a girl, people from Sicily and their descendants were slum dwellers, so it was believed, because they were Sicilians. The unslumming and self-diversification within the North End has nothing to do with Sicily. It has to do with the vigor of metropolitan economies, and with the choices and opportunities (some good, some bad) that these energetic economies produce.

This energy and its effects—so different from immemorial peasant life—are so obvious in great cities, and so much taken for granted, that it is curious that our planning fails to incorporate them as a major and salient reality. It is curious that city planning neither respects spontaneous self-diversification among city populations nor contrives to provide for it. It is curious that city designers seem neither to recognize this force of self-diversification nor to be attracted by the esthetic problems of expressing it.

These odd intellectual omissions go back, I think, to

the Garden City nonsense, as so many of the unspoken presuppositions of city planning and city design do. Ebenezer Howard's vision of the Garden City would seem almost feudal to us. He seems to have thought that members of the industrial working classes would stay neatly in their class, and even at the same job within their class; that agricultural workers would stay in agriculture; that businessmen (the enemy) would hardly exist as a significant force in his Utopia; and that planners could go about their good and lofty work, unhampered by rude nay-saying from the untrained.

It was the very fluidity of the new nineteenth-century industrial and metropolitan society, with its profound shiftings of power, people and money, that agitated Howard so deeply—and his more dedicated followers (like the American Decentrists and Regional Planners) after him. Howard wanted to freeze power, people, and the uses and increments of money into an easily manageable and static pattern. Indeed, he happened to want a pattern that was already obsolete. "How to stem the drift from the country is one of the main problems of the day," said he. "The laborer may perhaps be restored to the land, but how will the country industries be restored to rural England?"

Howard aimed at outfoxing the bewildering new city merchants and other entrepreneurs who seemed to spring up inexhaustibly from nowhere. How to leave them no scope in which to pursue their operations, except under the tight directives of a monopolistic corporate plan—this was one of Howard's chief preoccupations in devising his Garden Cities. Howard feared and rejected the energetic forces inherent in urbanization combined with industrialization. He permitted them no part in overcoming slum life.

The restoration of a static society, ruled—in everything that mattered—by a new aristocracy of altruistic planning experts, may seem a vision remote from modern American slum clearing, slum shifting and slum immuring. But the planning derived from these semifeudal objectives has never been reassessed. It has been employed to deal with real twentieth-century cities. And this is one reason why, when American city slums do unslum, they do so in spite of planning and counter to the ideals of city planning.

For the sake of its own internal consistency, conventional planning embodies a fantasy about the bewildering presence of people in "slums" whose incomes do not conform to slum dwellers' incomes. Such people are characterized as victims of inertia, who need a push. (The comments of those who are unctuously given this information about themselves are unprintable.) Clearance, even though they protest it, does them a favor, according to this fantasy, by forcing them to better themselves. Bettering themselves means finding their squadron of price-tagged population and marching with it.

Unslumming and its accompanying self-diversification—possibly the greatest regenerative forces inherent in energetic American metropolitan economies—thus appear, in the murky light of conventional planning and rebuilding wisdom, to represent mere social untidiness and economic confusion, and they are so treated.

16

GRADUAL MONEY AND CATACLYSMIC MONEY

Thus far, I have been writing almost entirely about the qualities at work for *inherent* success in cities. To make an analogy, it is as if I had been discussing farming almost entirely in terms of soil, water, machinery, seed and fertilizer requirements for good crops, but said nothing about the financial means of getting those things.

To understand why the financial means and methods used for buying the agricultural necessities mattered greatly, we would first have to understand why the crop-growing requirements themselves mattered greatly, and something about their own nature. Without that understanding, we might ignore the problem of how to finance a reliable water supply and enthusiastically tie ourselves up instead with methods to finance ever more elaborate fencing. Or, knowing that water was somehow important, but understanding little about its possible sources for our purposes, we might spend our substance on rain dances and have no financial arrangements to buy pipes.

Money has its limitations. It cannot buy inherent success for cities where the conditions for inherent success are lacking and where the use of the money fails to supply them. Furthermore, money can only do ultimate harm where it destroys the conditions needed for inherent success. On the other hand, by helping to supply the requirements needed, money can help build inherent success in cities. Indeed, it is indispensable.

For these reasons, money is a powerful force both for city decline and for city regeneration. But it must be understood that it is not the mere availability of money, but how it is available, and for what, that is all important.

Three principal kinds of money finance and shape most of the changes that occur in residential and business properties in cities. Because this money is so powerful an *instrument*—as it goes, so go our cities.

The first, and most important, of the three kinds of money is the credit extended by conventional, non-governmental lending institutions. In order of size of their mortgage holdings, the most important of these institutions are: savings and loan associations, life insurance companies, commercial banks and mutual savings banks. Added to these are various categories of minor mortgage lenders—some of them growing rapidly, such as pension funds. By far the lion's share of building, remodeling, rehabilitation, replacement and expansion that occurs in cities (as well as in the suburbs beyond cities) is financed by this kind of money.

The second kind of money is that provided by government, either out of tax receipts or through governmental borrowing power. Aside from the city building which is traditionally governmental (schools, highways, etc.), residential and business properties are also financed in some cases by this money. Still more are shaped and influenced by the fact that it can be drawn on for partial financing, or for insurance of other loans. Land-clearance subsidies from the federal and city governments to make privately financed redevelopment and renewal projects financially feasible, are among the uses of this money; so are housing projects underwritten by federal, state or city governments. In addition, the federal government will guarantee as much as 90 percent of the value of residential mortgages financed by conventional lenders—and will even buy up guaranteed mortgages from lenders—provided that the developments whose mortgages have thus been guaranteed conform to standards of planning approved by the Federal Housing Administration.

The third kind of money comes from a shadow world of investment, an underworld of cash and credit, so to speak. Where this money comes from ultimately, and by what avenues it finds its way, is concealed and devious. This money is lent at interest rates starting at about 20 percent and ranging as high as the market will bear, apparently in some cases up to 80 percent in combinations of interest rates and arrangers' fees and cuts. In does many jobs—a few of which are actually constructive and useful—but it is most notable for financing exploitative conversions of humdrum buildings to slum buildings at exorbitant profits. This money is to the mortgage market what loan-shark money is to personal finance.

All three of these kinds of money behave differently in important respects. Each does its part in financing city property changes.

With full awareness of their differences—and especially the moral difference between the shadow-world money and the legitimate private and governmental money—I plan to point out that the behavior of these three kinds of money is similar in one respect. In sum, this money shapes cataclysmic changes in cities. Relatively little of it shapes gradual change.

Cataclysmic money pours into an area in concentrated form, producing drastic changes. As an obverse of this behavior, cataclysmic money sends relatively few trickles into localities not treated to cataclysm.

Putting it figuratively, insofar as their effects on most city streets and districts are concerned, these three kinds of money behave not like irrigation systems, bringing life-giving streams to feed steady, continual growth. Instead, they behave like manifestations of malevolent climates beyond the control of man—affording either searing droughts or torrential, eroding floods.

This is, of course, no constructive way to nurture cities. City building that has a solid footing produces continual and gradual change, building complex diversifications. Growth of diversity itself is created by means of changes dependent upon each other to build increasingly effective combinations of uses. Unslumming—much as it should be speeded up from the glacial pace at which it now proceeds—is a process of steady but gradual change. All city building that retains staying power after its novelty has gone, and that preserves the freedom of the streets and upholds citizens' self-management, requires that its locality be able to adapt, keep up to date, keep interesting, keep convenient, and this in turn requires a myriad of gradual, constant, close-grained changes.

To bring city streets and districts up to good operating condition (which means, mainly, supplying the conditions to generate diversity), and to keep them there, is a job that cannot be begun too soon. But on the other hand, it is also a job that is never over and done with, and never will be, in any given place.

The kind of money necessary for capitalizing upon,

building upon and supplementing what exists is gradual money. But this indispensable instrument is lacking.

This is far from an inevitable situation. On the contrary, it has taken considerable well-intended ingenuity (along with a certain amount of drifting) to bring us to this pass. The "inevitable," as Holmes said, comes about only through great effort; this is so with respect to the cataclysmic use of money in cities. As one obvious indication of this, if all the pep talks and brochures urging investment in sweeping renewal cataclysms were bound together, they would make a volume at least fifty times the size of this book. And yet, notwithstanding all this promotion, and the immense data-collecting and legislative work behind it, so cumbersome is this form of city investment that it serves better, in many instances, to paralyze and to penalize the use of money rather than to stimulate and to reward it. Ever greater incentives must constantly be contrived to give investment in this type of cataclysm another shot and another shove. As Arthur H. Motley, president of the U. S. Chamber of Commerce, commented at a renewal conference late in 1960, "Some cities using federal funds have acquired so much land without rebuilding that the Federal Housing and Home Finance Agency has become the largest grower of ragweed."

Motley's bleak realism was not in the spirit of such conferences, which run mainly to platitudes about the "challenge," and "the businessman's stake in healthy and beautiful cities," and to such sage remarks as "The key to future investment in this field is the profit factor."

Behind the use of mortgage and building money is, to be sure, concern about the profit factor—in most cases legitimate concern about legitimate profits. But in addition, behind the use of this money stand more abstract ideas about cities themselves, and these ideas are mighty determinants of what is done with money in cities. No more than park designers or zoners do mortgage lenders operate in an ideological or legislative vacuum.

Let us begin with the existence and the effects of money droughts, for droughts of mortgage money are the cause of much otherwise unnecessary city decline.

"If the power to tax is the power to destroy . . . then the credit authority is not only the power to destroy but the power to create and the power to divert," says Professor Charles M. Haar of the Harvard Law School in an analysis of federal incentives for home-building investment.

The power to destroy which is possessed by authority over credit or by management of credit is negative: it is the power to withhold credit.

To understand the effects of this action on city neighborhoods we can best begin by looking into a couple of miracles—for the purpose of understanding that it does take miracles to overcome this force for decline.

The North End of Boston represents escape by miracle.

Following the Great Depression and then the war, periods in which virtually no building was done in any case, the North End was blacklisted by conventional lending institutions as a locality for mortgage loans. This meant that the North End was cut off from building, expansion or rehabilitation credit from the American lending systems almost as effectively as if it were a community in Tasmania.

For thirty years, beginning with the Depression and moving on into the period of Blacklist, the largest conventional mortgage loans made in this district were for $3,000, and these have been rare. The most affluent suburb, one would surmise, could hardly have held up over such a period under such terms. Material improvement would be miraculous.

Owing to a peculiarly fortunate circumstance, the North End did manage such a miracle. Among its residents and businessmen and their relatives and friends, it happens that there are many persons engaged in the building trades: masons, electricians, carpenters, contractors. These people have contributed their services in some cases and bartered them in others to modernize and rehabilitate North End buildings. Costs have been mainly costs of materials, and it has been possible to finance these pay-as-you-go, out of savings. In the North End, a businessman or landlord has to have the money *first*, to finance improvements which he anticipates will justify the expenditure by returning it.

In short, the North End reverted to primitive methods of barter and hoard that worked before there were banking systems. To do so was a given condition for continued unslumming and for community survival.

These methods, however, cannot be stretched to cover the financing of the new construction which should be introduced into the North End, as into any living city neighborhood, gradually.

The North End, as things stand, can get new construction only by submitting to a cataclysm of renewal and redevelopment—a cataclysm which would destroy its complexity, disperse its people and wipe out its businessmen.* It would also cost an immense amount of money in comparison with the North End's needs for money to finance steady, continual improvement and replacement of what wears out.

The Back-of-the-Yards in Chicago survived and improved after its death warrant had seemingly been sealed; it did so with a different kind of extraordinary resource. So far as I know the Back-of-the-Yards is the only city district which has met the common problem of credit blacklisting head on and overcome it by direct means. To understand how it was able to do so, it is necessary to understand a little of the history of this district.

The Back-of-the-Yards used to be a notorious slum. When the great muckraker and crusader, Upton Sinclair, wanted to describe the dregs of city life and human exploitation in his book, *The Jungle,* it was the Back-of-the-Yards and its associated stockyards he chose to portray. People from there who sought jobs outside the district gave false addresses, as late as the 1930's, to avoid the discrimination that then attached to residence there. Physically, as recently as 1953, the district, a hodgepodge of weather-beaten buildings, was a classic example of the sort of locality which it is conventionally believed must be bulldozed away entire.

In the 1930's the breadwinners of the district worked principally in the stockyards, and during that decade the district and its people became deeply involved in union-

---

* The first stage of such a cataclysm is already being prepared in plan, in the form of a scheme for massive clearance around historic buildings. Boston—or at least the custodians of its tradition—are ashamed that at present tourists and school children may be distracted by the irrelevant North End while taking in the meaning of American freedom.

izing the packing plants. Building upon the new militancy, and resolving to seize the opportunity it offered for submerging old nationality antagonisms that had previously set the district asunder, a number of very able men started an experiment in local organization.* Called the Back-of-the-Yards Council, the organization adopted the brave slogan, "We, the people, will work out our own destiny." The Council has come to operate much as a government does. It possesses a more inclusive and formal organization than the usual citizens' association, and much greater power, both for carrying out public services of its own and for exerting its will on the municipal government. Policies are set by a kind of legislature of two hundred elected representatives from smaller organizations and street neighborhoods. The district's power to get from city hall the municipal services, facilities, regulations, and exceptions to regulations it needs is regarded with considerable awe throughout Chicago. In short, the Back-of-the-Yards is no portion of the body politic to take on lightly or unthinkingly in a fight, which is a point of major significance to this story.

In the interval between the formation of the Council and the early 1950's, the people of the district and their children made other kinds of advancement. Many graduated into skilled industrial, white-collar or professional jobs. The "inevitable" next move at this stage should have been a mass emigration to income-sorting suburbs, with a new wave of people possessing little choice

* The leaders were Bishop Bernard J. Sheil, Saul D. Alinsky, sociologist and criminologist, and Joseph B. Meegan, then a neighborhood park director. Alinsky has described the theory and means of organizing in a book, *Reveille for Radicals*.

sweeping into the abandoned district. Backward, the perpetual slum.

Like people generally in unslumming city neighborhoods, however, the people of this district wanted to stay. (That is why they had already been uncrowding and unslumming within their neighborhoods.) The existing institutions, especially the churches, wanted them to stay.

At the same time, however, thousands of residents also wanted to improve their dwellings beyond the uncrowding and the small amount of refurbishing or refurnishing already accomplished. They were no longer slum dwellers and they did not wish to live as if they were.

The two desires—to stay and to improve—were incompatible because nobody could get a loan for an improvement. Like the North End, the Back-of-the-Yards was blacklisted for mortgage credit.

But in this case an organization capable of dealing with the problem existed. A survey by the Council turned up the information that businesses, residents and institutions within the district had deposits in some thirty of Chicago's savings and loan associations and savings banks. Within the district, it was agreed that these depositors—institutions and businesses as well as individuals —would be prepared to withdraw their deposits if lending institutions continued to blacklist the district.

On July 2, 1953, representatives of the banks and the savings and loan associations turned up by the Council's survey were invited to a meeting. The mortgage problem of the district was presented and discussed amiably. Comments were dropped by Council spokesmen, politely, about the numbers of depositors in the district . . . the extent of their deposits . . . the difficulty of understanding why investment of savings by city dwellers seemed so little available for use in cities . . . the solid concern about the problem within the district . . . the value of public understanding.

Before the meeting was over, several of the lenders pledged their help—that is, favorable consideration of requests for loans. The same day, the Council began negotiating for a site for forty-nine new dwellings. Soon afterward, the most squalid row of slum apartments was equipped with indoor plumbing and otherwise modernized, by means of a $90,000 loan. Within three years, some five thousand houses had been rehabilitated by their owners, and the number rehabilitated since has been so great it has not been kept track of. In 1959, construction of several small apartment houses was begun. The Council, and people within the district, refer to the banks' interest and cooperation in their improvement with gratitude. And the banks, in their turn, speak admiringly of the area as a location for sound investment. Nobody was thrown out of the district and "relocated." No businesses were destroyed. Unslumming, in short, has proceeded, even though the process reached a point—as it eventually does everywhere—when the need for credit becomes crucial.

Credit blacklisting of city localities is impersonal. It operates not against the residents or businessmen, as persons, but against their neighborhoods. For example, a merchant with whom I am acquainted in the blacklisted district of East Harlem in New York, unable to get a $15,000 loan for expanding and modernizing his successful business there, had no difficulty raising $30,000 to build a house on Long Island. Similarly, a person in the North End, purely by being alive and by holding a job as a bricklayer or a bookkeeper or a boltmaker, can easily borrow thirty years' worth of money, at the going rate, for the purpose of buying a house in a suburban development. But attached to the North End, neither he, nor his neighbors, nor their landlords, are worth a penny's credit.

This is outrageous and destructive, but before becoming outraged, it is well to pause and consider that the banks and other conventional lenders who blacklist city localities have done no more than take seriously the conventional lessons of city planning. They are not villainous. Credit-blacklist maps are identical, both in conception and in most results, with municipal slum clearance maps. And municipal slum-clearance maps are regarded as responsible devices, used for responsible purposes—among their purposes is, in fact, that of warning lenders not to invest here.

Sometimes the planners anticipate the lenders; sometimes the lenders anticipate the planners; both of them know what they are doing because they have both learned so much about Radiant Garden City Beautiful planning. The two devices—blacklist maps and slum-clearance maps—came into common use at about the same time, in the early 1940's. With the lenders, they first started as maps of areas in which there had been large numbers of foreclosures during the Great Depression, and which hence were presumably poor risks for future loans. This criterion, however, receded into the background. (It was confusing. The Grand Central office area in New York had one of the worst foreclosure records in the country; did this mean it was a poor risk for future investment?) The modern criterion is the lenders' decision that such-and-such a place is already a slum, or else is destined to become a slum. Its future, insofar as it is considered, is thus conceived in terms of orthodox city planning remedies: eventual erasure, and in the meantime, decline.

In choosing to use the power of credit to destroy, lenders operate on the premise, therefore, that their actions register an inevitability and, in the light of that inevitability, no more than prudence. They are making prophecies.

Usually their prophecies are borne out, too. Consider, for example, the case of a New England city (not Boston this time) with an extensive and well-publicized redevelopment program. As a foundation for its work, the redevelopment staff prepared a map that showed where decay had proceeded so far that clearance was deemed necessary. After the map was made, the planners discovered that it coincided, exactly, with the maps prepared by the city's bankers many years previously, designating localities into which no loans would be made. The bankers had prophesied these places would become hopeless slums, and their prognoses were accurate. Only one minor discrepancy showed between the two maps. This was a case in which the planners' map prescribed not complete clearance, but instead spot clearance. In this one instance, a blacklisted locality, including parts of its small business district, had not seemed too far gone for limited conservation. This locality alone had its independent source of credit: a small, family-run bank, a vestige of earlier days, an oddity that did make loans within its blacklisted area.

Such business expansion and refurbishing, such upkeep as the locality had, was financed by it. This, for instance, was the source of credit that had enabled the neighborhood's outstanding commercial establishment—a restaurant drawing customers from all over the city—to acquire good equipment and to expand and refurbish as needed.

Credit-blacklisting maps, like slum-clearance maps, are accurate prophecies because they are self-fulfilling prophecies.

In the cases of the North End and the Back-of-the-Yards, the blacklist maps were inaccurate prophecies. But no one would ever know they had been inaccurate estimates of the potentiality, were it not for the miraculous ability of these places to evade their sentences.

Other city neighborhoods of vitality often show resistance to the death sentence. My own neighborhood did for twelve years (this was a case in which the planners led the way with a slum-clearance map and the lenders followed). A few streets of East Harlem have stood up under blacklisting since 1942, by means of loans made back and forth among families and relatives.*

There is no telling how many city district have been destroyed by blacklisting. The Lower East Side of New York, an area of great potential—at least as great a poten-

---

*In 1960, property owners on one of these streets got what appear to be the first conventional mortgage loans made into East Harlem in eighteen years. They were obtained through the good offices of John J. Merli, city councilman and a potent figure in the New York County Committee of the Democratic party. Mr. Merli himself first advanced the money for buying necessary materials, and arranged for labor barter and labor donation in the fashion of the North End. After the work was done, he managed to get bank loans for the property owners concerned, with which they could repay the loans he had made them for materials.

tial as Greenwich Village—was doomed by blacklisting. The Society Hill district in Philadelphia, on which great sums of public renewal money are now to be spent to "bring back the middle class" officially, was chosen by many middle-income people on their own initiative in years past—only to be unchosen when they could not get loans to buy or to rehabilitate there.

Unless a neighborhood does possess extraordinary vitality, along with some form of extraordinary resource, a drought of conventional money inexorably enforces deterioration.

The worst cases are neighborhoods that are already stagnant, with much that is inherently wrong. These localities, which are losing their former residents anyway, often undergo a special form of investment cataclysm. Within a short interval after they are blacklisted for conventional credit, there may come into the vacuum money from the shadow world of investment. It pours in, buying up property for which there are no other purchasers now, and presumably will not be, and to which their current owners or users have no great, effective attachment. Quick conversions of buildings to the most exploitative slums follow. Shadow-world cataclysmic money is filling in the gap left by conventional money.

This sequence occurs in most great cities, and seems to be taken for granted, although few studies have been made of it. One of these few was a research report on a cataclysmically deteriorated area of New York's West Side, by Dr. Chester A. Rapkin, an economist and planner. Rapkin's report described the imposition of a money drought from conventional sources, the appearance of high-interest and unscrupulous money in its stead, the inability of property owners to make changes except for the sale of their property to exploitative purchasers. The *New York Times,* quoting James Felt, Chairman of the City Planning Commission, for which the report was prepared, summed it up both neatly and dispassionately:

> He said that it disclosed the almost complete termination of new construction in the twenty-block area. He said it also showed a halt in the flow of bank and other institutional mortgage loans on real property, a turnover of property to a new type of investor, a growth of absentee ownership and the transformation of much of the housing occupancy in the area into furnished-room occupancy.

All three kinds of cataclysmic money have been involved in this debacle, as they often are in city decay. First the withdrawal of all conventional money; then ruination financed by shadow-world money; then selection of the area by the Planning Commission as a candidate for cataclysmic use of government money to finance renewal clearance. This last stage makes possible cataclysmic re-entry of conventional money for financing renewal-project construction and rehabilitation. So well do these three different kinds of money prepare the way for each other's cataclysms that one would be impelled to admire the process, as a highly developed form of order in its own right, were it not so destructive to every other form of city order. It does not represent a "conspiracy." It is a logical outcome of logical men guided by nonsensical but conventional city planning beliefs.

The remarkable fact, however—and a great testimony to the strength and magnetism of many city neighborhoods in adversity—is the degree to which they resist their financial death decrees. This was discovered in New York City during the 1950's, after new laws required central heating in tenement buildings. Landlords were to be recompensed for the improvements by rent increases or tax abatements. The arrangement ran into unexpected obstacles, and precisely in places where no particular obstacles would have been anticipated: in socially stable areas, holding up well, where the tenants could have absorbed the increases. Money to do the work (at rates under 20 percent interest) was generally unobtainable.

The difficulties of one landlord, haled into court for violation of the law, were reported in the newspapers in December 1959, because he happened to be a Congressman, Representative Alfred E. Santangelo, and was therefore newsworthy. Santangelo reported that the central heating had been installed since inspection, and went on to recount that it had cost $15,000 for each of six buildings his family owned, or a total of $90,000. "Of this," he said, "we could get only $23,000 from banks by extending a mortgage for five years, and by getting a personal bank loan. We had to do the rest with personal family monies."

Santangelo did very well with the banks, considering the usual treatment of requests for loans into blacklisted localities. From time to time, the New York newspapers print letters about the problem. One such, from a lawyer of a landlords' association early in 1959, said:

> It is common knowledge that banks and insurance companies have refrained from making loans or mortgages to owners of tenement houses, espe-

cially those located in what have been marked as undesirable areas in the city. Mortgages upon expiration are not renewed and owners are frequently compelled to resort to moneylenders who exact interest as high as 20% [Note: this is conservative] for short-term loans . . . There are owners who desire to do more than just install central heating. They would modernize apartments by enlarging rooms, placing new equipment in kitchens, installing adequate wiring . . . With doors to financing closed to them, owners have appealed to the city for aid and none has been forthcoming . . . No agency exists to help with the problem.

The type of building involved, whether it is a tenement or historically valuable old town house or a purely commercial property, makes little difference, actually, in a blacklisted area. Just as it is not persons who are blacklisted, as such, neither are buildings, as such, but rather the locality, as such.

During 1959, New York embarked on a small experimental program for conserving neighborhoods in Manhattan that on the one hand were getting no new building, but on the other hand were judged to be far from hopeless physically and much worth saving socially. Unfortunately, lenders had already judged just these neighborhoods to be hopeless. *Merely so that building violations could be corrected,* the city found it necessary to obtain state legislation setting up a $15,000,000 public loan fund for property owners in such neighborhoods to draw upon. Money for gradual change is so hard to get that a new loan authority has had to be created to supply even a pittance for the most rock-bottom purposes. The legislation was drawn up so ineptly that the fund, as this is written, is almost unusable; and it is so small it cannot, in any case, make much difference to the city.

As already indicated, blacklisted localities can get money from conventional lenders again if the money comes in the form of a cataclysm, and if it is thus employed to sort out incomes and uses in some approximation of Radiant Garden City.

Dedicating a privately financed Radiant City project in Harlem the Borough President of Manhattan hailed the occasion as most significant because "in getting private financing the project sponsors have broken the barrier that banks have long maintained against substantial investment in new housing for Harlem."

The barrier, however, has been broken for no other type of investment in Harlem than investment in project cataclysms.

Conventional credit will reappear too in a blacklisted district if the federal government will guarantee mortgages as generously as it does for suburban development and for new Radiant Garden City projects. But the federal government does not guarantee mortgages in sufficient amount to stimulate spot building or rehabilitation except in certified renewal areas with an approved plan. An approved plan means that even existing buildings must help shape the area into the nearest possible approximation of Radiant Garden City. Usually these renewal plans disperse—even from low-density areas—between one-half and two-thirds of the original population. Again the money is used to finance cataclysms. And it is not used to build city diversity but to erase it. When I asked an official involved in arrangements for a "spot-clearance" renewal district why dispersed commerce was to be rooted out (instead of more of it stimulated), and why business was to be confined to a monopolistic shopping center, imitating suburban life, he said, first, that that represented good planning. He then added, "The question is academic anyhow. We couldn't get FHA approval on loans with mixed uses like that." He is right. There is no appreciable money available today for nurturing city districts fit for city life, and this is a situation encouraged and often enforced by government. We have, therefore, no one to blame for this but ourselves.

Still another form of respectable money is available to blacklisted districts: public housing project money. Although there is much prating about "vest-pocket projects," the vest in question seems to be Paul Bunyan's. This too is money that comes, almost invariably, in cataclysmic form, and always in the form of sorting out and price-tagging populations.

East Harlem—like the Lower East Side—has received floods of such money. Back in 1942, East Harlem would have looked at least as good a possibility for unslumming as the North End. Only five years before, in 1937, a sober study of the area, sponsored by the city, saw so much of hope and improvement occurring that it projected East Harlem as the logical center in New York of Italian-influenced culture. The district possessed thousands of businessmen, handling businesses so stable and successful that in many cases the second or third generation was now running them. It had hundreds of cultural and social organizations. It was an area of much worn-out and poor housing (along with some good housing and considerable unslumming housing), but also of immense vitality and with a great hold on many of its people. The district also possessed the city's main Puerto Rican community, which was miserably housed, but which contained many first-comers of the Puerto Rican immigration who were already emerging as leaders, and it contained an immense array of Puerto Rican cultural, social and business establishments.

After East Harlem was written off by lenders in 1942, it too had little miracles. One area, near the foot of the Tri-borough Bridge, continued unslumming and rehabilitating in spite of every obstacle. The Housing Authority's own site managers, when they had to drive the people out so that a huge immured slum, Wagner Houses, could be built there instead, were amazed and mystified that improvements so substantial and plentiful should be wiped away. No miracle sufficiently sensational turned up to save East Harlem. To carry out their plans (even where these were not directly overridden by the city's plans), too many people eventually had to leave. Those who stayed in spite of the discouragement to improvement, and in spite of the havoc of the shadow-world money which poured into every cranny it could find, hung on by extraordinary measures and tenacity.

For it was as if East Harlem, in effect, had been decreed a backward and deprived country, financially apart from our normal national life. Even the branch banks were closed down throughout an area of more than 100,000 people and thousands of businesses; merchants had to go out of the area simply to deposit their day's receipts. Even the system of school savings accounts was removed from the district's schools.

Eventually, much as the generosity of a rich nation might well extend massive aid to a deprived and backward country, into this district poured massive "foreign" aid, according to decisions by absentee experts from the remote continent inhabited by housers and planners. The aid poured in for rehousing people—some three hundred million dollars' worth. The more that poured in, the worse became the turmoils and troubles of East Harlem, and still more did it become like a deprived, backward country. More than 1,300 businesses which had the misfortune to occupy sites marked for housing were wiped away, and an estimated four-fifths of their proprietors ruined. More than 500 noncommercial "store-front" establishments were also wiped away. Virtually all the unslummed population which had hung on was rooted out and dispersed to "better itself."

Lack of money has hardly been the trouble in East Harlem. After the drought came fantastic floods. The money poured into East Harlem alone from the public housing treasuries is about as much as was lost on the Edsel. In the case of a mistake like the Edsel, a point is reached when the expenditure is reappraised and halted. But in East Harlem, citizens today have to fight off still more money for repetitions of mistakes that go unappraised by those who control the money floodgates. I hope we disburse foreign aid abroad more intelligently than we disburse it at home.

Lack of gradual money wastes city districts already inherently fit for city life, and therefore with a great potential for rapid improvement. It also means there is no hope for districts that lack one or more of the conditions for generating diversity, and need help in acquiring these supplements, as well as money for normal changes and for worn-out structures.

Where is the money from conventional sources, which might be going into gradual change? Where does it go instead?

Some of it goes into planned cataclysms of redevelopment and renewal; more is going into the self-destruction of diversity, to the ruination of outstanding city success.

Much is not going into cities at all, but instead into the outskirts of cities.

As Haar said, the credit authority is not only the power to destroy but the power to create and the power to divert. He was writing specifically of the government's credit authority, and the use of that authority to encourage suburb building rather than city building.

The immense new suburban sprawls of American cities have not come about by accident—and still less by the myth of free choice between cities and suburbs. Endless suburban sprawl was made practical (and for many families was made actually mandatory) through the creation of something the United States lacked until the mid-1930's: a national mortgage market specifically calculated to encourage suburban home building. Because of the certitude offered by government mortgage guarantees, a bank in New Haven could, would and does buy up mortgages on suburban housing in Southern California. A bank in Chicago buys up mortgages on suburban housing in Indianapolis one week, while an Indianapolis bank, the next week, buys them up for suburban housing outside Atlanta or Buffalo. Nor, nowadays, must these mortgages necessarily be government guaranteed. They can be a repetition, without the guarantees, of the kind of planning and building that is made routine and accepted by the guarantees.

A national mortgage market has obvious advantages in bringing the demand for money together with a distant supply of money quickly and sensitively. But, particularly when it is diverted so heavily into one kind of growth, it has its disadvantages too.

As the people of the Back-of-the-Yards found out, there is apt to be no relationship between city-created and city-needed savings, and city building investment. So remote is the relationship that in 1959 when one of the savings banks in Brooklyn announced that 70 percent of its loans had been made close to home, the *New York Times* considered the fact sufficiently newsworthy to give it a big play on the business pages. Close to home is a definition with some elasticity. The 70 percent, it turned out, had been used in Nassau County, a huge mess of new suburban sprawl on Long Island, out beyond Brooklyn. Meantime, much of Brooklyn lies under the sentence of the blacklist.

City people finance the building of suburbs. To be sure, one of the historic missions of cities, those marvelously productive and efficient places, is to finance colonization.

But you can run anything into the ground.

Obviously there have been changes in the sources of money for city building during the past thirty years. Money lending and spending have become more institutionalized than in the past. The counterparts of individuals who might have been lending money in the 1920's, for example, are today apt to be putting it into income tax and life insurance, and insofar as it is spent or lent for city building, it is spent or lent by the government or the life insurance company. Small local banks, like the New England oddity that lent money within its otherwise blacklisted neighborhood, disappeared in the Depression and in mergers after that time.

Does this mean, however, that our more institutionalized money nowadays can be used only cataclysmically? Are the great bureaucracies of money such big fish that they can operate only in cities of big fish, huge borrowers, immense and abrupt changes? Is a system which is able in one of its manifestations to retail credit, gently, for the purchase of encyclopedias and vacation trips, able in other manifestations only to distribute credit violently in wholesale lots?

This city building money operates as it does not because of its own internal necessities and forces. It operates cataclysmically because we, as a society, have asked for just this. We thought it would be good for us, and we got it. Now we accept it as if it were ordained by God or the system.

Let us look, from the point of view of what we have asked for and what we have explicitly permitted, at the three kinds of money which shape our cities—beginning with the most important, the conventional, nongovernmental sources of credit.

The idea of diverting huge sums of money to thin suburban growth *at the expense of starving city districts* was no invention of the mortgage lenders (although they, as well as suburban builders, have now acquired a vested interest in this routine). Neither the ideal nor the method of accomplishing it originated logically within our credit system itself. It originated with high-minded social thinkers. By the 1930's, when the FHA methods for stimulating suburban growth were worked out, virtually every wise man of government—from right to left—was in favor of the objectives, although they might differ with one another on methods. A few years previously, Herbert Hoover had opened the first White House Conference on Housing with a polemic against the moral inferiority of cities and a panegyric on the moral virtues of simple cottages, small towns and grass. At an opposite political pole, Rexford G. Tugwell, the federal administrator responsible for the New Deal's Green Belt demonstration suburbs, explained, "My idea is to go just outside centers of population, pick up cheap land, build a whole community and entice people into it. Then go back into the cities and tear down whole slums and make parks of them."

The cataclysmic use of money for suburban sprawl, and the concomitant starvation of all those parts of cities that planning orthodoxy stamped as slums, was what our wise men wanted for us; they put in a lot of effort, one way and another, to get it. We got it.

The deliberate social sponsorship of cataclysmic private credit for redevelopment and renewal projects is even more obvious. In the first place, society puts its own land clearance subsidy funds into these cataclysmic changes, purely to make financially possible the subsequent cataclysmic private investment. Society also oversees that the private investment is used *specifically* to create forms of pseudo-city and to combat urban diversity. Society goes still further, with its incentive of renewal mortgage guarantees, but insists that the creation thus guaranteed be as static as man can make it throughout the life of investment. Gradual change is outlawed for the future.

Social sponsorship of these cataclysms is taken for granted. This is the public's contribution to city rebuilding.

The public understands less well that in sponsoring these cataclysmic uses of private investment in cities, it has also made and enforced choices among various differing forms of private investment.

To understand this, we must understand that public subsidies for land clearance or spot clearance are far from the only subsidies. Involuntary subsidies, immense in the aggregate, go into these enterprises too.

When land is acquired for redevelopment or renewal, it is acquired through the power of eminent domain, a power which belongs only to governments. In addition, threat of acquisition under eminent domain is used to enforce compliance to renewal schemes in parcels of property not actually acquired.

The power of eminent domain, long familiar and useful as a means of acquiring property needed for public use, is extended, under redevelopment law, to acquisition of property intended for private use and private profit. This distinction was the point on which the constitutionality of redevelopment and renewal law hung. The Supreme Court declared that society did have the right—through the medium of its legislatures—to make that kind of choice between private entrepreneurs and owners; it could take the property of the one to benefit the other, as a means of achieving objects which, in the legislature's judgment, were for the public good.

This use of the power of eminent domain does more than make physically possible the assembly of project tracts. It also makes them financially possible, owing to the involuntary subsidy entailed. This point of the involuntary subsidy was well explained by Anthony J. Panuch, a management expert, in a 1960 report on New York City's housing and redevelopment snarl prepared for the Mayor:

> The direct consequence of the exercise of the power of eminent domain on the commercial tenant is drastic and often ruinous. When the government condemns property it is required to pay only for what it *acquires* for itself and not for what it *takes* from the owner.
>
> The government is *not* in condemnation acquiring a business but only the premises. It need only pay for the premises. The proprietor gets nothing for the loss of his business or goodwill, nor even for his unexpired lease because leases universally provide that upon condemnation the owner's lease contract with the tenant is automatically terminated with no compensation to the tenant.
>
> Although his entire property and his full investment is taken from him, he receives substantially nothing.

The report goes on to give an illustrative case:

> A druggist purchased a drug store for more than $40,000. A few years later, the building in which his store was located was taken in condemnation. The total sum which he eventually received

was an award of $3,000 for fixtures and that sum
had to be paid over to the chattel mortgagee. Thus
his total investment was completely wiped out.

This is a sad and common story on housing or
renewal sites, and is one reason these schemes are fought
so desperately by site businessmen. They are subsidizing
these schemes, not with a fraction of their tax money, but
with their livelihoods, with their children's college
money, with years of their past put into hopes for the
future—with nearly everything they have.

The Panuch report goes on to suggest what innumerable letters to editors, citizens at public hearings, and
newspaper editorials have already, in their own words,
suggested: "The community as a whole should bear the
expense of community progress and that cost should not
be imposed upon the unfortunate victim of community
progress."

The community as a whole has not yet seen fit to bear
that whole expense, and it is never going to. Redevelopment officials and housing experts blanch when it is suggested. The expense of bearing the whole cost would
make public subsidy costs for redevelopment and for
housing projects too heavy. At present, redevelopment
for private profit is ideologically and fiscally justified on
the grounds that the public subsidy investment will be
returned over a reasonable period in the form of increased
taxes from the improvement. Were the involuntary subsidies which make these schemes possible included as
public costs, the enlarged public costs would bear no conceivable relationship to anticipated tax returns. Public
housing on its part is held to a current cost of $17,000 per

dwelling unit. Were the involuntary subsidies absorbed as public cost, the expense of these dwellings would soar to politically unrealistic levels. Both of these operations, "renewal" projects and public housing projects, with their wholesale destruction, are inherently wasteful ways of rebuilding cities, and in comparison with their full costs make pathetic contributions to city values. At present, society is protected from these facts of life because so high a proportion of the costs is visited upon involuntary victims and is not officially added in. But the cost is there. Project building as a form of city transformation makes no more sense financially than it does socially.

When a life insurance company or a union pension fund pours cataclysmic amounts of money into a regimented project or renewal scheme for a price-tagged population, it is not indulging in behavior somehow necessary to twentieth-century investment funds. It is doing, rather, what society has specifically asked for and has made possible only by employing quite extraordinary and ruthless social powers.

In the case of the cataclysmic use of conventional credit for the self-destruction of diversity, the situation is different. The cataclysmic effects in such cases arise, not from vast wholesaling of credit at all, but from the aggregate of many individual transactions which happen to be heavily concentrated in one locality in one period of time. Society has produced no deliberate stimulants to this destruction of outstanding city success. But neither has society done anything to hamper or to divert this form of city-destroying money flood.

Private investment shapes cities, but social ideas (and laws) shape private investment. First comes the image of what we want, then the machinery is adapted to turn out that image. The financial machinery has been adjusted to create anti-city images because, and only because, we as a society thought this would be good for us. If and when we think that lively, diversified city, capable of continual, close-grained improvement and change, is desirable, then we will adjust the financial machinery to get that.

As for the cataclysmic use of public funds for city rebuilding, there is even less reason than in the case of private credit to suppose that this just happens because it happens. Public housing money is employed cataclysmically instead of for gradual, steady street and district improvement, because we thought cataclysms would be good for our slum dwellers—and a demonstration to the rest of us of the good city life.

There is no inherent reason why tax funds and public credit cannot be used to speed unslumming instead of slum shifting and slum immuring. Methods entirely different from those now employed are possible for subsidizing housing. I shall discuss this question in the next chapter.

Nor is there any inherent reason why public buildings must be sorted out and assembled into civic and cultural cataclysms. They can be built and located as ingredients of gradual change, to supplement and enliven their matrix of living city. We only do it the other way because we think it is right.

The shadow-world money is hard to control socially, but we could do much to hamper at least its cataclysmic effects. Blacklisting of localities opens wonderful opportunities to the cataclysmic use of exploitative money. To this degree, the problem is hardly the exploitative money itself, but the (socially encouraged) withholding of conventional investment.

Cataclysmic use of governmental money also affords, as a by-product, wonderful opportunities for the money from the shadow world. To understand why this is so, we must understand that slum landlords, unlike the drugstore proprietor in the Panuch report, benefit handsomely from blanket use of the powers of eminent domain. When a building is bought under the powers of eminent domain, three factors are customarily taken into account in setting the award (sale price). These are the assessed value of the property, the replacement value of the building, and the current earning power of the *building* (as distinguished from the earning power of a business which may be conducted within it). The more exploited a building, the higher its earning power, and the more the owner is given. So profitable are such condemnation sales for slum landlords that some of them make a business of buying up buildings in areas already condemned, overcrowding them, and raising rents, less for the profits to be made in the interim than for the profits to be made by the building's sale to the public. To combat this particular racket, some cities have passed "quick-take" laws technically transferring to public ownership the title of properties on a condemned site the day condemnation is approved—leaving negotiations on sale prices and appraisals to be worked out later.*

* The point of these laws, of course, is to prevent ownership from changing in the interim, and thus increasing costs to the city beyond those anticipated. Quick-take laws succeed in this, but as a by-product they work even greater hardship than usual upon legitimate site owners. In

Wherever exploited buildings exist, their owners are enriched from slum clearance. They can, and apparently often do, use their condemnation awards to buy more property than they formerly had, in new localities which they propose to convert to slums. If the new slum is later condemned, so much the better for such an investor's multiplying fortunes and holdings. In New York, some investors of this kind take not only their money with them to a new location, but also their former tenants, thereby helping the city solve the "relocation" problem. Slum shifting has its own efficiencies. It is self-financing.

Again, the cataclysmic use of shadow-world money to create new slums is hardly a problem entailing only the shadow-world money itself. To a degree, it is a problem that arises from (socially encouraged) slum shifting.

Finally, the cataclysmic use of shadow-world money could be better controlled through taxation, as explained in the Panuch report:

No amount of code enforcement or tax abated housing rehabilitation by the New York City Housing Authority will be able to keep pace with slum formation, *until and unless the profit is taken out of slums by taxation.* [Taxation on the basis of profits

---

Boston's West End, for example, owners who occupied their own buildings were reduced to desperation by the quick-take law. From the day of condemnation, their tenants began paying their rent to the city instead of to the former owner, and the owners also had to begin paying rent to the city. This went on month after month—in some cases about a year— while the former owner of the building was unable to move because he had not received his money and had no idea, furthermore, what he would get. Eventually he would accept almost anything.

is necessary] to overcome the effect of the Federal Income Tax structure, the depreciation and capital gains provisions of which make slum ownership a highly profitable speculation for slumlords. . . .

A slum owner in a congested area, where need for shelter is desperate and where the rents are what the traffic will bear, need not maintain the property. He pockets his annual depreciation allowance year after year, and after he has written down the book value of his slum property to zero, he then sells it at a price that *capitalizes his high rent roll.* Having made the sale, he pays a 25% capital gains tax on the difference between the book value and the sales price. He then acquires another slum property and goes through the same process again. [Saturation inspection by the Bureau of Internal Revenue of the income returns of owners of slum properties would] determine the amount of back taxes and penalties due as a result of their pocketing any improperly claimed depreciation allowance.

Cynics—or at least the cynics I talk to—think that pickings are made so easy nowadays for exploitative money in cities because the investment shadow world represents powerful interests, with a big say somewhere behind the legislative and administrative scenes. I have no way of knowing whether this is true. However, I should think that apathy on the part of the rest of us has something to do with the situation. Some professional housers, today, have a plausible rationalization for the profits the shadow world takes as a by-product of city rebuilding operations. "Society has created the slums," they say, "and it is only right that society should pay what is needed to wipe them out." Putting it in these terms, however, evades the question of who is being paid by society, and where the money goes next. The apathy is abetted, also, by the comfortable thought that the problem of slums is being overcome anyway by wiping out old slum buildings. Nothing could be less true.

It is so easy to blame the decay of cities on traffic . . . or immigrants . . . or the whimsies of the middle class. The decay of cities goes deeper and is more complicated. It goes right down to what we think we want, and to our ignorance about how cities work. The forms in which money is used for city building—or withheld from use— are powerful instruments of city decline today. The forms in which money is used must be converted to instruments of regeneration—from instruments buying violent cataclysms to instruments buying continual, gradual, complex and gentler change.

PART FOUR

DIFFERENT TACTICS

17

SUBSIDIZING DWELLINGS

Most of the aims I have been writing about, aims such as unslumming slums, catalyzing diversity, nurturing lively streets, are unrecognized today as objectives of city planning. Therefore, planners and the agencies of action that carry out plans possess neither strategies nor tactics for carrying out such aims.

However, although city planning lacks tactics for building cities that can work like cities, it does possess plenty of tactics. They are aimed at carrying out strategic lunacies. Unfortunately, they are effective.

In this section, I am going to deal with several subjects that, in themselves, are already well recognized as within the province of city planning: subsidized dwellings, traffic, city visual design, analytical methods. These are all matters for which conventional modern planning does have objectives and therefore does possess tactics—so many tactics, so well entrenched, that when their purposes are questioned they are generally justified *in terms of the conditions laid down by still other tactics* (e.g., We must do this for the purpose of getting the federal loan guarantees). We become the prisoners of our tactics, seldom looking behind them at the strategies.

As good a place as any to begin is with the tactics for subsidizing dwellings, because the tactics devised and embroidered over the years to make project communities a reality for the poor have deeply infected planning tactics for all purposes. "Did public housing fail completely?" housing expert Charles Abrams has asked, after castigating it as ill-conceived for its purposes and as having, in combination with urban-renewal clearance, attained "absurdity."

He went on to answer:

> No. It proved many things . . . It proved that large blighted areas are assemblable, replannable and rebuildable. It won public acceptance of large-scale urban improvement and established the legal base for it. It proved that . . . housing bonds are AAA investments; that public provision of shelter is a government duty; that the housing authority mechanism can at least operate without graft. All this is no small accomplishment.

All that is indeed no small accomplishment. The devices of large-scale clearance, slum shifting, slum immuring, project planning, income sorting, use sorting have become so fixed as planning images and as collections of tactics that city rebuilders, and most ordinary citizens too, face a blank when they try to think of city rebuilding without these means. To get past this obstacle, we must understand the original misconception on which the rest of the fancy structure rests.

A friend of mine reached the age of eighteen believing that babies were born through their mothers' navels. She got the idea as a small child, and whatever she heard from then on, she modified and embroidered into her initial mistake, for she was bright and ingenious. The more she learned, the more support, therefore, she seemed to have for her notion. She was exercising, somewhat bizarrely, one of the most universal, ingenious and distressing of human talents. She grew a new rationalization for every one demolished, so it was impossible to clear away her misunderstanding by chopping around in its outer reaches. To topple her fancy intellectual concoction, it was necessary to begin with the anatomy of the navel. When her first simple misunderstanding about the nature and use of the navel was cleared up thus by her family, she promptly exercised another clever and more heartening human talent. She cleared away the rest of her thicket of misunderstanding with such ease that she became a biology teacher (and subsequently produced a large family too).

The thicket of confusion about the workings of cities which has grown around and upon the subsidized housing project notion is no longer just in our minds. By now it is also a thicket of legislative, financial, architectural and analytical devices applied to cities.

Our cities contain people too poor to pay for the quality of shelter that our public conscience (quite rightly, I think) tells us they should have. Furthermore, in many cities the sheer supply of dwellings is too small to accommodate the population without overcrowding, and the quantity of additional dwellings needed does not necessarily match up with the direct ability of the people concerned to pay for them. Because of these reasons, we need subsidies for at least some portion of city dwellings.

These seem like simple and straightforward reasons for dwelling subsidies. They also leave a large leeway as to how subsidies might be applied, both financially and physically.

But let us see how involuted and rigid these reasons can become—have become—by giving another seemingly simple but slightly different answer to the question: What is the reason for subsidizing dwellings in cities?

The answer we long ago accepted went like this: The reason we need dwelling subsidies is to provide for that part of the population which cannot be housed by private enterprise.

And, the answer went on, so long as this is necessary anyway, the subsidized dwellings should embody and demonstrate the principles of good housing and planning.

This is a terrible answer, with terrible consequences. A twist of semantics suddenly presents us with *people who cannot be housed by private enterprise,* and hence must presumably be housed by someone else. Yet in real life, these are people whose housing needs are not in themselves peculiar and thus outside the ordinary province and capability of private enterprise, like the housing needs of prisoners, sailors at sea or the insane. Perfectly ordinary housing needs can be provided for almost anybody by private enterprise. What is peculiar about these people is merely that *they cannot pay for it.*

Quicker than the eye can see, however, "people who cannot be housed by private enterprise" have been turned into a statistical group with peculiar shelter requirements, like prisoners, on the basis of one statistic: their income. To carry out the rest of the answer, this statistical group becomes a special collection of guinea pigs for Utopians to mess around with.

Even if the Utopians had had schemes that made sense socially in cities, it is wrong to set one part of the population, segregated by income, apart in its own neighborhoods with its own different scheme of community. Separate but equal makes nothing but trouble in a society where people are not taught that caste is a part of the divine order. Separate but better is an innate contradiction wherever the separateness is enforced by one form of inferiority.

The notion that the fact of a subsidy required that these people be housed by someone other than private enterprise and normal landlords was an aberration in itself. The government does not take over the landlordship or ownership or management of subsidized farms or of subsidized airlines. Government does not, as a rule, take over the running of museums that receive subsidies from public funds. It does not take over the ownership or management of voluntary community hospitals whose construction is today frequently made possible by government subsidies.*

Public housing stands apart from other, logically analogous forms of capitalism and of government partnership which we have evolved; it incorporates the belief that government must take over a facility *purely* because government contributes subsidy funds.

Because we lack any ideology that puts government as the landlord and owner of public housing in context with the rest of our national life, we have no sense about

*The late Marshall Shaffer, the brilliant U. S. Public Health Service official who developed the federal program of hospital construction aid and administered it for many years, kept pasted in his desk drawer a piece of paper he looked at from time to time to remind himself of something. It said, "A fool can put on his own clothes better than a wise man can do it for him."

how to contend with such a thing. The bureaucracies that build and run these places—always in terror lest their capricious masters, the taxpayers, find fault with the tenants' housekeeping, morals or standards of amenity and blame the bureaucrats—are in some things impossibly arrogant and in others impossibly timid.

Because the government is a landlord, it is in potential competition with private landlords, and to prevent the competition from being unfair, cartel arrangements are necessary. The population itself must be cartelized, with people moved from the province of one cartel to another on the basis of the money they make.

The answer that these are people "who cannot be housed by private enterprise" was absolutely disastrous for cities too. Quicker than the eye can see, the city as an organism has disappeared. It becomes, in theory, a static collection of sites for planting these sorted-out sets of statistics.

From the beginning, the whole conception was irrelevant to the nature of the problem, irrelevant to the plain financial need of the people concerned, irrelevant to the needs and workings of cities, irrelevant to the rest of our economic system, and even irrelevant to the meaning of home as it has evolved otherwise in our tradition.

The best that can be said of the conception is that it did afford a chance to experiment with some physical and social planning theories which did not pan out.

The problem of how to administer subsidies for people unable to carry their own dwelling costs is fundamentally the problem of how to make up the difference between what they can pay and what their shelter costs. The shelter can be provided by private owners and landlords, and the difference made up to the owners—either directly to them in the form of subsidy payments, or indirectly in the form of rent supplements to the tenants themselves. There is no end of tactics by which the subsidy can be injected—in old buildings, new buildings, rehabilitated buildings.

I shall suggest one method here—not because it is the only reasonable method by any means, but because it is a method capable of helping to solve some of the most currently difficult problems of city improvement. In particular, it is a means of introducing new construction gradually instead of cataclysmically, of introducing new construction as an ingredient of neighborhood diversity instead of as a form of standardization, of getting new private construction into blacklisted districts, and of helping to unslum slums more rapidly. It can do its share toward helping to solve other problems too, as we shall see, along with its basic usefulness as shelter.

This method I am proposing can be called the guaranteed-rent method. The physical units involved would be buildings, not projects—buildings to go among other buildings, old and new, on city streets. These guaranteed-rent buildings would be of different kinds and sizes, depending on their kind of neighborhood, the size of the plot, and all such considerations as normally influence the size and type of more or less average dwellings.

To induce private owners to erect these buildings in neighborhoods where they are needed to replace worn-out buildings or to augment the supply of dwellings, the government agency involved, which I shall call the Office of Dwelling Subsidies (ODS), would make two kinds of guarantees to builders.

The Death and Life of Great American Cities

First, the ODS would guarantee to the builder that he would get the financing necessary for construction. If the builder could get a loan from a conventional lending institution, the ODS would guarantee the mortgage. If he could not get such a loan, however, the ODS would itself lend the money—a backstop facility necessary because of the existence of concerted credit blacklisting of city localities by conventional lenders, and necessary only to the extent that loans from conventional sources, at reasonably low interest rates for guaranteed mortgages, were unobtainable for the program.

Second, the ODS would guarantee to these builders (or to the owners to whom the buildings might subsequently be sold) a rent for the dwellings in the building sufficient to carry them economically.

In return for making financing available, and for guaranteeing the building an assured rental income for all occupied apartments, the ODS would require that the owner (a) build his building in a designated neighborhood and sometimes in a designated spot there, and (b) in most cases, that he select his tenants from among applicants within a designated area or designated group of buildings. This would usually be from an area close by, but in some cases might not be. We shall see soon why such conditions are useful, but first it is necessary to mention the third, and last, function of the subsidizing agency, the ODS.

After the landlord had selected his tenants from among the applicants, the ODS would then look into the incomes of the tenants selected. It would not be empowered to examine any other facts about them, other than their incomes and the fact that they had come from the area or buildings designated. We possess bodies of law and agencies of action on all relevant associated matters, such as landlord-tenant obligations, police powers, social welfare, and the ODS should assume no such functions for itself. This is no vague, futile and humiliating transaction in all-purpose uplift of the human soul. It is a dignified, businesslike transaction in shelter rental, no more, no less.

Those tenants who could not pay an economic rent (their full share of costs) would, at least in the beginning of such a program, be most or all of the tenants applying. The ODS would make up the difference. These examinations of income, taking the size of the household into consideration, would be on an annual basis, similar to income tax declaration. This is a concept already used in public housing (where it is combined with too much gratuitous snooping and talebearing about other matters entirely), and it is a concept we use, quite well, for many other purposes. For instance, colleges and universities use this technique in allocating scholarship funds granted on the basis of need.

If a household's income improved, its proportion of the rent would go up, and the proportion provided by the subsidy would go down. If and when a household reached the point of paying a full economic rent, it would thereafter—for as long as this was true—be no concern of the ODS. Such a household or individual could stay on in the dwelling forever, paying the economic rent.

The more successfully such guaranteed-rent buildings were able to hold tenants as their financial condition improved, the more rent subsidy would be available for more buildings, and for other households. The degree to which the program encouraged stability and accompanying self-diversification among people would be directly tied to the degree and speed with which the construction program could expand on a given amount of rent subsidy. It would have to be responsive to the needs of people who develop choice, and to the principles of building magnetic, safe, interesting neighborhoods in which people stay by choice. Insofar as it might fail in these respects, its own failure would automatically hamper its expansion. Expansion would represent no threat to private builders and landlords (as the expansion of public housing does), because private builders and landlords would be the direct proprietors of the expansion. Nor need it represent any threat to private lending institutions, for the functions of these institutions would be supplanted only insofar as they themselves did not wish to participate in the capital cost financing.

The guarantee of annual economic rent to the owner would extend over the amortization period for the mortgage. This might vary between thirty and fifty years, and such variation would be desirable because it would be one of the factors encouraging different types of buildings, and also because it would introduce variability in the age at which the rent-guaranteed building could be torn down or converted to quite different uses. To be sure, as time wore on, simply the gradual continuity of new building in a district, by this means and by other means, would bring an eventual variation in the time at which the buildings' lives, or original uses, could terminate if necessary.

A definition of economic rent would include fixed amortization and debt service costs, maintenance and running expenses which would have to be adjusted to meet changes in purchasing power (a common condition taken into account for many otherwise fixed rental or carrying charge costs), a profit or profit-and-management figure, and real estate taxes, a point to which I shall return later in this chapter.

The owner could be required to put into the building an equity slightly below that currently required for FHA guaranteed loans to suburban development, to help begin redressing the balance which has been draining cities of building money.

In the end, most of the subsidy involved in guaranteed-rent dwellings would be subsidy to pay for capital costs of building—just as this is the use of the subsidy in public housing. However, tactically, the process would be the opposite from the method used in public housing.

In public housing, the capital costs of building are directly borne by government. The local housing authorities issue long-term bonds to cover construction costs. Federal grants (in some cases, state grants) cover these bond payments. The rents of the low-income tenants pay only for local administrative costs, running expenses and maintenance—all of which, incidentally, are very high in public housing. Public housing tenants buy, with their rent money, more mimeograph paper, more conference time, and more combaters of vandalism than any renters since the world began. In public housing, rents are subsidized by the device of subsidizing capital costs directly, and removing them from the equation.

Under the guaranteed-rent system, the capital costs would be kept in the rent equation. The amortization of capital would be included in the rent, and insofar as it was necessary to subsidize rents, capital cost would be subsidized automatically. Either way, directly or through rents, capital costs have to be paid. The advantage of subsidizing them through rent subsidy is this: The capital subsidy becomes much more flexible in its application to tenants. It need not in the least be used to sort out people of this income and that income, as must be done when the capital subsidy is a fixed factor, built rigidly into the fact of tenancy itself.

Another fixed factor which segregates people by income today in subsidized construction could be eliminated under a system of guaranteed-rent construction. This is the matter of real estate tax abatement or tax elimination. Under public ownership, most low-income projects pay no real estate taxes. Many middle-income projects are given tax abatements or tax postponements to help bring down their rents or, in the case of cooperatives, their carrying charges. These are all forms of subsidy, and they require concomitant income limitations on tenants— at the very least, at their time of entry—so that those who are best able to pay real estate taxes as a part of their shelter costs will not be getting too blatant a free ride on other taxpayers.

Under a guaranteed-rent system, real estate taxes could and should be included in the rent; as in the case of capital costs, the degree to which these were subsidized for a household or individual would not be a rigid, built-in factor of the building, but would vary depending on the tenants' own (varying) abilities to carry their share of rental costs.

Since rent subsidies would have to come from federal grants, as almost all public housing subsidies do today, this would make the federal government, in effect, an indirect but substantial contributor to municipal real estate tax funds derived from dwellings. But again, the difference is mainly one of tactics in the use of subsidies. At present, federal housing subsidies are buying, directly and indirectly, many facilities and operations which are in essence normal city running expenses, warped into abnormal forms to fit the physical and financial formulas demanded by the project conception. For instance, federal grants pay for capital costs of project Turfs and public meeting rooms, game rooms, clinic spaces, and the like; indirectly—by picking up so much of the total tab—they pay for housing authority police and housing authority social and community workers. If the subsidy excluded such expenses—because they would no longer be relevant to the product—but included real estate tax, this could help pay for some of the things cities need desperately, such as well-placed neighborhood *public* parks instead of hostile project Turfs, police instead of authority police, building violation inspectors instead of authority maintenance checkers.

Aside from some requirements as to numbers of rooms in dwelling units (so that too many dwellings would not end up the same size), the ODS should have no responsibility or power to enforce its own standards of design or of construction. The physical standards and regulations applying should be those embodied in a city's own codes and body of regulations, and should therefore be the same for guaranteed-rent dwellings as they would be for any unsubsidized building at the same place. If it is public policy to improve or to change dwelling standards for safety, sanitation, amenity or street design, then this public policy must be expressed for the public—not for an arbitrarily selected, guinea-pig part of the public.

If the owner of a guaranteed-rent building wished to include commerce or other nonresidential use on the ground or basement floors, or both, the pro-rated costs of this space would simply not be included in the rent guarantee or financing guarantee. Both his costs and his income from this show of salutary enterprise would be over and above his arrangements with the ODS.

Since this kind of subsidized construction would not entail large-scale assembly and clearance, plots of land for guaranteed-rent dwellings would, in most cases, hardly require use of the power of eminent domain. Sales of plots within neighborhoods designated as eligible could normally be made as they generally are in private building operations, based on who is willing to sell at what price. To be sure, the cost of the plot would have to be absorbed, but let us remember that with such a system as this we are eliminating the necessity for the large-scale land clearance costs we now find it necessary to subsidize.

In cases where powers of eminent domain were used, the purchase price should include the realistic, full costs—such as value of unexpired business leases, or full and realistic moving and relocation costs for business, as is done in the case of private sales where business tenants are hardly expected to ante up a self-destroying involuntary subsidy toward someone else's plan.*

* This policy is already sometimes applied to purchases under eminent domain, when cities are aware that injustice to victims of their plans will result in bad political trouble for their plans. Thus New York City, in buying land upstate to be flooded for water supply operations, has obtained state enabling legislation to permit it to pay fair and full costs to dislocated businesses, even including purchase of business goodwill.

The purpose of paying, rather than exacting unjust involuntary subsidies, would be to avoid killing off city diversity gratuitously. To have to pay would, on the one hand, make it realistically possible for dislocated enterprises to relocate and continue to live (preferably within the neighborhood) and would, on the other hand, enforce automatic selectivity of what was destroyed. This kind of selectivity—allowing that which is worth more to remain—is utterly missing from current city rebuilding tactics, and is one reason why these are so fantastically wasteful of city economic assets. The point behind guaranteed-rent dwellings would be to build further on whatever success, or potentiality for success, already exists.

Again, because the method would entail no necessity for large-scale clearance and rebuilding, the program could include great numbers of builders and owners, thousands of them. It is ridiculous to consider that our great cities—various, vital, ever changing—should depend for rebuilding on a handful of authorities and huge builder barons. Owners of multiple-dwelling guaranteed-rent buildings should, if they wished, be able themselves to live in the buildings—just as if they were tenants—and this would be salutary, as on-the-spot ownership so often is. It should by no means be a requirement, but it could be encouraged by encouraging such participation in the building program or, more realistically, by not preventing sale by builders to such owners.

If we possessed such a tactic as guaranteed-rent construction, how might we use it?

Previously, I mentioned two conditions which it would be necessary to require of owners, in return for the guarantees given them: The buildings must go within designated neighborhoods and sometimes in a designated spot; and in most cases it would be required that tenants be selected from among applicants currently living within some area, or along some street, or in some group of buildings designated.

With these two simple conditions on builders, it would be possible to accomplish deliberately several different things, depending on the specific problems of a specific place.

It would be possible, for instance, to stimulate new construction in currently blacklisted localities where the lack becomes crucial, and to do it by helping to retain, at the same time, people already within the neighborhood.

It would be possible deliberately to increase net numbers of dwelling units in neighborhoods where this is needed, and to combine this increase with simultaneous uncrowding of nearby older buildings (the legal occupancy rates of which could become, at last, practical to enforce).

It would be possible to retain in a neighborhood people whose present dwelling must be demolished, either to make way for another use or because they are worn out.

It would be possible to introduce, or to increase to effective proportions, residence as an ingredient of primary use—where that primary use is needed as a supplement to other primary ingredients of the city mixture, such as work.

It would be possible to help fill in gaps that occur in new frontages created where new streets are cut through blocks that were previously too long.

It would be possible to add to an area's basic stock of diversity in building ages and types.

It would be possible to bring down densities of dwelling units in those exceptional areas where dwelling densities are too high, and it could do this sufficiently gradually to avoid cataclysmic mass upheavals of population.

And it would be possible to do these things while mixing income levels and encouraging the mixture to increase with time.

These are all means for abetting stability of population and diversity of population—some of them directly, by helping to make it possible for people who want to stay put in a neighborhood to stay put; and some of them indirectly (insofar as *one* portion of *one* of the many different uses in a city can do its share), by helping to create lively, safe, interesting, varied streets and districts in which people will stay put by choice.

Furthermore, because such a program would introduce into any one place gradual money and gradual change, it would not prevent concurrent or subsequent entrance into the neighborhood of people with choice, or of unsubsidized building. (Let us hope that this would be halted short of the self-destruction of diversity.) Nor would it prevent entrance into the neighborhood of other newcomers, including those whose only choice is expediency. For there would be in a neighborhood, at any one time, many other buildings which were not deliberately being used for relocation stability, and to which geographical origin of tenants would therefore not apply.

No matter how old the buildings in a locality, no matter how great the necessity for eventual replacement of all or nearly all, this process should not occur in one swoop.*

Too rapid replacement, besides militating economically against city diversity, and bringing on the standardized, denatured effect of project building, would also work at cross-purposes to the aim of holding as many people as possible by choice over time—people in old buildings as well as new, and people with ideas of their own about building or rehabilitation.

There is, of course, much opportunity for corruption or chiseling in a system of rent guarantees and guaranteed financing for new building. Corruption, chiseling and finagling we can hold down reasonably well, when we choose to. (Think how lucky we are to live in a country where we can do so.) More difficult to combat is stultification.

We may be sure that any specific tactics for subsidizing dwellings arc almost certain to get more and more routine, with more rigid results, diverging steadily, as time goes on, from the needs of the real world. Any imagination comes in at the beginning, and is inexorably whittled down from then on. Corruption, on the other hand—either corruption for the sake of money or corruption for the sake of power—has a different nature from that of strait-laced

*A word here about rats. This is one of the elementary evils that new housing is supposed to eliminate and the presence of old housing to perpetuate. But rats do not know that. Unless they are exterminated, when old rat-infested buildings are torn down, the rats simply move into the next inhabited area. One of the severe problems in the Lower East Side of New York, as this is written, is the influx of rats and other vermin from the demolished buildings on the site of a huge new cooperative project, Seward Houses. When a large part of the downtown of St. Louis

bureaucracy. Corruption grows more inventive, rather than less so, the longer it has an object to play with.

To combat both stultification and corruption, we ought, every eight or ten years at least, to try out new methods of subsidizing dwellings or add variations to old ones that are working well enough for us to retain. We ought even to call into being entirely new agencies for these new jobs, from time to time, and let old ones fade away. In any case, it is always necessary to check tactics against the specific needs that become evident in specific places. We should always be asking, "Does this device do the job needed *here*? And if not, what would?" Deliberate, periodic changes in tactics of subsidy would afford opportunity to meet new needs that become apparent over time, but that nobody can foresee in advance. This observation is, obliquely, a warning against the limitations of my own prescriptions in this book. I think they make sense for things as they are, which is the only place

---

was demolished,the displaced rats invaded buildings over many square miles. If extermination is not practiced in new buildings, the progeny of the rats come right back there too. Most cities have legal requirements that rats be exterminated in any building demolished; in New York, the going rate in 1960 for a lying certificate of extermination, paid by corrupt owners to corrupt exterminators, is $5. How public agencies, like the Housing Authority, evade the law I do not know, but to know that they do evade it one need only go look at the fearful rat festivals and exoduses at twilight from their sites in process of demolition. New buildings do not get rid of rats. Only people get rid of rats. This can be done in old buildings about as easily as in new ones. Our building was overrun with rats—big ones—when we got it. It costs $48 a year to keep it thoroughly rid of them and all other vermin. A live man does it. The notion that buildings get rid of rats is worse than a delusion because it becomes an excuse for not exterminating rats. ("We are soon going to get rid of these rat-infested buildings.") We expect too much of new buildings, and too little of ourselves.

ever possible to begin. But that does not mean that they would make the best sense, or even good sense, after our cities had undergone substantial improvement and great increase in vitality. Nor may they make sense if the current mishandling of our cities continues, and we lose constructive forms of behavior and forces on which we can still depend and still build.

Many variations are possible, even today, among methods of subsidy, so long as these are based on flexible and gradual change instead of cataclysms. James Rouse, a Baltimore mortgage banker and a civic leader in various city renewal and rebuilding efforts, has suggested, for example, a variation leading to eventual ownership by tenants—an idea most reasonable for places where row housing is a predominant dwelling type:

> Public housing is not properly an end in itself. It can only be justified as a means to an end of making our cities fit places in which to live. What kind of public housing should it be? . . . The tenant's rent should be increased with his increase in income and he should not be evicted as an over-income tenant. When his increasing rent reaches the point at which it will cover debt service, on liberal mortgage terms, then the property should be deeded to him at its book value and his rent converted into a mortgage payment. Such a program would move not only the individual but also his home back into the free market stream. This would block off the formation of public housing ghettos and it would curtail the empire protection complex which now surrounds the program . . .

Charles Platt, a New York architect, has long advocated the use of subsidized new dwellings in combination with older nearby buildings as a tool of uncrowding and thereby of two improvements in one. William Wheaton, professor of city planning at the University of Pennsylvania, has made eloquent pleas for the concept of a revolving supply of public housing, and for its indistinguishability from the variety of private housing in a community. Vernon De Mars, California architect, has proposed a system of privately built and owned housing, much like that I have called the guaranteed-rent system, for which anyone would be eligible and to which government housing agencies could also send subsidized tenants.

Stanley Tankel, a planner for the Regional Plan Association in New York, has asked:

> Why is it just occurring to us to see if the slums themselves have some of the ingredients of a good housing policy? We are discovering suddenly . . . that slum families don't necessarily move when their incomes go up; that independence in slums is not stifled by paternalistic management policy; and finally (incredible!) that slum people, like other people, don't like being booted out of their neighborhoods . . . The next step will require great humility, since we are now so prone to confuse big building projects with big social achievements. We will have to admit that it is beyond the scope of anyone's imagination to create a community. We must learn to cherish the communities we have; they are hard to come by. "Fix the buildings but leave the people." "No relocation outside the neigh-

borhood."—These must be the slogans if public
housing is to be popular.

Virtually all observers of public housing have, sooner or
later, inveighed against the destructiveness of tenant
income limitations and have advocated their abandonment.* The proposal of guaranteed-rent dwellings which
I have suggested contains no original ideas of my own; I
have simply combined into one related system ideas put
forward by many others.

Why have such ideas not already been incorporated
into the concept of public housing?

The answer is already given within the question.

The ideas are not used precisely because they are generally conceived and proposed as modifications to be
incorporated either into the project conception itself, or else
into the conception of public ownership of subsidized
housing. Both these basic ideas of public housing are
hopelessly unfit for good city building in our society. The
tactics shaped to achieve them—slum immuring, slum
shifting, income sorting, standardization—are bad in
human terms and bad in terms of city economic needs,
but they are good and logical tactics for project building
or for bureaucratic ownership and management. Indeed,
any other tactics for these ends are so illogical and forced,
that attempts to *incorporate* them peter out before the ink
is dry on the public relations releases.

We need new tactics for subsidizing dwellings, but

---

*Many of these ideas, and others, turned up in a symposium, "The
Dreary Deadlock of Public Housing," published by *Architectural Forum*
in June 1957.

hardly because the existing tactics need fiddling and diddling with. We need them because we require different
aims of city building, and new strategy for overcoming
slums and for retaining diversity of population, too, in
places that are no longer slums. The different aims and
the new strategy need their own appropriate and entirely
different tactics.

18

EROSION OF CITIES OR
ATTRITION OF AUTOMOBILES

Today everyone who values cities is disturbed by automobiles.

Traffic arteries, along with parking lots, gas stations
and drive-ins, are powerful and insistent instruments of
city destruction. To accommodate them, city streets are
broken down into loose sprawls, incoherent and vacuous
for anyone afoot. Downtowns and other neighborhoods
that are marvels of close-grained intricacy and compact
mutual support are casually disemboweled. Landmarks
are crumbled or are so sundered from their contexts in
city life as to become irrelevant trivialities. City character
is blurred until every place becomes more like every other
place, all adding up to Noplace. And in the areas most
defeated, uses that cannot stand functionally alone—
shopping malls, or residences, or places of public assembly, or centers of work—are severed from one another.

But we blame automobiles for too much.

Suppose automobiles had never been invented, or
that they had been neglected and we traveled instead in
efficient, convenient, speedy, comfortable, mechanized
mass transit. Undoubtedly we would save immense
sums which might be put to better use. But they might
not.

For suppose we had also been rebuilding, expanding

and reorganizing cities according to the project image and the other anti-city ideals of conventional planning.

We would have essentially the same results as I blamed on automobiles a few paragraphs back. These results can be repeated word for word: The city streets would be broken down into loose sprawls, incoherent and vacuous for anyone afoot. Downtowns and other neighborhoods that are marvels of close-grained intricacy and compact mutual support would be casually disemboweled. Landmarks would be crumbled or so sundered from their contexts in city life as to become irrelevant trivialities. City character would be blurred until every place became more like every other place, all adding up to Noplace. And in the areas most defeated, etc.

And then the automobile would have to be invented or would have to be rescued from neglect. For people to live or work in such inconvenient cities, automobiles would be necessary to spare them from vacuity, danger and utter institutionalization.

It is questionable how much of the destruction wrought by automobiles on cities is really a response to transportation and traffic needs, and how much of it is owing to sheer disrespect for other city needs, uses and functions. Like city rebuilders who face a blank when they try to think of what to do instead of renewal projects, because they know of no other respectable principles for city organization, just so, highwaymen, traffic engineers and city rebuilders, again, face a blank when they try to think what they can realistically do, day by day, except try to overcome traffic kinks as they occur and apply what foresight they can toward moving and storing more cars in the future. It is impossible for responsible and practi-

cal men to discard unfit tactics—even when the results of
their own work cause them misgivings—if the alternative
is to be left with confusion as to what to try instead and
why.

Good transportation and communication are not only
among the most difficult things to achieve; they are also
basic necessities. The point of cities is multiplicity of
choice. It is impossible to take advantage of multiplicity of
choice without being able to get around easily. Nor will
multiplicity of choice even exist if it cannot be stimulated
by cross-use. Furthermore, the economic foundation of
cities is trade. Even manufacturing occurs in cities mainly
because of attached advantages involving trade, not
because it is easier to manufacture things in cities. Trade
in ideas, services, skills and personnel, and certainly in
goods, demands efficient, fluid transportation and communication.

But multiplicity of choice and intensive city trading
depend also on immense concentrations of people, and on
intricate minglings of uses and complex interweaving of
paths.

How to accommodate city transportation without
destroying the related intricate and concentrated land
use?—this is the question. Or, going at it the other way,
how to accommodate intricate and concentrated city land
use without destroying the related transportation?

Nowadays there is a myth that city streets, so patently
inadequate for floods of automobiles, are antiquated vestiges of horse-and-buggy conditions, suitable to the traffic
of their time, but . . .

Nothing could be less true. To be sure, the streets of
eighteenth- and nineteenth-century cities were usually

well adapted, as streets, to the uses of people afoot and to the mutual support of the mingled uses bordering them. But they were miserably adapted, as streets, to horse traffic, and this in turn made them poorly adapted in many ways to foot traffic too.

Victor Gruen, who devised a plan for an automobile-free downtown for Fort Worth, Texas, about which I shall say more later in this chapter, prepared a series of slides to explain his scheme. After a view of a street with a familiar-looking automobile jam, he showed a surprise: just about as bad a jam of horses and vehicles in an old photograph of Fort Worth.

What street life was like for really big and intense cities and their users in the horse-and-buggy days has been described by an English architect, the late H. B. Creswell, who wrote for the British *Architectural Review* of December 1958 a description of London in 1890, when he was a young man:

> The Strand of those days . . . was the throbbing heart of the people's essential London. Hedged by a maze of continuous alleys and courts, the Strand was fronted by numbers of little restaurants whose windows vaunted exquisite feeding; taverns, dives, oyster and wine bars, ham and beef shops; and small shops marketing a lively variety of curious or workaday things all standing in rank, shoulder to shoulder, to fill the spaces between its many theatres . . . But the mud!* And the noise! And the smell! All these blemishes were [the] mark of [the] horse . . .

*A euphemism.

The whole of London's crowded wheeled traffic—which in parts of the City was at times dense
beyond movement—was dependent on the horse:
lorry, wagon, bus, hansom and "growler," and
coaches and carriages and private vehicles of all
kinds, were appendages to horses. Meredith refers
to the "anticipatory stench of its cab-stands" on railway approach to London: but the characteristic
aroma—for the nose recognized London with gay
excitement—was of stables, which were commonly
of three or four storeys with inclined ways zigzagging up the faces of them; [their] middens kept the
castiron filigree chandeliers, that glorified the reception rooms of upper and lower middle class homes
throughout London, encrusted with dead flies and,
in late summer, veiled with jiving clouds of them.

A more assertive mark of the horse was the
mud that, despite the activities of a numerous corps
of red-jacketed boys who dodged among wheels
and hooves with pan and brush in service to iron
bins at the pavement-edge, either flooded the streets
with churnings of "pea soup" that at times collected
in pools over-brimming the kerbs, and at others covered the road-surface as with axle grease or bran-
laden dust to the distraction of the wayfarer. In the
first case, the swift-moving hansom or gig would
fling sheets of such soup—where not intercepted by
trousers or skirts—completely across the pavement,
so that the frontages of the Strand throughout its
length had an eighteen-inch plinth of mud-parge
thus imposed upon it. The pea-soup condition was
met by wheeled "mud-carts" each attended by two
ladlers clothed as for Icelandic seas in thigh boots,
oilskins collared to the chin, and sou'westers sealing

in the back of the neck. Splash Ho! The foot passenger now gets the mud in his eye! The axle-grease
condition was met by horse-mechanized brushes
and travellers in the small hours found fire-hoses
washing away residues . . .

And after the mud the noise, which, again
endowed by the horse, surged like a mighty heart-
beat in the central districts of London's life. It was a
thing beyond all imaginings. The streets of workaday London were uniformly paved in "granite" sets
. . . and the hammering of a multitude of iron-shod
hairy heels upon [them], the deafening, side-drum
tatoo of tyred wheels jarring from the apex of one
set to the next like sticks dragging along a fence; the
creaking and groaning and chirping and rattling of
vehicles, light and heavy, thus maltreated; the jan-
gling of chain harness and the clanging or jingling of
every other conceivable thing else, augmented by
the shrieking and bellowings called for from those of
God's creatures who desired to impart information
or proffer a request vocally—raised a din that . . . is
beyond conception. It was not any such paltry thing
as noise. It was an immensity of sound . . .

This was the London of Ebenezer Howard, and it is
hardly surprising that he regarded city streets as unfit for
human beings.

Le Corbusier, when he designed his Radiant City of
the 1920's, as a park, skyscraper and automobile freeway
version of Howard's small-town Garden City, flattered
himself that he was designing for a new age and, along
with it, for a new system of traffic. He was not. So far as
the new age was concerned, he was merely adapting in a

shallow fashion reforms that had been a response to nostalgic yearnings for a bygone simpler life, and a response also to the nineteenth-century city of the horse (and the epidemic). So far as the new system of traffic was concerned, he was equally shallow. He embroidered (I think that is a fair word for his approach) freeways and traffic onto his Radiant City scheme in quantities that apparently satisfied his sense of design, but that bore no relationship whatsoever to the hugely greater quantities of automobiles, amounts of roadway and extent of parking and servicing which would actually be necessary for his repetitive vertical concentrations of people, separated by vacuities. His vision of skyscrapers in the park degenerates in real life into skyscrapers in parking lots. And there can never be enough parking.

The present relationship between cities and automobiles represents, in short, one of those jokes that history sometimes plays on progress. The interval of the automobile's development as everyday transportation has corresponded precisely with the interval during which the ideal of the suburbanized anti-city was developed architecturally, sociologically, legislatively and financially.

But automobiles are hardly inherent destroyers of cities. If we would stop telling ourselves fairy tales about the suitability and charm of nineteenth-century streets for horse-and-buggy traffic, we would see that the internal combustion engine, as it came on the scene, was potentially an excellent instrument for abetting city intensity, and at the same time for liberating cities from one of their noxious liabilities.

Not only are automotive engines quieter and cleaner than horses but, even more important, fewer engines than horses can do a given amount of work The power of mechanized vehicles, and their greater speed than horses, can make it easier to reconcile great concentrations of people with efficient movement of people and goods. At the turn of the century, railroads had already long demonstrated that iron horses are fine instruments for reconciling concentration and movement. Automobiles, including trucks, offered, for places railroads could not go, and for jobs railroads could not do, another means of cutting down the immemorial vehicular congestion of cities.

We went awry by replacing, in effect, each horse on the crowded city streets with half a dozen or so mechanized vehicles, instead of using each mechanized vehicle to replace half a dozen or so horses. The mechanical vehicles, in their overabundance, work slothfully and idle much. As one consequence of such low efficiency, the powerful and speedy vehicles, choked by their own redundancy, don't move much faster than horses.

Trucks, by and large, do accomplish much of what might have been hoped for from mechanical vehicles in cities. They do the work of much greater numbers of horse-drawn vehicles or of burden-laden men. But because passenger vehicles do not, this congestion, in turn, greatly cuts down the efficiency of the trucks.

Today, those in despair at the war between those potential allies, automobiles and cities, are apt to depict the impasse as a war between automobiles and pedestrians.

It is fashionable to suppose that the solution lies in designating certain places for pedestrians, and certain other places for vehicles. We may be able to make such separations eventually, if we find we really want to. But such schemes are only practical, in any case, if they *pre-suppose* a spectacular decline in the absolute numbers of automobiles using a city. Otherwise, the necessary parking, garaging and access arteries around the pedestrian preserves reach such unwieldy and deadening proportions that they become arrangements capable only of city disintegration, not of city saving.

The most famous of pedestrian schemes is the Gruen plan for the downtown of Fort Worth. The firm of Victor Gruen Associates, architects and planners, proposed that an area of roughly a square mile be circled with a ring road feeding into six huge, oblong garages, holding ten thousand cars each, which would each penetrate from the ring-road perimeter deep into the downtown area. The rest of the area would be kept free of automobiles and would be intensively developed as a downtown of mixed uses. The scheme has run into political opposition in Fort Worth, but imitative plans have been proposed for more than ninety cities and have been tried in a few. Unfortunately, the imitators ignore the salient fact that the scheme treated the entire part of Fort Worth which could be described as citylike in the form of one interlocked, uninterrupted whole, and in these terms it made sense; to this extent, it was an instrument of concentration rather than separation; to this extent, it fostered greater complexity rather than greater simplicity. In the imitations, the idea is almost invariably perverted into dinky and timid designs for isolating a few shopping streets in the fashion of suburban shopping malls, and surrounding them with dead borders of parking and access.

This is about all that can be done—and indeed it is all that could have been planned for Fort Worth—unless a problem much more difficult than shrub-planting and bench-installing is faced. This problem is how to cut down drastically the absolute numbers of vehicles using a city.

In the case of the Gruen plan for Fort Worth, Gruen had to presuppose such a decrease, even though the city is relatively small and simple in comparison with our great cities, and even though the arrangements for cars were enormous and elaborate. Part of Gruen's scheme included arrangements for express bus service tying the downtown into the whole city and its suburbs, and absorbing a far higher ratio of downtown users than is now served by public transportation. Without such an arrangement and such a presupposition, the ring-road scheme would have been unrealistic embroidery in the Le Corbusier tradition of wishful frivolity, or else—the difficulties faced realistically—it would have meant converting virtually the entire downtown to garages and rendering the ring road inadequate for access. To be sure, a greatly enlarged perimeter might have served, with the garages disposed far out, but then the practicality of a concentrated, intense district, readily used on foot, would have been defeated. The plan would have no point.

Some varieties of traffic separation, conceived for heavily congested downtown streets, envision not a horizontal separation as in the Gruen scheme, but a vertical separation with either the pedestrians put above the automobiles on an upper street level, or the automobiles put above the pedestrians. But removing pedestrians gives very little more room to cars. To provide roadbeds of the dimensions needed for the cars that bring in the pedestrians—which is the cause of the congestion and the reason

for the separation—means stretching the dimensions of
the corresponding pedestrian levels to the point of self-
cancellation of pedestrian convenience. These schemes
too, to be practical either for cars or for the pedestrians,
must presuppose a drastic reduction in absolute numbers
of automobiles, and much greater dependence on public
transportation instead.

And there is another difficulty behind pedestrian
schemes. Most city enterprises which are a response to
pedestrian street use, and which, reciprocally, generate
more pedestrian street use, themselves need convenient
access to vehicles for services, supplies or transport of
their own products.

If vehicular and pedestrian traffic are completely separated, one of two alternatives must be accepted.

The first alternative is that the preserves for the
pedestrians must be streets which do not contain such
enterprises. This is automatically an absurdity. These
absurdities can be found, in real life, and just as might be
expected, the preserves are empty. The pedestrians are in
the vehicular streets, where the enterprises are. This type
of built-in contradiction afflicts much grandiose "city of
tomorrow" planning.

The other alternative is that it is necessary to devise
schemes of vehicular servicing, separated from the pedestrian preserves.

Gruen's scheme for Fort Worth handled the servicing
problem with a system of underground tunnels for trucks
and for taxi service to hotels, with access through base-
ment-level loading.

As a variant, the scheme also proposed a highly developed system of "post officing," a method also worked out

many years ago by Simon Breines, a New York architect, in a proposal for a pedestrian midtown New York. "Post officing" means a system of central sorting for all freight and other deliveries within a zone. The sorted materials of *all* kinds from *all* sources to each destination are then combined and their distribution rationalized, much as incoming mail is sorted at a post office and distributed. In this case, the point is to cut down numbers of truck deliveries drastically; the reduced numbers of deliveries (and dispatches) can then be made when few pedestrians are around, preferably at night. The car-pedestrian separation, so far as trucking is concerned, thus becomes principally a separation in time, rather than in space. It involves considerable expense, because it involves an extra step of materials handling.

Except in the most intensively used central downtown areas, it hardly seems that the service complications accompanying thoroughgoing separation of pedestrians and vehicles are justified.

I am doubtful as to whether the advantages of thoroughgoing separation are, in any case, very great. The conflicts between pedestrians and vehicles on city streets arise mainly from overwhelming numbers of vehicles, to which all but the most minimum pedestrian needs are gradually and steadily sacrificed. The problem of vehicular dominance, beyond toleration, is not exclusively a problem involving automobiles. Obviously, excessive numbers of horses produced similar conflicts; people who have experienced an Amsterdam or New Delhi rush hour report that bicycles in massive numbers become an appalling mixture with pedestrians.

Where opportunity affords, I have been watching

how people use pedestrian streets. They do not sally out in the middle and glory in being kings of the road at last. They stay to the sides. In Boston, which has experimented with closing two of its downtown shopping streets (the deliveries were the knotty problem, of course), it was quite a sight to see the almost empty roadbeds and the very crowded, very narrow sidewalks. On the other side of the continent, the same phenomenon occurs in the model Main Street of Disneyland. The only vehicles on the Disneyland town's roadbed are a trolley which comes by at rather long intervals, for kicks, and once in a while a horse and buggy. Nevertheless, visitors there use the sidewalks in preference to walking down the middle of the street; the only times I saw them choose the street instead were, perversely, when one of the vehicles or a parade went by. Then they went out to *join* what was in the street.

A certain amount of such inhibition in Boston or in Disneyland may be caused by the fact that we have all been so conditioned to respect the curbs. Paving which merged roadbed and sidewalk would probably induce more pedestrian use of roadbed space; certainly, where sidewalks are wide (even in Boston) people do not bunch themselves up to the laughable degree that they do in Disneyland or on the narrow downtown Boston sidewalks.

However, that is apparently only part of the answer. In suburban shopping centers where "streets" are wide but thoroughly pedestrian and without curbs, people stay to the sides also except where something interesting to see has been deliberately placed out in the "street." It takes tremendous numbers of pedestrians to populate the whole width of a roadbed, even in scatterings. The only times pedestrians seem to use, or want to use, a street roadbed in this fashion are in cases of extraordinary floods of pedestrians, as in the Wall Street district or the Boston financial area when the offices let out, or during the Easter parade on Fifth Avenue. In more ordinary circumstances, people are attracted to the sides, I think, because that is where it is most interesting. As they walk, they occupy themselves with seeing—seeing in windows, seeing buildings, seeing each other.

In one respect, however, people on the pedestrian streets of Boston, of Disneyland, or of shopping centers do behave differently from people on ordinary city streets heavily used by vehicles. The exception is significant. People cross over from one side to the other freely, and in using this freedom they do not seem to be inhibited by the curbs. These observations, coupled with the way people are forever sneaking across streets at forbidden places if they can get away with it—even at risk to their lives— and coupled with the palpable impatience people so often exhibit at crossings, lead me to believe that the main virtue of pedestrian streets is not that they completely lack cars, but rather that they are not overwhelmed and dominated by floods of cars, and that they are easy to cross.

Even for children the point may be less to segregate the cars than to reduce the domination by cars and combat the erosion of sidewalk play space by cars. It would, of course, be ideal to dispose of cars entirely on city streets where children play; but worse troubles still are harvested if this means disposing of the other utilitarian purposes of sidewalks, and along with them, supervision. Sometimes such schemes, too, are automatically self-canceling. A housing project in Cincinnati affords an illustration. The houses in this project front on pedestrian precincts of lawns and sidewalks, and they back up on service alleys for cars and deliveries. All the casual coming and going occurs between the houses and the alleys and therefore, functionally, the backs of the houses have become the fronts and vice versa. Of course the alleys are where the children all are too.

Life attracts life. Where pedestrian separation is undertaken as some sort of abstract nicety and too many forms of life and activity go unaccommodated or are suppressed to make the nicety work, the arrangement goes unappreciated.

To think of city traffic problems in oversimplified terms of pedestrians versus cars, and to fix on the segregation of each as a principal goal, is to go at the problem from the wrong end. Consideration for pedestrians in cities is inseparable from consideration for city diversity, vitality and concentration of use. In the absence of city diversity, people in large settlements are probably better off in cars than on foot. Unmanageable city vacuums are by no means preferable to unmanageable city traffic.

The problem that lies behind consideration for pedestrians, as it lies behind all other city traffic difficulties, is how to cut down absolute numbers of surface vehicles and enable those that remain to work harder and more efficiently. Too much dependence on private automobiles and city concentration of use are incompatible. One or the other has to give. In real life, this is what happens. Depending on which pressure wins most of the victories, one of two processes occurs: erosion of cities by automobiles, or attrition of automobiles by cities.

To understand the pros and cons of any city traffic tactics, we have to understand the nature of these two processes, and their implications. We also have to be aware that surface traffic in cities exerts pressures upon *itself*. Vehicles compete with each other for space and for convenience of their arrangements. They also compete with other uses for space and convenience.

Erosion of cities by automobiles entails so familiar a series of events that these hardly need describing. The erosion proceeds as a kind of nibbling, small nibbles at first, but eventually hefty bites. Because of vehicular congestion, a street is widened here, another is straightened there, a wide avenue is converted to one-way flow, staggered-signal systems are installed for faster movement, a bridge is double-decked as its capacity is reached, an expressway is cut through yonder, and finally whole webs of expressways. More and more land goes into parking, to accommodate the ever increasing numbers of vehicles while they are idle.

No one step in this process is, in itself, crucial. But cumulatively the effect is enormous. And each step, while not crucial in itself, is crucial in the sense that it not only adds its own bit to the total change, but actually accelerates the process. Erosion of cities by automobiles is thus an example of what is known as "positive feedback." In cases of positive feedback, an action produces a reaction which in turn intensifies the condition responsible for the first action. This intensifies the need for repeating the first action, which in turn intensifies the reaction, and so on, ad infinitum. It is something like the grip of a habit-forming addiction.

A striking statement of the positive feedback traffic

process—or part of it—was worked out by Victor Gruen in 1955, in connection with his Fort Worth plan. Gruen, in order to understand the size of problem he had in hand, began by calculating the potential business that Fort Worth's currently underdeveloped and stagnating— but traffic-jammed—downtown ought to be doing by 1970, based on its projected population and trading area. He then translated this quantity of economic activity into numbers of users, including workers, shoppers and visitors for other purposes. Then, using the ratio of vehicles per downtown users current in Fort Worth, he translated the putative future users into numbers of vehicles. He then calculated how much street space would be required to accommodate the numbers of these vehicles apt to be on the streets at any one time.

He got an outlandish figure of roadbed needed: sixteen million square feet, not including parking. This is in comparison with the five million square feet of roadbed the underdeveloped downtown now possesses.

But the instant Gruen had calculated his sixteen million square feet, the figure was already out of date and much too small. To obtain that much roadbed space, the downtown would have to spread out physically to an enormous extent. A given quantity of economic uses would thereby be spread relatively thin. To use its different elements, people would have to depend much less on walking and much more on driving. This would further increase the need for still more street space, or else there would be a terrible mess of congestion. Differing uses, necessarily strung out in such relatively loose fashion, would be so far from one another that it would become necessary to duplicate parking spaces themselves, because uses bringing people at different hours would not be sufficiently compact for much staggered use of the same accommodations.* This would mean spreading the downtown even thinner, in turn requiring still more use of cars, traveling greater absolute distances internally. Very early in the process, public transportation would be thoroughly inefficient, from both the customer's and the operator's point of view. In short, there would be no coherent downtown, but a great, thin smear, incapable of generating the metropolitan facilities, diversity and choices theoretically possible for the population and economy concerned.

As Gruen pointed out here, the more space that is provided cars in cities, the greater becomes the need for use of cars, and hence for still more space for them.

In real life, we do not suddenly jump five million square feet of city roadbed to sixteen million square feet, and so the implications of accommodating a few more cars and a few more cars and a few more cars are a little harder to see. But swiftly or slowly, the positive feedback is at work. Swiftly or slowly, greater accessibility by car is inexorably accompanied both by less convenience and efficiency of public transportation, and by thinning-down and smearing-out of uses, and hence by more need for cars.

---

*This type of waste already occurs frequently in downtowns where dribbled use is deliberately planned. Thus Pittsburgh's new civic center, dribbled and buffered off at the edge of downtown, must provide, for evening use, parking accommodations that are duplicated in the working part of downtown and go empty in the evenings. Joint support of any type of city facility, including parking and pavement as surely as parks and stores, requires great compactness.

The paradox of increasing car accessibility and decreasing intensity of users can be seen at its extreme in Los Angeles, and to almost as great a degree in Detroit. But the combination is just as inexorable in cities at an earlier stage of the erosion process, where only a small minority of users are accommodated by the increase in surface traffic flow. Manhattan is a case in point. One method adopted there to palliate vehicular congestion is to speed traffic by making the wide north-south avenues one-way. Buses, instead of running both ways on an avenue, must, of course, like the other vehicles, run north on one avenue, south on another. This can, and often does, mean two long blocks of otherwise unnecessary walking by bus users, in the course of reaching a given destination.

Not surprisingly, when an avenue is made one-way in New York, a drop in bus patronage follows. Where do these former bus riders go? Nobody knows, but the bus company's theory is that this fraction of its riders represents persons on a borderline of choice. Some, the company officials think, are on a borderline of choice as to whether to use buses or to use individual vehicles; others, who have come into the district from outside, are on a borderline of choice as to whether to make the effort to use the district, and there may be other choices, such as not making the internal trip. Whatever their choices, convenience differentials have shifted sufficiently for these people to change their minds. What is indisputable is that the increased traffic flow, with its by-the-way depressing effect on public transportation, does bring into play an increase in numbers of vehicles. It also cuts down pedestrian convenience by forcing longer waits than formerly at crossings on the affected avenues.

With one palliative and another, Manhattan enabled, during the eight-year period 1948-56, 36 percent more vehicles to enter it daily from outside, although this still represents a small fraction of Manhattan's users from outside, 83 percent of whom arrive by public transportation. During this same interval there was a 12-percent decline in public transportation passengers from outside, leaving a "deficit" of about 375,000 human users a day from outside. Increased city accessibility by cars is *always* accompanied by declines in service of public transportation. The declines in transit passengers are always greater than increases in private automobile passengers. With greater accessibility to a district by cars, total cross-use of the district by people thus invariably declines, and this is a serious matter for cities, where one of the great jobs of transportation is to permit and encourage cross-use.

Results like this—increased accessibility, decreased intensity—stir panic in certain breasts. To counter the drop in intensity of use, the standard remedy is to try to increase further the accessibility by cars—usually, first, by making parking easier for them. Thus, taking another Manhattan example, one of the remedies fervently advocated by the traffic commissioner, as a palliative for department stores, is a series of city-owned parking garages. This palliative would erode some ten blocks or so of midtown Manhattan land, including many hundreds of small businesses.*

Thus does erosion, little by little, subtract reasons for

---

* At one of the garage sites the traffic commissioner advocates—very "logically" located between a department store and the foot of a bridge—I counted 129 businesses, including several unique spice shops to which customers come from all over the metropolitan area, a couple

using an eroded district, and at the same time make it less
lively, less convenient, less compact, less safe, for those
who continue to have reason to use it. The more concentrated and genuinely urban an area, the greater the contrast between the smallness of what is delivered and the
significance of what is lost by the process of erosion.

If vehicular traffic in cities represented some fixed
quantity of need, then the action of providing for it would
produce a satisfying and fulfilling reaction. Something,
at least, would be solved. But because the need for more
vehicles grows with the palliatives, the solution keeps
receding.

Even so, there should be at least a theoretical point of
solution—a point when increasing accessibility and
decreasing intensity of use reach a state of equilibrium or
balance. At this point, the traffic problem should be
solved in the sense that there would be no more pressure
from vehicles unsatisfied for movement and storage
room. With progressive erosion, traffic pressures upon
the various parts of a city should be gradually equalized,
and then the continued sprawl should satisfy these equalized pressures. When a city has become a sufficiently

---

of art galleries, some dog beauty parlors, a couple of very good restaurants, a church, and a great many residences, including several recently
rehabilitated old houses. The businesses include those which would be
taken, and those facing, on the opposite sides of the streets, for these
make a unit; the businesses left, facing a huge deadening garage, would
be amputated from their constellation of mutual support, and deadened
too. To its credit, the City Planning Commission is opposing the traffic
commissioner's garage scheme, as this is written, and is opposing it for
the right reasons: on the grounds that encouragement to more vehicles
will be destructive to other values.

homogeneous and thin smear, it should have the traffic problem, at any rate, in hand. Such a state of equilibrium is the only possible solution to a positive feedback process like city erosion.

This point of equilibrium has not yet been approached in any American city. Our real-life examples of big cities subjected to erosion illustrate, as yet, only the stage of ever growing pressure. It would seem that Los Angeles ought to be approaching the point of equilibrium because 95 percent of travel within Los Angeles is now done by private automobile. Yet, even so, the pressures have not been sufficiently equalized, for into Los Angeles' eroded and drab downtown 66 percent of users still come by public transportation. When a strike of transit workers in 1960 brought out more cars in Los Angeles than usual, air photos showed freeways and surface roads alike jammed at crawling bumper-to-bumper capacity, and news reports told of fist fights between harried drivers competing for insufficient parking places. Los Angeles' transit system, once considered the best in the United States (some experts say in the world), has declined to a slow and inconvenient vestige of public transportation, but it obviously still has a reservoir of users for whom there is no room on the highways and parking lots. Moreover, the parking pressure generally is still on the increase there. A few years ago, two parking places per apartment were considered ample for those moving back into the "city." Today the new apartment houses are providing three parking places per apartment, one for the husband, one for the wife, and an average of one per apartment for other household members or visitors. No fewer will do in a city where it is hard to buy a pack of cigarets without an automobile; and when someone gives a party even an average allotment of three parking spaces per apartment becomes a squeeze. Nor has the pressure been lifted yet for cars in motion under normal, everyday conditions. As Harrison Salisbury has written in the *New York Times:*

> Time and again, Los Angeles freeway movement is impeded by accidents. So chronic is the problem that the engineers propose to remove stalled cars from the highways by helicopter. The truth is that a horse and buggy could cross Los Angeles almost as fast in 1900 as an automobile can make this trip at 5 P.M. today.

The point of equilibrium, wherever it may lie, lies beyond the point where problems even more serious than traffic bottlenecks are generated. It lies beyond the point of safety from other human beings for persons afoot upon streets. It lies beyond the point of casual city public life. It lies far beyond the point of any relationship between investment and productivity. Quoting Salisbury again:

> The drawback is that as more and more space is allotted to the automobile, the goose that lays the golden eggs is strangled. Enormous areas go from the tax rolls and are rendered unsuitable for productive economic purposes. The community's ability to foot the ever-multiplying costs of freeways dwindles . . . At the same time traffic movement becomes more and more random . . . It is from Los Angeles that the most anguished cries are heard for rescue from the rubber-tired incubi. It is Los Angeles that threatens to prohibit new cars unless they

are fitted with devices to prevent the discharge of smog-creating hydrocarbon fractions . . . It is in Los Angeles that serious officials say that the system is exhausting the elements necessary for human life— land, air and water.

Los Angeles did not plan to cultivate such problems, any more than New York and Boston and Philadelphia and Pittsburgh, eating themselves away with express-ways, are planning to chop up and eat themselves away. One seemingly logical step is taken after another, each step plausible and apparently defensible in itself; and the peculiar result is a form of city which is not easier to use and to get around in, but on the contrary more scattered, more cumbersome, more time wasting, expensive and aggravating for cross-use. A New York manufacturer who makes many business calls in other cities tells me he must devote almost twice as much time in Los Angeles as in San Francisco or New York to achieve a given number of calls and completed work. The head of a branch office of a consulting firm in Los Angeles tells me he ought to have two more staff members than are needed in Chicago, just to make an equivalent number and range of contacts.

Yet although erosion solves nothing, and creates great inefficiency, there is never a good or obvious point at which to swear off; for as the process proceeds, from its small and apparently innocuous beginnings, it becomes continually harder to halt or reverse it and seem-ingly, at least, more impractical to do so.

The tactics of erosion, destructive as they are to cities, and poor as they are at solving anything, cannot be blamed for all that is cumbersome and progressively

impractical and expensive in city transportation, however. Many city districts, without benefit of erosion, are
thin and impractical for use except by private automobiles and always were—even before automobiles.

We are all familiar with the great need for automobiles in suburbs. It is common for wives in suburbs to
chalk up more errand mileage in a day than their husbands chalk up in commuting mileage. Duplication of car
parking is also familiar in suburbs: the schools, the supermarkets, the churches, the shopping centers, the clinics,
the movie, all the residences, must have their own parking lots and all this duplicate parking lies idle for much
of the time. Suburbs, at least while they remain suburbs,
can stand this land waste and this high ratio of private
automobile travel, because of their lack of concentration.
(Here, it would seem, is that elusive point of equilibrium;
yet the moment work is introduced into the mixture, even
in a suburb, the equilibrium is lost.)

Much the same need, both for automobiles as a constant necessity and for duplicated parking, can occur in
cities where conditions for city diversity—including sufficiently high densities—are lacking. "I am the one who
commutes in this family," explains my friend Mrs.
Kostritsky. The Kostritskys live in inner Baltimore, where
they are close to Mr. Kostritsky's work. But his wife, using
a car (nothing else is practical), must "commute" to get
her children to school, to do any shopping more extensive
than that involving a loaf of bread, a can of soup and a
head of withered lettuce, to use a library, to see a show,
to attend meetings; and, like any mother already out in
the suburbs, this inner-city mother too must drive to a
suburban shopping center to buy children's clothing. Not

only are there no such stores near her home, but the downtown stores no longer have enough demand to carry a good range of children's clothing. By dark it is dangerous to travel except by car. The district's thinness, moreover, cannot justify tolerable public transportation, either within the district itself or to other parts of the city, and this would be so whether or not automobiles existed.

Such city districts are like suburbs in requiring constant automobile use. But, on the other hand, unlike suburbs, their concentration of people is too high for suburban accommodation of all the automobiles and parking necessary. "In-between" densities—too low for cities, too high for suburbs—are as impractical for transportation as they are for other economic or social purposes.

The common fate of such districts nowadays is to be abandoned by people with choice, in any case. If the very poor inherit them, the transportation and use impracticalities may not cause serious traffic problems, because the inhabitants may not be able to afford enough traffic to make a problem. When they are able to, they are apt to leave.

But when such districts are purposely "renewed to bring back the middle class," or if they are the objects of conservation, to retain a population that has not yet deserted, the need to provide very extensive car accommodations immediately becomes a chief and overriding consideration. The existing deadness and thinness of use are thereby reinforced.

The Great Blight of Dullness is allied with the blight of traffic congestion.

The more territory, *planned or unplanned*, which is dull, the greater becomes the pressure of traffic on lively districts. People who *have* to use automobiles to use their dull home territory in a city, or to get out of it, are not merely capricious when they take the cars to a destination where the cars are unnecessary, destructive and a nuisance to their own drivers.

Territories exhibiting the Great Blight of Dullness need to be supplied with whatever conditions they lack for generating diversity. This is their basic need, regardless of traffic. But it is an aim which becomes impossible to further, if accommodations for huge numbers of cars get first consideration, and other city uses get the leftovers. A strategy of erosion by automobiles is thus not only destructive to such city intensity as already exists; it also conflicts with nurturing new or additional intensity of use where that is needed.

City uses and interests of various kinds are forever interfering with the erosion process. One reason that erosion occurs as gradually as it does in most cities is the exorbitant cost of buying up so much land which is already in use for other purposes. But no end of other factors besides expense exert friction on unlimited flow of surface traffic. The many corners where pedestrians are allowed to cross streets, for instance, exert friction.

To get a sharp impression of the conflict that is waged between the pressures for accommodating more vehicles and the pressures exerted by many other uses, one need go no farther than the nearest public hearing about a street widening, a route for a city expressway, a bridge approach, a road in a park, a switch to one-way traffic, a new group of public garages, or any other officially sponsored erosion proposal that requires a hearing.

Such occasions bring forward a different viewpoint from that of the erosion advocates. Citizens whose neighborhoods or property will be affected usually turn up to combat the plan, sometimes protesting not only with their voices and petitions, but with demonstrations and signs.* They sometimes cite much the same line of general argument against erosion that I have touched on, quoting Salisbury or Gruen or Wilfred Owens' book, *Cities in the Motor* Age, or Lewis Mumford's arguments for balanced and varied transportation.

However, generalities and philosophy about whither the cities are heading are not really the meat of the citizens' arguments, nor does such comment make up their most fervent and convincing points.

What the citizens really attack is the *specific* destruction that will be wrought on their homes, their streets, their businesses, their community. Often their localized minor elected officials turn up to join the protest; if they did not, they would never be elected again.

The planners, traffic commissioners, major elected officials, and other remote people at the top of the municipal apparatus expect this procedure. They know all about such protesters: well-meaning people but, in the nature of things, untrained in these problems, concerned with parochial interests, unable to see "the big picture."

But what these citizens say is worth listening to.

The very earthiness and directness of their reasoning about concrete and specific local effects is the key, I think,

---

*Edmund Bacon, the director of Philadelphia's planning commission, tells me that citizens against an expressway he was for turned up with signs reading "Fry Bacon."

to rescuing cities from destruction by traffic, a point I shall return to soon. It is also a reminder that erosion is unpopular, for very tangible reasons, with great numbers of city people.

While protests, the necessity for hearings themselves, and the direct expenses required for many erosive changes all represent some of the forms of friction exerted by cities on the erosion process, they do not represent any reversal of the erosion process. At the most, they represent stalemate.

If the triumph of other pressures over traffic is carried a step further, however, so as to *diminish* vehicular traffic, then we have an example of attrition of automobiles by cities.

Attrition of automobiles by cities is today almost always happenstance. Attrition, unlike erosion, is seldom deliberately planned by anybody, and it is neither recognized nor practiced as policy. Nevertheless, it does occur.

Many of its occurrences are ephemeral. For instance, when an off-Broadway theater was opened at the intersection of several narrow streets in Greenwich Village, the added intensity of use at that spot, between the acts and after the show, hampered traffic. The patrons used the street roadbed as an outdoor lobby because the sidewalk was so narrow, and they were slow to get out of the way. A similar blockage of a much wider street can be seen in New York when Madison Square Garden lets out after some event at night. So great is the press of the crowds that they ignore the rights of vehicles. They do not respect the cars' turns at the lights. Traffic halts and backs up for many blocks. In either of these cases, if drivers on the borderline of choice decide not to try to bring the car next time, attrition is operating, although very ephemerally.

Another common form of attrition of automobiles by cities is represented in the garment district of New York City which generates a great deal of truck traffic. These trucks, in competition for road space, operate inefficiently; their numbers are so great that they render inefficient other forms of automobile traffic. People in private passenger cars learn to avoid the garment district. When those on borderlines of choice decide instead to walk or use the subway between their points of travel, attrition is operating. Indeed, so difficult has it become to move into the garment district by taxi or private car that in recent years most of Manhattan's fabric firms, which used to be in a quiet backwater in downtown Manhattan, have moved up into the garment district where they can be within walking distance of their customers. While such a move adds to concentration and intensity of city land use, it cuts down on city vehicular use, and is an example of attrition carried to the point that the *need* for cars is reduced.

Attrition of automobiles by cities is so seldom deliberate that it is hard to find recent examples. (The closing of streets for pedestrian use, being almost always accompanied by compensating provisions for vehicles, is not attrition but rearrangement of traffic.) However, the closing of Washington Square Park in New York to automobiles, beginning in 1958, affords an instance and is worth examining.

Washington Square Park, about seven acres in size, terminates the southern end of Fifth Avenue. However, until 1958, it did not terminate north-south traffic on Fifth Avenue. A roadway arrangement, originally a carriage drive, carried traffic through the park between Fifth Avenue's terminus and other north-south roadways below the park.

Over the years, traffic, of course, gradually increased on this park roadway link and it was always a nuisance to other users who patronize this park heavily and continuously. Back in the 1930's, Robert Moses, in his capacity as parks commissioner, attempted to remove this road. But his plan was to compensate for it—much more than compensate for it—by trimming down the sides of the park to widen the narrow perimeter streets, and thus to encircle the park with a major, high-speed traffic artery. This scheme, locally christened "the bathmat plan" (describing what would be left of the park) was fought and defeated. Stalemate.

Then in the mid-1950's, Mr. Moses came up with a new plan for erosion. This one involved a major depressed highway cutting through the center of the park, as a link for carrying a heavy volume of high-speed traffic between midtown Manhattan and a vast, yawning Radiant City and expressway which Mr. Moses was cooking up south of the park.

At first most of the local citizens opposed the proposed depressed highway, anticipating nothing beyond a stalemate. However, two daring women, Mrs. Shirley Hayes and Mrs. Edith Lyons, were less conventional in their thinking. They took the remarkable intellectual step of envisioning improvement for certain city uses, such as children's play, strolling, and horsing around, at the expense of vehicular traffic. They advocated eliminating the existing road, that is, closing the park to all automobile traffic—but at the same time, *not* widening the perimeter roads either. In short, they proposed closing off a roadbed without compensating for it.

Their idea was popular; the advantages were evident to anyone who used the park. Furthermore, it began to dawn on the theorists in the community that stalemate did not exist as a choice this time. For when other parts of the Moses Radiant City and Downtown Expressway scheme were eventually developed, the road through the park would begin to get automobiles in express-highway quantities. It was noticed that the old road, although a nuisance, was being used well below its capacity, and would be quite a different and intolerable affair when it carried a share of the proposed future expressway-destined load.

Instead of staying on the defensive, majority opinion in the community took to the offensive.

The city officials insisted that if the roadway were closed—a step they appeared to think insane—the only possible alternatives must be to widen the streets at the park perimeter, or else bring them to a state of frantic and frenetic congestion. The Planning Commission, after a hearing, turned down the proposals for closure, and approved instead what its members called a "minimum roadway" through the park, on the grounds that if the community got its foolish way the citizens would regret it. The streets surrounding the park, they said, would be swamped with diverted traffic. The traffic commissioner forecast an immediate annual increase of millions of cars in the nearby streets. Mr. Moses predicted that if the community got its way, the citizens would soon be back begging him to reopen the road and build a highway, but the mess they were in would serve them right and teach them a lesson.

All these dire predictions would likely have come true *if* compensating provision had been made for cars diverted from the park. However, before any alternate arrangements were made—even arrangements for speed-up of flow on existing perimeter roadbeds—the community, by exerting rather tough political pressure abruptly, got the park road closed, first on a trial basis and then permanently.

None of the predictions of increased traffic around the park were borne out. These predictions could not be borne out because these perimeter streets, narrow, beset with many lights, cluttered with parked cars, whimsically used by jaywalkers, replete with hard-to-negotiate corners, were already a most aggravating and slow route for automobiles. The route through the park, the route that was being closed, was much the best immediate north-south route.

Every traffic count taken around the park perimeter since the closing has shown no increase in traffic; most counts have shown a slight reduction. On lower Fifth Avenue, the traffic counts dropped appreciably; apparently a considerable amount of its traffic had been through traffic. Far from bringing new problems of congestion, the obstacle resulted in slight relief of previous congestion.

Where have the traffic commissioner's annual millions of cars gone instead?

This is the most interesting and significant part of the story. They have not noticeably gone anywhere else instead. The through avenues east and west of Fifth

Avenue, and parallel to it, which might have been expected to take the brunt of the diverted load, did not seem to receive an extra load. At least the running time of the buses, a factor sensitive to increases or decreases in total traffic, reflected no change. Nor did the bus drivers detect a difference from observation. (The traffic commissioner, who has the means for making counts of the extent needed, and for doing origin-destination trip studies, appeared uninterested in learning where, if anywhere, his vanished hordes departed. He does not like to talk about it.)

Like the vanished bus riders on the one-way avenues, these cars—or *some* cars—disappeared into thin air. Their disappearance is no more mysterious, and no less to be expected, than the disappearance of the bus riders. For just as there is no absolute, immutable number of public transportation riders in a city, so is there no absolute, immutable number of private automobile riders; rather, the numbers vary in response to current differentials in speed and convenience among ways of getting around.

Attrition of automobiles operates by making conditions *less* convenient for cars. Attrition as a steady, gradual process (something that does not now exist) would steadily decrease the numbers of persons using private automobiles in a city. If properly carried out—as one aspect of stimulating diversity and intensifying city use—attrition would decrease the need for cars simultaneously with decreasing convenience for cars, much as, in reverse, erosion increases need for cars simultaneously with increasing convenience for cars.

In real life, which is quite different from the life of

dream cities, attrition of automobiles by cities is probably the only means by which absolute numbers of vehicles can be cut down. It is probably the only realistic means by which better public transportation can be stimulated, and greater intensity and vitality of city use be simultaneously fostered and accommodated.

However, a strategy of attrition of automobiles by cities cannot be arbitrary or negative. Nor is such a policy capable of giving dramatic results suddenly. Although its cumulative effects should be revolutionary, like any strategy aimed at keeping things working it has to be engaged in as a form of evolution.

What sort of tactics are suitable to a strategy of attrition of automobiles by cities? Many of the tactics become obvious at once, if we understand that the point is not attrition of automobiles *in* cities but rather the attrition of automobiles *by* cities. Tactics are suitable which give room to other necessary and desired city uses that happen to be in competition with automobile traffic needs.

Consider, for example, the problem of accommodating the sidewalk uses, from outdoor store displays to children's play, that people attempt in popular streets. These need broad sidewalks. In addition, double rows of trees might be splendid on some sidewalks. An attrition tactician would look for sidewalks getting heavy or various use, and would seek to widen and enhance them as a gain for city life. Automatically, this would narrow the vehicular roadbed.

If and when our cities learn to foster deliberately the four basic generators of diversity, popular and interesting streets will grow ever more numerous. As soon as such streets, by their use, earn sidewalk widening, it should be offered.

Where would the money come from? From the same place the money now comes that is misapplied to sidewalk narrowing.*

There are many variants to physical subtraction of roadbed space for the benefit of other, already evident uses. Spots of intense congregation outside schools, some theaters, certain store groupings, could be given outdoor lobbies intruding partially into the vehicular roadbed, thus making their attrition value permanent instead of ephemeral. Small parks could be carried across a street, thereby creating dead ends. These would still permit, from either direction, vehicular service access to a street. But they would prevent vehicular through traffic except in emergency. Park roads, where parks get enough use to justify this, could be closed off as in Washington Square.

Aside from these and other variants of intrusion on roadbed space, shorter blocks (and therefore many crossings) which are a necessity in any case for generating diversity, also interfere with traffic flow.

In the next chapter, on visual order, I shall make further specific suggestions for tactics that simultaneously are of positive benefit for city life and happen to frustrate automobile traffic. Possibilities for adding to convenience, intensity and cheer in cities, while simultaneously hampering automobiles, are limitless. Today we automati-

*Manhattan alone widened 453 street roadbeds in the years 1955-58, and its borough president announced that this was only a start. A sensible attrition program there would eliminate sidewalk narrowing, would aim—among other things—at widening the sidewalks of at least 453 streets in a four-year period, and would consider this only a start.

cally, if sometimes regretfully, rule out most amenities—
to say nothing of pure functional necessities like easy and
frequent pedestrian crossings—because these are in conflict with the voracious and insatiable needs of automobiles. The conflict is real. There is no need to invent tactics
artificially.

Nor is there any need to foist such improvements
where they are not wanted. Streets and districts where
appreciable numbers of people want and will enjoy such
changes should get them; not streets or districts whose
people will give them no support.

So close and so organic is the tie between vital,
diverse city districts and a reduction in absolute numbers
of vehicles using their streets, that, except for one serious
problem, a good strategy of attrition could be based
purely on building lively, interesting city districts, and all
but ignoring the by-the-way effects on automobile traffic—which would automatically be effects of attrition.

Attrition must come about with a certain selectivity.
As mentioned earlier in this chapter, traffic exerts pressures upon *itself*; vehicles compete with each other, as
well as with other uses. Just as other uses and traffic adapt
and adjust to each other, thus giving rise to the processes
of erosion or attrition, so do vehicles adapt and adjust to
the presence of each other. For instance, the inefficiency of
trucks in cities is, in large part, an adaptation by trucks to
the competition of so many vehicles. If the inefficiency
becomes sufficiently great, the enterprises concerned may
move or go out of business, which is another aspect of
erosion and thinning down in cities. I have already given
an example of differential convenience among vehicles
themselves: the differing effects upon private automo-

biles and upon buses of making an avenue one-way. The advantage to the automobiles is a penalty to the buses.

Utterly unselective attrition of vehicles could be, in many streets, as discouraging to trucks and to buses as to private automobiles.

Trucks and buses are themselves important manifestations of city intensity and concentration. And as I shall soon indicate, if their efficiency is encouraged, this too results in further attrition of automobiles, as a side effect.

I am indebted for this line of thought to William McGrath, traffic commissioner of New Haven, who has conceived several means by which already familiar traffic techniques can be used deliberately for selective vehicular encouragement and discouragement. The very idea of doing such a thing at all is brilliant; McGrath says it occurred to him gradually, over a period of four years of working with New Haven planners, during which he realized that techniques for moving and storing more cars and for putting every foot of roadbed to maximum use, as he learned in school, was a most lopsided way of dealing with city streets.

One of McGrath's aims is to encourage greater efficiency of public transportation, which in New Haven today means buses. To achieve this, the buses going into and through downtown must be speeded up. This can be done without doubt, says McGrath, by regulating the traffic light frequencies to short intervals and not staggering them. Owing to the corner pick-up stops required in any case by buses, the short signal frequencies interfere with bus travel time less than long signal frequencies. These same shorter frequencies, unstaggered, constantly hold up and slow down private transportation, which would thereby be discouraged from using these particular streets. In turn, this would mean still less interference and more speed for buses.

McGrath thinks that the realistic way to get pedestrian streets where these may be desirable in a heavily used downtown is to bollix up the use of the street for cars—largely by bollixing up the signal system—to the point that "only a driver with a hole in his head would pick such a route after he tried it a time or two," and also by forbidding parking and standing. After such a street has reached the point that it is being used only by trucks making or picking up deliveries there, and by few other vehicles, its status as a pedestrian street can be formalized without much jolt to anybody and without the necessity to compensate by throwing heavy flow and burdensome parking upon some other street. The necessary changes in habits will already have been absorbed, by attrition.

Theoretically, city expressways are always presented as means for taking cars off of other streets, and thereby relieving city streets of traffic. In real life, this works only if and when the expressways are well under capacity use; left unconsidered is the eventual destination, off the expressway, of that increased flow of vehicles. Instead of serving as bypassers, expressways in cities serve too frequently as dumpers. Mr. Moses' proposed plan for a downtown expressway in Manhattan, for instance—the one with repercussions on Washington Square—is always presented appealingly as a fast route between the East River bridges and the Hudson River tunnels to keep through traffic out of the city. And yet the actual plan for it includes a spaghetti-dish of ramps into the city. It will be a dumper, and by thus accommodating traffic aimed for the heart of the city, it will actually tend to choke up, instead of aid, city bypass traffic.

McGrath thinks that if expressways are genuinely meant to relieve city streets, their full effects must be taken into account. There must, for one thing, be no increased parking to be reached through city streets that are theoretically supposed to be relieved of cars. Nor should it be possible at exit ramps, McGrath believes, for drivers to thread their way through theoretically relieved streets. McGrath works this out as follows: Streets that could possibly be used as alternates to the artery when the artery chokes up, should be protected by judiciously placed dead ends; these would not interfere with localized use of streets but would thoroughly thwart drivers trying to knit them with expressway or arterial routes. With such devices, expressways could serve as bypass routes only.

Certain ramps, which do lead into dense cities, could be limited to trucks and buses.

Extending the basic McGrath idea of selectivity further, trucks in cities could be greatly helped. Trucks are vital to cities. They mean service. They mean jobs. At present, we already have, in reverse, truck selectivity traffic tactics on a few city streets. On Fifth and Park avenues in New York, for instance, trucks are forbidden, except for those making deliveries.

This is a reasonable policy for some streets, but under a strategy of attrition of automobiles, the same tactics can be used wrong-side-out on other streets. Thus, where streets are narrowed or bottlenecked to the point that a choice must be made as to what vehicles can use them, precedence can go to trucks, with other vehicles

permitted only if *they* are making (passenger) deliveries
or pickups.

Meantime, the fastest lanes in multilane arteries or
on wide avenues could be reserved for trucks only. This
is no more than a reversal, for example, of the amazingly
frivolous New York policy of designing the speediest
expressway arteries, along the densest parts of the city,
deliberately to exclude trucks, and forcing even long-dis-
tance trucking into local streets.

Trucks, favored by selective attrition, would do considerable self-sorting. Long-haul vehicles would, in the
main, use fast arteries. Narrow or bottlenecked streets
would be used primarily for deliveries or pickups.

In a city district where attrition of automobiles had
steadily and selectively occurred, we could expect to find
trucks forming a much higher proportion of total surface
vehicles than is the case today. This does not mean there
would be more trucks, but rather fewer passenger automobiles; the more effective the attrition on private cars,
the less ubiquitous we might expect the trucks to be,
because they would not be halted and idled to the extent
they are now. Furthermore, trucks which are used *for*
work, instead of for getting to and from work, spread out
their use through the working day instead of piling up in
wild peaks.

As between taxis and private passenger automobiles,
inadequate parking selectively favors taxis. This can be a
useful form of traffic selectivity too, because taxis do so
many more times the work of equivalent private cars.
Khrushchev, when he visited this country, understood
this differential in efficiency very quickly. After watching
the traffic in San Francisco, he commented to the mayor in

wonder at the waste, and evidently thought over what he had seen, because when he reached Vladivostok on his way home he announced that it would be his policy to encourage fleets of taxis in Soviet cities rather than private automobiles.

Selectivity, which would have to be part of a successful strategy of attrition wherever the competition among vehicles warranted it, means very little, however, by itself. It has point only as part of a broad strategy of cutting down absolute numbers of vehicles in cities.

In considering suitable tactics and principles of attrition, it is worth taking another look at the process of erosion. Erosion of cities by automobiles, while anything but admirable in its effects, presents much to admire in certain of its principles of operation. Anything so effective has something to teach, and is worth respect and study from that point of view.

The changes required or wrought by erosion always occur piecemeal—so much so that we can almost call them insidious. In the perspective of a city's life as a whole, even the most drastic steps in the process are piecemeal changes. *Therefore, each change is absorbed piecemeal, as it occurs.* Each erosive change requires changes in the habits which people follow to get around in a city, and changes in the ways that they use a city, but not everybody needs to change his habits at once, nor does anybody (except those displaced) have to change too many habits at once.

Attrition of automobiles requires changes in habits and adjustments in usage too; just as in the case of erosion it should not disrupt too many habits at once.

The desirability of piecemeal, evolutionary attrition has a bearing, too, on the development of public transportation. At present public transportation languishes, but not from lack of potential technical improvement. A wealth of ingenious technique lies in limbo because there is no point in developing it during an era of city erosion, no funds for it, no faith in it. Even if public transportation is stimulated by increase in usage, under tactics of automobile attrition, it is unrealistic to expect that revolutionary improvement will be accomplished abruptly, or wished into being. The development of twentieth-century public transportation (something we have never possessed) has to follow a rise in custom and clearly anticipated custom, just as decline in public transportation has followed a drop in custom and anticipated drop in custom.

The piecemeal erosive changes that cumulatively eat away a city are by no means all thought out in advance, in some Olympian scheme or master plan. If they were, they would not be nearly as effective as they are. In the main, they occur as direct, practical responses to direct, practical problems as those problems appear. Every move thus counts; few are gestures and boondoggles. In the case of attrition of automobiles, this same kind of opportunism will give maximum results, and also best results in terms of city utility and improvement. Attrition tactics should be applied where conflicts exist between traffic flow and other city uses, and as new conflicts of this kind develop.

Finally, city eroders always approach the problems to be solved in positive fashion. There is some talk, mostly on rarefied and abstract levels, about using highways for the side *purpose* of slum clearance. But in real life, nobody either promotes or supports highways with the negative *purpose* of getting rid of something else. Increased, or supposedly increased, convenience, speed or access are the purposes.

Attrition, too, must operate in positive terms, as a means of supplying positive, easily understood and desired improvements, appealing to various specific and tangible city interests. This is desirable not because such an approach is a superior persuasive and political device (although it is), but because the objects should be the tangible and positive objects of increasing, in specific places, city diversity, vitality and workability. To concentrate on riddance as the primary purpose, negatively to put taboos and penalties on automobiles as children might say, "Cars, cars, go away," would be a policy not only doomed to defeat but rightly doomed to defeat. A city vacuum, we must remember, is not superior to redundant traffic, and people are rightly suspicious of programs that give them nothing for something.

What if we fail to stop the erosion of cities by automobiles? What if we are prevented from catalyzing workable and vital cities because the practical steps needed to do so are in conflict with the practical steps demanded by erosion?

There is a silver lining to everything.

In that case we Americans will hardly need to ponder a mystery that has troubled men for millennia: What is the purpose of life? For us, the answer will be clear, established and for all practical purposes indisputable: The purpose of life is to produce and consume automobiles.

It is not hard to understand that the producing and

consuming of automobiles might properly seem the purpose of life to the General Motors management, or that it
might seem so to other men and women deeply committed economically or emotionally to this pursuit. If they so
regard it, they should be commended rather than criticized for this remarkable identification of philosophy
with daily duty. It is harder to understand, however, why
the production and consumption of automobiles should
be the purpose of life for this country.

Similarly, it is understandable that men who were
young in the 1920's were captivated by the vision of the
freeway Radiant City, with the specious promise that it
would be appropriate to an automobile age. At least it
was then a new idea; to men of the generation of New
York's Robert Moses, for example, it was radical and
exciting in the days when their minds were growing and
their ideas forming. Some men tend to cling to old intellectual excitements, just as some belles, when they are old
ladies, still cling to the fashions and coiffures of their
exciting youth. But it is harder to understand why this
form of arrested mental development should be passed
on intact to succeeding generations of planners and
designers. It is disturbing to think that men who are
young today, men who are being trained now for their
careers, should accept *on the grounds that they must be
"modern" in their thinking,* conceptions about cities and
traffic which are not only unworkable, but also to which
nothing new of any significance has been added since
their fathers were children.

19

VISUAL ORDER: ITS LIMITATIONS AND POSSIBILITIES

When we deal with cities we are dealing with life at its most complex and intense. Because this is so, there is a basic esthetic limitation on what can be done with cities: *A city cannot be a work of art.*

We need art, in the arrangements of cities as well as in the other realms of life, to help explain life to us, to show us meanings, to illuminate the relationship between the life that each of us embodies and the life outside us. We need art most, perhaps, to reassure us of our own humanity. However, although art and life are interwoven, they are not the same things. Confusion between them is, in part, why efforts at city design are so disappointing. It is important, in arriving at better design strategies and tactics, to clear up this confusion.

Art has its own peculiar forms of order, and they are rigorous. Artists, whatever their medium, *make selections* from the abounding materials of life, and organize these selections into works that are under the control of the artist. To be sure, the artist has a sense that the demands of the work (i.e., of the selections of material he has made) control him. The rather miraculous result of this process—if the selectivity, the organization and the control are consistent within themselves—can be art. But the essence of this process is disciplined, highly discriminatory selectivity *from* life. In relation to the inclusiveness and the literally endless intricacy of life, art is arbitrary, symbolic and abstracted. That is its value and the source of its own kind of order and coherence.

To approach a city, or even a city neighborhood, as if it were a larger architectural problem, capable of being given order by converting it into a disciplined work of art, is to make the mistake of attempting to substitute art for life.

The results of such profound confusion between art and life are neither life nor art. They are taxidermy. In its place, taxidermy can be a useful and decent craft. However, it goes too far when the specimens put on display are exhibitions of dead, stuffed cities.

Like all attempts at art which get far away from the truth and which lose respect for what they deal with, this craft of city taxidermy becomes, in the hands of its master practitioners, continually more picky and precious. This is the only form of advance possible to it.

All this is a life-killing (and art-killing) misuse of art. The results impoverish life instead of enriching it.

To be sure, it is possible for the creation of art not to be so individualistic a process as it usually is in our society.

Under certain circumstances, the creation of art can apparently be done by general, and in effect anonymous, consensus. For instance, in a closed society, a technologically hampered society, or an arrested society, either hard necessity or tradition and custom can enforce on everyone a disciplined selectivity of purposes and materials, a discipline by consensus on what those materials demand of their organizers, and a disciplined control over the forms thereby created. Such societies can produce villages, and maybe even their own kinds of cities, which look to us like works of art in their physical totality.

But this is not the case with us. For us, such societies may be interesting to ponder; and we may regard their harmonious works with admiration or a kind of nostalgia and wonder wistfully why we can't be like that.

We can't be like that because the limitations on possibilities and the strictures on individuals in such societies extend much beyond the materials and conceptions used in creating works of art from the grist of everyday life. The limitations and strictures extend into every realm of opportunity (including intellectual opportunity) and into relationships among people themselves. These limitations and strictures would seem to us an unnecessary and intolerable stultification of life. For all our conformity, we are too adventurous, inquisitive, egoistic and competitive to be a harmonious society of artists by consensus, and, what is more, we place a high value upon the very traits that prevent us from being so. Nor is this the constructive use we make of cities or the reason we find them valuable: to embody tradition or to express (and freeze) harmonious consensus.

Nineteenth-century Utopians, with their rejection of urbanized society, and with their inheritance of eighteenth-century romanticism about the nobility and simplicity of "natural" or primitive man, were much attracted to the idea of simple environments that were works of art by harmonious consensus. To get back to this condition has been one of the hopes incorporated in our tradition of Utopian reform.

This futile (and deeply reactionary) hope tinctured the Utopianism of the Garden City planning movement too and, at least ideologically, somewhat gentled its more dominant theme of harmony and order imposed and frozen by authoritarian planning.

The hope for an eventual, simple environment formed of art by consensus—or rather, a ghostly vestige of that hope—has continued to flit through Garden City planning theory when it has kept itself pure from Radiant City and City Beautiful planning. Thus, as late as the 1930's, Lewis Mumford in *The Culture of Cities* gave an importance, which would be puzzling indeed in the absence of this tradition, to pursuits like basket weaving, pottery making and blacksmithing in the planned communities he envisioned for us. As late as the 1950's, Clarence Stein, the leading American Garden City planner, on the occasion of receiving the American Institute of Architects' gold medal for his contributions to architectural progress, was casting about for some object which might suitably be created by harmonious consensus in the ideal communities he envisioned. He suggested that citizens could be allowed to build a nursery school, of course with their own hands. But the gist of Stein's message was that, aside from the conceded nursery school, the complete physical environment of a community and all the arrangements that comprise it must be in the total, absolute and unchallenged control of the project's architects.

This is, of course, no different from the Radiant City and City Beautiful assumptions. These always were primarily architectural design cults, rather than cults of social reform.

Indirectly through the Utopian tradition, and directly through the more realistic doctrine of art by imposition, modern city planning has been burdened from its beginnings with the unsuitable aim of converting cities into disciplined works of art.

Like the housers who face a blank if they try to think what to do besides income-sorting projects, or the highwaymen who face a blank if they try to think what to do besides accommodate more cars, just so, architects who venture into city design often face a blank in trying to create visual order in cities except by substituting the order of art for the very different order of life. They cannot do anything else much. They cannot develop alternate tactics, for they lack a strategy for design that will help cities.

Instead of attempting to substitute art for life, city designers should return to a strategy ennobling both to art and to life: a strategy of illuminating and clarifying life and helping to explain to us its meanings and order—in this case, helping to illuminate, clarify and explain the order of cities.

We are constantly being told simple-minded lies about order in cities, talked down to in effect, assured that duplication represents order. It is the easiest thing in the world to seize hold of a few forms, give them a regimented regularity, and try to palm this off in the name of order. However, simple regimented regularity and significant systems of functional order are seldom coincident in this world.

To see complex systems of functional order as order, and not as chaos, takes understanding. The leaves dropping from the trees in the autumn, the interior of an airplane engine, the entrails of a dissected rabbit, the city desk of a newspaper, all appear to be chaos if they are seen without comprehension. Once they are understood as systems of order, they actually *look* different.

Because we use cities, and therefore have experience with them, most of us already possess a good groundwork for understanding and appreciating their order. Some of our trouble in comprehending it, and much of the unpleasant chaotic effect, comes from lack of enough visual reinforcements to underscore the functional order, and, worse still, from unnecessary visual contradictions.

It is fruitless, however, to search for some dramatic key element or kingpin which, if made clear, will clarify all. No single element in a city is, in truth, the kingpin or the key. The mixture itself is kingpin, and its mutual support is the order.

When city designers and planners try to find a design device that will express, in clear and easy fashion, the "skeleton" of city structure (expressways and promenades are current favorites for this purpose), they are on fundamentally the wrong track. A city is not put together like a mammal or a steel frame building—or even like a honeycomb or a coral. A city's very *structure* consists of mixture of uses, and we get closest to its structural secrets when we deal with the conditions that generate diversity.

Being a structural system in its own right, a city can best be understood straightforwardly in its own terms, rather than in terms of some other kinds of organisms or objects. However, if the slippery shorthand of analogy can help, perhaps the best analogy is to imagine a large field in darkness. In the field, many fires are burning. They are of many sizes, some great, others small; some far apart, others dotted close together; some are brightening, some are slowly going out. Each fire, large or small, extends its radiance into the surrounding murk, and thus it carves out a space. But the space and the shape of that space exist only to the extent that the light from the fire creates it.

The murk has no shape or pattern except where it is carved into space by the light. Where the murk between the lights becomes deep and undefinable and shapeless, the only way to give it form or structure is to kindle new fires in the murk or sufficiently enlarge the nearest existing fires.

Only intricacy and vitality of use give, to the parts of a city, appropriate structure and shape. Kevin Lynch, in his book *The Image of the City*, mentions the phenomenon of "lost" areas, places that the people he interviewed completely ignored and were actually unaware of unless reminded, although it would seem the locations of these "lost" places by no means merited this oblivion, and sometimes his observers had just traversed them in actuality or in imagination.*

Wherever the fires of use and vitality fail to extend in a city is a place in the murk, a place essentially without city form and structure. Without that vital light, no seeking for "skeletons" or "frameworks" or "cells" on which to hang the place can bring it into a city form.

These metaphoric space-defining fires are formed—to

---

*About a similar phenomenon, regarding highways, Professor Lynch makes this comment: "Many [Los Angeles] subjects had difficulty in making a mental connection between the fast highway and the remainder of the city structure, just as in the Boston case. They would, in imagination, even walk across the Hollywood Freeway as if it did not exist. A high-speed artery may not necessarily be the best way of visually delimiting a central district."

get back to tangible realities—by areas where diverse city uses and users give each other close-grained and lively support.

This is the essential order which city design can assist. These areas of vitality need to have their remarkable functional order clarified. As cities get more such areas, and less gray area or murk, the need and the opportunities for clarification of this order will increase.

Whatever is done to clarify this order, this intricate life, has to be done mainly by tactics of emphasis and suggestion.

Suggestion—the part standing for the whole—is a principal means by which art communicates; this is why art often tells us so much with such economy. One reason we understand this communication of suggestion and symbol is that, to a certain extent, it is the way all of us see life and the world. We constantly make organized selections of what we consider relevant and consistent from among all the things that cross our senses. We discard, or tuck into some secondary awareness, the impressions that do not make sense for our purposes of the moment— unless those irrelevant impressions are too strong to ignore. Depending on our purposes, we even vary our selections of what we take in and organize. To this extent, we are all artists.

This attribute of art, and this attribute in the way we see, are qualities on which the practice of city design can bank and which it can turn to advantage.

Designers do not need to be in literal control of an entire field of vision to incorporate visual order in cities. Art is seldom ploddingly literal, and if it is, it is poor stuff. Literal visual control in cities is usually a bore to everybody but the designers in charge, and sometimes after it is done, it bores them too. It leaves no discovery or organization or interest for anybody else.

The tactics needed are suggestions that help people make, for themselves, order and sense, instead of chaos, from what they see.

Streets provide the principal visual scenes in cities.

However, too many streets present our eyes with a profound and confusing contradiction. In the foreground, they show us all kinds of detail and activity. They make a visual announcement (very useful to us for understanding the order of cities) that this is an intense life and that into its composition go many different things. They make this announcement to us not only because we may see considerable activity itself, but because we see, in different types of buildings, signs, store fronts or other enterprises or institutions, and so on, the inanimate evidences of activity and diversity. However, if such a street goes on and on into the distance, with the intensity and intricacy of the foreground apparently dribbling into endless amorphous repetitions of itself and finally petering into the utter anonymity of distance, we are also getting a visual announcement that clearly says endlessness.

In terms of all human experience, these two announcements, one telling of great intensity, the other telling of endlessness, are hard to combine into a sensible whole.

One or the other of these two conflicting sets of impressions has to take precedence. The viewer has to combat or try to suppress the other set of impressions. Either way, it is difficult not to sense confusion and disorder. The more lively and varied the foreground (that is, the better its innate order of diversity), the sharper, and therefore the more disturbing, the contradiction of the two announcements can be. If too many streets embody this conflict, if they stamp a district or a whole city with this equivocation, the general effect is bound to be chaotic.

There are, of course, two ways of trying to see such a street. If a person gives the long view precedence, with its connotations of repetition and infinity, then the close-up scene and the intensity it conveys seem superfluous and offensive. I think this is the way that many architecturally trained viewers see city streets, and this is one reason for the impatience, and even contempt, that many (not all) of those who are architecturally trained express for the physical evidences of city diversity, freedom and life.

If the foreground view, on the other hand, takes precedence, then the endless repetition and continuation into lost, indefinite distances becomes the superfluous, offensive and senseless element. I think this is the way most of us look at city streets most of the time, because this is the viewpoint of a person whose purpose it is to use what exists on that street, rather than to look at it in detachment. Looking at the street in this way, the viewer makes sense, and at least a minimum amount of order, from the intimate view, but only at the price of considering the distance as a deplorable mishmash, better dismissed from mind if possible.

To bring even a chance for visual order to most such streets—and to districts in which such streets predominate—this basic contradiction of strong visual impressions has to be dealt with. I think this is what European visitors are getting at when they remark, as they often do, that the ugliness of our cities is owing to our gridiron street systems.

The functional order of the city demands that the intensity and diversity be there; their evidences can be removed from the street only at the cost of destroying necessary functional order. On the other hand, however, the order of the city does not demand the impression of endlessness; this impression can be minimized without interfering with functional order. Indeed, by so doing, the really significant attribute of intensity is reinforced.

Therefore a good many city streets (not all) need visual interruptions, cutting off the indefinite distant view and at the same time visually heightening and celebrating intense street use by giving it a hint of enclosure and entity.

Old parts of our cities which have irregular street patterns frequently do this. However, they have the disadvantage of being difficult to understand as street systems; people easily get lost in them and have a difficult time keeping them mapped out in their heads.

Where the basic street pattern is a gridiron plan, which has many advantages, there are two main ways, nevertheless, of introducing sufficient visual irregularities and interruptions into the city scene.

The first means is by adding additional streets where the streets of the gridiron plan are too far apart from each other—as on the West Side of Manhattan, for example; in short, where additional streets are necessary in any case for the functional purpose of helping to generate diversity.

If such new streets are added economically, with a

decent respect and restraint for saving the most valuable, the most handsome, or the most various among buildings that lie in their potential paths, and also with the aim of incorporating sides or rears of existing buildings into their frontages wherever possible, to give a mixture of age, then these new streets are seldom going to be straight for great length. They are going to have bends in them and sometimes a considerable tangent. Even a straight street cutting one former large block into two small blocks will not likely form a continuous straight line with its extensions through the next block and the next and next, indefinitely. There are certain to be T junctures where these offset street segments meet intersecting streets at right angles. Ordinary prudence and respect for city variety, combined with an awareness that irregularity in these cases is an advantage in itself, can determine the best of various potential alternative paths for new extra streets. The least material destruction should be combined with maximum visual gain; these two aims are not in conflict.

Subsidiary irregularity within a dominant grid system is not difficult to understand. Extra streets like these, introduced in between the grid streets, could even be named in recognition of their relationship to the grid.

The combination of a basic, easily understandable grid system, together with purposely irregular streets dropped in where the grid is too large for good city functioning, could be, I think, a distinctive and most valuable American contribution to the tactics of city design.

The second means for introducing irregularities and visual interruptions where they are insufficient, is on grid streets themselves.

San Francisco is a city with many natural visual interruptions in a gridiron street pattern. San Francisco's streets, in general, are regular gridiron arrangements in two-dimensional plan; however, in three-dimensional topography they are masterpieces of visual interruption. The many and abrupt hills constantly make separations between the nearby scene and the distance, and this is true whether one is looking along a street toward a rise, or looking down a slope. This arrangement greatly emphasizes the intimate and immediate street scenes, without sacrificing the clarity of gridiron organization.

Cities without such topography cannot reproduce any such happy accident by natural means. However, they too can introduce visual interruptions into straight and regular street patterns without sacrificing clarity of organization and movement. Bridges that connect two buildings up above a street sometimes do this service; so do buildings which themselves bridge a street. Occasional large buildings (preferably with public significance) can be placed across straight streets at ground level. Grand Central Terminal in New York is a well-known example.*

Straight, "endless" streets can be interrupted and the street itself divided around a square or plaza forming the interruption; this square can be occupied by a building. In cases where vehicular traffic can actually be dead-ended on straight streets, small parks could be thrown across

---

*It also provides an example of an extra street, Vanderbilt Avenue, with T terminations, and at Vanderbilt's northern T is a handsome new building, Union Carbide, which in effect bridges the sidewalk; the short blocks between Vanderbilt and Madison are illustrative, by the way, of the liveliness and pedestrian convenience natural to short blocks in cities.

from sidewalk to sidewalk; the visual interruption or diversion would be provided here by groves of trees or by small (and, let us hope, cheerful) park structures.

In still other cases, a visual diversion need not extend across a straight street, but can be in the form of a building or group of buildings set forward from the normal building line to make a jog, with the sidewalk cut underneath. Another form of jog is a plaza at one side of the street, which makes the building beyond stand out as a visual interruption.

It might be supposed that all this visual emphasis on intensity of street use would be rather overwhelming or even inhuman. But this is not so. Districts with many visual street interruptions do not, in real life, tend to intimidate or overwhelm people; they are more apt to be characterized as "friendly" and also to be comprehensible as districts. After all, this is intensity of human life which is being acknowledged and emphasized and, what is more, emphasized in its understandable, close-up aspect. It is city infinity and repetition which generally seem overwhelming, inhuman and incomprehensible.

There can be pitfalls, however, in the use of visual street interruptions.

First, there is little point in using them where there is no visual tale of street intensity and detail to tell. If a street is, in truth, a long repetition of one kind of use, providing thin activity, then visual interruption does not clarify the existing form of order here. Visual enclosure of practically nothing (in terms of city intensity) can hardly be more than a design affectation. Visual interruptions and vistas will not, in themselves, *bring* city vitality and intensity or their accompaniments of safety, interest, casual public life and economic opportunity. Only the four basic generators of diversity can do that.

Second, it is unnecessary, and would even become boring in its own way, for all city streets to have visual interruptions. After all a big city is a big place, and there is nothing wrong in acknowledging or stating this fact too from time to time. (Another of the advantages of San Francisco's hills, for instance, is that the views from them do precisely this, and they do it at the same time as they are separating the distance from the immediate street view.) Occasional endlessness, or else focal endings far in the distance on streets, lend variety. Some streets that run into borders such as bodies of water, campuses or large sports grounds should be left without visual interruptions. Not every street that terminates in a border need reveal this fact, but some of them should, both to introduce distant glimpses of what is different, and to convey casual messages about the whereabouts of the border—a form of orientation clue, incidentally, that Lynch found very important to the people he interviewed for his study of city "imageability."

Third, visual street interruptions should be, in functional terms, not dead ends, but "corners." Actual physical cut-offs to foot traffic in particular are destructive in cities. There should always be a way around the visual interruption or through it, a way that is obvious as a person reaches it, and that then lays out before the eyes a new street scene. This seductive attribute of designed interruptions to the eye was summed up neatly by the late architect Eliel Saarinen, who is reported to have said, in explaining his own design premises, "There must always be an end in view, and the end must not be final."

Fourth, visual interruptions get their force partially from being exceptions to the rule. Too many of the same kind can cancel themselves out. For instance, if plazas along the side of a street are plentiful, the street disintegrates visually as a street, to say nothing of going dead functionally. Jogs with arcades beneath, if they are plentiful instead of exceptional, just give us a narrower street and can even become claustrophobic in their effect.

Fifth, a visual street interruption is a natural eye-catcher and its own character has much to do with the impressions made by the entire scene. If it is banal, vacuous or merely messy, it might better not exist. A gas station or a bunch of billboards or a vacant and neglected building in such a place casts a pall out of all proportion to its size. A visual street interruption which is also beautiful is great luck, but when we go after beauty too solemnly in cities we usually seem to end up with pomposity. Beauty is not around for the asking, but we can ask that visual interruptions be decent and even interesting.

Landmarks, as their name says, are prime orientation clues. But good landmarks in cities also perform two other services in clarifying the order of cities. First, they emphasize (and also dignify) the diversity of cities; they do this by calling attention to the fact that they are different from their neighbors, and important because they are different. This explicit statement about themselves carries an implicit statement about the composition and order of cities. Second, in certain instances landmarks can make important to our eyes city areas which are important in functional fact but need to have that fact visually acknowledged and dignified.

By understanding these other services, we can understand why many different uses are eligible and useful as city landmarks, depending on their contexts in the city.

Let us first consider the role of landmarks as announcers and dignifiers of diversity. One reason a landmark can be a landmark is, of course, that it is in a spot where it shows to advantage But in addition, it is necessary that the landmark be distinctive as a thing itself, and it is this point with which we are now concerned.

Not all city landmarks are buildings. However, buildings are the principal landmarks in cities and the principles which make them serve well or ill apply also to most other kinds of landmarks, such as monuments, dramatic fountains, and so on.

Satisfying distinction in the appearance of a building almost always grows out of distinction in its use, as discussed in Chapter Twelve. The same building can be physically distinctive in one matrix because its use is distinctive in that context, but can be undistinctive in another setting where its use is the rule rather than the exception. The distinctiveness of a landmark depends considerably on reciprocity between the landmark and its neighbors.

In New York, Trinity Church, at the head of Wall Street, is a well-known and effective landmark. But Trinity would be relatively pallid as an element of city design if it were merely one among an assemblage of churches or even of other symbolic-looking institutions. Trinity's physical distinction, which is anything but pallid in its setting, depends partly on its good landmark site—at a T intersection and a rise in ground—but it also depends greatly on Trinity's functional distinction in its context of office buildings. So dominant is this fact of difference that Trinity makes a satisfying climax for its street scene, even though it is much smaller than its neighbors. An office building of this size (or any size) at this same advantageous spot, in this context, simply could not perform this service nor convey this degree of visual order, let alone do it with such unlabored and "natural" rightness.

Just so, the New York Public Library building, set in its commercial matrix at Fifth Avenue and Forty-second Street, forms an excellent landmark, but this is not true of the public libraries of San Francisco, Pittsburgh and Philadelphia, as examples. These have the disadvantage of being set among institutions which contrast insufficiently in function or—inevitably—in appearance.

Back in Chapter Eight, which deals with the need for mixed primary uses, I discussed the functional value of dotting important civic buildings within the workaday city, instead of assembling them into cultural or civic projects. In addition to the functional awkwardnesses and the economic waste of primary diversity that these projects cause, the buildings assembled into such islands of pomp are badly underused as landmarks. They pale each other, although each one, by itself, could make a tremendously effective impression and symbol of city diversity. This is serious, because we badly need more, not fewer, city landmarks—great landmarks and small.

Sometimes attempts are made to give a building landmark quality simply by making it bigger than its neighbors, or by turning it out with stylistic differences. Usually, if the use of such a building is essentially the same as the uses of its neighbors, it is pallid—try as it might. Nor does such a building do us that extra service of clarifying and dignifying diversity of uses. Indeed, it tries to tell us that what is important in the order of cities are mere differences in size or outward dress. Except in very rare cases of real architectural masterpieces, this statement that style or size is everything gets from city users, who are not so dumb, about the affection and attention it deserves.

However, it should be noted that some buildings which depend on size for their distinction do provide good landmark orientation service and visual interest for people *at a distance*. In New York, the Empire State Building and the Consolidated Edison Tower with its great illuminated clock are examples. For people seeing them from the streets close by, these same buildings, inconsequential in their differences from neighboring buildings, are inconsequential as landmarks. Philadelphia City Hall, with its tower surmounted by the statue of William Penn, makes a splendid landmark from afar; and its true, not superficial, difference within its intimate matrix of city also makes it a splendid landmark from close by. For distant landmarks, size can sometimes serve. For intimate landmarks, distinction of use and a statement about the importance of differences are of the essence.

These principles apply to minor landmarks too. A grade school can be a local landmark, by virtue of its special use in its surroundings, combined with visibility. Many different uses can serve as landmarks, provided they are special in their own context. For instance, people from Spokane, Washington, say that a physically distinctive and beloved landmark there is the Davenport Hotel, which serves, as hotels sometimes do, also as a unique and major center of city public life and assembly. In a place that is mainly residential, working places that are well seen can make landmarks, and often do.

Some outdoor spaces that are focal centers, or, as they are sometimes called, nodes, behave very much like landmarks and get much of their power as clarifiers of order from the distinctiveness of their use, just as in the case of landmark buildings. The plaza at Rockefeller Center in New York is such a place; to users of the city on the ground in its vicinity it is much more of a "landmark" than the towering structure behind it or the lesser towers further enclosing it.

Now let us consider that second extra service which landmarks can perform to clarify the order of cities: their ability to help state explicitly and visually that a place is important which is in truth functionally important.

Centers of activity, where the paths of many people come together in concentrated fashion, are important places economically and socially in cities. Sometimes they are important in the life of a city as a whole, sometimes to a particular district or neighborhood. Yet such centers may not have the visual distinction or importance merited by the functional truth. When this is the case, a user is being given contradictory and confusing information. The sight of the activity and the intensity of land use says Importance. The absence of any visual climax or dignifying object says Unimportance.

Because commerce is so predominant in most city centers of activity, an effective landmark in such a place usually needs to be overtly uncommercial.

People become deeply attached to landmarks that occur in centers of activity and in this their instincts about city order are correct. In Greenwich Village, the old

Jefferson Market Courthouse, now abandoned as a court-house, occupies a prominent site abutting on one of the community's busiest areas. It is an elaborate Victorian building, and opinions differ radically as to whether it is architecturally handsome or architecturally ugly. How-ever, there is a remarkable degree of unanimity, *even among those who do not like the building as a building,* that it must be retained and used for something. Citizens from the area, as well as architectural students working under their direction, have devoted immense amounts of time to detailed study of the building interior, its condition and its potentialities. Existing civic organizations have put time, effort and pressure into the job of saving it, and a new organization was even started to finance the repair of the public clock on the tower and get it going! The Public Library system, having been shown the architec-tural and economic practicality, has now asked the city for funds to convert the building to a major branch library.

Why all the to-do over a peculiar building on a cen-trally located site which could make a lot of quick money for somebody and some extra taxes for the city, if it were used for commerce and residences, like most sites around it?

Functionally, it happens that just such a difference in use as a library is needed here, to help counter the self-destruction of diversity. However, few people are aware of this functional need, or conscious that just such a build-ing can help to anchor diversity. Rather, there seems to be a strong popular agreement that *visually* the whole busy neighborhood of this landmark will lose its point—in short, its order will blur rather than clarify—if this landmark is replaced by a duplication of the uses that already exist around it.

Even an inherently meaningless landmark in a center of activity seems to contribute to the users' satisfaction. For instance, in St. Louis there stands a tall concrete column in the middle of a down-at-heel commercial center in declining, gray area surroundings. It once served as a water tower. Many years ago, when the water tank was removed, the local citizens prevailed on City Hall to save the pedestal, which they themselves then repaired. It still gives to the district its name, "The Watertower," and it still gives a bit of pathetic distinction to its district too, which would otherwise hardly even be recognizable as a place.

As clarifiers of city order, landmarks do best when they are set right amidst their neighbors, as in the case of all the examples I have mentioned. If they are buffered off and isolated from the generalized scene, they are contradicting, instead of explaining and visually reinforcing, an important fact about city differences: that they support each other. This too needs to be said by suggestion.

Eye-catchers, as already mentioned in the case of visual street interruptions, have an importance in city appearance out of all proportion to the physical space they occupy.

Some eye-catchers are eye-catchers just by virtue of *what* they are, rather than because of precisely *where* they are: an odd building for instance, or a little group of differing buildings standing out, because of themselves, in the wide-angle view across a park space. I think it is neither necessary nor desirable to try deliberately to create or to control this category of eye-catchers. Where diversity is generated, where there is mixture in building ages and types, and where there are opportunity and welcome for many people's plans and tastes, eye-catchers of this kind always turn up, and they are more surprising, various and interesting than anyone, aiming primarily at city design, could deliberately plan. Truth is stranger than fiction.

Other eye-catchers, however, are eye-catchers because of *precisely where* they are, and these are necessary to consider as a deliberate part of city design. First of all, there must be spots that, simply as locations, do catch the eye—for example, visual street interruptions. Second, these spots must count for something. These highly visible spots are few and exceptional; they are only one or two among many scores of buildings and locations comprising a street scene. We cannot therefore depend on the law of averages or on chance alone to deliver us visual accents in exactly these natural eye-catcher spots. Often, no more is needed than a good paint color (and a subtraction of billboards) on a building that already exists. Sometimes a new building or new use is needed in these spots—even a landmark. By taking care with the relatively very few spots that are inevitable eye-catchers, much character, interest and accent can be given to a whole scene by suggestion, and with the least design regimentation and the greatest economy of means and tactics.

The importance of such places, and the importance of making them count are points well made in *Planning and Community Appearance,* a booklet prepared by a committee of New York planners and architects formed to investigate the problems of municipal design control. The committee's principal recommendation was that the crucial visual spots in a community be identified, and that *these small spots be zoned to require exceptional treatment.* No good can come, said the committee's report, of blandly including such eye-catching locations in general schemes of zoning and planning.* Their locations alone give buildings on these few sites special and exceptional significance, and when we ignore that fact we are ignoring the most tangible realities.

There are some city streets which, in the absence of excellent eye-catchers, or even in addition to eye-catchers, need another kind of design help too. They need unifying devices, to suggest that the street, with all its diversity, is also an entity.

I have mentioned, in Chapter Twelve, a tactic suitable for some streets of mixed residences and commerce, to prevent them from being visually exploded or disintegrated by incongruously large uses. The suitable tactic for visual unity on these streets, as already explained, is to zone a limit on the length of street frontage permitted any single enterprise.

For another family of street unifying tactics, we can exploit the principle that a strong, but otherwise unobtrusive, design element can tie together in orderly fashion much happenstance detail. This kind of unification can be

---

*This booklet, obtainable from the New York Regional Plan Association, also discusses the legislative, regulatory and tax arrangements required by such an approach, and is thus valuable to anyone seriously interested in city visual order.

useful on streets that are heavily used, much seen and contain much detail without much real variety of use—streets almost entirely commercial, for instance.

One of the simplest such devices is trees along the stretch to be unified, but trees planted close enough together to give a look of continuity when they are seen close up, as well as when the space between them is elided by distance. Pavements have possibilities as unifiers; that is, sidewalk pavements with strong, simple patterns. Awnings in strong colors have possibilities.

Each street that needs this kind of help is its own problem, and probably needs its own solution.* There is a pitfall inherent in unification devices. One reason for a unifier's power is that it is special to a place. The sky itself, in a way, ties together nearly every scene, but its very ubiquity makes it an ineffective visual unifier of most scenes. A unifier supplies only the visual suggestion of entity and order; the viewer does most of the job of unifying by using the hint to help him organize what he sees. If he sees exactly the same unifier in otherwise disparate places and scenes, he will soon unconsciously discount it.

All these various tactics for capturing city visual order are concerned with bits and pieces in the city—bits and pieces which are, to be sure, knit into a city fabric of use that is as continuous and little cut apart as possible. But emphasis

---

*The effects of various kinds of unifiers—as well as of visual interruptions good and bad, landmarks and much else—are pictured and explained in two remarkable books on design in English cities, towns and countryside, *Outrage* and *Counter Attack*, both by Gordon Cullen and Ian Nairn.

on bits and pieces is of the essence: this is what a city is, bits and pieces that supplement each other and support each other.

Perhaps this all seems very commonplace compared with the sweep and swoop of highways, or the eerily beautiful beehive huts of tribal kraals. But what we have to express in expressing our cities is not be be scorned. Their intricate order—a manifestation of the freedom of countless numbers of people to make and carry out countless plans—is in many ways a great wonder. We ought not to be reluctant to make this living collection of interdependent uses, this freedom, this life, more understandable for what it is, nor so unaware that we do not know what it is.

20

SALVAGING PROJECTS

One of the unsuitable ideas behind projects is the very notion that they *are* projects, abstracted out of the ordinary city and set apart. To think of salvaging or improving projects, *as projects,* is to repeat this root mistake. The aim should be to get that project, that patch upon the city, rewoven back into the fabric—and in the process of doing so, strengthen the surrounding fabric too.

Reweaving projects back into the city is necessary not only to bring life to dangerous or inert projects themselves. It is also necessary for larger district planning. Cut up physically by projects and their border vacuums, handicapped socially and economically by the isolation of too small neighborhoods, a city district cannot be a district in truth, coherent enough and large enough to count.

The underlying principles for bringing life to a project site itself and to the borders where it must be rejoined with the district are the same as the principles for helping any city area where vitality is low. The planners have to diagnose which conditions for generating diversity are missing here—whether there is a lack of mixed primary uses, whether the blocks are too large, whether there is insufficient mixture in ages and types of buildings, whether the concentration of people is great enough. Then, whatever among those conditions is missing has to be supplied—usually gradually and opportunistically—as best it can be.

511

In the case of housing projects, the fundamental problems can be much like those presented by unplanned,
low-vitality gray areas and engulfed former suburbs. In
the case of nonresidential projects, such as cultural or
civic centers, the fundamental problems can be much like
those presented by has-been parts of downtowns which
have suffered the self-destruction of diversity.

However, because projects and their borders present
special kinds of obstacles to supplying the conditions necessary for generating diversity (and sometimes special
kinds of obstacles to the process of unslumming too),
their salvage does require some special tactics.

The projects that today most urgently need salvaging are
low-income housing projects. Their failures drastically
affect the everyday lives of many people, especially children. Moreover, because they are too dangerous, demor-
alizing and unstable within themselves, they make it too
hard in many cases to maintain tolerable civilization in
their vicinities. Immense investments have gone into fed-
eral- and state-financed housing projects; these expenditures, in spite of having been ill conceived, are too large to
write off, even for a country as rich as ours. To salvage the
investments themselves, the projects must be converted
into the assets to human life and to cities that it was hoped
they would become.*

These projects, like any slums, need to be unslummed.
This means, among other things, that they must be capa-

---

*The silliest conception of salvage is to build a duplicate of the first fail-
ure and move the people from the first failure into its expensive duplicate so the first failure can be salvaged! This is a stage of slum shifting

ble of holding their populations through *choice*. It means they must be safe and otherwise workable for city life. They need, among other things, casual public characters, lively, well-watched, continuously used public spaces, easier and more natural supervision of children, and normal city cross-use of their territory by people from outside it. In short, in the process of being rejoined into the city fabric, these projects need to take on the qualities of healthy city fabric themselves.

The easiest way to get at this problem mentally is to imagine, first, that the project ground level, right up to its perimeter roadbeds, is virtually a clean and empty slate. Above it float the apartment houses, attached to the ground only by their stairs and elevator stacks. All kinds of things can be done on this almost clean slate.

In real life, to be sure, this theoretical clean slate will not always be so clean as that. Sometimes there are other fixed features besides elevators and stairs on that ground-level plane. Some projects contain on their grounds schools or settlement houses or churches. Once in a while there are large trees that ought to be kept if possible, and

---

and slum duplicating that our cities are reaching, however. Buffalo, for example, has a low-income project named Dante Place, built with federal funds in 1954. Dante Place has speedily become a festering sore; it "represented an obstacle to the development of the land adjacent to it," in the words of the city's Housing Authority director. Solution: A new project, much like Dante Place, has been built in another part of town, and the inhabitants of Dante Place are to be moved there to fester so Dante Place can be salvaged—which means so it can be converted to a middle-income project. This process of correcting mistakes by compounding them was hailed in November 1959 by the New York State Commissioner of Housing as progress that "may well set a pattern for other housing authorities."

very occasionally indeed there is some outdoor space which works well enough and is unique enough to hold on to.

The grounds of newer projects—and especially most of those built since 1950—automatically make much cleaner ground-level slates than older projects, when thought of in this way. This is because, as time has gone on, housing project design has become ever more a routine matter of plunking down ever higher towers in ever more vacuous settings.

On this slate new streets must be designed: real streets which are to receive buildings and new uses along them; not "promenades" through vacuous "parks." These streets must be laid out in small blocks. Small public parks should be included to be sure, and sports or play areas, but only in quantities and in places where busy new streets and their uses can enforce safety and insure attraction.

The placement of these new streets will be influenced by two principal physical considerations: First, they must tie in with streets beyond the project borders, because the prime object is to knit this site with what lies around it. (An important part of the problem will be the redesign and added uses for the project's side of its border street itself.) Second, the new streets must also tie into the few fixed features within the project site. The apartment buildings, which we have been thinking of as floating above the site, attached only by elevators and stairs, can become street buildings, with their ground floors redesigned and incorporated into street-side uses; or if they are "missed" by the street, their access points can be gotten to by short walks or spurs leading off streets between new street-side buildings. The existing towers, in any case, will now rise here and there above the new streets, the new buildings, the new city which will lie below them.

Of course, it will typically be impossible to design streets that tie into the city surrounding, into the immutable fixed site features, and are at the same time straight, regular grid patterns on the site. As in the case of new streets cut through other city blocks that are too long, they will likely have bends, jogs and T intersections. So much the better, as I have argued in the previous chapter.

What sorts of new street uses and street buildings are possible?

The general aim should be to bring in uses different from residence, because lack of enough mixed uses is precisely one of the causes of deadness, danger and plain inconvenience. These different uses can occupy entire new street-side buildings, or merely the first floors or basements of buildings. Almost any kind of work use would be especially valuable; also evening uses and general commerce, particularly if these will draw good crossuse from outside the project's former boundaries.

Getting this diversity is more easily said than done, because buildings on new streets on a project site will carry the serious economic burden of being composed of virtually all new construction, instead of being of mingled ages. This is a truly formidable handicap; there is no way of overcoming it ideally—it is one of the handicaps we inherit in inheriting projects. However, there are several ways of minimizing this.

One means, possibly the most promising, is to

depend in part upon vendors who use carts and do not require buildings. This is a partial economic substitute for the missing old, low-overhead store space.

Deliberate street arrangements for vendors can be full of life, attraction and interest, and because of bargains are excellent stimulators of cross-use. Moreover, they can be delightful-looking. A Philadelphia architect, Robert Geddes, has designed an interesting vendor area for a proposed commercial renewal street in that city. In the street problem which Geddes had, the vendor area was to be a market plaza, across the street from a small public building; on its side of the street the plaza was enclosed on two sides by the sides of adjoining store and apartment buildings, but there was nothing enclosing it across the rear (it penetrated only half through its block and abutted parking). Geddes designed, as a backdrop, an attractive but economical shed for garaging the carts after business hours.

A street-side shed for cart garaging could be used along stretches of project streets, just as well as it can be used in a plaza design.

Outdoor vending would be an excellent eye-catcher for extending across T intersections or street bends. You will recall that what goes into an eye-catching street site has much to do with giving an impression of character to a whole scene. One of the difficult visual problems of project salvage will be to make these places look lively and urban enough; they have so much grimness and visual repetition to overcome.

Another possible means for partially overcoming the handicap of too much new construction would depend on the device of guaranteed-rent dwellings. These buildings could be placed on project streets, the same as on any other city streets, as described in Chapter Seventeen. However, they could be specified as row houses, or as double duplexes (one duplex on top of another, making four stories). Just as rows of old city brownstones have proved convertible to many kinds of different city uses and combinations of uses, generally one or two buildings at a time, or even one or two floors at a time, so would these basically similar small buildings be inherently flexible. They would represent, from the beginning, a use-conversion reservoir.

Still another possibility has been worked out by Perkins & Will, Chicago and White Plains architects, who, as a public service, devised for Union Settlement in New York a number of new ideas in public housing project design. Among the Perkins & Will proposals were four-story flats, placed on stilts to form an open "basement," with the basement floor either at ground level or four feet below ground level; one purpose was to make possible cheap enclosure of space for stores or other uses. The half-level basements made the flats above only a half-story instead of a full story above ground; this arrangement, besides being economical, would make a good street variation, because stores or workshops in basements, reached by a few steps down from the street, are often popular and attractive.

Still another possibility is to build some of the street-side edifices in cheap and makeshift fashion (which does not necessarily mean they must be ugly), with the intention of making overhead low at the most economically difficult stage, and their replacement practical in future when economic success warrants it. This is not as promising as the other methods, however, because buildings built well enough to stand five years or ten years have to be built well enough to stand a great deal longer. It is hard to give buildings a calculated built-in obsolescence and make really appreciable savings.

All housing projects with tall buildings are especially handicapped in supervision of children, and even after salvage work it will still be impossible to supervise children from the high apartments in the way that children on normal city sidewalks can be supervised from the windows of flats, houses or tenements above. This is one reason it is so imperative to get adults circulating around and spreading themselves through time in all public spaces at ground level, to get small businessmen with their typical propensity for public law and order, to get other public characters too, and to have streets sufficiently active and interesting so that they will be watched reasonably well from dwellings in at least the first three or four stories of buildings, the floors from which surveillance counts most.

One of the project planning delusions has been the notion that projects can evade the general workings of city land economics. To be sure, by making use of subsidies and of the powers of condemnation, it is possible to evade the *financial* need for good economic environment for city commerce and other uses. However, it is one thing to get around a financial problem, and another to evade basic economic functioning. Project sites are of course as dependent as any other fragments of city geography on intensity of use, and to get it they have to have a good economic environment for it. How good this economic environment can be depends in part on the new arrangements and new mixtures of uses within former project grounds, and on gradual unslumming and self-diversification in the project population. But it also depends on how well the surrounding territory is generating diversity and cross-use.

If the area as a whole, along with its former projects, becomes lively, improving and unslumming, the non-housing uses on former project grounds should eventually be able to produce a good return. But these grounds have so many handicaps to begin with, and so much needs to be done from scratch, that considerable public money will be needed for salvage: money will be needed for site replanning and designing itself, which will take a heavy investment in time and imagination because this time it cannot be done routinely or by people ignorant of what they are doing and why; money will be needed for construction of streets and other public spaces; and probably money will be needed for subsidy to at least some of the new building construction.

Whether or not the ownership of the already existing dwellings themselves remains with the housing authorities, the new streets and new uses, including new dwellings mixed with them, cannot be the property and responsibility of these agencies, putting them into a politically impossible (and unwise) competition with private building owners. Nor should housing authorities be given the responsibility of reweaving their old baronies back into the free city, a responsibility for which they are in no way whatever equipped. This land was taken by governmental powers for the authorities. It can be taken from them by governmental powers, replanned, and lots for building sold off or rented under long-term leases. Portions, of course, should go under the jurisdiction of appropriate city agencies, such as the department of parks and the department of streets.

Apart from physical and economic improvements at ground level such as those suggested, the salvage of public housing requires some other changes.

The corridors of the usual high-rise, low-income housing building are like corridors in a bad dream: creepily lit, narrow, smelly, blind. They feel like traps, and they are. So are the elevators that lead to them. These traps are what people mean when they say, time and again, "Where can we go? Not to a project! I have children. I have young daughters."

Much has been written about the fact that children urinate in housing project elevators. It is an obvious problem because it leaves a smell and corrodes the machinery. But this is perhaps the most innocuous misuse of project self-service elevators. More serious is the terror that people can feel in them, with good reason.

The only solution that I can see to this problem, and to the related corridor problem, is to provide elevator attendants. Nothing else, not guards on the grounds, not doormen, no form of "tenant education" can make these buildings tolerably safe or their people tolerably secure from predators coming both from outside the project and from within.

This too will take money, but little compared to the tremendous investments that have to be salvaged—as much as $40,000,000 in single projects. I mention $40,000,000 because that happens to be the public investment in Frederick Douglass Houses, a new project on the Upper West Side of Manhattan, where there has occurred, along with all the usual terrors, an elevator crime so appallingly savage that the newspapers have taken notice of it.

In Caracas, Venezuela, where the deposed dictator left a large legacy of similar projects with similar dangers, an experiment in improving elevator and corridor safety is reported to have helped. Women tenants who can manage full- or part-time jobs are hired as regular elevator attendants from 6:00 A.M. to 1:00 A.M., when elevator service is discontinued. Carl Feiss, a U.S. planning consultant who has done considerable work in Venezuela tells me that the buildings are safer, and that general communication and social tone have also been somewhat improved because the elevator operators have become rudimentary public characters.

Women tenants as attendants might work well in our projects too during the day, when the principal elevator misuses are extortion and sexual molestation of younger children by older children. I suspect that the night shift, when adult attacks, muggings and robberies are a greater danger, would require men as attendants. It is also doubtful that the night service cut-off would work for us, first, because too many tenants in these projects have night jobs and, second, because too many arbitrary rules, different from those applying to other people, already set the projects apart and feed residents' resentments and bitterness.*

To unslum, public housing projects must be capable of

*Nowadays, relatively few people enter low-income projects by free choice; rather, they have been thrown out of their previous neighborhoods to make way for "urban renewal" or highways and, especially if they are colored and therefore subject to housing discrimination, have holding people by choice when they develop choice (which means they must become gladly attached before they have choice), and for this the kinds of salvage already suggested, outside and inside, are necessary. However, in addition, people must of course be permitted to stay by choice, which means that maximum income limits must be abandoned. It is not enough to raise limits; the tie of residency to income price tags must be abandoned altogether. So long as it remains, not only will all the most successful or lucky inexorably be drained away, but all the others must psychologically identify themselves with their homes either as transients or as "failures."

Rents should be increased in accord with increased incomes, up to the point where full economic rent is paid, as in the proposed guaranteed-rent system, already explained. This economic rent figure would have to include pro-rated amortization and debt service, to work capital costs back into the rent equation.

No one, or even two, of the suggestions I have made will be effective as an all-purpose salvager in itself. All three—grounds reconverted and woven back into surrounding city; safety inside buildings; removal of maximum income limits—are necessary. Naturally, the

---

had no other choice. Among the dislocated, only about 20 percent (in Philadelphia, Chicago and New York, for which figures have been published) go into public housing; among those who do not are many who are eligible but will not go because they can find some other way out. Describing this maddening obstinacy of those still lucky enough to have some choice, a New York City housing official cited 16 dislocated families who were eligible for three-bedroom apartments, which were waiting for them, in public housing. "They had eviction papers in their hands, but not one would take public housing."

quickest positive results can be expected in the projects where demoralization and the going-backward process of the perpetual slum have wreaked the least harm.

Middle-income housing projects are not so urgent a salvage problem as low-income projects, but in some ways they are more baffling.

Unlike low-income project tenants, many middle-income project tenants appear to favor sorting themselves into islands distinctly apart from other people. My impression, which I admit is shaky, is that middle-income projects, as they age, tend to contain a significant (or at least articulate) proportion of people who are fearful of contact outside their class. How much such tendencies are innate to people who have chosen to live in class-segregated and regimented projects, and to what extent these feelings are cultivated and developed by Turf living itself, I do not know. My acquaintances in a number of middle-income projects tell me they have observed in their neighbors the growth of hostility to the city outside their project borders as disturbing incidents have occurred in their own elevators and in their own grounds—incidents for which outsiders are invariably blamed, with or without evidence. The growth and hardening of Turf psychology because of real dangers—or the concentration together of appreciable numbers of people already beset with xenophobia, whichever it may be—is a serious problem for big cities.

People who live behind project borders and who feel estranged and deeply unsafe about the city across those borders are not going to be much help in eliminating district border vacuums, or even in permitting replanning aimed at rejoining them with the fabric of a city district.

It may be that districts which contain projects exhibiting advanced xenophobia must simply proceed to improve, as districts, in spite of this handicap, as best they can. If the streets outside such projects can nevertheless be catalyzed into greater safety, diversity and vitality, and increased stability of population, and if at the same time, within the project borders, the built-in dangers resulting from vacuity are ameliorated in any ways that do prove acceptable to the project residents and to the insurance companies, labor unions, cooperatives and private entrepreneurs who own these places, perhaps in time it will be possible to knit them in with the living city. Certainly the hope of doing so grows less and less, the more the district around them is converted into stereotyped and dangerous projects too.

Nonresidential projects, such as cultural or civic centers, can probably in a few cases employ ground replanning tactics to weave them back into the city fabric. The most promising cases are centers located at the edges of downtowns, with little but the buffers and border vacuums resulting from their own presence between themselves and potentially supplementary high-intensity uses. One side of Pittsburgh's new civic center, at least, might be rewoven into the downtown, from which it is now buffered. Parts of San Francisco's civic center might be rewoven into the city with new streets and new uses added.

The main difficulty with civic centers, especially those that contain buildings such as auditoriums and halls, bringing huge concentrations of people for relatively brief times, is to find other primary uses at least roughly proportionate in the concentrations of people that they can supply at other times of day. There still has to be room, somewhere, for the range and amount of secondary diversity that these combined intensive uses can support; and of course the problem exists of insufficient older buildings for a good range of secondary diversity. In short, the trouble is that many civic and cultural center components make sense only as elements of intensive downtown or central use, and to try to make them serve so, once they have been abstracted into islands, means trying to move the mountain to Mahomet.

A more practical way to approach reintegration in most cases, I think, is to aim at disassembling these centers, over periods of time. Disassembly can occur as opportunity and expediency permit it. The point is to watch for the opportunities. Such an opportunity occurred, for example, in Philadelphia, at the time the downtown Broad Street Station and Pennsylvania Railroad track embankment were removed, and the office-transportation-hotel project of Penn Center was planned in their place. The Philadelphia Free Library, stuck off on a cultural-center boulevard where it gets shockingly little use, was at this time in need of major rehabilitation. Its officials tried hard and long to persuade the city that, instead of redoing the old building, it would be better to move the library out of the cultural center and into the downtown, as part of the Penn Center plan. Apparently nobody responsible in the city government saw that just this kind of reinfiltration of central cultural facilities into the downtown was necessary—for the downtown and for the vitality of the cultural facilities themselves.

If assembled components of cultural and civic islands

are disassembled and leave their islands, one by one, as opportunity affords, entirely different uses can be put in their places—preferably uses that will not only be different rather than similar, but that, in their differences, will supplement what remains in the project.

Philadelphia, while perpetuating its old library mistake, at least saved itself from piling on another mistake—because by this time Philadelphia has had enough experience with a cultural center to be somewhat disenchanted with the supposed vitalizing powers of such a place. When the Academy of Music, which is in the downtown, needed rehabilitation a few years ago, almost nobody took seriously the idea that it should be transplanted to the culture reservation. It was kept where it belongs, downtown. Baltimore, after playing around for years with this plan and that for an abstracted and isolated civic-cultural center, has decided instead to build downtown, where these facilities can count most both as needed primary uses and as landmarks.

This is, of course, the best way to salvage any kind of sorted-out project, up to the time it is actually built: Think better of it.

21

GOVERNING AND
PLANNING DISTRICTS

A public hearing in a big city is apt to be a curious affair, simultaneously discouraging and heartening. The ones I know best are held in New York's City Hall, alternate Thursdays, on measures that require decision by the city's chief governing body, the Board of Estimate. The subjects have appeared on the day's hearing calendar by prior pushing, pulling and contriving on the part of somebody either in government or out.

Citizens who wish to speak their minds address the Mayor, the five Borough Presidents, the Comptroller and the President of the City Council, who sit behind a raised semicircular bench at one end of a large and handsome room filled with high-backed white pews for the public. Public officials, elected and appointed, turn up on those pews too, to oppose or to advocate controversial items. Sometimes the sessions are calm and speedy; but often they are tumultuous and last not only all day, but far into the night. Whole segments of city life, problems of neighborhood upon neighborhood, district upon district, parades of remarkable personalities, all come alive in this room. The members of the Board listen, interject and sometimes hand down decrees on the spot, like rulers holding court in the manor during medieval days.

I became an addict of the Board of Estimate sessions

as a fierce and rooted partisan at just such hearings, and I cannot lose my habit of involvement as some other district's problems are cried out here or some other neighborhood's cause is pled. In one sense, the whole affair is exasperating. So many of the problems need never have arisen. If only well-meaning officials in departments of the city government or in freewheeling authorities knew intimately, and cared about, the streets or districts which their schemes so vitally affect—or if they knew in the least what the citizens of that place consider of value in their lives, and why. So many of the conflicts would never occur if planners and other supposed experts understood in the least how cities work and respected those workings. Still other issues, it appears, involve forms of favoritism, deals or arbitrary administrative acts which outrage voters but for which they can find no effective place to pin responsibility or seek repair. In many cases too (not all), the hundreds of people who have lost a day's pay, or have made arrangements for care of their children, or have brought their children along and sit hour upon hour with youngsters fidgeting in their laps, are being hoaxed; it has all been decided before they are heard.*

Even more discouraging than all this is the sense one soon gets of problems which are out of the control of everyone. Their ramifications are too complex; too many

---

*Thus in a letter to the *New York Times* on charter revision, Stanley M. Isaacs, City Councilman and former Borough President of Manhattan, writes: "Will they hold hearings? Of course. But we who are experienced know what that means. These will be hearings like those regularly held these days by the Board of Estimate. They will hold an executive session first"; [executive sessions are on Wednesdays, the day before public hearings] "everything will be decided; and then the public will be listened to with complete courtesy and with deaf ears."

different kinds of trouble, need and services are inter-locked in a given place—too many to be understood, let alone helped or handled when they are attacked, one-sidedly and remotely, by the sprawling municipal gov-ernment's separate administrative empires, each by each. It is the blind men feeling the elephant again. Helpless-ness, and its partner futility, become almost palpable dur-ing these hearings.

On the other hand, though, the proceedings are heart-ening, because of the abounding vitality, earnestness and sense with which so many of the citizens rise to the occa-sion. Very plain people, including the poor, including the discriminated against, including the uneducated, reveal themselves momentarily as people with grains of great-ness in them, and I do not speak sardonically. They tell with wisdom and often eloquence about things they know first-hand from life. They speak with passion about concerns that are local but far from narrow. To be sure, foolish things are said too, and untrue things, and things brazenly or suavely self-seeking; and it is good, too, to see the effects of these remarks. We listeners are seldom fooled, I think; it is clear from our responses that we understand and rate these sentiments for what they are. There is experience at living, responsibility and concern in abundance among the city's people. There is cynicism but there is also faith, and this is, of course, what counts most.

The eight rulers who sit behind the raised bench (we cannot call them servants of the people as the conventions of government have it, for servants would know more of their masters' affairs), these rulers are not sorry specimens either. Most of us present, I think, are grateful that we have at least a dim and glimmering chance (so seldom fulfilled) of prevailing upon them to protect us from the oversimplifications of the experts, the blind men feeling the elephant. We watch and study our rulers as best we can. Their energy, wits, patience and human responsiveness are, on the whole, creditable. I see no reason to expect great improvement from finding better. These are not boys sent on a man's errand. These are men sent on a superman's errand.

The trouble is, they are trying to deal with the intimate details of a great metropolis with an organizational structure to back them up, advise them, inform them, guide them and pressure them, that has become anachronistic. There is no villainy responsible for this situation, not even the villainy of pass-the-buck; the villainy, if it can be called that, is a most understandable failure by our society to keep abreast of demanding historical changes.

The historical changes relevant in this case are not only an immense increase in the size of great cities, but also the immensely increased responsibilities—for housing, for welfare, for health, for education, for regulatory planning—which have been taken on by the governments of great municipalities. New York is not unique in failing to match such profound changes in circumstances with appropriate functional changes in administrative and planning structure. Every great American city is at a similar impasse.

When human affairs reach, in truth and in fact, new levels of complication, the only thing that can be done is to devise means of maintaining things well at the new level. The alternative is what Lewis Mumford has aptly called "unbuilding," the fate of a society which cannot maintain the complexity on which it is built and on which it depends.

The ruthless, oversimplified, pseudo-city planning and pseudo-city design we get today is a form of "unbuilding" cities. But although it was shaped and sanctified by reactionary theories actually glorifying the "unbuilding" of cities, the practice and influence of this kind of planning today rests not on theory alone. Insensibly and gradually, as city administrative organization has failed to evolve suitably along with city growth and complexity, city "unbuilding" has become a destructive but practical necessity for planning and other administrative staffs, whose members are also being sent on supermen's errands. Routine, ruthless, wasteful, oversimplified solutions for all manner of city physical needs (let alone social and economic needs) *have* to be devised by administrative systems which have lost the power to comprehend, to handle and to value an infinity of vital, unique, intricate and interlocked details.

Consider, for a moment, the kind of goals at which city planning must begin to aim, if the object is to plan for city vitality.

Planning for vitality must stimulate and catalyze the greatest possible range and quantity of diversity among uses and among people throughout each district of a big city; this is the underlying foundation of city economic strength, social vitality and magnetism. To do this, planners must diagnose, in specific places, specifically what is lacking to generate diversity, and then aim at helping to supply the lacks as best they can be supplied.

Planning for vitality must promote continuous networks of local street neighborhoods, whose users and

532   The Death and Life of Great American Cities

informal proprietors can count to the utmost in keeping the public spaces of the city safe, in handling strangers so they are an asset rather than a menace, in keeping casual public tabs on children in places that are public.

Planning for vitality must combat the destructive presence of border vacuums, and it must help promote people's identification with city districts that are large enough, and are varied and rich enough in inner and outer contacts to deal with the tough, inescapable, practical problems of big-city life.

Planning for vitality must aim at unslumming the slums, by creating conditions aimed at persuading a high proportion of the indigenous residents, whoever they may be, to stay put by choice over time, so there will be a steadily growing diversity among people and a continuity of community both for old residents and for newcomers who assimilate into it.

Planning for vitality must convert the self-destruction of diversity and other cataclysmic uses of money into constructive forces, by hampering the opportunities for destructiveness on the one hand, and on the other hand by stimulating more city territory into possessing a good economic environment for other people's plans.

Planning for vitality must aim at clarifying the visual order of cities, and it must do so by both promoting and illuminating functional order, rather than by obstructing or denying it.

To be sure, this is not quite so formidable as it sounds, because all such aims are interrelated; it would be impossible to pursue any one of them effectively without simultaneously (and, to an extent, quite automatically) pursuing the others. Nevertheless, aims of this kind cannot be pursued unless those responsible for diagnosis, for devising tactics, for recommending actions and for carrying out actions know what they are doing. They must know it not in some generalized way, but in terms of the precise and unique places in a city with which they are dealing. Much of what they need to know they can learn from no one but the people of the place, because nobody else knows enough about it.

For this kind of planning, it is not enough for administrators in most fields to understand specific *services* and *techniques*. They must understand, and understand thoroughly, specific *places*.

Only supermen could understand a great city as a total, or as whole groups of districts, in the detail that is needed for guiding constructive actions and for avoiding unwitting, gratuitous, destructive actions.

There is a widespread belief among many city experts today that city problems already beyond the comprehension and control of planners and other administrators can be solved better if only the territories involved and problems entailed are made larger still and can therefore be attacked more "broadly." This is escapism from intellectual helplessness. "A Region," somebody has wryly said, "is an area safely larger than the last one to whose problems we found no solution."

Big-city government is today nothing more than little-city government which has been stretched and adapted in quite conservative fashion to handle bigger jobs. This has had strange results, and ultimately destructive results, because big cities pose operational problems that are innately different from those posed by little cities.

There are similarities, of course. Like any settlement, a big city has a territory to be administered, and various services to be administered for it. And just as in most smaller settlements, it is logical and practical in big cities to organize these services vertically: that is, each service has its own organization, e.g., city-wide parks departments, health departments, traffic departments, housing authorities, departments of hospitals, departments of water supply, departments of streets, licensing departments, police departments, sanitation departments and the like. From time to time new services are added—departments to combat air pollution, redevelopment agencies, transit authorities and so on.

However, because of the enormous amount of work these agencies must do in big cities, even the most traditional have had to make, over the course of time, numerous internal divisions.

Many of these divisions are themselves vertical: the agencies are divided internally into fractions of responsibility, each fraction again applying to the city as a whole. Thus, for example, departments of parks are apt to have separate lines of responsibility for forestry, maintenance, playground design, recreation programs, and so on, coming together under top commands. Housing authorities have separate lines of responsibility for site selection and design, maintenance, social welfare, tenant selection and so on, each line a complex agency in itself, coming together under top commands. The same is true of boards of education, welfare departments, planning commissions and so on.

Besides these vertical divisions of responsibility many administrative agencies also have horizontal divisions: they are divided into *territorial* segments, for gathering information or for getting the work done, or both. Thus, for example, we have police precincts, health districts, welfare districts, subadministrative school and park districts, and so on. In New York, the five territorial borough presidents' offices have full responsibility over a few services, mainly streets (but not traffic) and various engineering services.

Each of the many internal divisions of responsibility, vertical or horizontal, is rational in its own terms, which is to say rational in a vacuum. Put them all together in terms of a big city itself and the sum is chaos.

The result is inherently different in a little city, no matter what internal divisions of services may be made. Consider for a moment such a city as New Haven, which has only 165,000 people. At this little-city scale, the head of an administrative agency and his staff members can easily and naturally communicate and coordinate with administrative heads and staffs in other services entirely, if they want to. (Whether they have good ideas to communicate and coordinate is, of course, another matter.)

Even more important, agency heads and their staffs, at little-city scale, can be experts in two matters simultaneously: they can be experts in their own responsibilities, and they can also be experts on the subject of New Haven itself. The only way an administrator (or anybody else) gets to know and understand a place well is partly from first-hand information and observation over time, and still more from learning what other people, both in government and out of government, know about the place. Some of this information can be mapped or tabulated; some of it cannot. New Haven is understandable, by combinations of all these means, to normally bright intellects. There are no other means, either for the bright or for the stupid, of understanding a locality intimately.

In short, New Haven, as an administrative structure, has a relative coherence built right into it, as one factor of its size.

The relative coherence of a place like New Haven is taken for granted, administratively. There may be ways to improve administrative efficiency and other facets of performance, but certainly nobody is under the delusion that the way to do so is to reorganize New Haven so it possesses one-eighth of a parks department, six and a quarter health districts, one-third of a welfare district, a thirteenth of a planning staff, half of one school district, a third of a second school district and two-ninths of a third school district, two and a half police departments, and a passing glance from a traffic commissioner.

Under such a scheme as that, even though it has only 165,000 persons, New Haven would not be understood as a place by anyone responsible. Some would see only a fraction of it; others would see it whole but only superficially, as a relatively inconsequential fraction of something much larger. Nor could its services, including planning, be efficiently or even sanely administered on such a scheme.

Yet this is the way we try to gather intelligence, administer services and plan for places within big cities. Naturally, problems which nearly everyone wants to solve, and which are capable of solution, are out of everyone's comprehension and control.

Multiply the imaginary fractionation I have outlined for New Haven by ten or by fifty for cities ranging from populations of one and a half million to eight million (and remember that the inherent complications to be understood and handled are increasing, not arithmetically with the population, but geometrically). Then sort out the differing responsibilities from their jackstraw disorder in localities, and combine them into great departmental and bureaucratic empires.

Mazes of coordination, conference and liaison tenuously connect these sprawling and randomly fractionated empires with one another. The mazes are too labyrinthine even to be kept mapped and open, let alone to serve as reliable and sensitive channels of interdepartmental understanding, or channels of pooled information about specific places, or channels of action for getting things done. Citizens and officials both can wander indefinitely in these labyrinths, passing here and there the bones of many an old hope, dead of exhaustion.

Thus, in Baltimore, a sophisticated citizens' group, which had the advantage of inside advice, and which made no false or unnecessary moves, engaged in conferences, negotiations and series of referrals and approvals extending over an entire year—merely for permission to place a sculpture of a bear in a street park! Innately simple achievements become monumentally difficult in these mazes. Difficult achievements become impossible.

Consider this item from the *New York Times* in August 1960 about a fire which had injured six persons in a tenement owned by the city. The tenement, reports the paper, "had been described as a firetrap in February in a Fire Department report to the Department of Buildings." The Commissioner of Buildings, defending his department, said that building inspectors had been trying to get into the building for a long time, including the period after May 16 when the city acquired title. The news story goes on:

> In fact, the Real Estate Department [the city agency which owned the building] did not notify the Buildings Department that it had acquired the property until July 1, the Commissioner said. And not until twenty-five days later did the notification complete its journey through channels from the Buildings Department on the twentieth floor to the housing division [of the Buildings Department] on the eighteenth floor of the Municipal Building. When the information arrived in the housing division on July 25, a telephone call was made to the Real Estate Department requesting access for inspection. At first the Real Estate Department said it did not have keys to the building, the Commissioner [of Buildings] said. Negotiations were undertaken . . . They were still under way when the fire occurred Saturday [Aug. 13]. They were renewed the following Monday by a Buildings Department official who had not heard about the fire . . .

If all this inanity concerning sheer communication is too cumbersome, futile and tedious to follow, consider how much more cumbersome, futile and tedious it is to contend with. Persons of hope, energy and initiative who enter into the service of these empires almost have to become uncaring and resigned, for the sake of their self-preservation (not for job preservation, as is so often thought, but for *self*-preservation).

And if useful communication of intelligence and effective coordination of action are baffling from within the government, consider also how baffling and frustrating they are for those who must deal with it from without. Difficult, time consuming—and expensive too—as group political pressure is to organize and exert on elected officials, the citizens of big cities learn that this is often the only practicable way to bypass or undercut still more difficult and time-consuming procedures of the nonelected bureaucracy.*

Political action and pressure will always be necessary, and rightly so in a self-governing society, to battle and settle real conflicts of interest and opinion. It is another matter to find, as we find today, in all the biggest cities, that it takes enormous effort—usually never put forth— merely to bring together and try to interest the appropriate experts of several different services that are necessarily involved in handling a single problem or need of a single place. And it is still more ridiculous that if these "arrangements to formulate a liaison"—as they seem to be called in the New York City Planning Commission—are at last arranged and formulated, they are

*Special interests sometimes hire "influence" to overcome—in their own interest of course—frustrations similar to those that impel ordinary citizens to exert group leverage on administrators via elected officials. Thus one aspect of New York's urban redevelopment scandals concerned payments made to Sydney S. Baron (press chief of Democratic Party leader Carmine G. DeSapio) by six sponsors of federally subsidized redevelopment projects. One of the sponsors explained, according to the *New York Post*, "It would be fantastic to tell you we hired Baron for any other reason than his influence. We would wait months for meetings with Commissioners—like the Health, Fire and Police Departments— but then he would go to the phone and, immediately, we would have action." The news report goes on to say, "Baron flatly denied that he was primarily hired to 'expedite with city agencies.' 'I only set up two conferences, one with Health, one with Fire,' he said."

apt to be liaisons of expert ignorance meeting with expert ignorance. You never realize how complicated a neighborhood within a big city is until you try to explain it to experts in fractionated responsibility. It is like trying to eat through a pillow.

Citizens of big cities are forever being berated for not taking sufficiently active interest in government. It is amazing, rather, that they keep trying.

Again and again in his penetrating *New York Times* articles on delinquency, reporter Harrison Salisbury cites the seemingly immovable obstacles to improvement that are posed by wildly fragmented information, fragmented administration, fragmented responsibility, fragmented authority. "The real jungle is in the office of the bureaucrats," he quotes one student of delinquency. And Salisbury himself sums up, "Conflict, confusion, overlapping authority are the order of the day."

It seems to be frequently supposed that this obstructionism and inertia are deliberate, or are at least the by-products of various nasty administrative traits. "Hypocrisy," "bureaucratic jealousy," "vested interest in the status quo," "they don't care," are words and phrases that constantly crop up in despairing descriptions by citizens, telling of their frustrations in the labyrinths of city empires. To be sure, these nasty qualities can be found—they thrive in milieus where it takes so many to accomplish so little in the face of such need—but neither personal evil nor orneriness contrives this mess. Saints could not run such systems well.

The administrative structure itself is at fault *because it has been adapted beyond the point that mere adaptations can serve*. This is how human affairs often evolve. There comes a point, at increased levels of complication, when actual invention is required.

Cities have made one considerable attempt at invention to deal with this problem of fragmented administration—the invention of the planning commission.

In city administrative theory, planning commissions are the grand administrative coordinators. They are rather new as significant features of American city government, most of them having been instituted only within the past twenty-five years as a direct response to the glaringly obvious fact that city administrative departments are unable to coordinate various schemes entailing city physical changes.

The invention was a poor one for the reason that it duplicated, and in some ways reinforced, the very flaws it was intended to overcome.

Planning commissions are organized, just as the other bureaucratic empires are, in fundamentally vertical fashion, with vertical fractionated responsibility and, as need and expediency have dictated, into random horizontal divisions here and there (renewal districts, conservation areas, etc.), coming together under top commands. Under this arrangement, it still remains that nobody, including the planning commission, is capable of comprehending places within the city other than in either generalized or fragmented fashion.

Furthermore, as coordinators of the physical plans of other city agencies, planning commissions deal mainly with proposals only *after* the officials of other agencies have at least tentatively figured out what they want to do. From dozens of sources these proposals come to the ken of the planning commission, which is *then* supposed to see whether they make sense in light of each other and in light of the planning commission's own information, conceptions and visions. But the vital time for coordinating intelligence is before and during the time that even tentative proposals are conceived or tactics worked out for any specific service in any specific place.

Naturally, under a system as unrealistic as this, the coordinators are unable to coordinate, even for themselves, let alone for others. Philadelphia's planning commission is widely admired as one of the best in the country, and it probably is, considering. But when one attempts to find out why the planning commission's pet esthetic creations, the Greenway "promenades,"* do not have the physical appearance in reality that they had in the planners' renderings, one learns from the planning director himself that the department of streets did not get the idea or something, and has not provided the proper pavements, the parks department or the housing authority or the redeveloper did not get the idea or something, and has not done right with the abstract open spaces, the many city departments concerned with street furniture did not get the idea or something—and above all, the citizens do not get the idea or something. All these details are so wearying and frustrating, it is more rewarding to create new visions of what might "ideally" be for some other place than it is to wander the labyrinths trying futilely to put together the pieces of last year's vision. Yet these are innately simple matters compared with the coordination required to attack such really tough plan-

---

*Which of course have no promenaders.

ning problems as unslumming, safety, clarifying the order of cities, and better economic environment for diversity.

Under the circumstances, planning commissions have become, not effective instruments for comprehending and coordinating a necessary infinity of complex city detail, but rather destructive instruments, of greater or lesser effectiveness, for "unbuilding" and oversimplifying cities. It cannot be helped, as things are. Their staffs do not and cannot know enough about places within cities to do anything else, try as they might. Even should their ideologies of planning switch from Radiant Garden City Beautiful visions to *city* planning, they could not do city planning. They do not even have the means of gathering and comprehending the intimate, many-sided information required, partly because of their own unsuitable structures for comprehending big cities, and partly because of the same structural inadequacies in other departments.

Here is an interesting thing about coordination both of information and of action in cities, and it is the crux of the matter: The principal coordination needed comes down to coordination among different services within localized places. This is at once the most difficult kind of coordination, and the most necessary. Coordination up and down the line of fractionated vertical responsibilities is simple in comparison, and less vital too. Yet vertical coordination is made easiest by the administrative structure, and all other kinds more difficult, with locality coordination made impossible.

Intellectually, the importance of locality coordination is little recognized or acknowledged in city administrative theory. Planning commissions themselves are again a prime case in point. Planners like to think they deal in grand terms with the city as a whole, and that their value is great because they "grasp the whole picture." But the notion that they are needed to deal with their city "as a whole" is principally a delusion. Aside from highway planning (which is done abominably, in part because nobody understands the localities involved), and the almost purely budgetary responsibility for rationalizing and allocating the sum of capital improvement expenditures presented in tentative budgets, the work of city planning commissions and their staffs seldom deals, in truth, with a big city as a total organism.

In truth, because of the nature of the work to be done, almost all city planning is concerned with relatively small and specific acts done here and done there, in specific streets, neighborhoods and districts. To know whether it is done well or ill—to know what should be done at all— it is more important to know that specific locality than it is to know how many bits in the same category of bits are going into other localities and what is being done with them there. No other expertise can substitute for locality knowledge in planning, whether the planning is creative, coordinating or predictive.

The invention required is not a device for coordination at the generalized top, but rather an invention to make coordination possible where the need is most acute—in specific and unique localities.

In short, great cities must be divided into administrative districts. These would be horizontal divisions of city government but, unlike random horizontality, they would be common to the municipal government as a whole. The administrative districts would represent the primary, basic subdivisions made within most city agencies.

The chief officials of an agency, below the top commissioner, should be district administrators. Each district administrator would supervise all aspects of his department's service within his district; working under him would be the staff for supplying his service to the locality. The same district boundaries would be common to each department which acts directly on district life or planning—such as traffic, welfare, schools, police, parks, code enforcement, health, housing subsidy, fire, zoning, planning.

That district, as well as his own service, would be each district administrator's specific business. This double knowledge is not too much for normally bright intellects—particularly when districts include other men and women looking at the same place from other angles, and also responsible for understanding and serving the place as a place.

These administrative districts would have to correspond with reality, instead of fragmenting it under a new device. They would have to correspond with districts that now operate—or can potentially operate—as social and political Things in the manner described in Chapter Six.

With this kind of framework of governmental intelligence and action at hand, we could expect that many citywide voluntary agencies of public service would also adapt themselves to district administration.

The idea of horizontal municipal administration is, as already indicated, not a new idea. There are precedents for it in the random, unreconciled horizontality already resorted to by much city administration. There are precedents also in the designations, which have become common today, of renewal or conservation districts. When New York began to try neighborhood conservation in a handful of places, the administrators of this program promptly discovered they could get nothing useful done unless they made special and exceptional arrangements with at least the buildings department, the fire department, the police department, the health department and the sanitation department to supply staff members specifically responsible for that *place*. This has been necessary merely to coordinate a modicum of improvement in the simplest matters. The city describes this arrangement of reconciled horizontality as "a department store of services for the neighborhood," and it is recognized by both the city itself and the citizens concerned as one of the chief benefits received by a neighborhood which is declared a conservation area!

Among the most telling precedents for horizontal administration and responsibility are the settlement houses of big cities, which have always organized themselves with a piece of territory as their prime concern, rather than as a disembodied collection of vertical services. This is a main reason why settlement houses have been so effective, why their staffs usually know a place as thoroughly as they know their jobs, and why settlement house services, as a rule, neither become obsolescent nor work at cross-purposes to one another. Different settlement houses in a big city typically work together to quite a degree—fund raising, finding personnel, exchanging ideas, pressuring for legislation—and in this sense they are more than horizontal organizations. They are simultaneously horizontal and vertical in effect, but structurally the coordination is made easiest where inherently it is hardest.

Nor is the idea of administrative districts for American cities new, either. It has been proposed from time to time by citizens' groups—in New York it was suggested in 1947 by the competent and well-informed Citizens' Union, which went so far as actually to map out feasible administrative districts, based on empirical city districts; the Citizens' Union district map remains to this day the most understandable and logical mapping of New York City.

Usually, suggestions of big-city district administration wander off along unprofitable intellectual trails, however, and I think this is one reason they get nowhere. They are sometimes conceived of, for example, as organs of formalized "advice" to government. But in real life, advisory bodies lacking authority and responsibility are worse than useless for district administration. They waste everyone's time and inevitably succeed no better than anyone else in threading the impossible labyrinths of fractionated bureaucratic empires. Or administrative districts are sometimes conceived of in terms of a single "kingpin" service, such as planning for example, and this too turns ineffectual for solving anything of much importance; for to work usefully as instruments of government, administrative districts must encompass the many-sided activities of government. And sometimes the idea gets diverted into the aim of building local "civic centers," so that its importance is confused with the superficial aim of providing a new kind of project ornament for cities. The offices of district administration would have to be within the district concerned, and they should be close together.

However, the virtue of this arrangement is hardly anything visible or materially impressive. The most important visible manifestation of district administration would be the sight of people talking together without having first had "arrangements to formulate a liaison."

District administration, as a form of municipal government structure, is inherently more complex than the adapted little-city administrative structures we now have. City administration needs to be more complex in its fundamental structure so it can *work* more simply. The present structures, paradoxically, are fundamentally too simple.

For it must be understood that district administration in big cities cannot be "pure" or doctrinaire, with the vertical connections forgotten. A city, however big, is still a city, with great interdependence among its places and its parts. It is not a collection of towns and if it were it would be destroyed as a city.

Doctrinaire reorganization of government into pure horizontal administration would be as fatally simple and as chaotically unworkable as the present messes. It would be impractical if for no other reason than that taxation and the overall allocation of funds must be centralized city functions. Furthermore, some city operations transcend district administration completely; intimate and intricate details of district knowledge are largely irrelevant to them, and those that are relevant could be easily and quickly comprehended by gathering the necessary intelligence from district administrators who do understand the place. Water supply, air pollution control, labor mediation, management of museums, zoos and prisons are examples. Even within some departments, some services are illogical as district functions while others are logical; for instance, it would be foolish for a department of licenses to dispense taxi licenses as a district function, but secondhand dealers, places of entertainment, vendors, key makers, employment agencies, and many other operations requiring licenses would be sensibly dealt with under district organization.

In addition, certain specialists can be afforded by big cities and can be useful to them, although they would not be needed constantly in any one administrative district. Such people can serve as roving technicians and experts within a service, *under* the district administrator to whom they are assigned as needed.

A city instituting district administration should attempt to convert every service to which district knowledge is relevant into this new kind of structural organization. However, for some services, and portions of services, it would be necessary to see how it worked. Various adjustments could be made. The system does not need to be preceded by a copper-riveted, immutable scheme of operation. Indeed to put it into effect, and to make changes after it was in effect, would require no more formal powers than are now required when services make their hit-and-miss adaptations of organization. What would be needed to put it in force would be a strong mayor with a convinced belief in popular government (the two usually go together).

In short, vertical city-wide service departments would still exist and would internally pool information and ideas among districts. But in nearly all cases, the internal organizations of varying services would be rationalized and automatically matched up with one another, to make innate functional sense with respect to both their dealings among themselves and their dealings with localities. In the case of planning, a city planning service would exist, but nearly all its staff (and, let us hope, its brightest staff) would be serving the city in decentralized fashion, in administrative districts, at the only scale where planning for city vitality can be comprehended, coordinated and carried out.

Administrative districts in a big city would promptly begin to act as political creatures, because they would possess real organs of information, recommendation, decision and action. This would be one of the chief advantages of the system.

Citizens of big cities need fulcrum points where they can apply their pressures, and make their wills and their knowledge known and respected. Administrative districts would inevitably become such fulcrum points. Many of the conflicts that are today fought out in the labyrinths of vertical city government—or that are decided by default because the citizens never know what hit them—would be transferred to these district arenas. This is necessary for big-city self-government, whether self-government is considered as a creative or as a supervisory process (of course it is both). The larger, the more impersonal, the more incomprehensible big-city government becomes, and the more blurred in the total localized issues, needs and problems become, the more attenuated and ineffectual becomes either citizen action or citizen supervision. It is futile to expect that citizens will act with responsibility, verve and experience on big, city-wide issues when self-government has been rendered all but impossible on localized issues, which are often of the most direct importance to people.

As a political creature, an administrative district would need a head man, and would certainly get one, either formally or informally. A formal means, and on paper the neatest, might be to appoint a deputy "mayor," responsible to the city mayor. However, an appointive official as *head man* would soon be undercut by an elected official of some sort, for the simple reason that groups of citizens will always apply their pressures on an elected official if they can—and back him up with their support if he comes through—when they are maneuvering to get administration to see things their way. Voters, perceiving alternatives for applying their influence, are intelligent enough to use their power where it has a handle. Almost inevitably, some elected official with a constituency corresponding at least roughly to the district would become, in function, a sort of local "mayor." This is what happens now wherever big-city districts are socially and politically effective.*

---

*Local "mayors" in this sense seem to evolve as a combination of two factors: their own accessibility and success in delivering what is asked, and their scale of constituency. Because of the first factor, the formal offices they hold are likely to differ within a single city. But the second factor is important too. Thus, although in many cities councilmen are apt to be local "mayors," this is unusual in New York, where city councilmen's constituencies (about 300,000 people) are too big for the purpose; instead, local "mayors" are more frequently state assemblymen who, purely because of the circumstance that they have the smallest scale of constituencies in the city (about 115,000 people) are typically called upon to deal with the city government. Good state assemblymen in New York City deal much more with the city government on behalf of the citizens than they do with the state; they are sometimes vital in this way as city officials, although this is entirely aside from their theoretical responsibilities. It is an outcome of district political make-do.

What is the right size for an administrative district?

Geographically, empirical city districts that work effectively as districts are seldom larger than about a mile and a half square in area, and they are usually smaller.

However, there is at least one striking exception to this, and it may be significant. The Back-of-the-Yards district in Chicago is roughly one and a half by three miles, about twice maximum size for an effective district, according to evidence of other places.

In effect, the Back-of-the-Yards already operates as an administrative district, not formally or theoretically, but in fact. In the Back-of-the-Yards, the local government that counts most, as government, is not the generalized city government but rather the Back-of-the-Yards Council, which I described briefly in Chapter Sixteen. Decisions of the kind that can be carried out only under the formal powers of government are transmitted by the Council to the city government, which is, shall we say, extremely responsive. In addition, the Council itself provides some services which, if provided at all, are apt customarily to be provided by formal government.

It may be this ability of the Back-of-the-Yards to function as a true, though informal, unit of governmental power that makes possible its untypically large geographic size. In short, effective district identity, which usually depends almost wholly on internal cross-use for its foundation, has the reinforcement here of solid governmental organization.

This could be significant for the areas of big cities where residence is one of the chief primary uses, but where densities are too low to reconcile sufficient numbers of people with usual, viable district area. In time,

such areas ought gradually to be brought up to city concentration of use, and eventually a single geographically
large area like this might become a couple of districts; but
in the meantime, if the Back-of-the-Yards clue means
what I think it means, the cohesion introduced by district
administration might make it possible for these too-thin
areas to operate as districts politically and socially, as well
as administratively.

Outside of downtowns, or of huge manufacturing
constellations, residence is almost always one of the main
primary uses of a city district; population size is thus
important in considering district size. In Chapter Six, on
city neighborhoods, empirically useful districts were
defined as places big enough (in population) to swing
weight in the city as a whole, but small enough so that
street neighborhoods were not lost or ignored. This might
vary from as little as 30,000 people in cities like Boston
and Baltimore to a minimum of about 100,000 in the
largest cities, with a possible maximum of about 200,000.
I think 30,000 is low for efficient district administration;
50,000 would be a more realistic minimum. The maximum of about 200,000 holds for administration, however,
as it does for a district considered as a social and political
organ, because anything much larger than that exceeds a
unit that can be comprehended both whole and in sufficient detail.

Big cities have become, in themselves, only parts of still
larger units of settlement, known in the census figures as
Standard Metropolitan Areas. A Standard Metropolitan
Area includes a major city (sometimes more, as in the
New York-Newark or San Francisco-Oakland Standard

Metropolitan Areas for example), along with the related towns, smaller satellite cities, villages and suburbs that lie outside a major city's political boundaries but within its economic and social orbit. The size of Standard Metropolitan Areas, both geographically and in population, has of course been growing extraordinarily in the past fifteen years. This is partly because of cataclysmic money that has flooded city outskirts and starved cities as explained in Chapter Sixteen, partly because big cities have failed to work well enough as *cities*, and partly because suburban and semisuburban growth from these two reasons has engulfed formerly discrete villages and towns.

Many problems, particularly planning problems, are common to these governmentally separate settlements of a metropolitan area. This—not the big city—is the unit that means most with respect to overcoming water pollution, or major transportation problems, or major land waste and misuse, or conservation of water tables, wild land, big recreation sites and other resources.

Because these real and important problems exist, and because we have, administratively, no very good ways of getting at them, a concept called "Metropolitan Government" has been developed. Under Metropolitan Government, politically separate localities would continue to have a political identity and autonomy in purely local concerns, but they would be federated into a super-area government which would have extensive planning powers and administrative organs for carrying the plans into action. Part of the taxes from each locality would go to the Metropolitan Government, thus helping also to relieve great cities of part of the financial burden they carry, unrecompensed, for major central city facilities used by the hinterland. Political boundaries, as barriers to joint planning and joint support of common metropolitan facilities, would thus, it is reasoned, be overcome.

Metropolitan Government is a popular idea not only with many planners; it seems to have appealed to numerous big businessmen, who explain in many a speech that this is the rational way to handle the "business of government." Advocates of Metropolitan Government have standard exhibits to show how impossible metropolitan area planning is at present. These exhibits are political maps of greater metropolitan areas. Somewhere near the center is a conspicuously large, neat entity, representing the government of the largest city involved, the metropolis. Outside it is a welter of overlapping, duplicating, strangulated, town, county, small-city and township governments, together with all manner of special administrative districts evolved by expediency, some of them overlapping the big city.

The Chicago metropolitan area, for instance, has about a thousand different contiguous or overlapping local government units, in addition to the municipal government of Chicago itself. In 1957, our 174 metropolitan areas contained a mélange of 16,210 separate units of government.

"Government crazy quilt" is the standard description, and it is in some ways an apt one. The moral drawn is that crazy quilts like these cannot function sensibly; they provide no workable basis either for metropolitan planning or action.

Every so often in a metropolitan area, Metropolitan Government is put up to the voters. The voters inexorably and invariably turn it down.*

The voters are right, in spite of the fact that there is great need for common and coordinated action (and financial support) on many metropolitan area problems, and still more need for localized coordination here and there among different governmental units within a metropolitan area. The voters are right because in real life we lack strategies and tactics for making large-scale metropolitan government and planning work.

The maps that are supposed to explain the situation as it exists contain a monstrous fiction. The conspicuously neat, clean entity representing the "unified" government of the major metropolis is, of course, an administrative crazy quilt even madder than that formed by the governmental fragments that lie outside it.

The voters sensibly decline to federate into a system where bigness means local helplessness, ruthless, over-simplified planning, and administrative chaos—for that is just what municipal bigness means today. How is helplessness against "conquering" planners an improvement over no planning? How is bigger administration, with labyrinths nobody can comprehend or navigate, an improvement over crazy-quilt township and suburban governments?

We already have governmental units which cry out for new and workable strategies and tactics of big metro-

*With the exception of voters in the Miami metropolitan area. However, in order to get Metropolitan Government accepted there, its proponents put so little power in the hands of the Metropolitan Government that what was voted in was little more than a gesture.

politan administration and planning, and these are the great cities themselves. Workable metropolitan administration has to be learned and used, first, *within* big cities, where no fixed political boundaries prevent its use. This is where we must experiment with methods for solving big common problems without, as a corollary, wreaking gratuitous mayhem on localities and on the processes of self-government.

If great cities can learn to administer, coordinate and plan in terms of administrative districts at understandable scale, we may become competent, as a society, to deal too with those crazy quilts of government and administration in the greater metropolitan areas. Today we are not competent to do so. We have no practice or wisdom in handling big metropolitan administration or planning, except in the form of constantly more inadequate adaptations of little-city government.

22

THE KIND OF
PROBLEM A CITY IS

Thinking has its strategies and tactics too, much as other forms of action have. Merely to think about cities and get somewhere, one of the main things to know is what *kind* of problem cities pose, for all problems cannot be thought about in the same way. Which avenues of thinking are apt to be useful and to help yield the truth depends not on how we might prefer to think about a subject, but rather on the inherent nature of the subject itself.

Among the many revolutionary changes of this century, perhaps those that go deepest are the changes in the mental methods we can use for probing the world. I do not mean new mechanical brains, but methods of analysis and discovery that have gotten into human brains: new strategies for thinking. These have developed mainly as methods of science. But the mental awakenings and intellectual daring they represent are gradually beginning to affect other kinds of inquiry too. Puzzles that once appeared unanalyzable become more susceptible to attack. What is more, the very nature of some puzzles are no longer what they once seemed.

To understand what these changes in strategies of thought have to do with cities, it is necessary to understand a little about the history of scientific thought. A splendid summary and interpretation of this history is included in an essay on science and complexity in the *1958 Annual Report of the Rockefeller Foundation,* written by Dr. Warren Weaver upon his retirement as the foundation's Vice-President for the Natural and Medical Sciences. I shall quote from this essay at some length, because what Dr. Weaver says has direct pertinence to thought about cities. His remarks sum up, in an oblique way, virtually the intellectual history of city planning.

Dr. Weaver lists three stages of development in the history of scientific thought: (1) ability to deal with problems of simplicity; (2) ability to deal with problems of disorganized complexity; and (3) ability to deal with problems of organized complexity.

Problems of simplicity are problems that contain two factors which are directly related to each other in their behavior—two variables—and these problems of simplicity, Dr. Weaver points out, were the first *kinds* of problems that science learned to attack:

> Speaking roughly, one may say that the seventeenth, eighteenth and nineteenth centuries formed the period in which physical science learned how to analyze two-variable problems. During that three hundred years, science developed the experimental and analytical techniques for handling problems in which one quantity—say a gas pressure—depends primarily upon a second quantity—say, the volume of the gas. The essential character of these problems rests in the fact that . . . the behavior of the first quantity can be described with a useful degree of accuracy by taking into account only its dependence upon the second quantity and by neglecting the minor influence of other factors.

These two-variable problems are essentially simple in structure . . . and simplicity was a necessary condition for progress at that stage of development of science.

It turned out, moreover, that vast progress could be made in the physical sciences by theories and experiments of this essentially simple character . . . It was this kind of two-variable science which laid, over the period up to 1900, the foundations for our theories of light, of sound, of heat, and of electricity . . . which brought us the telephone and the radio, the automobile and the airplane, the phonograph and the moving pictures, the turbine and the Diesel engine and the modern hydroelectric power plant . . .

It was not until after 1900 that a second method of analyzing problems was developed by the physical sciences.

Some imaginative minds [Dr. Weaver continues] rather than studying problems which involved two variables or at most three or four, went to the other extreme, and said, "Let us develop analytical methods which can deal with two billion variables." That is to say, the physical scientists (with the mathematicians often in the vanguard) developed powerful techniques of probability theory and of statistical mechanics which can deal with what we may call problems of *disorganized complexity* . . .

Consider first a simple illustration in order to get the flavor of the idea. The classical dynamics of the nineteenth century was well suited for analyzing and predicting the motion of a single ivory ball as it moves about on a billiard table . . . One can, but with a surprising increase in difficulty, analyze the motion of two or even three balls on a billiard table . . . But as soon as one tries to analyze the motion of ten or fifteen balls on the table at once, as in pool, the problem becomes unmanageable, not because there is any theoretical difficulty, but just because the actual labor of dealing in specific detail with so many variables turns out to be impractical.

Imagine, however, a large billiard table with millions of balls flying about on its surface . . . The great surprise is that the problem now becomes easier: the methods of statistical mechanics are now applicable. One cannot trace the detailed history of one special ball, to be sure; but there can be answered with useful precision such important questions as: On the average how many balls per second hit a given stretch of rail? On the average how far does a ball move before it is hit by some other ball? . . .

. . . The word "disorganized" [applies] to the large billiard table with the many balls . . . because the balls are distributed, in their positions and motions, in a helter-skelter way . . . But in spite of this helter-skelter or unknown behavior of all the individual variables, the system as a whole possesses certain orderly and analyzable average properties . . .

A wide range of experience comes under this label of disorganized complexity . . . It applies with entirely useful precision to the experience of a large telephone exchange, predicting the average frequency of calls, the probability of overlapping calls of the same number, etc. It makes possible the financial stability of a life insurance company . . . The

motions of the atoms which form all matter, as well
as the motions of the stars which form the universe,
all come under the range of these new techniques.
The fundamental laws of heredity are analyzed by
them. The laws of thermodynamics, which describe
basic and inevitable tendencies of all physical systems, are derived from statistical considerations.
The whole structure of modern physics . . . rests on
these statistical concepts. Indeed, the whole question of evidence, and the way in which knowledge
can be inferred from evidence, is now recognized to
depend on these same ideas . . . We have also come
to realize that communication theory and information theory are similarly based upon statistical
ideas. One is thus bound to say that probability
notions are essential to any theory of knowledge
itself.

However, by no means all problems could be probed
by this method of analysis. The life sciences, such as biology and medicine, could not be, as Dr. Weaver points out.
These sciences, too, had been making advances, but on
the whole they were still concerned with what Dr.
Weaver calls preliminary stages for application of analysis; they were concerned with collection, description, clas-
sification, and observation of apparently correlated
effects. During this preparatory stage, among the many
useful things that were learned was that the life sciences
were neither problems of simplicity nor problems of disorganized complexity; they inherently posed still a different kind of problem, a kind of problem for which
methods of attack were still very backward as recently as
1932, says Dr. Weaver.

Describing this gap, he writes:

> One is tempted to oversimplify and say that scientific methodology went from one extreme to the other . . . and left untouched a great middle region. The importance of this middle region, moreover, does not depend primarily on the fact that the number of variables involved is moderate—large compared to two, but small compared to the number of atoms in a pinch of salt . . . Much more important than the mere number of variables is the fact that these variables are all interrelated . . . These problems, as contrasted with the disorganized situations with which statistics can cope, *show the essential feature of organization.* We will therefore refer to this group of problems as those of *organized complexity.*
>
> What makes an evening primrose open when it does? Why does salt water fail to satisfy thirst? . . . What is the description of aging in biochemical terms? . . . What is a gene, and how does the original genetic constitution of a living organism express itself in the developed characteristics of the adult? . . .
>
> All these are certainly complex problems But they are not problems of disorganized complexity, to which statistical methods hold the key. They are all problems which involve dealing simultaneously with a *sizable number of factors which are interrelated into an organic whole.*

In 1932, when the life sciences were just at the threshold of developing effective analytical methods for handling organized complexity, it was speculated, Dr. Weaver tells us, that if the life sciences could make significant progress in such problems, "then there might be opportunities to extend these new techniques, if only by helpful analogy, into vast areas of the behavioral and social sciences."

In the quarter-century since that time, the life sciences have indeed made immense and brilliant progress. They have accumulated, with extraordinary swiftness, an extraordinary quantity of hitherto hidden knowledge. They have also acquired vastly improved bodies of theory and procedure—enough to open up great new questions, and to show that only a start has been made on what there is to know.

But this progress has been possible only because the life sciences were recognized to be problems in organized complexity, and were thought of and attacked in ways suitable to understanding that *kind* of problem.

The recent progress of the life sciences tells us something tremendously important about other problems of organized complexity. It tells us that problems of this *kind* can be analyzed—that it is only sensible to regard them as capable of being understood, instead of considering them, as Dr. Weaver puts it, to be "in some dark and foreboding way, irrational."

Now let us see what this has to do with cities.

Cities happen to be problems in organized complexity, like the life sciences. They present "situations in which a half-dozen or even several dozen quantities are all varying simultaneously *and in subtly interconnected ways.*" Cities, again like the life sciences, do not exhibit *one* problem in organized complexity, which if understood explains all. They can be analyzed into many such problems or segments which, as in the case of the life sciences, are also related with one another. The variables are many, but they are not helter-skelter; they are "interrelated into an organic whole."

Consider again, as an illustration, the problem of a city neighborhood park. Any single factor about the park is slippery as an eel; it can potentially mean any number of things, depending on how it is acted upon by other factors and how it reacts to them. How much the park is used depends, in part, upon the park's own design. But even this partial influence of the park's design upon the park's use depends, in turn, on who is around to use the park, and when, and this in turn depends on uses of the city outside the park itself. Furthermore, the influence of these uses on the park is only partly a matter of how each affects the park independently of the others; it is also partly a matter of how they affect the park in combination with one another, for certain combinations stimulate the degree of influence from one another among their components. In turn, these city uses near the park and their combinations depend on still other factors, such as the mixture of age in buildings, the size of blocks in the vicinity, and so on, including the presence of the park itself as a common and unifying use in its context. Increase the park's size considerably, or else change its design in such a way that it severs and disperses users from the streets about it, instead of uniting and mixing them, and all bets are off. New sets of influence come into play, both in the park and in its surroundings. This is a far cry from the simple problem of ratios of open space to ratios of population; but there is no use wishing it were a simpler problem or trying to make it a simpler problem, because in real life it is not a simpler problem. No matter what you try to do to it, a city park *behaves* like a problem in organized complexity, and that is what it is. The same is true of all other parts or features of cities. Although the interrelations of their many factors are complex, there is nothing accidental or irrational about the ways in which these factors affect each other.

Moreover, in parts of cities which are working well in some respects and badly in others (as is often the case), we cannot even analyze the virtues and the faults, diagnose the trouble or consider helpful changes, without going at them as problems of organized complexity. To take a few simplified illustrations, a street may be functioning excellently at the supervision of children and at producing a casual and trustful public life, but be doing miserably at solving all other problems because it has failed at knitting itself with an effective larger community, which in turn may or may not exist because of still other sets of factors. Or a street may have, in itself, excellent physical material for generating diversity and an admirable physical design for casual surveillance of public spaces, and yet because of its proximity to a dead border, it may be so empty of life as to be shunned and feared even by its own residents. Or a street may have little foundation for workability on its own merits, yet geographically tie in so admirably with a district that is workable and vital that this circumstance is enough to sustain its attraction and give it use and sufficient workability. We may wish for easier, all-purpose analyses, and for simpler, magical, all-purpose cures, but wishing cannot change these problems into simpler matters than organized complexity, no matter how much we try to evade the realities and to handle them as something different.

Why have cities not, long since, been identified, understood and treated as problems of organized complexity? If the people concerned with the life sciences were able to identify their difficult problems as problems of organized complexity, why have people professionally concerned with cities not identified the *kind* of problem they had?

The history of modern thought about cities is unfortunately very different from the history of modern thought about the life sciences. The theorists of conventional modern city planning have consistently mistaken cities as problems of simplicity and of disorganized complexity, and have tried to analyze and treat them thus. No doubt this imitation of the physical sciences was hardly conscious. It was probably derived, as the assumptions behind most thinking are, from the general floating fund of intellectual spores around at the time. However, I think these misapplications could hardly have occurred, and certainly would not have been perpetuated as they have been, without great disrespect for the subject matter itself—cities. These misapplications stand in our way; they have to be hauled out in the light, recognized as inapplicable strategies of thought, and discarded.

Garden City planning theory had its beginnings in the late nineteenth century, and Ebenezer Howard attacked the problem of town planning much as if he were a nineteenth-century physical scientist analyzing a two-variable problem of simplicity. The two major variables in the Garden City concept of planning were the quantity of housing (or population) and the number of jobs. These two were conceived of as simply and directly related to each other, in the form of relatively closed systems. In turn, the housing had its subsidiary variables, related to it in equally direct, simple, mutually independent form: playgrounds, open space, schools, community center, standardized supplies and services. The town as a whole was conceived of, again, as one of the two variables in a direct, simple, town-greenbelt relationship. As a system of order, that is about all there was to it. And on this simple base of two-variable relationships was created an entire theory of self-contained towns as a means of redistributing the population of cities and (hopefully) achieving regional planning.

Whatever may be said of this scheme for isolated towns, any such simple systems of two-variable relationships cannot possibly be discerned in great cities—and never could be. Such systems cannot be discerned in a town either, the day after the town becomes encompassed in a metropolitan orbit with its multiplicity of choices and complexities of cross-use. But in spite of this fact, planning theory has persistently applied this two-variable *system of thinking and analyzing* to big cities; and to this day city planners and housers believe they hold a precious nugget of truth about the *kind* of problem to be dealt with when they attempt to shape or reshape big-city neighborhoods into versions of two-variable systems, with ratios of one thing (as open space) depending directly and simply upon an immediate ratio of something else (as population).

To be sure, while planners were assuming that cities were properly problems of simplicity, planning theorists and planners could not avoid seeing that real cities were not so in fact. But they took care of this in the traditional way that the incurious (or the disrespectful) have always regarded problems of organized complexity: as if these puzzles were, in Dr. Weaver's words, "in some dark and foreboding way, irrational."*

Beginning in the late 1920's in Europe, and in the 1930's here, city planning theory began to assimilate the newer ideas on probability theory developed by physical science. Planners began to imitate and apply these analyses precisely as if cities were problems in disorganized complexity, understandable purely by statistical analysis, predictable by the application of probability mathematics, manageable by conversion into groups of averages.

This conception of the city as a collection of separate file drawers, in effect, was suited very well by the Radiant City vision of Le Corbusier, that vertical and more centralized version of the two-variable Garden City. Although Le Corbusier himself made no more than a gesture toward statistical analysis, his scheme assumed the statistical reordering of a system of disorganized complexity, solvable mathematically; his towers in the park were a celebration, in art, of the potency of statistics and the triumph of the mathematical average.

The new probability techniques, and the assumptions about the *kind* of problem that underlay the way they have been used in city planning, did not supplant the base idea of the two-variable reformed city. Rather these new ideas were added. Simple, two-variable systems of order were still the aim. But these could be organized even more "rationally" now, from out of a supposed existing system of disorganized complexity. In short, the new probability and statistical methods gave more "accuracy,"

---

*E.g., "a chaotic accident," "solidified chaos," etc.

more scope, made possible a more Olympian view and treatment of the supposed problem of the city.

With the probability techniques, an old aim—stores "properly" related to immediate housing or to a preordained population—became seemingly feasible; there arose techniques for planning standardized shopping "scientifically"; although it was early realized by such planning theorists as Stein and Bauer that pre-planned shopping centers within cities must also be monopolistic or semimonopolistic, or else the statistics would not predict, and the city would go on behaving with dark and foreboding irrationality.

With these techniques, it also became feasible to analyze statistically, by income groups and family sizes, a given quantity of people uprooted by acts of planning, to combine these with probability statistics on normal housing turnover, and to estimate accurately the gap. Thus arose the supposed feasibility of large-scale relocation of citizens. In the form of statistics, these citizens were no longer components of any unit except the family, and could be dealt with intellectually like grains of sand, or electrons or billiard balls. The larger the number of uprooted, the more easily they could be planned for on the basis of mathematical averages. On this basis it was actually intellectually easy and sane to contemplate clearance of all slums and re-sorting of people in ten years and not much harder to contemplate it as a twenty-year job.

By carrying to logical conclusions the thesis that the city, as it exists, is a problem in disorganized complexity, housers and planners reached—apparently with straight faces—the idea that almost any specific malfunctioning could be corrected by opening and filling a new file drawer. Thus we get such political party policy state-ments as this: "The Housing Act of 1959 . . . should be supplemented to include . . . a program of housing for moderate-income families whose incomes are too high for admission to public housing, but too low to enable them to obtain decent shelter in the private market."

With statistical and probability techniques, it also became possible to create formidable and impressive planning surveys for cities—surveys that come out with fanfare, are read by practically nobody, and then drop quietly into oblivion, as well they might, being nothing more nor less than routine exercises in statistical mechan-ics for systems of disorganized complexity. It became pos-sible also to map out master plans for the statistical city, and people take these more seriously, for we are all accus-tomed to believe that maps and reality are necessarily related, or that if they are not, we can make them so by altering reality.

With these techniques, it was possible not only to con-ceive of people, their incomes, their spending money and their housing as fundamentally problems in disorganized complexity, susceptible to conversion into problems of simplicity once ranges and averages were worked out, but also to conceive of city traffic, industry, parks, and even cultural facilities as components of disorganized complexity, convertible into problems of simplicity.

Furthermore, it was no intellectual disadvantage to contemplate "coordinated" schemes of city planning embracing ever greater territories. The greater the terri-tory, as well as the larger the population, the more ratio-nally and easily could both be dealt with as problems of disorganized complexity viewed from an Olympian vantage point. The wry remark that "A Region is an area safely larger than the last one to whose problems we found no solution" is not a wry remark in these terms. It is a simple statement of a basic fact about disorganized complexity; it is much like saying that a large insurance company is better equipped to average out risks than a small insurance company.

However, while city planning has thus mired itself in deep misunderstandings about the very nature of the problem with which it is dealing, the life sciences, unburdened with this mistake, and moving ahead very rapidly, have been providing some of the concepts that city planning needs: along with providing the basic strategy of recognizing problems of organized complexity, they have provided hints about analyzing and handling this *kind* of problem. These advances have, of course, filtered from the life sciences into general knowledge; they have become part of the intellectual fund of our times. And so a growing number of people have begun, gradually, to think of cities as problems in organized complexity—organisms that are replete with unexamined, but obviously intricately interconnected, and surely understandable, relationships. This book is one manifestation of that idea.

This is a point of view which has little currency yet among planners themselves, among architectural city designers, or among the businessmen and legislators who learn their planning lessons, naturally, from what is established and long accepted by planning "experts." Nor is this a point of view that has much appreciable currency in schools of planning (perhaps there least of all).

City planning, as a field, has stagnated. It bustles but it does not advance. Today's plans show little if any perceptible progress in comparison with plans devised a generation ago. In transportation, either regional or local, nothing is offered which was not already offered and popularized in 1938 in the General Motors diorama at the New York World's Fair, and before that by Le Corbusier. In some respects, there is outright retrogression. None of today's pallid imitations of Rockefeller Center is as good as the original, which was built a quarter of a century ago. Even in conventional planning's *own given terms,* today's housing projects are no improvement, and usually a retrogression, in comparison with those of the 1930's.

As long as city planners, and the businessmen, lenders, and legislators who have learned from planners, cling to the unexamined assumptions that they are dealing with a problem in the physical sciences, city planning cannot possibly progress. Of course it stagnates. It lacks the first requisite for a body of practical and progressing thought: recognition of the kind of problem at issue. Lacking this, it has found the shortest distance to a dead end.

Because the life sciences and cities happen to pose the same *kinds* of problems does not mean they are the *same* problems. The organizations of living protoplasm and the organizations of living people and enterprises cannot go under the same microscopes.

However, the tactics for understanding both are similar in the sense that both depend on the microscopic or detailed view, so to speak, rather than on the less detailed, naked-eye view suitable for viewing problems of simplicity or the remote telescopic view suitable for viewing problems of disorganized complexity.

In the life sciences, organized complexity is handled by identifying a specific factor or quantity—say an enzyme—and then painstakingly learning its intricate relationships and interconnections with other factors or quantities. All this is observed in terms of the behavior (not mere presence) of other specific (not generalized) factors or quantities. To be sure, the techniques of two-variable and disorganized-complexity analysis are used too, but only as subsidiary tactics.

In principle, these are much the same tactics as those that have to be used to understand and to help cities. In the case of understanding cities, I think the most important habits of thought are these:

1. To think about processes;

2. To work inductively, reasoning from particulars to the general, rather than the reverse;

3. To seek for "unaverage" clues involving very small quantities, which reveal the way larger and more "average" quantities are operating.

If you have gotten this far in this book, you do not need much explanation of these tactics. However, I shall sum them up, to bring out points otherwise left only as implications.

Why think about processes? Objects in cities—whether they are buildings, streets, parks, districts, landmarks, or anything else—can have radically differing effects, depending upon the circumstances and contexts in which they exist. Thus, for instance, almost nothing useful can be understood or can be done about improving city dwellings if these are considered in the abstract as "housing." City dwellings—either existing or potential—are *specific* and particularized buildings *always involved in* *differing, specific processes* such as unslumming, slumming, generation of diversity, self-destruction of diversity.*

This book has discussed cities, and their components almost entirely in the form of processes, because the subject matter dictates this. For cities, processes are of the essence. Furthermore, once one thinks about city processes, it follows that one *must* think of catalysts of these processes, and this too is of the essence.

The processes that occur in cities are not arcane, capable of being understood only by experts. They can be understood by almost anybody. Many ordinary people already understand them; they simply have not given these processes names, or considered that by understanding these ordinary arrangements of cause and effect, we can also direct them if we want to.

Why reason inductively? Because to reason, instead, from generalizations ultimately drives us into absurdities—as in the case of the Boston planner who knew (against all the real-life evidence he had) that the North End had to be a slum because the generalizations that make him an expert say it is.

This is an obvious pitfall because the generalizations on which the planner was depending are themselves so nonsensical. However, inductive reasoning is just as important for identifying, understanding and constructively using the forces and processes that actually are relevant to cities, and therefore are not nonsensical. I have generalized about these forces and processes consider-

*Because this is so, "housers," narrowly specializing in "housing" expertise, are a vocational absurdity. Such a profession makes sense only if it is assumed that "housing" per se has important generalized effects and qualities. It does not.

ably, but let no one be misled into believing that these generalizations can be used routinely to declare what the particulars, in this or that place, *ought* to mean. City processes in real life are too complex to be routine, too particularized for application as abstractions. They are always made up of interactions among unique combinations of particulars, and there is no substitute for knowing the particulars.

Inductive reasoning of this kind is, again, something that can be engaged in by ordinary, interested citizens, and again they have the advantage over planners. Planners have been trained and disciplined in *deductive* thinking, like the Boston planner who learned his lessons only too well. Possibly because of this bad training, planners frequently seem to be less well equipped intellectually for respecting and understanding particulars than ordinary people, untrained in expertise, who are attached to a neighborhood, accustomed to using it, and so are not accustomed to thinking of it in generalized or abstract fashion.

Why seek "unaverage" clues, involving small quantities? Comprehensive statistical studies, to be sure, can *sometimes* be useful abstracted measurements of the sizes, ranges, averages and medians of this and that. Gathered from time to time, statistics can tell too what has been happening to these figures. However, they tell almost nothing about how the quantities are working in systems of organized complexity.

To learn how things are working, we need pinpoint clues. For instance, all the statistical studies possible about the downtown of Brooklyn, N.Y., cannot tell us as much about the problem of that downtown and its cause as is

told in five short lines of type in a single newspaper advertisement. This advertisement, which is for Marboro, a
chain of bookstores, gives the business hours of the chain's
five stores. Three of them (one near Carnegie Hall in Manhattan, one near the Public Library and not far from Times
Square, one in Greenwich Village) stay open until midnight. A fourth, close to Fifth Avenue and Fifty-ninth
Street, stays open until 10 P.M. The fifth, in downtown
Brooklyn, stays open until 8 P.M. Here is a management
which keeps its stores open late, if there is business to be
had. The advertisement tells us that Brooklyn's downtown
is too dead by 8 P.M., as indeed it is. No surveys (and certainly no mindless, mechanical predictions projected forward in time from statistical surveys, a boondoggle that
today frequently passes for "planning") can tell us anything so relevant to the composition and to the need of
Brooklyn's downtown as this small, but specific and precisely accurate, clue to the *workings* of that downtown.

It takes large quantities of the "average" to produce
the "unaverage" in cities. But as was pointed out in Chapter Seven, in the discussion on the generators of diversity,
the mere presence of large quantities—whether people,
uses, structures, jobs, parks, streets or anything else—
does not guarantee much generation of city diversity.
These quantities can be working as factors in inert, low-
energy systems, merely maintaining themselves, if that.
Or they can make up interacting, high-energy systems,
producing by-products of the "unaverage."

The "unaverage" can be physical, as in the case of
eye-catchers which are small elements in much larger,
more "average" visual scenes. They can be economic, as
in the case of one-of-a-kind stores, or cultural, as in the

case of an unusual school or out-of the-ordinary theater. They can be social, as in the case of public characters, loitering places, or residents or users who are financially, vocationally, racially or culturally unaverage.

Quantities of the "unaverage," which are bound to be relatively small, are indispensable to vital cities. However, in the sense that I am speaking of them here, "unaverage" quantities are also important as analytical means—as clues. They are often the only announcers of the way various large quantities are behaving, or failing to behave, in combination with each other. As a rough analogy, we may think of quantitatively minute vitamins in protoplasmic systems, or trace elements in pasture plants. These things are necessary for proper functioning of the systems of which they are a part; however, their usefulness does not end there, because they can and do also serve as vital clues to *what is* happening in the systems of which they are a part.

This awareness of "unaverage" clues—or awareness of their lack—is, again, something any citizen can practice. City dwellers, indeed, are commonly great informal experts in precisely this subject. Ordinary people in cities have an awareness of "unaverage" quantities which is quite consonant with the importance of these relatively small quantities. And again, planners are the ones at the disadvantage. They have inevitably come to regard "unaverage" quantities as relatively inconsequential, because these are *statistically* inconsequential. They have been trained to discount what is most vital.

Now we must dig a little deeper into the bog of intellectual misconceptions about cities in which orthodox reformers and planners have mired themselves (and the rest of us). Underlying the city planners' deep disrespect for their subject matter, underlying the jejune belief in the "dark and foreboding" irrationality or chaos of cities, lies a long-established misconception about the relationship of cities—and indeed of men—with the rest of nature.

Human beings are, of course, a part of nature, as much so as grizzly bears or bees or whales or sorghum cane. The cities of human beings are as natural, being a product of one form of nature, as are the colonies of prairie dogs or the beds of oysters. The botanist Edgar Anderson has written wittily and sensitively in *Landscape* magazine from time to time about cities as a form of nature. "Over much of the world," he comments, "man has been accepted as a city-loving creature." Nature watching, he points out, "is quite as easy in the city as in the country; all one has to do is accept Man as a part of Nature. Remember that as a specimen of *Homo sapiens* you are far and away most likely to find that species an effective guide to deeper understanding of natural history."

A curious but understandable thing happened in the eighteenth century. By then, the cities of Europeans had done well enough by them, mediating between them and many harsh aspects of nature, so that something became popularly possible which previously had been a rarity—sentimentalization of nature, or at any rate, sentimentalization of a rustic or a barbarian relationship with nature. Marie Antoinette playing milkmaid was an expression of this sentimentality on one plane. The romantic idea of the "noble savage" was an even sillier one, on another plane. So, in this country, was Jefferson's intellectual rejection of cities of free artisans and mechanics, and his dream of an ideal republic of self-reliant rural yeomen—a pathetic dream for a good and great man whose land was tilled by slaves.

In real life, barbarians (and peasants) are the least free of men—bound by tradition, ridden by caste, fettered by superstitions, riddled by suspicion and foreboding of whatever is strange. "City air makes free," was the medieval saying, when city air literally did make free the runaway serf. City air still makes free the runaways from company towns, from plantations, from factory-farms, from subsistence farms, from migrant picker routes, from mining villages, from one-class suburbs.

Owing to the mediation of cities, it became popularly possible to regard "nature" as benign, ennobling and pure, and by extension to regard "natural man" (take your pick of how "natural") as so too. Opposed to all this fictionalized purity, nobility and beneficence, cities, not being fictions, could be considered as seats of malignancy and—obviously—the enemies of nature. And once people begin looking at nature as if it were a nice big St. Bernard dog for the children, what could be more natural than the desire to bring this sentimental pet into the city too, so the city might get some nobility, purity and beneficence by association?

There are dangers in sentimentalizing nature. Most sentimental ideas imply, at bottom, a deep if unacknowledged disrespect. It is no accident that we Americans, probably the world's champion sentimentalizers about nature, are at one and the same time probably the world's most voracious and disrespectful destroyers of wild and rural countryside.

It is neither love for nature nor respect for nature that

leads to this schizophrenic attitude. Instead, it is a sentimental desire to toy, rather patronizingly, with some
insipid, standardized, suburbanized shadow of nature—
apparently in sheer disbelief that we and our cities, just by
virtue of being, are a legitimate part of nature too, and
involved with it in much deeper and more inescapable
ways than grass trimming, sunbathing, and contempla-
tive uplift. And so, each day, several thousand more acres
of our countryside are eaten by the bulldozers, covered by
pavement, dotted with suburbanites who have killed the
thing they thought they came to find. Our irreplaceable
heritage of Grade I agricultural land (a rare treasure of
nature on this earth) is sacrificed for highways or supermarket parking lots as ruthlessly and unthinkingly as the
trees in the woodlands are uprooted, the streams and
rivers polluted and the air itself filled with the gasoline
exhausts (products of eons of nature's manufacturing)
required in this great national effort to cozy up with a fictionalized nature and flee the "unnaturalness" of the city.

The semisuburbanized and suburbanized messes we
create in this way become despised by their own inhabitants tomorrow. These thin dispersions lack any reasonable degree of innate vitality, staying power, or inherent
usefulness as settlements. Few of them, and these only the
most expensive as a rule, hold their attraction much
longer than a generation; then they begin to decay in the
pattern of city gray areas. Indeed, an immense amount of
today's city gray belts was yesterday's dispersion closer
to "nature." Of the buildings on the thirty thousand acres
of already blighted or already fast-blighting residential
areas in northern New Jersey, for example, half are less
than forty years old. Thirty years from now, we shall have

The Death and Life of Great American Cities

accumulated new problems of blight and decay over acreages so immense that in comparison the present problems of the great cities' gray belts will look piddling. Nor, however destructive, is this something which happens accidentally or without the use of will. This is exactly what we, as a society, have willed to happen.

Nature, sentimentalized and considered as the antithesis of cities, is apparently assumed to consist of grass, fresh air and little else, and this ludicrous disrespect results in the devastation of nature even formally and publicly preserved in the form of a pet.

For example, up the Hudson River, north of New York City, is a state park at Croton Point, a place for picnicking, ballplaying and looking at the lordly (polluted) Hudson. At the Point itself is—or was—a geological curiosity: a stretch of beach about fifteen yards long where the blue-gray clay, glacially deposited there, and the action of the river currents and the sun combined to manufacture clay dogs. These are natural sculptures, compacted almost to the density of stone, and baked, and they are of a most curious variety, from breathtakingly subtle and simple curving forms to fantastic concoctions of more than Oriental splendor. There are only a few places in the entire world where clay dogs may be found.

Generations of New York City geology students, along with picnickers, tired ballplayers and delighted children, treasure hunted among the clay dogs and carried their favorites home. And always, the clay, the river and the sun made more, and more, and more, inexhaustibly, no two alike.

Occasionally through the years, having been introduced to the clay dogs long ago by a geology teacher, I would go back to treasure hunt among them. A few summers ago, my husband and I took our children to the Point so they might find some and also so they might see how they are made.

But we were a season behind improvers on nature. The slope of muddy clay that formed the little stretch of unique beach had been demolished. In its place was a rustic retaining wall and an extension of the park's lawns. (The park had been augmented—statistically.) Digging beneath the new lawn here and there—for we can desecrate the next man's desecrations as well as anyone—we found broken bits of clay dogs, mashed by the bulldozers, the last evidence of a natural process that may well have been halted here forever.

Who would prefer this vapid suburbanization to timeless wonders? What kind of park supervisor would permit such vandalism of nature? An all too familiar kind of mind is obviously at work here: a mind seeing only disorder where a most intricate and unique order exists; the same kind of mind that sees only disorder in the life of city streets, and itches to erase it, standardize it, suburbanize it.

The two responses are connected: Cities, as created or used by city-loving creatures are unrespected by such simple minds because they are not bland shadows of cities suburbanized. Other aspects of nature are equally unrespected because they are not bland shadows of nature suburbanized. Sentimentality about nature denatures everything it touches.

Big cities and countrysides can get along well together. Big cities need real countryside close by. And countryside—from man's point of view—needs big cities,

with all their diverse opportunities and productivity, so
human beings can be in a position to appreciate the rest of
the natural world instead of to curse it.

Being human is itself difficult, and therefore all kinds
of settlements (except dream cities) have problems. Big
cities have difficulties in abundance, because they have
people in abundance. But vital cities are not helpless to
combat even the most difficult of problems. They are not
passive victims of chains of circumstances, any more than
they are the malignant opposite of nature.

Vital cities have marvelous innate abilities for understanding, communicating, contriving and inventing what
is required to combat their difficulties. Perhaps the most
striking example of this ability is the effect that big cities
have had on disease. Cities were once the most helpless
and devastated victims of disease, but they became great
disease conquerors. All the apparatus of surgery, hygiene,
microbiology, chemistry, telecommunications, public
health measures, teaching and research hospitals, ambu-
lances and the like, which people not only in cities but
also outside them depend upon for the unending war
against premature mortality, are fundamentally products
of big cities and would be inconceivable without big
cities. The surplus wealth, the productivity, the close-
grained juxtaposition of talents that permit society to support advances such as these are themselves products of
our organization into cities, and especially into big and
dense cities.

It may be romantic to search for the salves of society's
ills in slow-moving rustic surroundings, or among inno-
cent, unspoiled provincials, if such exist, but it is a waste
of time. Does anyone suppose that, in real life, answers to

any of the great questions that worry us today are going to come out of homogeneous settlements?

Dull, inert cities, it is true, do contain the seeds of their own destruction and little else. But lively, diverse, intense cities contain the seeds of their own regeneration, with energy enough to carry over for problems and needs outside themselves.

INDEX

587

A NOTE ON THE TYPE

The principal text of this Modern Library edition
was composed in a digitized version of Palatino,
a contemporary typeface created by Hermann Zapf,
who was inspired by the sixteenth-century calligrapher
Giambattista Palatino, a writing master of Renaissance Italy.
Palatino was the first of Zapf's typefaces
to be introduced in America.